613.52
H488s

FOR REFERENCE

Do Not Take From This Room

**Renner Learning Resource Center
Elgin Community College
Elgin, IL 60123**

A Reader's Guide
to the Short Stories of
ERNEST HEMINGWAY

*A
Reference
Publication
in
Literature*

James Nagel
Editor

A Reader's Guide to the Short Stories of
ERNEST HEMINGWAY

Paul Smith

G.K.HALL&CO.
70 LINCOLN STREET, BOSTON, MASS.

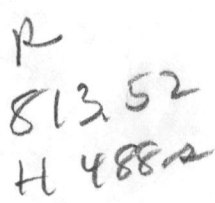

Passages from the papers of Ernest Hemingway in the Ernest Hemingway Collection of the John F. Kennedy Library are published with the permission of the Ernest Hemingway Foundation (d.b.a. The Hemingway Society). Copyright the Ernest Hemingway Foundation.

A Reader's Guide to the Short Stories of Ernest Hemingway
Paul Smith

Copyright 1989 by Paul Smith
All rights reserved.
Published by G. K. Hall & Co.
70 Lincoln Street
Boston, Massachusetts 02111

Book production by Patricia D'Agostino

Typeset in 11 pt. Garamond
by Williams Press, Albany, N.Y.

Printed on permanent/durable acid-free paper
and bound in the United States of America

Library of Congress Cataloging-in-Publication Data

Smith, Paul. 1925—
   A reader's guide to the short stories of Ernest Hemingway / Paul Smith.
      p. cm. — (A Reference publication in literature)
   Includes bibliographies and index.
   ISBN 0-8161-8794-0 (alk. paper)
   1. Hemingway, Ernest, 1899–1961—Criticism and interpretation.
2. Short story.   I. Title.   II. Series.
PS3515.E37Z864   1989
813'.52—dc19   88-34944
                                                                            CIP

Contents

The Author	viii
Preface	ix
Acknowledgments	xiii
Introduction	xv
A Note on Sources	xxiii
Prologue: Oak Park and Chicago, 1916–1921	xv
Three Stories and Ten Poems (July 1923)	1
1. Up in Michigan (Fall 1921; February 1922)	3
2. My Old Man (July-September 1922)	10
3. Out of Season (April 1923)	16
In Our Time (October 1925)	23
4. A Very Short Story (June-July 1923)	25
5. The Revolutionist (June-July 1923)	30
6. Indian Camp (November 1923-February 1924)	34
7. Cat in the Rain (February 1923-March 1924)	43
8. The End of Something (March 1924)	50
9. The Three-Day Blow (March 1924)	56
10. The Doctor and the Doctor's Wife (March-April 1924)	61
11. Soldier's Home (April 1924)	68
12. Mr. and Mrs. Elliot (April 1924)	75
13. Cross-Country Snow (April 1924)	81
14. Big Two-Hearted River (May-November 1924)	85
15. The Undefeated (September-November 1924) *Men Without Women*	102
16. Banal Story (January-February 1925) *Men Without Women*	110
17. The Battler (December 1924-March 1925)	115
Men Without Women (October 1927)	123
18. Fifty Grand (January 1924-November 1925)	125
19. An Alpine Idyll (April 1926)	132
20. The Killers (September 1925-May 1926)	138
21. Today Is Friday (May 1926)	154
22. A Canary for One (August-September 1926)	159
23. In Another Country (September-November 1926)	164
24. Now I Lay Me (November-December 1926)	172
25. A Pursuit Race (November 1926-February 1927)	180
26. A Simple Enquiry (November 1926-February 1927)	185

27.	On the Quai at Smyrna (Winter 1926-1927) *In Our Time* (1930)	189
28.	Che Ti Dice la Patria? (April-May 1927)	193
29.	Ten Indians (September 1925-May 1927)	197
30.	Hills Like White Elephants (May 1927)	204

Winner Take Nothing (October 1933) — 215
31.	Wine of Wyoming (October 1928-May 1930)	217
32.	The Sea Change (January 1930-June 1931)	223
33.	A Natural History of the Dead (January 1929-August 1931)	231
34.	After the Storm (April 1928-June 1932)	240
35.	God Rest You Merry, Gentlemen (February-December 1932)	246
36.	Homage to Switzerland (March-June 1932)	252
37.	The Light of the World (May-July 1932)	257
38.	The Mother of a Queen (Fall 1931-August 1932)	264
39.	A Way You'll Never Be (May-November 1932)	268
40.	A Clean, Well-Lighted Place (Fall 1932)	277
41.	The Gambler, the Nun, and the Radio (Summer 1931-Fall 1932)	289
42.	One Reader Writes (February 1932-February 1933)	297
43.	A Day's Wait (March-July 1933)	302
44.	Fathers and Sons (November 1932-August 1933)	307

The Fifth Column and the First Forty-nine Stories (October 1938) — 319
45.	The Capital of the World (November 1935-February 1936)	321
46.	The Short Happy Life of Francis Macomber (November 1934-April 1936)	327
47.	The Snows of Kilimanjaro (February-April 1936)	349
48.	Old Man at the Bridge (April 1938)	362

The Fifth Column and Four Stories of the Spanish Civil War (August 1969) [Magazine Publication] — 367
49.	The Denunciation (May-September 1938) [November 1938]	369
50.	The Butterfly and the Tank (July-September 1938) [December 1938]	375
51.	Night Before Battle (September-October 1938) [February 1939]	378
52.	Nobody Ever Dies (October-November 1938) [March 1939] *The Complete Stories*	382
53.	Under the Ridge (February 1939) [October 1939]	385

The Complete Short Stories of Ernest Hemingway:
The Finca Vigia Edition (November 1987) [Magazine Publication] — 389
54/55.	Get a Seeing-Eyed Dog (March 1954-July 1956) [November 1957]	391
	A Man of the World (May-June 1957) [November 1957]	391

Epilogue: Excluded Stories, 1921-1987 395

Index of Hemingway's Works 397

General Index 401

Parenthetical dates after story titles designate the period in which the story was composed; dates of magazine publication are indicated in brackets; where a story was published in a later collection, the title of the volume is given in italics.

The Author

Paul Smith is James J. Goodwin Professor of English at Trinity College in Hartford, Conn. He is the coauthor (with Robert Foulke) of *An Anatomy of Literature* (New York: Harcourt, 1972), and has published articles on Melville, Shelley, critical theory, and the curriculum in English. He was the founding president of the Hemingway Society and has published on Hemingway in the *Journal of Modern Literature,* the *Hemingway Review, American Literature, Resources for American Literary Study,* and several anthologies of Hemingway criticism.

Preface

The Scope of this Guide

This book takes as its domain the fifty-five works of fiction Hemingway offered to his readers as short stories in his lifetime, all but seven of which he saw published in five collections between 1923 and 1938, and those seven published in magazines. The remaining twenty that some will claim deserve inclusion have been excluded or only briefly reviewed for three reasons: either Hemingway did not consider them short stories, or he did not see them into print, or they tell us little if anything more of how he mastered the genre than do the fifty-five stories considered here. Those twenty excluded or reviewed works are cited in the Epilogue.

The Organization of this Guide

The fifty-five short stories are considered here in the chronology of their composition from "Up in Michigan" in the fall of 1921 to "A Man of the World" in the spring of 1957. The sequence is derived largely from the evidence of the stories' manuscripts, lists of titles, memoirs, biographies, critical studies, Hemingway's published and unpublished correspondence, and then some speculation. For some stories the date of composition can be precisely determined—"Old Man at the Bridge" was written in Barcelona in the late evening of 17 April 1938 (Watson 154–55). For others only the earliest and latest dates of composition can be suggested with an inference drawn for the story's probable date of completion—"Ten Indians" was begun in September 1925, substantially revised in May 1926, and given a new ending in May 1927.

This chronology differs, of course, from that of the stories' publication and their arrangement in the five collections, and, incidentally, at some crucial points from that followed by Hemingway's biographers and critics.

Each chapter, with the exception of the last on "Two Tales of Darkness," considers one story under the following headings:

Composition History (Date or Period of Composition)

This section dates and reviews the writing of the story, describing each of its more important manuscripts, noting their differences from the published text, and summarizing the relevant bibliographical studies.

Hemingway's most common practice in writing a story followed these stages: first, a pencil or ink manuscript, revised slightly as he wrote, and then again when the draft was finished, with additions more often than deletions, except for the few large excisions of beginnings and endings; second, his own typescript, incorporating the manuscript revisions and adding others, and at times, if these were major, a third typescript; then a final typescript, usually by another typist; if the revisions here were slight, this version was often submitted for publication.

Once a story was accepted for publication and in proof, there is evidence—albeit heretical to some Hemingway scholars—that Hemingway's reading of proofs was cursory; and once published he rarely revised the first printed text. Perhaps remembering the rejection slips from 1919 to 1922, or even the theft of his early work, he felt that making it into print at last was enough for the time being—and then, of course, there were other stories to write.

Publication History (Dates of First Publication and First Collection)

Since Audre Hanneman's *Ernest Hemingway: A Comprehensive Bibliography* (1967) and its *Supplement* (1975) provide the publication history of the fifty-five stories, this section reviews only the circumstances leading to the story's first and subsequent publications before its inclusion in one of Hemingway's collections.

A few of these sections are more detailed when the later history of publication reveals something of Hemingway's commitment to the story—as in his futile efforts to include "Up in Michigan" in the collections from 1925 to 1933—or when a crucial change was made in the text—as in the waiters' dialogue in "A Clean, Well-Lighted Place."

Sources and Influences

This section summarizes the more influential events, places, and individuals in Hemingway's experience and the works of other writers—journalists, essayists, and, most important, recent or contemporary authors of short stories—that served as sources or informing influences on his short fiction. Here, too, are noted the more substantive relationships among his own stories.

However often Hemingway criticism and the recent biographies by Peter Griffin, Jeffrey Meyers, Michael Reynolds, and Kenneth Lynn have found threads, from gossamer to steel, running from the life to the fiction and back to the life again, relatively little scholarship has ventured beyond the earlier, and perhaps strained, literary influence of Gertrude Stein and Sherwood

Anderson. James Joyce and T. S. Eliot have yet to be recognized in detail for their influence; and Mark Spilka's recent work on that of the lesser Victorians and Frederick Marryat points to other largely unexplored sources.

Those critical studies that primarily identify biographical origins or literary analogues are reviewed in this section; others that draw on those sources to reorient the interpretation of a story are considered in the final section.

Critical Studies

Some principle of selection was essential in this section, especially for the stories with what sometimes seems unending bibliographies—"Big Two-Hearted River," "The Killers," "A Clean, Well-Lighted Place," and "The Short Happy Life of Francis Macomber." The intent of this section is to review the more important critical issues raised by a story and to note or summarize those critical studies that, in meeting those issues, have advanced or redirected Hemingway scholarship. Critical studies of Hemingway are perhaps not unique in being—to put it politely—sometimes redundant; and when they are, this section will pass quietly by. (The bibliographies consulted appear in "A Note on Sources" following this preface.)

The reviews of critical studies follow one of two structures: historical, for those stories with relatively few commentaries, like "Out of Season"; and thematic, that is to say, considering those critical studies together that gather about a single theme or issue, like Mrs. Macomber's guilt or innocence. In the latter case, those commentaries on a single issue are reviewed chronologically, so the reader may follow the exchange in a critical controversy.

These surveys often conclude with a comment on those questions scholarship has not—perhaps cannot—resolve, but still deserve attention, or with a note on those issues overlooked in the critical history of the stories. Again, the intent of this book is to acknowledge the good criticism of the past, to suggest where it deserves reconsideration, and to offer some suggestions for new work on the stories that have been neglected only because so many others have captured and still challenge our imagination.

Works Cited

Hanneman, Audre. *Ernest Hemingway: A Comprehensive Bibliography*. Princeton: Princeton UP, 1967.

———. *Supplement to Ernest Hemingway: A Comprehensive Bibliography*. Princeton: Princeton UP, 1975.

Spilka, Mark. "A Source for the Macomber 'Accident': Marryat's *Percival Keene*." *Hemingway Review* 3 (Spring 1984): 29–37.

Watson, William B. " 'Old Man at the Bridge': The Making of a Short Story." *Hemingway Review* 7 (Spring 1988): 152–65.

Acknowledgments

Any author of a book like this one owes more than can be acknowledged to generations of students, colleagues down the hall, and scholars afar. For all my students in Hemingway courses over the years, let my graduate students of 1988 who tried out many of these chapters accept my appreciation. For colleagues come and gone, let Charles Ross (University of Hartford), James Wheatley, and Dirk Kuyk, Jr., (Trinity College) bear my thanks for their long-standing friendship and support. For Hemingway scholars at large, let "The Thompson Island Forty"—the charter members of the Hemingway Society who met there in Boston Harbor in 1980 to open the Kennedy Library's collection—pass on my gratitude to the others whose work I depend on in these chapters.

While writing this book I had behind me, and sometimes far ahead, research assistants who made the hard work of library searches easier: Sarah Brown, Karen Albano, Amy Rebovich, and Jennifer and Paula Smith, who also kept something in the family.

Then, the librarians, without whom nothing. At the Kennedy Library: Jo August Hills gathered the vast collection of Hemingway manuscripts, letters, photographs, and memorabilia and described them with scrupulous intelligence in the *Catalog of the Ernest Hemingway Collection at the John F. Kennedy Library*, 2 vols. (Boston: Hall, 1982). She knew the collection by heart, and she shared her knowledge with grace and generosity. Joan O'Connor carried on her efforts; and, recently, Megan Desnoyers has been instrumental in organizing the collection, reporting new acquisitions, and making it more widely accessible to scholars requesting photocopies. All have served this rich collection well, realizing the intent of Mary Hemingway's generous gift and the support of John and Patrick Hemingway, to whom all of us are indebted.

At the Trinity College Library, I have had the ready assistance of its reference librarians: Peter Knapp, Patricia Bunker, and Linda McKinney—who delighted in discovering the color of Austrian army uniforms in 1917.

Many of these chapters were read and revised by scholars with a special interest in a story or its context. For their careful readings and comments I am indebted to: Susan Beegel (University of Massachusetts), Gerry Brenner (University of Montana), Scott Donaldson (College of William and Mary), Robert Fleming (University of New Mexico), Allen Josephs (University of

West Florida), Robert Lewis (University of North Dakota), George Monteiro (Brown University), James Nagel (Northeastern University), and Alice Hall Petry (Rhode Island School of Design).

Others have commented on my related research or assisted in the search for manuscripts: Jackson Benson (San Diego State University), Richard Davison (University of Delaware), E. R. Hagemann (University of Louisville), James Hinkle (San Diego State University), Wayne Kvam (Kent State University), Kenneth Lynn (Johns Hopkins University), Bruce Stark (University of Wisconsin, Milwaukee), Linda Wagner-Martin (University of North Carolina), and William Watson (Massachusetts Institute of Technology).

I am obliged to the administration and Faculty Research Committee of Trinity College for their generous and continuing support with a sabbatical leave and extension for 1986–87, to the American Council of Learned Societies for a 1986 grant-in-aid, and to the Goodwin family for the research support in the endowment of the James J. Goodwin Professorship.

I owe a great deal to two persons representative of the last two generations of Hemingway scholarship. The late Carlos Baker read some of these chapters, and in his last year searched his extensive files and answered my questions with postcards or encouraging letters. Michael Reynolds was at work on his Hemingway biography during the years I wrote this book. We corresponded, talked expensively on the telephone, and on long drives along the Dordogne, or through late nights at Caux, to and from conferences, we argued over and resolved, usually, the points where our manuscripts met. So now I could not say where this book does *not* owe something to his imaginative research, disciplined scholarship, and steady conviction—when mine wavered—that it was all worth doing.

Introduction

When Ernest Hemingway arrived in Paris in December 1921, his literary baggage was as light as his letters of introduction heralding him were heavy. Sherwood Anderson had written extolling Hemingway's extraordinary promise and sophistication to Gertrude Stein, Ezra Pound, Sylvia Beach, a friend to James Joyce, and Lewis Galantière, familiar with all of Paris and its literati. Whatever manuscripts he had with him would hardly prove that promise: some imitative poems, the beginning of a novel, perhaps some sketches, and for certain a draft of "Up in Michigan." That he left the other stories of the last two years behind when he embarked for France argues that he knew the high standards Paris would set for prose and that, perhaps for the moment, a poet was the thing to be. Hadley Richardson, his wife of three months, had liked the poems.

Three Stories and Ten Poems (1923)

With Galantière's help the young couple found an apartment on rue du Cardinal Lemoine and immediately set off for a skiing holiday at Chamby-sur-Montreux in Switzerland. It had been raining in Paris, a flu epidemic threatened, and there were those promissory letters with little currency behind them. When they returned in February 1922, he revised "Up in Michigan" and in the late summer finished "My Old Man." Then in December, just a year after his arrival, everything he had brought with him or had written recently, except those two stories, was stolen from Hadley in a Paris station as she was on her way to join him in Switzerland. That loss, recollected years later in *A Moveable Feast,* was one of the earliest of Hemingway's uncanny strokes of luck. If the lost stories were like those he had written in Chicago, it was time to clear his desk and begin again. Ezra Pound advised him that if a lost story's form had been right at first, then "one ought to be able to reassemble it from memory," but if it "won't reform then it has no proper construction, and never *wd.* have been *right*" (Hagemann 207). Years later Hemingway agreed that it "was probably good for me to lose early work" (*Moveable Feast* 74).

After a few dark months in early 1923, he wrote "Out of Season" in a fury over an argument with Hadley. Then with that story and the two that escaped the loss, "Up in Michigan" and "My Old Man," Hemingway published his first collection in the summer of 1923, *Three Stories and Ten Poems*. He was still placing bets in both genres, but with those three stories he had found his voice and answered the promise of Anderson's letters of introduction.

In Our Time (1925)

During the summer of 1923 he worked on the early chapters of *in our time* (published in 1924), of which two ("A Very Short Story" and "The Revolutionist") were to become "short stories"; then returned to Toronto with Hadley in the fall for the birth of their son "Bumby" and a brief but restive stint reporting for the *Toronto Star*. He resigned on New Year's Day and they fled back to Paris.

Then the miraculous year—in the twelve months after February 1924, Hemingway wrote twelve short stories: he finished eight of them by May ("Indian Camp," "Cat in the Rain," "The End of Something," "The Three-Day Blow," "The Doctor and the Doctor's Wife," "Soldier's Home," "Mr. and Mrs. Elliot," and "Cross-Country Snow"); began "Big Two-Hearted River" in May and revised it by November; finished "The Undefeated" in December, "Banal Story" in January 1925; and when Boni and Liveright objected to "Up in Michigan" for *In Our Time,* he wrote "The Battler" by March.

Later, as if for good measure, he wrote the first draft of *The Sun Also Rises* (1926) in six weeks of the summer of 1925, and between April 1926 and April 1927 another twelve stories for *Men Without Women* (1927)— but by then he had practiced. However remarkable these later achievements, the writing of *In Our Time* first seems the greater and, at last, an inexplicable mystery.

Certainly, after chafing under the *Star*'s editor, Hemingway was determined to write himself free of journalism, but sometimes the will's not the way. The manuscripts of those stories at times show how he labored over them, but at others how often his first draft was the right one. So one may wonder whether early drafts of the *In Our Time* stories were among those that were stolen at the Gare de Lyon in 1922. Apparently Hadley remembered them as Nick Adams stories, but that was much later. If some of the lost manuscripts had been drafts of the stories of early 1924, then perhaps Ezra Pound was right when he told Hemingway that those stories with a significant form will be remembered and those without, fortunately forgotten. That, at least, would account for the creation of eight stories, several among his finest, in the remarkable first three months of 1924.

Men Without Women (1927)

After the marathon writing and months of revising *The Sun Also Rises* and, by the way, ten days dashing off *Torrents of Spring,* Hemingway wrote "An Alpine Idyll" in April 1926 and, during a lonely May day in Madrid, returned to two manuscripts he had begun for "The Killers" and "Ten Indians," brought them close to completion, and wrote "Today Is Friday."

By the end of the summer his marriage to Hadley was over. They separated, and for a month he wrote little more than sad, self-incriminating letters. Then in September he drew on his last train ride with Hadley for "A Canary for One." Somehow, writing that story initiated the first two stories of woundings in war as well as in marriage, "In Another Country" and "Now I Lay Me," followed by two unusual tales, "A Pursuit Race" and "A Simple Enquiry," as well as "On the Quai at Smyrna."

Between his divorce from Hadley in January 1927 and marriage to Pauline Pfeiffer in May, he turned his *New Republic* article into "Che Ti Dice la Patria?", revised the ending of "Ten Indians," and wrote "Hills Like White Elephants"—in the idyllic setting of Grau du Roi he would return to in *The Garden of Eden.* With "The Undefeated" from the fall of 1924, "Fifty Grand" and "Banal Story" finished in January 1925, he had his usual fourteen stories for a collection, and "On the Quai at Smyrna" to use later as an introduction to Scribner's 1930 reissue of *In Our Time. Men Without Women* was an early and tentative choice for a title in February 1927, when Hemingway listed ten stories (including "Up in Michigan"), in "almost" all of which, he wrote, "the softening feminine influence through training, discipline, death, and other causes [was] absent" (*Letters* 245). By the time he had relented on including "Up in Michigan," added "A Canary for One" and "Now I Lay Me," and had written "Che Ti Dice la Patria?", "Ten Indians," and "Hills Like White Elephants," the title was no more and perhaps less descriptive of the collection. Training and discipline may account for the absence of women in the stories of bullfighters and boxers (including that champion Christ of "Today Is Friday"), but that fact is irrelevant; wives die in "An Alpine Idyll" and "In Another Country," but Olz's simple "I loved her, . . . I loved her fine" in the first and the extremity of the major's grief in the second both imply ways in which love instructs us to bear its loss.

The stories Hemingway either did not mention ("A Canary for One" and "Now I Lay Me") or mentioned but, for good reasons, did not submit to *Scribner's Magazine* ("A Pursuit Race" and "A Simple Enquiry") say something of the "other causes" he had in mind for these men without women. Some were close to home: divorce and its unspoken provocations ("A Canary for One") and the binding ties of incompatability ("Now I Lay

Me"); others he had witnessed from Kansas City to Paris: homosexuality ("A Simple Enquiry") and addiction to drugs and alcohol ("A Pursuit Race").

If, finally, Hemingway's title was better than he first thought, it is because the completed collection ranged over a variety of dramatic situations delineating not only the lives of men without women, but also those of men with women who are less than they deserve, Nick's mother, or more, Jig in "Hills Like White Elephants." And not by coincidence, as Hemingway's purview widened, so did his exploration of modes of narrative and narration, to extend his sense of the art of the short story.

Winner Take Nothing (1933)

From March to August 1928 Hemingway wrote the first draft of *A Farewell to Arms* and revised it for nearly another year. Two years later *Death in the Afternoon,* on his mind for some time, claimed his attention from the summer of 1930 to the early winter of 1932. With the novel the early reviewers took as fact and a work of nonfiction now read as a fiction, both written in these years, it is not surprising that more of the *Winner Take Nothing* stories seem closer to the life than those in the earlier collections: "Wine of Wyoming," "The Gambler, the Nun, and the Radio," "A Day's Wait," and "Fathers and Sons." Four draw on the accounts of others: Bra Saunders's tale in "After the Storm," Sidney Franklin's in "The Mother of a Queen," and, from Carlos Baker's evidence, the anonymous letter-writers behind "God Rest You Merry, Gentleman" and "One Reader Writes" *(Ernest Hemingway: A Life Story 227)* The fragments from early 1929 through the late summer of 1931 that became "A Natural History of the Dead," first submitted as a short story, then included in *Death in the Afternoon,* and finally reinstated as a story, are central documents for all these stories challenging the claims along the boundaries of fiction and nonfiction.

Nor is it surprising that ten of these fourteen stories were begun and revised over a period of one or two years; and not simply because the second novel and the bullfighting book intervened, but because Hemingway was, once again, testing the limits of his art, some of which he had set by 1930 and his readers had come to expect—and demand, for many reviews were critical.

Although "A Clean, Well-Lighted Place" became the thematic centerpiece of this volume and of nearly all his fiction, and "The Light of the World" filled in part of the Nick Adams's saga, Hemingway was about other business as well. Only recently Joseph Flora has shown that "Wine of Wyoming," "A Day's Wait," and "Fathers and Sons" form a sequence of late "marriage tales" like the earlier sequence from "Out of Season" to "A Canary for One," which most had missed the first time. "Homage to Switzerland," perhaps Hemingway's most ambitious but unrealized experiment, joins the end of a marriage with the theme of homosexuality; and that story, with "The Sea Change" before it and "Mr. and Mrs. Elliot" from *In Our Time,* form another sequence that associates varieties of sexual experience with the writer's creative act, a sequence that ended with *The Garden of Eden.*

Among these stories of the early 1930s is his last on the wounded Nick Adams, "A Way You'll Never Be," another experimental story with a technique realized in "The Snows of Kilimanjaro." This story with the late marriage tales and the studies of lesbianism and male homosexuality repeat the themes of the stories from late 1926 and early 1927 with which he rounded out *Men Without Women.*

The Fifth Column and the First Forty-nine Stories (1938)

With *Winner Take Nothing* complete in the spring of 1933, except for revising "Fathers and Sons," Hemingway turned once again to a novel and, after the African safari in the winter of 1933-34, a long work of nonfiction. Although the first two sections of *To Have and Have Not* (1937) were published as stories in 1934 and 1936, from his first mention of them in a letter of February 1933, he thought of them as chapters in a novel. *Green Hills of Africa* (1935), again mixing the strategies of fiction in nonfiction, took up the months from March to November of 1934; but recalling the safari in that experimental genre led to the climax in Hemingway's career as a writer of short stories in the winter and spring of 1936.

Having begun "The Capital of the World" the preceding fall and "The Short Happy Life of Francis Macomber" perhaps a year before that, between February and April of 1936 he brought all three to brilliant conclusions. With the deaths of the Spanish waiter Paco and Francis Macomber—both killed by someone doing the work of a bull—he extended his experiments with various narrative points of view and the manipulation of time. "The Snows of Kilimanjaro" joins the *Green Hills of Africa* with scenes recollected later in *A Moveable Feast.* It, too, mingles the past and the present in a writer's memory, and at the end, leaps to the ultimate future in his vision of death.

The last story Hemingway collected during his lifetime was "Old Man at the Bridge." Begun as a Spanish Civil War dispatch in April but submitted as a story in May 1938, it recounts the narrator's meeting an old man with steel spectacles, too tired to retreat or even stand, resigned to his own death from the advancing troops but still concerned that he had left behind two goats, a cat, and four pairs of pigeons.

The Fifth Column and Four Stories of the Spanish Civil War (1969)

Although "Old Man at the Bridge" was the last story to be collected, it introduces the four stories of the Spanish Civil War and their sentimental Cuban epilogue, "Nobody Ever Dies," all written between May 1938 and February 1939, and published during those years in *Esquire* and *Cosmopolitan*. In "The Denunciation," "The Butterfly and the Tank," "Night Before Battle," and "Under the Ridge," Hemingway continued to probe the lines between fact and fiction in a series of related stories. The first three share settings in Chicote's bar in Madrid and a narrator with the conflicting roles of a detached observer and an engaged participant in the politics and bloodshed of that prophetic civil war. The stories themselves prophesied the next novel; and when he began writing *For Whom the Bell Tolls* (1940) in March 1939, they must have seemed to have served that purpose. They were collected in 1969, eight years after his death.

The Complete Short Stories of Ernest Hemingway (1987)

Hemingway's last two stories were published in response to a request from the *Atlantic Monthly* in early 1957 for its centenary issue. He began a memoir of Scott Fitzgerald, gave it up, wrote "A Man of the World" and with it finessed "Get a Seeing-Eyed Dog" from three years before, both under the title "Two Tales of Darkness." Each is more a sketch than a story, and blindness is their only unity. "Get a Seeing-Eyed Dog," set in Venice, is elegiac and contemplative; while "A Man of the World" is a brutal tale of violence told to a novice in a Wyoming saloon. Sounding with grim rage and whispers of self-pity, the last two stories published in his lifetime may echo that old king challenging the elements on a heath or bidding farewell to a loving daughter; but in the bright and enduring light of the stories from the twenties and thirties, they seem more like a voice from the depths.

Hemingway's art of the short story was born, flourished to greatness, and died within a brief life of some fifteen years, between 1923 and 1938, before the succession of novels in his last two decades. To come to Paris knowing as little of the art of fiction as he knew of French, to meet the promise of his mentors in two years, to lay claim a year later to an original and influential style, to become a master craftsman in the next two years in a guild to which he had so recently been apprenticed, and then in a final decade to give a new form and meaning to the art of the short story—to do all this in that brief time is the remarkable achievement this book will try to record and explain, knowing, of course, that the original sources of genius are beyond us all.

Works Cited

PRIMARY

A Moveable Feast. New York: Scribner's, 1964.

Ernest Hemingway: Selected Letters, 1917–1961. Ed. Carlos Baker. New York: Scribner's, 1981.

SECONDARY

Baker, Carlos. *Ernest Hemingway: A Life Story.* 1969. New York: Scribner's, 1988.

Flora, Joseph M. *Hemingway's Nick Adams.* Baton Rouge: Louisiana State UP, 1982.

Hagemann, E. R. " 'Dear Folks . . . Dear Ezra': Hemingway's Early Years and Correspondence, 1917–1924." *College Literature* 7 (1980): 202–12.

A Note on Sources

This book is meant to serve any serious reader of Hemingway's short stories, from students to scholars, with the will to look things up and the sense to question its assertions—or at least some of them. No book on Hemingway and certainly none on Hemingway criticism could, or even should, remain impartial. This one is meant to guide readers through the writing and publication and criticism of the stories with brief commentaries partial to the critical evidence and conclusions that will enlighten past readings of the stories and encourage the writing of original criticism in the future.

Almost all the manuscripts cited are in the Hemingway Collection of the John F. Kennedy Library, Columbia Point, Boston MA 02125, where photocopies of the manuscripts may be ordered. Those cited from other collections are similarly available. This book should demonstrate the critical importance of those manuscripts for any further study of Hemingway's fiction.

Texts:

The Short Stories of Ernest Hemingway (New York: Scribner's, 1938) for all the stories but the following.

The Nick Adams Stories (New York: Scribner's, 1972) for the deleted sections of "Indian Camp" and "Big Two-Hearted River";

The Fifth Column and Four Stories of the Spanish Civil War (New York: Scribner's, 1969) for "The Denunciation," "The Butterfly and the Tank," "Night Before Battle," and "Under the Ridge"; and

The Complete Short Stories of Ernest Hemingway (New York: Scribner's, 1987) for "Nobody Ever Dies," "Get a Seeing-Eyed Dog," and "A Man of the World."

(Two other books are cited in almost every chapter, and the reader would do well to have them both at hand: Carlos Baker's *Ernest Hemingway: A Life Story* (1969; New York: Scribner's, 1988), and *Ernest Hemingway: Selected Letters, 1917–1961*, ed. Carlos Baker (New York: Scribner's, 1981).

Bibliographies

The bibliographies consulted for the periods indicated are:

1923–1965—Audre Hanneman, *Ernest Hemingway: A Comprehensive Bibliography* (Princeton: Princeton UP, 1967) and

1966-1973—*Supplement to Ernest Hemingway: A Comprehensive Bibliography* (1975); and two other supplements,

1966-1970—Audre Hanneman, "Hanneman Addenda," *Fitzgerald/Hemingway Annual* (1970): 195-218, and William White, "Supplement to Hanneman: Articles, 1966-1970," *Hemingway Notes* 1 (Spring 1971): 3-12.

1971-1981—William White, "Current Bibliography," *Hemingway Notes* 1-6 (Spring 1971-Spring 1981) and *Hemingway Review* 1-7 (Fall 1981-Fall 1987).

1924-1974—"A Comprehensive Checklist of Hemingway Short Fiction Criticism, Explication, and Commentary," *The Short Stories of Ernest Hemingway: Critical Essays*, ed. Jackson J. Benson (Durham: Duke UP, 1975).

1974-1985—*MLA International Bibliography* (New York: Modern Language Association, 1974-85).

Abbreviations and Symbols

KL/EH	With a folder number, an item in the Hemingway Collection, John F. Kennedy Library.
Four Stories	*The Fifth Column and Four Stories of the Spanish Civil War.* New York: Scribner's, 1969.
Letters	*Ernest Hemingway: Selected Letters, 1917-1961.* Ed. Carlos Baker. New York: Scribner's, 1981.
Stories	*The Short Stories of Ernest Hemingway.* New York: Scribner's, 1938.
Complete Stories	*The Complete Short Stories of Ernest Hemingway.* New York: Scribner's, 1987.
| |	Material deleted from a manuscript.
/ /	Material inserted in a manuscript.

Prologue: Oak Park and Chicago, 1916–1921

Oak Park: The High School Stories, 1916–1917

Although recent biographies have searched Hemingway's childhood and school years to find him constricted by a conservative society moving upward from the middle class, bound for good and bad by a strenuous protestant morality, and determined to be distinguished from the "Hog Butcher for the World" to the east along the lake, none has any serious complaint with Hemingway's education in Oak Park High School. It had a fine curriculum in English language and literature, albeit as thin in American writers as most were in the early 1900s (Reynolds, *Hemingway's Reading* 39–43). Among its English faculty, Fannie Biggs was perhaps most influential in her courses on the short story and journalism (Lynn 25), although even she never taught him to spell: "The last thing I remember about English in High School," he once wrote, "was a big controversy on whether it was *already* or *all ready*. How did it ever come out?" (*Letters* xi).

During his last two years he spent most of his time writing a variety of articles and serving as editor for the school's newspaper, the *Trapeze*. One manuscript from that period shows that he was not beyond taking a speaker's address to the Mark Hanna Club—whose namesake made corporate business and Republicanism synonymous—to write a rousing tale of a massacre in the Philippines, the moral of which is "listen to your elders!" This piece, abandoned because a schoolmate wrote a detailed article on the talk, forecasts Hemingway's later use of a privileged narrator retelling the tale of an old hand.

In his junior and senior years (1916–17) Hemingway published in the school's literary magazine, *Tabula,* his first three stories: "Judgment of Manitou," 22 (February 1916); "A Matter of Colour," 22 (April 1916); and "Sepi Jingan," 23 (November 1916).

No manuscripts for these stories have turned up, the fate of most school fiction. The stories were first collected in Constance Cappel Montgomery, *Hemingway in Michigan* (Waitsfield: Vermont Crossroads, 1977); and then in *Ernest Hemingway's Apprenticeship,* ed. Matthew J. Bruccoli (Washington: NCR Microcard Editions, 1971).

Almost all the biographers cite these stories to demonstrate Hemingway's early reading, much of it outside his school courses, or to find harbingers of his later fiction. He had read Ring Lardner—even took the name Ring

Lardner, Jr., in his *Trapeze* articles—O. Henry, Jack London, Owen Wister's *The Virginian,* and Mark Twain's *Huckleberry Finn.* Stewart Edward White's title, *Silent Places,* provided a phrase for "Judgment of Manitou," and the "Twa Corbies" flew in from his school anthology to offer a grim allusion in that story (Reynolds, *Young Hemingway* 74).

Critics and biographers from Charles Fenton to Michael Reynolds, particularly Constance Montgomery, have found themes and techniques in these stories foretelling his later fiction: violent death, suicide, revenge, ineluctable fate, twist endings, inside narratives told in flavorful dialects and jargons—the usual matter and manner of high school writers.

The only detailed analysis of any of these stories is Gregory Green's of "A Matter of Colour"—perhaps the least of the three stories. He finds its source in a boxing anecdote told of Stanley Ketchel's plan to have Jack Johnson clubbed from behind a curtain in an exhibition bout only to be clubbed himself by mistake. This leads Green through a consideration of the racist attitudes that led to the cry in 1908 for a "Great White Hope" to defeat Johnson, the black heavyweight champion. That Ketchel nearly did defeat Johnson in 1909 then associates this school story with Hemingway's "The Light of the World" of 1932. Green's is an intricate and persuasive argument, but it seems to invest Hemingway as a teenager with a subtlety he only later achieved with "The Light of the World."

If all the prose in the *Trapeze* and *Tabula* were as predictive as Hemingway's, several of his classmates would have gone on to careers as great as his. His youngest sister, Carol, published "The Eleven o'Clock Mail Plane" in the 1930 *Tabula,* a story with as much promise as any Ernest wrote in his schooldays. It tells of a young boy, about Leicester Hemingway's age, sitting in class and hearing the drone of the mail plane and remembering the confusing events on the day he heard a shot in his father's bedroom at eleven o'clock in the morning, then the inquest at eleven the next day, and later the murmuring relatives and friends who came to visit and wondered about "another woman." His teacher notices the boy oddly distracted by the sound of the plane and later remarks that "half the fun of teaching children is surmising about what they'll be when they grow up." She is sure this one will be a "second Lindbergh." A cautionary tale for us all.

Chicago: The Manuscripts, 1919–1921

When Hemingway remembered the fall of 1919 in Petoskey, Michigan, he recalled shoveling gravel for the county to pay his rent and writing

> stories which I sent to the Saturday Evening Post. The Saturday Evening Post did not buy them nor did any other magazine and I doubt if

worse stories were ever written. I was always known in Petoskey as Ernie Hemingway who wrote for the Saturday Evening Post. . . . After Christmas when I was still writing for the Saturday Evening Post and had $20 left of my savings, I was promised a job in the pump factory . . . and was looking forward to laying off writing for the magazines for a time. (KL/EH 820)

Five of the thirteen manuscripts from this period were published in Peter Griffin's *Along with Youth* (Oxford: Oxford UP, 1985), and most confirm Hemingway's later judgment.

Two of these stories are among those written in Hemingway's "Chicago" style: the narrator often assumes the role of a privileged witness, recalling another's tale and mingling elaborate circumlocutions for his audience with colloquial diction to attest to his veracity. "The Ash Heel's Tendon" draws on the stereotypes of the tough detective and the ruthless hired gun, the latter with a fatal weakness punned upon in the title—his Italian love for opera. This story and "The Mercenaries" were completed in the fall of 1919, before the job at the pump factory offered some relief. The latter story, like "The Woppian Way" Michael Reynolds considers (*Young Hemingway* 58–59), draws on some of the Italian exploits Hemingway invented in 1918 and with which he regaled high school and ladies' club audiences on his return.

Two others, "The Current" and "Portrait of the Idealist in Love," are sentimental and dubious efforts from late 1921. In the first, a wealthy and philandering sportsman proves himself worthy of his beloved Dorothy Hadley by winning the middleweight boxing title—she would not be impressed by his skill in fly-fishing and, unfortunately, the polo season is over. The second, with a title Hemingway rejected, shows evidence of being another person's letter Hemingway hastily copied as a private joke, framed with a brief introduction and conclusion, and then set aside. He repeated this format in "One Reader Writes" with some success.

The last manuscript published in Griffin is the collection of five pieces titled "Crossroads—An Anthology." Michael Reynolds documented Hemingway's writing these sketches in the fall of 1919 on the model of E. W. Howe's "An Anthology of Another Town" from the *Saturday Evening Post* (Introduction, 3–6). They were brief, colloquial vignettes told in the local voice of the region around Horton Bay. Some of them, however, were more than imitations of Howe, for in them Hemingway found for a moment his first true style, which he perfected in the *in our time* chapters. Here, too, he discovered the rich vein of his Michigan stories: the portrait of "Pauline Snow" was a promising sample that led to "Up in Michigan" in the fall of 1921.

The Chicago manuscripts of 1919–21 argue that, above all, Hemingway was determined to be published in the popular magazines of the time and that he would imitate any style, from the tough reporter's to the glossy sentimentalist's, to get in print. But when he packed for Paris in December 1921, he knew which manuscripts to take, and he packed light. (For a fuller discussion of this period see Smith.)

Works Cited

PRIMARY

Ernest Hemingway: Selected Letters, 1917–1961. Ed. Carlos Baker. New York: Scribner's, 1981.

SECONDARY

Bruccoli, Matthew, ed. *Ernest Hemingway's Apprenticeship.* Washington: NCR Microcard Editions, 1977.

Green, Gregory. " 'A Matter of Colour': Hemingway's Criticism of Race Prejudice." *Hemingway Review* 1 (Fall 1981): 27–32.

Griffin, Peter. *Along with Youth: Hemingway, The Early Years.* Oxford: Oxford UP, 1985.

Lynn, Kenneth S. *Hemingway.* New York: Simon, 1987.

Montgomery, Constance Cappel. *Hemingway in Michigan.* Waitsfield: Vermont Crossroads, 1977.

Reynolds, Michael S. *Hemingway's Reading: 1910–1940.* Princeton: Princeton UP, 1981.

———. "Introduction: Looking Backward." *Critical Essays on Ernest Hemingway's "In Our Time."* Boston: Hall, 1983.

———. *The Young Hemingway.* Oxford: Blackwell, 1986.

Smith, Paul. "Hemingway's Apprentice Fiction: 1919–21." *American Literature* 58 (Dec. 1986): 574–86.

Three Stories
and
Ten Poems
(July 1923)

1
Up in Michigan

Composition History (Fall 1921; February 1922)

For years it was assumed that "Up in Michigan" was, if not the first, one of the earliest stories Hemingway wrote after his arrival in Paris in December 1921. When he mentioned the story in the later recollections of *A Moveable Feast*, he remembered showing it to Gertrude Stein sometime in March 1922 and being told that in her judgment the story was *inaccrochable*, unsuitable for public display (15). Although the anecdote is not corroborated by Stein in her *Autobiography of Alice B. Toklas*, the story's *second* version (KL/EH 799) bears editorial marks that seem to be hers.

This second version was a revision of an earlier manuscript and a related fragment (KL/EH 800, 801), probably written in Chicago in the early fall of 1921, when Sherwood Anderson suggested that the Hemingways go to Paris rather than to Italy and offered him letters of recommendation to Stein and Ezra Pound.

There is a third manuscript (KL/EH 798) from the summer of 1930 in which Hemingway revised and expurgated the narrative in an attempt to make it suitable for Scribner's reissue of the 1925 Boni and Liveright edition of *In Our Time* (Smith).

Publication History (July 1923; October 1938)

One of the nicest ironies in Hemingway's early career is that Stein's judgment of "Up in Michigan" as too graphic in its description of sex may well have preserved it for publication in his first volume, *Three Stories and Ten Poems*. For that reason, as Carlos Baker notes, the manuscript was "gathering dust in a drawer" in the fall of 1922 (*Ernest Hemingway: A Life Story* 103). When Hadley left Paris to join Ernest in Lausanne that December, she either overlooked it or was told not to include it among the manuscripts she packed in a valise for his working vacation. Whatever the reason, she boarded the train at the Gare de Lyon with a substantial number of his manuscripts and carbons—and they were stolen. This left him, according to his account, with two stories, this one and "My Old Man," which, by another stroke of luck, Lincoln Steffens had read in Lausanne and suggested submitting to *Cosmopolitan* that December.

Late the following January, Hemingway met Robert McAlmon, the wealthy publisher and novelist, and in May they traveled to Spain for Hemingway's first and formative encounter with bullfights. In Madrid they met William Bird, for whose Three Mountain Press edition of Ezra Pound's "inquest" series Hemingway had promised his work in progress. But on their return to Paris in June, McAlmon announced the forthcoming publications of Contact Editions, including "Short Stories" by Ernest Hemingway (Baker, *Ernest Hemingway: A Life Story* 111). By this time Hemingway had one other story he had written in April, "Out of Season," and ten poems, only four of which were unpublished. Perhaps they, like "Up in Michigan," had been gathering dust in a drawer or, like "My Old Man," were with Hemingway in Lausanne and escaped the loss.

The text of "Up in Michigan" in *Three Stories* is close to the version in manuscript 799. Gertrude Stein's editorial suggestions are crossed out in Hemingway's hand, and her deletions of the more explicit language at the story's climax are revoked with his words "Pay no attention." From this or a typescript similar to it, "Up in Michigan" found its way into print as the first story in his first book. And appropriately so: set in the countryside of his adolescence; marked by his initiation into his craft as a young man in Chicago; and, it is likely, the first fiction he revised at the beginning of his Parisian years, the story deserves that place.

That the story was not reprinted until the 1938 edition of *The First Forty-nine* was no fault of Hemingway's. Throughout those fifteen years his letters record his persistent efforts to convince, first, Boni and Liveright to include it in *In Our Time* (1925), and later, Scribner's to print it in *Men Without Women* (1927) and in their own 1930 reissue of *In Our Time*. In that last try he wrote out an expurgated version of the story (KL/EH 798), changing the characters' names, deleting some of their identifying features, and, ironically, crossing out many of those more breathless passages that Gertrude Stein had found objectionable in 1922. By 1938 such objections were even more irrelevant, and Hemingway could delight in suggesting to Max Perkins that he use as an advertisement for the volume the fact that "Up in Michigan" was "only obtainable in a book that now sells for $350. a copy" (*Letters* 474).

Sources and Influences

In its initial place among the published short stories it was perhaps inevitable that "Up in Michigan" would evoke more critical interest in its origins than in the story itself as an original work—a writer's first work must be derivative. Like the early reviews of *Three Stories,* the first commentaries picked the story up only to place it in one of two lines of literary influence, one from Sherwood Anderson and the other from Gertrude Stein.

Charles Fenton was the first to distinguish between the influences of Anderson and Stein on the story (149–59). Anderson's *Winesburg, Ohio,* which Hemingway had read avidly in the winter of 1920 in Toronto, would have confirmed his discovery in the previous fall of the drama in the ordinary lives of the Horton Bay villagers. Anderson's use of simple and colloquial speech, his interest in his characters' often bewildering passions and sentiments, seldom understood or articulated, and his then daring realism would have encouraged Hemingway to follow his example and, as always, try to surpass it.

When Fenton turned to the question of Stein's influence, he suspected that the story was written before Hemingway "could have fully grasped Miss Stein's teaching" (149); but Fenton then proceeded to an analysis of the story's crucial third paragraph ("Liz liked Jim very much.") to argue that Hemingway had learned the lesson of "repetition" from correcting proofs of Stein's *The Making of Americans* a year after the story had been published and three after he had written its first version.

Fenton's work in 1954 on Hemingway's apprenticeship—still an invaluable resource—set the terms for the discussion of literary influence. Since then the advantage of literary influence has swung to Anderson at times, to Stein at others, but most often has ended in a truce partitioning the territory of the story with Anderson claiming its subject and Stein its style. Philip Young, in a characteristic move, attempted to settle the controversy by stating that the story's prose was too "hardheaded" for Anderson and "cut off by its subject matter" from Stein (179). Earl Rovit turned the issue back to literary history with the suggestion that Hemingway himself "overestimated" the influence of Anderson, "which may account for the unnecessary savagery" of his attack on him in *Torrents of Spring* (43). Sheldon Grebstein later turned from the "texture" of the story, which he thought was influenced by both Anderson and Stein, to the perhaps more interesting fact of Hemingway's experiment with a point of view that is at first omniscient but, assuming the attitudes of the characters, especially Liz Coates's, becomes a variant of the first-person narrative perspective (80).

The question of influence depends in part, of course, upon the dating of the original manuscripts. If the first version of the story, with its crucial third paragraph nearly identical to the published version, can be dated in the fall of 1921 when it is unlikely that, as Fenton first noted, Hemingway could have been influenced by Stein, then the origin of the story's repetitive style might lie elsewhere. Michael Reynolds was the first to follow the leads in the Hemingway correspondence with his friend William B. Smith to suggest that the model he was imitating was E. W. Howe's "Anthology of Another

Town," a series of sketches appearing in the *Saturday Evening Post* through the fall and winter of 1919–20 (Reynolds 2–6). There is a clear line of influence from Howe's sketches to Hemingway's "Cross Roads: An Anthology," a manuscript of which has been published in Griffin (124–27). From that early series of sketches, particularly that of "Pauline Snow," there is a still discernible line to the style, the subject, and the narrative structure of "Up in Michigan" (Smith). The influences on Hemingway's early fiction, this research suggests, may be more native than was at first suspected.

When Hemingway himself attracted the interest of biographers, "Up in Michigan" was made to serve their purposes, some for literary history and not a few for gossip. The most detailed account of the original figures and places in Horton Bay—Jim Dilworth, the blacksmith, and his wife, Liz; the few houses of the town, the dock, and the view of Lake Charlevoix—is in Constance Montgomery's intimate study (119–23). Her book demonstrates that in this early story, as in "Cross Roads," Hemingway turned to what he had seen and heard during his summers in Michigan and away from the formula fiction he was writing for the popular magazines—the first important step he took toward becoming an original writer.

Then the gossip begins: Was he tattling on the Dilworths, or was he himself the rough-handed seducer? Who was the girl, and did she in fact get a hemlock sliver in her bottom for her pains? Speculations such as these began with Carlos Baker's biography (1969) and will not end with Jeffrey Meyers's (1985), even though what Hemingway had to know to describe the sexual scene he could have learned on any street corner or in any high school locker room of his youth.

Critical Studies

That "Up in Michigan" was later excluded from the volumes of Hemingway's short stories until *The First Forty-nine* in 1938 may account in part for its relatively few and brief critical considerations. By then the axiom that Hemingway was a man writing of and for men only might have obscured the fact that his first published story was almost wholly written from the point of view of a woman experiencing a ritual initiation, similar to that his young men go through, as a prologue to a life of violence, pain, and brutality (Young 179). So too that axiom might have diverted attention from the formal and thematic connections between this story and the later "marriage tales": its companion story, "Out of Season," as well as "Cat in the Rain," "A Canary for One," and "Hills Like White Elephants," all written between 1923 and 1927. Each of these later stories, reflecting the dissolution of Hemingway's first marriage, iterates one or more of the features of "Up in Michigan": all offer us singularly obtuse and unsympathetic male characters; two present the action as it is witnessed by a woman ("Cat in the Rain" and "Hills Like White Elephants"), and each of those women has a vision of the world that is more creative or poetic than her burdensome partner's—"Cat in the Rain" even repeats the stylistic features of the third paragraph of "Up in Michigan."

When Philip Young noted in 1952 that this story "is really the story Hemingway long continued to write" (177) for both men and women, and not only in the short stories, and Carlos Baker later identified its theme as the "attraction and repulsion between the two sexes" (*Writer as Artist* 135), it was as if the central critical question of the story was simply Hemingway's depiction, and thus his conception, of the relationship between the sexes. Most commentaries, however, finding nothing in Liz Coates that repelled Jim Gilmore, ignored or underestimated what she saw in him that was attractive. And so the story was read as the tale of, at best, a seduction and, at worst, a rape.

This range of readings of the story's climactic event is reviewed in its most recent and comprehensive study. Alice Hall Petry argues that the story centers on "the disparity between the male and female attitudes toward love and sex" and finds evidence for those attitudes in Jim Gilmore's perception of Liz in "exclusively sexual terms" and Liz Coates's consciousness of Jim determined by her innocent and "non-sexual romanticized attraction" to him. Given these attitudes, the climax was "destined . . . in view of both her ignorance, vulnerability, confusion, and awakening sexuality, as well as Jim's comparative experience" (23, 27).

Whether we assume that Jim is more sexually experienced—nothing in the story proves it—or that Liz, anticipating the event, does not encourage it, the story derives some persuasive and particular meaning from its setting and occasion. Petry has argued that the description of Horton Bay, its houses and its views, function in this story as does the heath in Hardy, and that Liz's view of the ore-barges, seeming fixed on the horizon when she sees them first but gone, inevitably, when she looks again, suggests the *destined* outcome of the evening (23, 25). That seems right, even though it begs a large question. The significance of the climactic union of Jim Gilmore and Liz Coates out there on the dock—in itself an unremarkable event—is not only that the one's passion coincided with the other's sentimental curiosity, but that it happened on the return from a hunt to something like a home.

Leslie Fiedler's dramatic reading of Hemingway's fiction draws on this story to exemplify in part the archetypal conflict between the hunter man and the homemaker woman—each a threat to the other (304 ff.). With something less of Fiedler's curious virulence toward Hemingway, that larger cultural theme still illuminates "Up in Michigan." Jim returns from the wilderness, bearded and impassioned from the kill and the whiskey, with the trophy of manhood embodied in a "big buck . . . stiff and hard," which both he and Liz admire. Liz and Mrs. Smith had cooked for four days to send the men off with home cooking. When Jim returns and presents his symbolic kill, the ritual drinking celebrating the masculine hunt and the dinner served by the women to the hunters combine to make the sexual union of their representational characters almost an anticlimax, when the buck comes alive, as it were, in the tumescence of the last scene—thus the title, as some have read it (Flora 466, Petry 26).

With this interpretation the story reaches beyond Hemingway's experience for its meaning and locates its depiction of passion and sentiment in a singular myth of American culture.

Works Cited

PRIMARY

Ernest Hemingway: Selected Letters, 1917-1961. Ed. Carlos Baker. New York: Scribner's, 1981.

A Moveable Feast. New York: Scribner's, 1964.

The Short Stories of Ernest Hemingway. New York: Scribner's, 1938, 81–86.

SECONDARY

Baker, Carlos. *Ernest Hemingway: A Life Story.* 1969. New York: Scribner's 1988

———. *Hemingway: The Writer as Artist.* 1952. Princeton: Princeton UP, 1972.

Fenton, Charles A. *The Apprenticeship of Ernest Hemingway: The Early Years.* New York: Farrar, 1954.

Fiedler, Leslie. *Love and Death in the American Novel.* Cleveland: Criterion Books, 1960.

Flora, Joseph M. "Hemingway's 'Up in Michigan.'" *Studies in Short Fiction* 6 (Summer 1969): 465–66.

Grebstein, Sheldon N. *Hemingway's Craft.* Carbondale: Southern Illinois UP, 1973.

Griffin, Peter. *Along with Youth: Hemingway, The Early Years.* Oxford: Oxford UP, 1985.

Meyers, Jeffrey. *Hemingway: A Biography.* New York: Harper, 1985.

Montgomery, Constance. *Hemingway in Michigan.* Waitsfield: Vermont Crossroads, 1977.

Petry, Alice Hall. "Coming of Age in Hortons Bay: Hemingway's 'Up in Michigan.'" *Hemingway Review* 3 (Spring 1984): 23–28.

Reynolds, Michael S. "Introduction: Looking Backward." *Critical Essays on Ernest Hemingway's "In Our Time."* Boston: Hall, 1983.

Rovit, Earl. *Ernest Hemingway.* New York: Twayne, 1963.

Smith, Paul. "Three Versions of 'Up in Michigan': 1921–1930." *Resources for American Literary Study* 15 (Autumn 1985): 163–77.

Stein, Gertrude. *The Autobiography of Alice B. Toklas.* New York: Harcourt, 1933.

Young, Philip. *Ernest Hemingway: A Reconsideration.* 1952. New York: Harcourt, 1966.

2

My Old Man

Composition History (July–September 1922)

The references in "My Old Man" to the Paris racing season of the summer of 1922 and Gregory Clark's letters to Hemingway that fall make the dating of its composition a relatively simple matter. Carlos Baker first noted the allusions to that racing season and that Hemingway had the manuscript in hand by late November (*Ernest Hemingway: A Life Story* 100). Recently Michael Reynolds has demonstrated that specific details—the famous horses, Kzar, Kircubbin, and Guildford ("Gilford" in the story), the odds, the winner's share, the track, and a variety of others—all come from that season in the summer of 1922 and from a race, albeit an honest one, on 2 July in which Kzar and Kircubbin were the favorites (3–8). Late July, then, is the earliest date for the composition of the story. On 2 September Gregory Clark, Hemingway's feature editor on the *Toronto Star,* wrote that he would "watch for [the] Old Man story"; and on 21 November, having read it, Clark wrote to him that "My Old Man is simply great" (KL/EH). Hemingway's reasons for sending Clark a draft may have been educational; for in an unpublished memoir of his Toronto days Hemingway recalled holding one thing against Clark, "he did not know . . . about horse racing" (Baker, *Ernest Hemingway: A Life Story* 121).

Hemingway gave the story to Lincoln Steffens in late November, who then submitted it with his recommendation to *Cosmopolitan.* Late September was taken up with a fishing trip to the Black Forest, and from then to late October Hemingway was in Constantinople writing articles for the *Toronto Star.* So the story must have been nearly completed by mid-September.

The manuscripts seem to support that date. There are two sets of typescripts in the Kennedy Collection, neither typed by Hemingway. Item 591 is a set of carbons of a title page and uncorrected pages numbered 119–40; the originals could have served as setting copy for *In Our Time.* Item 592 is a set of two carbons bearing Hemingway's Paris address for 1922; the pencil corrections on one set were incorporated in *Three Stories and Ten Poems* (1923). It is possible that Hemingway had these carbons and their originals with him in Lausanne to revise for submission. If so, that would account for the curious absence of both a holograph and a Hemingway typescript in the collection—they, too, might have been stolen from Hadley in December 1922.

The story is nearly three times as long as either of the other two in *Three Stories*. To have written a story that long and to have it typed (by Hadley or someone else) suggests the rather more leisurely period of composition in the summer. Finally, the story itself gives the impression of precise and recent memories of the race tracks in Milan and Paris and their environs. Hemingway had spent the first week of June at San Siro with Hadley, "playing the races with tremendous success" on her "clairevoyance" and the advice of a friend who "sleeps with the horses" (*Letters* 69). With these recollections of Milan fresh in his mind, followed the next month by the Kzar-Kircubbin race in Paris, one might expect the story's two settings and the immediacy of their details.

Publication History (July 1923; January 1924; October 1925)

For all Lincoln Steffens's good offices, *Cosmopolitan* rejected "My Old Man" in December 1922; but in the following February in Rapallo, Hemingway's luck changed when he met Edward O'Brien, who accepted the story for publication in *The Best Short Stories of 1923*. In April Hemingway submitted it to *Pictorial Review*—perhaps to meet the formality of previous magazine publication for O'Brien's series—and again it was rejected. But by then it was scheduled for publication in the summer with *Three Stories and Ten Poems*. The *Best Short Stories* edition of January 1924 reprinted that text; and with some minor changes "My Old Man" was published in the first edition of *In Our Time* of October 1925.

In spite of its two early rejections, "My Old Man" accumulated an impressive number of Hemingway "firsts": the first story begun in Europe, it was the first to be anthologized, the first to be published in the United States, and the first to win a literary honor. When Hemingway rather dispiritedly offered his manuscript to O'Brien in Rapallo, after losing most of what he had written a few months earlier, he was placing what he had left of his literary capital on a long shot; and—as in the story itself—it paid off handsomely.

Sources and Influences

Few who have commented on this story, including Scott Fitzgerald and Hemingway, have neglected its similarity to Sherwood Anderson's "I Want to Know Why" (1919). Fitzgerald thought it another one of those "sentimental 'horse stories'" (Stephens 18). In a letter to Edmund Wilson of November 1923, Hemingway said that both stories derive "from boys and horses," but that his is about "a boy and his father and race-horses," and that he wasn't "inspired" by Anderson (*Letters* 105). Hemingway implied that the apparent similarities between the two stories are inconsequential. Both are first-person narratives of young boys with a passion for horse-racing, and both boys' idolization of an older man is shattered in a disillusioning epiphany. Some of Hemingway's descriptions of the horses are close in their details to Anderson's; and Joe Butler's remark "But I don't know" seems a deliberate allusion to Anderson's title and the last line of his story, "I want to know why."

Few have remarked on the more important dissimilarities between the two stories. For all the shared colloquialisms (Somers 491–93), Anderson's diction and syntax are more formal than Hemingway's, and his story is "written" rather than "told." The conflict in Anderson is established in a Lawrentian moment when a boy and a horse-trainer are mystically united in their love for a horse; in Hemingway it is set in a son's love for his father. The disillusionment in Anderson comes with the realization that a man can love both fast horses and fast women; in Hemingway it comes with a boy's false sense that his dead father was, as he hears someone say, a crook.

However the similarities and differences between the two stories are tallied, it is at least as interesting that Hemingway called attention to them in a letter to a critic he knew would recognize what was derivative and hoped would see what was original. The story, like the letter to Wilson, deliberately challenges Anderson on his own turf. Gerry Brenner's analysis admits the imitation; but, unlike most commentators, he sees it as a thrown gauntlet: "*This*, Sherwood, is how you should have treated a story of self-pity" (8).

Just as Anderson's and Hemingway's stories both derived from "boys and horses," so each derived from Mark Twain. Philip Young made the most of the larger influence of Twain on Hemingway but did not note the indebtedness to Huck Finn's example of the wise but innocent narrator, as have David Seed (26) and Michael Reynolds (3). The young Joe Butler has Huck's early morning vision of the world and his intuitive wisdom of the large and simple matters of right and wrong. But like Huck, he can miss the more subtle issues of morality that trouble and complicate adult lives.

When Hemingway mentioned the story in a letter to Scott Fitzgerald in December 1925, he placed it in a class below "Indian Camp" and "Big Two-Hearted River," one that included "The Undefeated" and "Fifty Grand," and was "not the thing I'm shooting for" (*Letters* 180). It was the first of his stories to draw on the sporting world—like "The Battler" and the two he noted from 1925 and "A Pursuit Race" and "The Gambler, the Nun, and the Radio" from 1933. And its antecedents go back to an unpublished sketch of 1919 "The galleria in Milan . . ." (KL/EH 416).

To read "My Old Man" only in the context of the gambling sports is to risk the loss of much of its import. If, however, it is read as the first of his stories of a boy's initiation, irrespective of its setting, then the story assumes something of the larger meaning of stories like "The Killers." Joe Butler's implied dissatisfaction with George Gardner's comforting remarks comes close to Nick Adams's rejection of George's in the later story; and Joe seems about to make Nick's decision to "get out of this town," following Huck's to "light out for the territory."

Critical Studies

When the early reviewers and critics repeatedly identified "My Old Man" with "I Want to Know Why" for its subject or style, it was as if any further questions of character or meaning in Hemingway's story could be as simply resolved as those in Anderson's. Sheridan Baker in 1967 summarized that reading of the story as one "told by a boy, son of a crooked American jockey in Europe who is killed . . . when he buys a horse and tries to go straight. The little aging jockey, pathetically good as a father and bad as a man, is superb. The boy's idiom exactly conveys the irony of his imperceptions and his heartbreak" (26–27). This resembles Carlos Baker's interpretations (1952, 1969), Arthur Waldhorn's (1972), and that repeated in Meyers's biography (1985).

This interpretation of the story slights some of its own evidence: there *is* a resounding irony in Joe Butler's "imperceptions and his heartbreak," and it rests in the issue of the reliability of his narration, which Sheldon Grebstein briefly characterized as that of an "unreliable I-witness" (63). Moreover, this persistent reading of the story has passed over Sidney Krause's brief but important comment of 1962. He argued not only that Joe "cannot allow that his father may have done crooked things, of which we (and he) learn nothing in the story," but also that, in a "Jamesian twist," his father "was in fact militantly honorable—while the boy must be condemned to disbelieve in him" (Item 39).

Robert Lewis offered another Jamesian turn by arguing that "Joe is not as ignorant and naive as he pretends to be, but his innocence demands of him that he continue to delude himself" not only about his father but also about George Gardner, "his father's crooked friend." Thus he fails to appreciate "the slight but nonetheless important care of a friend who to him is a son of a bitch" (13).

The first detailed reading of the text was Ray Lanford's (1976); it related Joe Butler's gradual disillusionment, marked at three points in the narrative, with his "entrance into puberty," or at least his first interest in a girl—a point that others have overlooked (13). His reading contrasts the usual superficial interpretation with the evidence of Butler's refusal to throw the Premio Commercio race with George Gardner's complicity in the fixed Kzar-Kircubbin race.

The most recent interpretation of the story, Gerry Brenner's, slacks off the ironic turn in Lewis's analysis and centers on the story's two contradictory levels of meaning: that which offers the "sentimental" narrative of the boy's disillusionment at hearing that his father was a crook; and the "concealed" meaning that demonstrates his disillusionment was unfounded. His telling point is that "when crooks call a man a crook, naturally they testify to his honesty" (9).

There may be yet another "lower layer" if we insist on Brenner's point with George Gardner. He, after all, did throw the Kzar-Kircubbin race, and it is that that leads Joe to call him a son of a bitch, not his giving Butler a winner. And if Joe is as distraught as he is by the bettors who call his father a crook, he might well be as confused by George's judgment of his father as "one swell guy." Or perhaps not; perhaps he would agree that in one way his father was *one* swell guy and the *only* one among a collection of crooks that included George. His disillusionment with his father is, in any case, unfounded. The more important question is whether he understands the implications of both the bettors and George's remarks. Robert Lewis argued that Joe's "innocence demands . . . that he continue to delude himself." But Joe, finally, does not delude himself, he simply says, "I don't know." He is left desperately, as are we, between two opposed positions; and his last remark, "Seems like when they get started they don't leave a guy nothing," includes all those, Holbrook and the bettors and George, in a corrupt adult world whose morality cannot justify in any terms why a boy lost his father.

Although Lewis's interpretation serves his thesis on Hemingway's concern with the varieties of love and Brenner's his demonstration of Hemingway's "concealed" narratives, each reconsiders the potential ironies in the story that show Hemingway, very early on, moving beyond Sherwood Anderson toward Joseph Conrad and ultimately Henry James. Everything suggests that Hemingway was leaving Anderson with a deliberate challenge. But the story leaves us uncertain that he fully realized the complex implications of that narrative point of view Conrad and James had so brilliantly displayed. Like young Joe Butler, caught between two adults he cannot trust, Hemingway can only say, for now, "But I don't know."

Works Cited

PRIMARY

Ernest Hemingway: Selected Letters, 1917–1961. Ed. Carlos Baker. New York: Scribner's, 1981.

The Short Stories of Ernest Hemingway. New York: Scribner's, 1938, 191–205.

SECONDARY

Baker, Carlos. *Ernest Hemingway: A Life Story.* 1969. New York: Scribner's, 1988.

———. *Hemingway: The Writer as Artist.* 1952. Princeton: Princeton UP, 1972.

Baker, Sheridan. *Ernest Hemingway: An Introduction and Interpretation.* New York: Holt, 1967.

Brenner, Gerry. *Concealments in Hemingway's Works.* Columbus: Ohio State UP, 1983.

Krause, Sidney J. "Hemingway's 'My Old Man.'" *Explicator* 20 (January 1962), Item 39.

Lanford, Ray. "Hemingway's 'My Old Man.'" *Linguistics in Literature* 1 (1976): 11–19.

Lewis, Robert W., Jr. *Hemingway on Love.* 1965. New York: Haskell, 1973.

Meyers, Jeffrey. *Hemingway: A Biography.* New York: Harper, 1985.

Reynolds, Michael S. "Hemingway's 'My Old Man': Turf Days in Paris." Unpublished article.

Seed, David. "'The Picture of the Whole': *In Our Time.*" *Ernest Hemingway: New Critical Essays.* Ed. A. Robert Lee. London: Vision, 1983.

Somers, Paul P. "The Mark of Sherwood Anderson on Hemingway: A Look at the Texts." *South Atlantic Quarterly* 26 (1974): 487–503.

Stephens, Robert O., ed. *Ernest Hemingway: The Critical Reception.* N.p.: Burt Franklin, 1977.

Waldhorn, Arthur. *A Reader's Guide to Ernest Hemingway.* New York: Farrar, 1972.

Young, Philip. *Ernest Hemingway: A Reconsideration.* 1952. New York: Harcourt, 1966.

3
Out of Season

Composition History (April 1923)

The story of the composition of "Out of Season" has assumed the aspect of a legend in the biographical and critical studies of Hemingway. And little wonder, for after his journalistic quests to the Black Forest and Black Sea in the summer and fall of 1922 and the tragic loss of his manuscripts that winter, it is as if the pattern of a myth required the rebirth of his powers with a new theory in the spring to initiate the miraculous years of his early fiction.

All the evidence gathers to confirm that he wrote "Out of Season" in mid-April 1923 when, as he remembered, he "had first been able to write a story after losing everything" (*Moveable Feast* 75). After the loss of the manuscripts in late December, he and Hadley spent most of February in Italy, some of it in Rapallo with Ezra Pound, where he read T. S. Eliot's "The Waste Land" and sketched some notes for "Cat in the Rain." In March they went to Cortina d'Ampezzo for the end of the skiing season, where he completed the first six of the *In Our Time* chapters for the *Little Review*. Then he was called away to cover the Franco-German troubles in the Ruhr—and for that assignment he wrote some eight or nine articles. The *In Our Time* chapters, his preliminary notes for "Cat in the Rain," and the *Toronto Star* articles could have had as much to do with what he remembered as a lean period for fiction as did the loss of the manuscripts.

However discouraged Hemingway was when he returned to Cortina in April, it took no more than an argument with Hadley to inspire him again. In a letter to Fitzgerald in December 1925, he wrote that, with his ear sharpened by the row, "Out of Season" was "an almost literal transcription of what happened . . . when I came in from an unproductive fishing trip [and] wrote [it] right off on the typewriter without punctuation" (*Letters* 180–81). The story's only typescript confirms this: typed by Hemingway, its crossouts are struck so hard it is difficult to read the original words, and the dialogue between the young gentleman and his wife at the Concordia is not only unpunctuated and unparagraphed but is only slightly revised in the manuscript and setting copy (KL/EH 644, 203).

That typescript may confirm the quarrel that occasioned the story, but the letter to Fitzgerald seriously questions Hemingway's celebrated account of the discovery of his "theory of omission." In *A Moveable Feast* Hemingway claimed that the guide Peduzzi hanged himself and, in the letter, that he did so because "I reported him to the hotel owner." Both time and logic argue that, although the guide might have killed himself much later, his suicide could not have been "the thing left out," if the story, as more reliable evidence suggests, was written so soon after the day's dismal events (Smith 236–39).

The original typescript's pencil corrections were probably made within the week, and the revisions incorporated in the typescript for the setting copy of *Three Stories and Ten Poems* by the early summer of 1923.

Publication History (July 1923; October 1925)

Hemingway met Robert McAlmon in Rapallo in late February 1923, the month of good fortune when Edward O'Brien promised to publish "My Old Man." It is likely that McAlmon, the new editor and publisher of Contact Editions on the scene at Ezra Pound's literary headquarters, would have asked Hemingway to send him what he had, as Fenton states (203). What he had in hand then was only "Up in Michigan" and "My Old Man," probably the "two things" he told Gertrude Stein he had been working on and had done on 18 February (*Letters* 79). This might explain why McAlmon first announced Hemingway's volume as *2 Stories and Ten Poems* after their return from Spain in late May or early June (Fenton 284); but it raises the question of Hemingway's intention to include "Out of Season," presumably the third of the three stories, that late in the plan to publish. Hemingway's letters confuse matters a bit more: he wrote to William Horne on 17–18 July that he was reading proofs for the edition and on 5 August to McAlmon that he had just received them (*Letters* 87, 90).

In the late summer of 1923 the story was published, although badly edited, in *Three Stories and Ten Poems,* and Hemingway could pride himself on the fact that it "was the same gang that published Ulysses" the year before—and with as little care (*Letters* 89). The Boni and Liveright edition of *In Our Time* (1925) cleaned up its punctuation and typography, and "Out of Season" took its place in the canon.

Sources and Influences

Perhaps Hemingway's claim that "Out of Season" was inspired by his "new theory" of omission has diminished the interest of readers in finding models for the story; or it may be that since it is so distinct from either "Up in Michigan" or "My Old Man"—and thus innocent of the influence of Stein or Anderson—it seems more original than it is. That it is clearly different from its companion stories does mark some break from his earlier mentors.

Philip Young argued, rather half-heartedly, that Hemingway's example for "the feeling of things falling apart" and a "discomforting atmosphere" can be found in F. Scott Fitzgerald's *The Beautiful and the Damned* (1922) (178). When Carlos Baker suggested that the "theory of omission" had little if anything to do with the story, while the "metaphorical confluence of emotional atmospheres," associating the "out of season" fishing and the couple's marriage, was "the foremost esthetic discovery of Ernest's early career" (*Ernest Hemingway: A Life Story* 109), he implied that the literary influence of Eliot's "The Waste Land" was as important as any biographical matter involving the elusive Peduzzi and the discovery of a "new theory." Like "Cat in the Rain," this story brings together a rotten marital or sexual relationship and a day's or a season's weather. As "Cat in the Rain" echoes the accents of the neurotic woman and her silent companion in Eliot's "A Game of Chess," so "Out of Season" places an uncommunicative couple in a desolated scene with a turbid river by a dump heap in the unregenerative rain—all familiar images from Eliot's powerful poem.

This hint at an influence from the most influential poem of the period ("The Waste Land" was published in 1922) has been, at the least, slighted. Biographers now find the story's source in Hemingway's anger with Hadley over the theft of the manuscripts in December 1922, her announcement of her pregnancy in the following month, and his restive sense that his need to support himself and his incipient family with journalism was inhibiting his career as an artist. The inevitable assumption is that Hemingway suggested an abortion, the hidden issue the couple might be discussing at the Concordia and one that finds some support in the story's imagery (Johnston 41–46; Meyers 154; Lynn 202).

Critical Studies

Like its companion stories in *Three Stories and Ten Poems*, "Out of Season" has occasioned relatively few critical studies that are more than casual nods. One might expect that "Up in Michigan" and "My Old Man" would be dismissed as derivative; but this story is so obviously original and so promising, it is difficult to account for such a critical slighting. With the publication of *A Moveable Feast* (1964) it could be briefly introduced with the cachet of the theory of omission; and with Carlos Baker's biography (1969) it became perhaps too familiar as the first of the autobiographical "marriage tales." There the matter rests, with the exception of only four extended critical studies. Of interest in themselves, they also offer a history in little of Hemingway criticism in the last twenty years.

In 1963, the year before *A Moveable Feast,* Joseph DeFalco read the story as an ironic comedy, indistinguishable at times from an "outright joke." The "mock-figure" of Peduzzi as guide and teacher, the repeated identification of the husband as "the young gentleman," his recollection of Max Beerbohm, whose works suggest "preciosity and gentlemanliness," followed by a bilingual pun on the German word *Geld,* and, of course, the fact that the day's fishing is spoiled because the husband has no "lead," all suggest to DeFalco that the discord at the heart of the story derives from the couple's "sexual estrangement or incompatibility" and the husband's at least psychological castration (163–68). This reading may seem narrow—perhaps typical of the psychological quest for a critical alchemy that will change lead into *Geld*— for it glosses over the wasteland allusions that T. S. Eliot had informed with larger social and cultural meanings. However, it does direct attention toward the benighted and troubled couple, and it does find a central and dramatic function for Peduzzi in their conflict.

In 1971 Kenneth Johnston extended and modified DeFalco's earlier analysis with Hemingway's remarks in *A Moveable Feast* and Baker's biography, especially his summary of the letter Hemingway wrote to Scott Fitzgerald in late December 1925 on the composition of the story (*Ernest Hemingway: A Life Story* 581). He connects the story with the other marriage tales of reluctant fathers-to-be in "Cross-Country Snow" and "Hills Like White Elephants" and of a wife's desire for a child in "Cat in the Rain." With those stories stating or suggesting abortion, Gertrude Stein's recollection of Hemingway's remark that he was "too young to be a father" (262), and the image of fishing out of season, when the trout are protected to spawn, Johnston argues that the couple's "quarrel clearly appears to center on the question of abortion" (42).

His argument from the story's text, however, begins with an interpretation of a curious passage:

> "There," said Peduzzi, pointing to a girl in the doorway of a house they passed. "My daughter."
> "His doctor," the wife said, "has he got to show us his doctor?"
> "He said his daughter," said the young gentleman. (*Stories* 176)

Johnston concludes that this is a significant psychological mishearing: Peduzzi said, in the Tyroler German dialect, *tochter* (daughter); the wife heard the Italian word *dottore* (doctor); and this reveals the couple's "long-standing quarrel" over the question of a birth or an abortion. Perhaps, but it is clear that the wife speaks neither German nor Italian and knows that Peduzzi speaks no English. *Tochter* may sound more like *doctor* than *daughter* but not at all like *dottore;* which raises the finer question of whether a Freudian mishearing between two languages is at all significant, and the broader question of whether the couple's utter inability to communicate with each other or anyone else is more significant.

One should also question Johnston's note that the Cortina villagers' Catholicism accounts for their "stony silence" toward the couple arguing privately over an abortion, for their contempt is clearly directed at Peduzzi. However far the reach of this study, it is valuable for what it has grasped somewhat closer to the story's center.

The biographical evidence for an interpretation of this story raises some crucial questions: among them is whether or not the story of Peduzzi and his suicide was an invention, and in either case what Hemingway's motive for mentioning it might have been. Paul Jackson's article (1981) admits in a note that it might have been an invention but argues that if it was, "the invention itself would emphasize the importance [Hemingway] attached to Peduzzi" (12). That seems right, but it does not consider that the invention, given the story's personal origin, was meant to turn us away from rather than toward its significance; and later studies have made that point.

Jackson takes Carlos Baker's citation of the 1925 letter to Fitzgerald at close to face value to argue that the story's hidden and more important element is "Peduzzi's trauma," if not his tragedy. He suggests that his "social uncertainty," his being reduced to "manipulative flattery," and his great expectations for this and the next day's fishing end in Peduzzi's "anguish when his prospects collapse" (17). But for someone as tough as Peduzzi to start the day "quite drunk," down three grappas and later the better part of a bottle of marsala, walk to the river, and earn four lire for the little likelihood of the next day's fishing—this, as he says, is living. Any sentiment for Peduzzi—who could not hang himself if he wanted to—is wasted.

If this study seems misled by the assumption that Peduzzi is the central figure of the story, the critical analysis of its shifting point of view and its scenic structure is original and perspicuous, however little it supports the article's thesis. Jackson's analysis needs to be read, not only for its close and complex description of the story's structure but also as something of an historical moment, the first consideration after fifty years of the story as a form of fiction.

My article (1983), responding to Johnston and agreeing with Jackson's analysis of the story's structure, considered the manuscript evidence for the composition of the story and its implications. First, the evidence of this manuscript should lay to rest the legend of Peduzzi's suicide and the discovery of the "theory of omission" in April 1923. If the original of Peduzzi ever existed, he may have done himself in sometime between the spring of 1923 and December of 1925 but not in time to immortalize himself as the donné of Hemingway's first theory. Second, the manuscript confirms the impression that the heart of the story is in the Concordia scene and that it was written in quick anger, perhaps, as Hemingway recalled, as "an almost literal transcription" of a row with Hadley that went unrevised through the process of composition. And finally, this evidence calls attention to the story's structure, at the center of which is the Concordia scene and the wife's telling remark "It doesn't make any difference. . . . None of it makes any difference" (*Stories* 175). If *nothing* in their lives makes any difference, then what they are arguing about—birth or abortion or whatever—seems trivial next to that terrifying reality. As in "Hills Like White Elephants," neither an abortion nor a birth will teach these people to hear and understand one another. So this couple has come to the perfect setting for their brief and discordant conversation, the Concordia. The dialectical scene of the story, in which everyone misunderstands or miscontrues everyone else, is for them very much in season (249).

The critical commentary on this most important of Hemingway's first published stories needs some cumulative and judicial resolution. Too often slighted as a work of art and too often cited as proof positive of the myth Hemingway invented to give some form to his first venture into original fiction, "Out of Season" deserves a more ecumenical interpretation, one that joins the more persuasive of the biographical and psychological evidence with a cautious reading of the story as—for a change—a work of fiction.

Works Cited

PRIMARY

Ernest Hemingway: Selected Letters, 1917–1961. Ed. Carlos Baker. New York: Scribner's, 1981.

A Moveable Feast. New York: Scribner's, 1964.

The Short Stories of Ernest Hemingway. New York: Scribner's, 1938, 173–79.

SECONDARY

Baker, Carlos. *Ernest Hemingway: A Life Story.* 1969. New York: Scribner's, 1988.

DeFalco, Joseph. *The Hero in Hemingway's Short Stories.* Pittsburgh: U of Pittsburgh P, 1963.

Fenton, Charles A. *The Apprenticeship of Ernest Hemingway: The Early Years.* New York: Farrar, 1954.

Jackson, Paul R. "Hemingway's 'Out of Season.' " *Hemingway Review* 1 (Fall 1981): 11–17.

Johnston, Kenneth G. "Hemingway's 'Out of Season' and the Psychology of Errors." *Literature and Psychology* 21 (Nov. 1971): 41–46.

Lynn, Kenneth. *Ernest Hemingway: A Biography.* New York: Simon, 1987.

Meyers, Jeffrey. *Hemingway: A Biography.* New York: Harper, 1985.

Smith, Paul. "Some Misconceptions of 'Out of Season.' " *Critical Essays on Ernest Hemingway's "In Our Time."* Ed. Michael S. Reynolds. Boston: Hall, 1983.

Stein, Gertrude. *The Autobiography of Alice B. Toklas.* New York: Harcourt, 1933.

Young, Philip. *Ernest Hemingway: A Reconsideration.* 1952. New York: Harcourt, 1966.

In Our Time
(October 1925)

4

A Very Short Story

Composition History (June–July 1923)

When Ernest and Hadley returned to Paris after the rousing Pamplona fiesta of early July 1923, he had little more than a month to meet his second deadline for a book. After the loss of his manuscripts the previous December, *Three Stories and Ten Poems* had nearly exhausted the meager balance of his literary account. But he had agreed to contribute to Ezra Pound's "inquest into the state of contemporary English prose" for William Bird's Three Mountains Press with little more at hand than the first six *In Our Time* sketches—and those recently published in the spring issue of the *Little Review*. He did the natural, if not the only, thing—he made some minor revisions in the original six and wrote another twelve chapters. Although he may have sketched some of these out that spring and early summer of 1923, the likely date for setting typescripts was mid-August, for they were submitted to William Bird before Ernest and Hadley returned to Toronto for the birth of their first child. The tenth of the eighteen chapters was the untitled piece that began "One hot evening in Milan . . . ," the first published version of "A Very Short Story."

The earliest draft of this version (KL/EH 633) could have been written almost anyplace except at a writing desk. Like other early drafts of the second group of chapters, it resembles his journalistic field notes—two folded pages, heavily revised, with many of the transitional and subordinated sentences left for later, especially at the end of the sketch. A first-person account, with one revision to the third-person, it is set in Milan and identifies Ag, for Agnes von Kurowsky. On the last of the four sides of the two folded pages is a brief sketch of a rejected *In Our Time* chapter, a first-person account of the death of a soldier named Adams in an attack on the Germans. If these notes suggest a false start toward the two chapters on Nick's wounding and fear during a bombardment (*In Our Time,* chaps. 7 and 8), the two following the six published in the spring, then the first draft of "A Very Short Story" might have been written sometime in June or early July 1923 during the trip to Spain.

The second version of the story, a Hemingway typescript (KL/EH 94A), partially fills out the story, incorporating all but the more sentimental revisions in the first manuscript. Although like other typescripts of the second group of chapters it bears a heading "Blank. Sub-head—Love" (others were headed "Religion," "Youth," "Crime," "Toros y Toreros," and so on), suggesting a late but rejected format in early August, it is not the last stage of composition. This typescript does not include some twenty-five lines in the proofs of the 1924 *in our time* version. Those twenty-five lines expand on the lovers' playing at marriage, their quarrel, the conditions Ag sets for her return to the States, and—most important—the last five sentences of the story's penultimate paragraph in which the language of Ag's letter is recreated (*Stories* 142, "She was sorry . . . for the best").

The Cunard Line *Antonia*'s departure was delayed from the 17 to 26 August, giving Hemingway an unexpected nine days to expand the story further. It is unlikely that he would have left his typescript (KL/EH 94A) with so many holograph revisions for Bill Bird's setting copy, and so one can assume a missing typescript with the twenty-five lines that appeared in the proofs and the *in our time* version. Bird sent those proofs (KL/EH 94) to Toronto on 5 December 1923, but they could not have arrived much before the 15th. He might have saved himself the trouble, for Hemingway made only one change, which he immediately rescinded: he deleted "chapter 10," added the title "A Short Story," then deleted it and restored the chapter number. With no record, then, of a typescript sent to Bill Bird in the fall of 1923, those twenty-five lines not in KL/EH 94A were probably incorporated in a lost typescript in late August 1923.

Publication History (March 1924; October 1925)

Hemingway should have read the proofs more carefully, for when *in our time* was finally published in March 1924, the lovers quarrel on the train from "Padova to Milan" and then part "in the station at Padova" (*in our time* 19). This error is corrected in a Hemingway typescript (KL/EH 95) that was sent off with others for Don Stewart to offer to New York publishers in September 1924 (Baker 133).

In the *In Our Time* version of October 1925 the infected "sales girl from The Fair" is changed to one "in a loop department store," but the nurse is still "Ag" at Milan and later Torre di Mosta. Not until the 1930 Scribner's edition is she veiled as "Luz" in Padua and later Pordenone.

Sources and Influences

Ever since Carlos Baker revealed the details of Hemingway's "first adult love affair" (50) in 1969, "A Very Short Story" has been read as a close account of his relationship with Agnes von Kurowsky from July 1918 through March 1919. Michael Reynolds interviewed her in 1971 and published parts of that interview interspersed with a variety of related documents, letters, and passages from *A Farewell to Arms* in his 1976 study of the making of that novel (*Hemingway's First War* 181–219). He suggested that a letter from her of 22 December 1922, in answer to one of Hemingway's, may have initiated the story late in the following spring. The four biographers of 1985–87—Peter Griffin, Jeffrey Meyers, Michael Reynolds, and Kenneth Lynn—tell much the same story in different styles, from the laconic (Reynolds) to the melodramatic (Griffin), with speculative forays into the psychological origins of Hemingway's love for Agnes (Meyers and Lynn) and how far it went—Hemingway intimated broadly that it went the distance; she denied it.

The more innocent details of the story have been supported with letters, photographs, interviews with other nurses and patients who were there in the Red Cross Hospital in Milan, and family recollections of Hemingway's first few months home in 1919 (Baker 572, Griffin 239–41). What remains undocumented and private are the two passages added to the story between the first typescript and the first *in our time* proofs (KL/EH 94A and 94): the lovers' understanding that "he would not drink, and [that] he did not want to see his friends or anyone else in the States," and the recreated language of her letter (*Stories* 142). The curious agreement not to see his friends lends some support to Jeffrey Meyers's theory that Agnes suspected that James Gamble, then in the States, had a "homosexual attraction to Hemingway" (40). Long thought to be lost, Agnes's letter of rejection, dated 7 March 1919, is in a private collection and has been discussed by Scott Donaldson in an unpublished paper presented in December 1987. Donaldson confirms that Agnes addressed him as "Ernie dear boy," was concerned about Gamble's influence, thought that theirs was a boy-and-girl affair, and admitted that her decision to marry was a "sudden" one.

If there are any literary antecedents for this story, Hemingway, perhaps unfortunately, did not need them. Its primary importance in the canon, of course, derives from its place in the progression from his Chicago manuscripts on the war, through the Nick Adams chapters of *In Our Time,* to *A Farewell to Arms.*

Critical Studies

Almost all the critics have noticed "A Very Short Story," and most have commented in passing on the ironic contrast between the narrator's romantic expectations and the seemingly bitter remark that he "had contracted gonorrhea from a sales girl in a loop department store while riding in a taxicab through Lincoln Park" (*Stories* 142). Joseph DeFalco noted that the narrator had been afflicted with both a "physical and a psychological disease"—

the latter being his romantic expectations (163). Richard Peterson saw the ending as an expression of "outrage, hurt, and sorrow, the cruelty of life and love, and the pathetic victim they make of one" (72).

And that fairly sums up the critical responses to "A Very Short Story" as a fiction until Robert Scholes's semiotic study in 1982. His chapter "Decoding Papa" is unusual in recent Hemingway criticism in that it brings principles and procedures of semiotic criticism to an analysis of the story—admitting some similarities with conventional rhetorical strategies, but insisting on essential advantages in this approach—to demonstrate that the opposed codes of discourse or "oral presentation" conflict with those of the written or "referential" modes (111). His application of Roland Barthes's strategy—rewriting all third-person narration to first-person—to discover a "covert first-person narrator"—works neatly to confirm what the original manuscript (KL/EH 633) and the biographical evidence had already, for some, made evident. What is unusual here is that Scholes demonstrated with only the text and the codes of discourse and narration precisely what the manuscripts and all the biographical evidence could only argue but not ultimately prove. Scholes notes that when the narrator, now only slightly veiled in the third-person, remarks that Luz's fate is projected into infinity—she "did not marry . . . in the spring, or any other time" and "never got an answer to her letter" once she had been jilted (*Stories* 142)—"something punitive is going on here" (115). Only after this close textual and semiotic analysis demonstrating that the "third-person narrative of the original text is a disguise, a mask of pseudo-objectivity worn by the text for its own rhetorical purposes"—that is to say, Hemingway's—does Scholes then turn to the biographical evidence. That he concludes his chapter with a survey of that evidence does not suggest that he proved the obvious, but that his analysis of the text helps to validate a long history of biographical speculation.

This sort of open collaboration in the work of contemporary critics and literary biographers offers a model for others, and they could well begin with other stories—like the late stories of *Winner Take Nothing*—that at times seem to have a covert first-person narrator.

Works Cited

PRIMARY

In Our Time. New York: Boni and Liveright, 1925.

The Short Stories of Ernest Hemingway. New York: Scribner's, 1938, 141–42.

SECONDARY

Baker, Carlos. *Ernest Hemingway: A Life Story.* 1969. New York: Scribner's, 1988.

DeFalco, Joseph. *The Hero in Hemingway's Short Stories.* Pittsburgh: U of Pittsburgh P, 1963.

Donaldson, Scott. "The Jilting of Ernest Hemingway." Paper given at Modern Language Association meeting, Dec. 1987.

Griffin, Peter. *Along with Youth.* New York: Oxford UP, 1985.

Lynn, Kenneth S. *Hemingway.* New York: Simon, 1987.

Meyers, Jeffrey. *Hemingway: A Biography.* New York: Harper, 1985.

Peterson, Richard K. *Hemingway: Direct and Oblique.* The Hague: Mouton, 1969.

Reynolds, Michael S. *Hemingway's First War.* Princeton: Princeton UP, 1976.

———. *The Young Hemingway.* Oxford: Blackwell, 1986.

Scholes, Robert. *Semiotics and Interpretation.* New Haven: Yale UP, 1982.

5

The Revolutionist

Composition History (June–July 1923)

"The Revolutionist" is the second of the chapters of *in our time* raised to the status of a short story between March 1924 and the publication of *In Our Time* in October 1925. Unlike "A Very Short Story," it apparently was not begun with a manuscript sketch but was revised three times in its first set of typescripts (KL/EH 94A); and this suggests its composition in late June or July after the Pamplona trip of 1923.

The first of these collected typescripts is a brief one-page sketch outlining the narrator's meeting with the young revolutionist. The second typescript, headed "Blank |9| 10" and "Youth," bears heavy pencil revisions and adds the artists whose paintings the revolutionist had seen, Giotto, Masaccio, Piero della Francesca, and Mantegna, whom "he did not like," the reproductions "wrapped in a copy of *Avanti*," the narrator's suggestion the young man see the "Mantegnas in Milano," and the line "In spite of what had happened to him in Hungary, he believed altogether in the world revolution" (see *Stories* 157–58). The third typescript, headed "Blank 10" and "Youth," bears only a few minor revisions and could have served as setting copy for the *in our time* version.

The proofs for this version (KL/EH 94), like those for "A Very Short Story," show a momentary decision to delete "chapter 11" and add the title, which is then rescinded.

Publication History (March 1924; October 1925)

As with "A Very Short Story," Hemingway seems to have nodded over the proofs for this one. In the third typescript he had written "In spite of *Hungary* he believed altogether in the world revolution," which became "In spite of Italy . . ." in the proofs and was not corrected until *In Our Time* of 1925. The only remaining changes, other than typographical, between the 1924 and 1925 versions are the addition of the lines "I did not say anything" and "He loved the mountains in the autumn" (*Stories* 157–58). Sometime in summer of 1925, however, Hemingway typed out a list of titles for his next collection (KL/EH 97A) with "An Even Shorter Story" as an alternate title or subtitle and two others he rejected, "The Wounded Revolutionist" and "The Worried Revolutionist," also listed. Finally, with its present title it became a "short story" in October 1925.

Sources and Influences

Hemingway was far from Italy in September 1919, and although he might have sympathized with some socialist ambulance drivers the year before, he was never, like the narrator of "The Revolutionist," among the trusted comrades in Italy. But Anthony Hunt has offered a convincing argument for the story's sources in the "biographical and historical events of 1922–1923." From early April through late June 1922 more than twenty of his dispatches on the Genoa Conference appeared in the *Toronto Star;* he knew that Mussolini began his career in 1914 as the editor of *Avanti,* the socialist daily in Milan in which the young revolutionist wraps his Piero della Francesca reproductions (*Dateline* 173); Just after that conference, which made clear how badly the revolution had gone, Hemingway, with Hadley and Chink Dorman-Smith, reversed the revolutionist's route over the Saint Bernard pass and went on to Milan; later the Hemingways went on to his old front at Fossalta di Piave where some "bad things" had happened to him that night in July 1918. In February 1923, Hemingway walked with Ezra Pound "up into the Romagna," and it would be a wonder if they did not talk of Italy's recent political history as well as its more ancient battles (Baker 88–94, 107). All this Anthony Hunt brings to a focus on the story's symbolic geography, its political ironies, and the subtle relationship between the narrator and the revolutionist.

Hunt's essay may well explain why it is that when "In spite of Hungary" in the manuscripts became "In spite of Italy" in the *in our time* proofs, Hemingway did not catch the error; for if he was recollecting his own experiences of the last two years in Italy, then however illogical the mistake is in the story, it would have seemed right for Hemingway at the time.

Finally, "The Revolutionist" is intimately related to "A Very Short Story," and not only through their shared histories of composition, for each story is a narrative of disillusionment, one in the happy prospects for marriage and the other in the hopes for escape to Switzerland. And together the two stories foreshadow *A Farewell to Arms* (Johnston 90–91).

Critical Studies

The critical issue that divides most commentaries on the story rests in the character of the young revolutionary and whether he is "an innocent untouched by experience" in spite of his suffering, as Joseph DeFalco claimed

(89), or a "young man whose idealism has been tested in the crucible of pain, one of Hemingway's initiated who has suffered much," as Kenneth Johnston countered (90). Often this division depends on whether the critic gives primary emphasis to the significance of the pre-Renaissance Italian artists—Giotto, Masaccio, and Piero della Francesca, whom the revolutionist admires, and Andrea Mantegna, whose works he refuses to see—or to the Communist revolution in Hungary and the White counterrevolution led by Admiral Horthy in 1919 and from which the revolutionist has fled.

Barbara Groseclose contrasts the style Masaccio and Piero derived from Giotto, "a style of monumental simplicity and humanistic concern which depends on the creation of an ideal," with that of Mantegna, especially in "The Dead Christ" in Milan, which displays Christ "as a cadaver with no suggestion of the resurrection within the painting itself" (568-69). With this evidence, then, the youth seems to be affirming his idealism with the reproductions of the more "humanistic" painters and refusing to admit "the harsh view of reality that Mantegna represents" (570).

Kenneth Johnston's essay recalls the tragic conflicts in Hungary in the spring and summer of 1919: the ill-conceived attacks by the Red Guardsmen on the Catholic clergy and churches, and the "bloody reaction and brutal repression referred to as the White Terror" (89). If we assume the revolutionist was a victim of the White Terror, once called the "Christian Course," then the Mantegna painting might remind him of the "betrayal of the true revolution by the Horthy regime" (90).

Anthony Hunt went further to argue that Hemingway must have counted much less on his readers' familiarity with pre-Renaissance art history than on their "knowledge of significant contemporary places and situations in the political and cultural life of Europe" (205). In the light of those events of 1919, Hunt suggests that the narrator did not challenge the youth's precarious faith in the revolution "in deference to what he senses to be [his] fragile state of mind." The boy's faith "has been thoroughly shaken: he is disoriented, on the verge of lucidity through despair; he turns shy, afraid to talk too much, and he becomes a lover of peaceful quiet things like the natural surroundings of the Romagna and the high passes of the Alps in autumn"— and he knows the "weather will turn" (211-12). For Hunt this is not a meeting between an innocent and naive youth and an older, more cynical man of the world, but one between a wounded boy, desperately on the edge like Nick Adams, and a sympathetic adult who does what little he can to help his escape, however futile, to Switzerland.

This interpretation of the story nicely recognizes its complexity. But with that much complexity revealed even more is intimated. If this youth is in flight from the agony of Hungary in 1919 and the narrator recognizes his fragile and disoriented condition, might not the older man see the irony of a young and faithful Communist spending what little he had on reproductions of religious paintings and wrapping them in copies of *Avanti?* If the boy was a victim of both the outrages of the Red Guardsmen *and* the White Catholics and is torn by his own conflicting political and religious beliefs, then one may question the narrator's sensitivity, knowing what he must know, in suggesting—in spite of the boy's having seen enough of Mantegna—that he look again at his Christ as a cadaver. When the youth says " 'No,' . . . very shyly, he did not like Mantegna" (*Stories* 158), his shyness could just as well have been the polite embarrassment one feels when those, perhaps with the best intentions, fail to understand.

If so, then, "The Revolutionist," like the best of Hemingway's stories, still challenges our imagination.

Works Cited

PRIMARY

Dateline: Toronto. Ed. William White. New York: Scribner's, 1985.

The Short Stories of Ernest Hemingway. New York: Scribner's, 1938, 157–58.

SECONDARY

Baker, Carlos. *Ernest Hemingway: A Life Story.* 1969. New York: Scribner's, 1988.

DeFalco, Joseph. *The Hero in Hemingway's Short Stories.* Pittsburgh: U of Pittsburgh P, 1963.

Groseclose, Barbara. "Hemingway's 'The Revolutionist': An Aid to Interpretation." *Modern Fiction Studies* 17 (1971–72): 565–70.

Hunt, Anthony. "Another Turn for Hemingway's 'The Revolutionist': Sources and Meanings." *Fitzgerald/Hemingway Annual* (1977): 119–35; rpt. in *Critical Essays on Ernest Hemingway's "In Our Time."* Ed. Michael S. Reynolds. Boston: Hall, 1983, 203–17.

Johnston, Kenneth G. "Hemingway and Mantegna: The Bitter Nail Holes." *Journal of Narrative Technique* 1 (May 1971): 86–94.

6

Indian Camp

Composition History (November 1923–February 1924)

On 6 November 1923 Ernest Hemingway wrote to Sylvia Beach, "Have just ripped the beginning of a letter to [Larry Gains] out of the typer. Can't seem to write to him either" (*Letters* 97). That unfinished letter to his boxer friend was probably shuffled into a stack of fresh paper he packed for Paris two months later and came to the top either on the return voyage (19–30 January 1924) or soon after, for it appears on the back of page nine of the earliest manuscript of "Indian Camp" (KL/EH 493).

He might have been eight pages along in the manuscript when he started writing to Gains on 4 November, but that fall was a lean period for writing fiction. With several *Toronto Star* assignments away from home— one that kept him from Bumby's birth on 10 October—Hemingway complained in his letters that journalism was, once again, robbing him of time for his own writing. On 9 November he told Gertrude Stein he had "some good stories to write," and on the 20th he asked Edward O'Brien how many he would "need for a Boni Liveright book" (*Letters* 102, 104). The two months left before their sailing were taken up with the new baby, the holidays, his resignation from the *Star,* an elaborate plan to jump their lease, and packing for the return to Europe (Baker 122). And the prospect of Paris itself might have persuaded him to put off the "good stories" he had in mind for a "Boni Liveright book."

They landed at Cherbourg on 30 January, spent the first week of February finding an apartment, and on the 10th he wrote Ezra Pound, "I have about 7 stories to write. Dont know when or where able to write" (*Letters* 110). Ten days later, however, Hadley wrote to Grace Hemingway that "Ernie has written two dandy stories this week and is at his third this morning" (KL/EH, Hadley Hemingway to Grace Hemingway, 20 February 1924). One of those must have been "Indian Camp," for on 17 March he wrote again to Pound that Ford Madox Ford had accepted it for the April *Transatlantic Review* (*Letters* 112).

The story's manuscripts provide the earliest example of what came to be known as his "theory of omission"—or, at least, one aspect of it. (There are crucial differences between *omitting* something for which we have only Hemingway's word, like "all of Chicago" from "The Killers"; *replacing* something, like the original ending of "Big Two-Hearted River"; or, as with "Indian Camp," *deleting* a substantial part of the fiction [Smith, "Hemingway's Early Manuscripts" 277]). The first and untitled manuscript of twenty-nine pages (KL/EH 493) linked what was later published as "Three Shots" with this story (*Nick Adams Stories* 13–15). The two remaining manuscripts, however, confuse the question of when he decided to delete the original eight manuscript pages. Item 494 is typed in his hand, ordinarily the second stage in his composition (KL/EH). This seven-page typescript deletes "Three Shots," and is marked in his hand as "Published April 1924 in *Transatlantic Review*" with an alternate title, "One Night Last Summer." The usual last stage in composition is a professional typescript; but here that typescript was originally paginated 5–11 and renumbered as 1–7 with the title revised, "INDIAN |CAMP|/STORY/" (KL/EH 495).

Lifting the lid on those manuscripts lets loose some perplexities about Hemingway's early intentions for both "Three Shots" and "Indian Camp." He first thought of the two narratives as one. If Item 495 is closest to the version he submitted to the *Transatlantic Review*, then the decision was made, with or without Ford's advice, probably a week or two before 17 March, with the typescript pages renumbered. That he had the first four missing pages of Item 495 retyped, that he was considering other titles ("One Night Last Summer" and "Indian Story") for "Indian Camp" or for it and its original introduction, and that he agreed to the title "Work in Progress" for its first publication (Baker 125), argue that the decision to delete "Three Shots" was anything but final in March 1924. He knew he needed some ten to fifteen stories for the book he had in mind, and not even in his few moments of hope could he have predicted the close to miraculous half-year of writing that started with this story. Had he been pressed for pages when he put together *In Our Time,* he might well have begun that volume with a two-part version of the story beginning with "Three Shots" as he ended it with a two-part story, "Big Two-Hearted River." They would have made an interesting frame for the collection: two Nick Adams stories setting in opposition his youth and maturity and two fearful nights with two days in which he proves himself able to master—if only for the moment—not dissimilar fears. An appealing symmetry, perhaps, but it was not worth the risk. For in the months following February 1924 and "Indian Camp"—not in April 1923 and "Out of Season"—Hemingway first learned to delete a part of his story and so "make people feel something more than they understood" (*Moveable Feast* 75).

Publication History (April 1924; October 1925)

When Hemingway returned to Paris, Ezra Pound assumed his customary role as impresario and talked Ford Madox Ford into taking on "the finest prose stylist in the world" as a subeditor for the *Transatlantic Review* (Baker 123). However much Hemingway rankled at the task, he was in a perfect position to publish. It is almost as if the April number of the review was intended to prove Pound's judgment. It not only offered "Indian Camp" under the general title of *Works in Progress* with "selections from Tristan Tzara, the founder of literary Dadaism, and from Joyce's still-untitled *Finnegans Wake*," but it garnished the story with laudatory reviews of *Three Stories and Ten Poems* and *in our time* (Baker 125). "Indian Camp" was the fourth major story to be published and the first in an important literary journal.

When Hemingway first considered the *In Our Time* stories as a collection, he placed "Indian Camp" second after "Up in Michigan" (*Letters*, 12 September 1924, 123), and, through Donald Ogden Stewart, submitted it to George H. Doran a month later. Doran held it until January 1925 and then turned it down; but by then Hemingway had submitted it to Boni and Liveright's literary scout, and it was accepted by cable on 5 March (*Letters* 141, 156 n.). Hemingway returned the signed contract on 31 March and, in a prescient moment, wrote that the "book will be praised by highbrows and can be read by lowbrows" (*Letters* 154).

When Horace Liveright objected to the seamy sections of "Up in Michigan" and Hemingway readily agreed to replace it, "Indian Camp" took its rightful place as the first story in that remarkable collection. For once then, a benighted and overly scrupulous publisher moved a Hemingway story to its perfect position. And two months later Hemingway admitted as much when he wrote to Scott Fitzgerald that this story, after "Big Two-Hearted River," was "Grade I" and the thing he was "shooting for" (*Letters* 180).

Sources and Influences

Sometime in August 1924 Hemingway finished the original conclusion of "Big Two-Hearted River," an introspective review that centered on his experiences of that summer and his early years in Paris. He wrote that "everything good he'd ever written he'd made up. . . . Nick in the stories was never himself. . . . Of course he'd never seen an Indian woman having a baby. . . . He'd seen a woman have a baby on the road to Karagatch and tried to help her. That was the way it was" (*Nick Adams Stories* 237–38). Although Hemingway is not to be trusted, especially when he denies influences on his writing, there is little evidence to contradict him with "Indian Camp." What he wrote "was the way it was" everywhere, on the road to Karagatch or in Michigan's Upper Peninsula; and there is no one event in his life that initiated the story, as with "Out of Season," nor does the story have any single literary model, as does "My Old Man" in Sherwood Anderson's "I Want to Know Why."

He found the scene of the Indian barkpeelers' camp near the Hemingway cottage at Walloon Lake (Montgomery 58) and removed it to the Upper Peninsula, at least a half-day's trip from Saint Ignace and near the setting of "Big Two-Hearted River" (*Stories* 94). His characters' originals were at hand, too. His father was a general physician who had taken postgraduate courses in obstetrics, one in obstetrical surgery at the Mayo Clinic, and had delivered the children of some local families and ministered to the Indians in emergencies (Baker 10–11; Montgomery 58–63). The neighbors recognized Ernest's uncle, George Hemingway, in the story—somewhat to his displeasure. And always there were the Indians, whose often desperate lives on the edge of a growing resort were marked with poverty, drunkenness, suffering, and violent death, more than once by suicide. In the winter of 1918 Prudence Boulton, the original for Nick Adams's girl in several stories, was pregnant at sixteen when she and her lover swallowed strychnine (Smith, "Tenth Indian" 67, 74). Such violent conjunctions of death and birth were not unusual as the Indians faded north into Canada with the logging camps or served the vacationers from Chicago.

Hemingway's school fiction often drew on ironic coincidence and intimated a sinister fate at work in the lives of trappers and Indians ("Judgment of Manitou" and "Sepi Jingan"). But the image he recalled in "On Writing"— the one that "was the way it was"—appeared originally in a dispatch to the *Toronto Star* from Adrianople on 20 October 1922. It, too, conjoins birth and death and a silent retreat, but in open warfare between two nations: "A husband spreads a blanket over a woman in labor in one of the carts to keep off the driving rain. She is the only person making a sound. Her little daughter looks at her in horror and begins to cry. And the procession keeps moving" (*Dateline* 232). This dispatch provided the details of chapter 2 of *In Our Time* and the sentences: "There was a woman having a kid with a young girl holding a blanket over her and crying. Scared sick looking at it. It rained all through the evacuation." And in a nice coincidence, the chapter follows "Indian Camp" in *In Our Time* with another unusual birth in the proximity of death and witnessed by a horrified child (*Stories* 97). If that image from the dispatch initiated the story and the abundant particulars of his early experience provided the dramatic details, there is reason enough to understand the story's nearly uncontested originality.

Certainly, one can detect some traces of other writers. Sherwood Anderson's interest in the violent juxtaposition of opposites in stories of initiation— a whole collection, in fact—would have encouraged Hemingway here as it did in "Up in Michigan." And he could have learned from James Joyce's "Araby" how to end his story. The final paragraph in each story is introduced with a simple dialogue, which resonates with meaning back through the narrative; each story ends with a young boy's unexpected, even irrelevant, response to the events of the night; and neither story can be understood without some resolution of the apparent illogic of its final sentence.

Other more precise and persuasive literary sources for "Indian Camp" may be discovered. If not, then it could be argued that the story's originality derives not only from the particularity of its characters and setting but also, paradoxically, from the universal aspects of its narrative. It is an archetypal story that works some slight and some radical changes on an ancient tale, and so Hemingway's ultimate source was the shaping force of the human imagination.

Critical Studies

When Hemingway came to conclude "Indian Camp," he ended it, for the moment, with the penultimate paragraph and the journalist's symbol "30": "They were seated in the boat, Nick in the stern, his father rowing. The sun was coming up over the hills. A bass jumped, making a circle in the water. Nick trailed his hand in the water. It felt warm in the sharp chill of the morning."

He had ended "Up in Michigan" with a similar descriptive passage implying a unity, even a sympathetic identity, between the natural scene and a character's emotions; and he would do it again in "Ten Indians" and then brilliantly in *A Farewell to Arms*. But he must have sensed that the correlation between the objective scene and the subjective state is not obvious enough in this paragraph; and he added the story's last paragraph. He repeated from the previous paragraph the time, the place, and the position of the father and son; and then he added the last clause on which so much of the story's meaning turns: "|Sitting in the stern of the boat with| In the early morning on the lake/sitting in the stern of the boat with his father rowing/he felt quite sure he would never die" (KL/EH 493).

Every major commentary on the story has, at the least, noted that it is a tale of initiation—and they would have, even without the last sentence. But with that sentence and its unexpected revelation of Nick's sense "that he would never die," some have argued that the rite of passage has failed. Nick's feeling of immortality is "illusory and child-like because it is a romantic reaction to the experience" (DeFalco 32). If, as Arthur Waldhorn notes, a "caul of innocence protects [Nick] from more than partially comprehending the tragedy he has witnessed," there is still the potential for a later awareness, for when Nick trails his hand in the water, "he plucks from nature a sense of renewal and reassurance" (54–55). If so, it is still a romantic notion; and perhaps, as Bernard Oldsey has suggested, the story is Hemingway's version of Wordsworth's "Intimations" ode (217–18). Finally, George Monteiro's suggestion—that since Nick has witnessed *only* a suicide, he can assure himself that he will never die *that* way—makes a certain though still illusory sense (155).

With the publication of "Three Shots" in 1972, the story's crucial last line was read as either doubly ironic or not at all. Larry Grimes used the rejected introduction to illustrate Nick's fear of death "as a result of a child's . . . fantasy life," and "Indian Camp" to demonstrate that "death is the stuff from which adult nightmares . . . are made." It is ironic, then, that Nick is capable of ignoring the "raw and grotesque" evidence of those fears only "in the reassuring presence of his father" (414). Dick Penner agrees that in "Three Shots" Nick has only sensed death "in the abstract, as a vague and unknown presence," and so knows fear. In "Indian Camp" he comes to "experience death," to "know its reality," and more. For in his final conversation with his father, Nick realizes his father's love, and "that love reinforces his sense of being, and of immortality. Thus the ending is appropriate in a sense that is neither illusory nor ironic" (202).

This reading is persuasive for it responds to the syntax of the final sentence Hemingway carefully revised. Its four introductory phrases are more than adverbial. They serve as necessary conditions for the rest of the sentence: *only* in the early morning *and* on the lake *and* sitting in the stern of the boat *and* with his father rowing, could Nick "feel *quite* sure that he would never die." Which is not to say that elsewhere or at another time or alone he would be so certain—he was far from it when the Indian rowed and his father sat in the stern with his arm around him. So Nick's feeling is more reasonable and less illusory than it seems at first, and it returns our attention to the central issue of any male initiation story, the relationship between the figures of the father and son.

Critics have brought three critical disciplines to the story—psychoanalytic, sociological, and archetypal—and considered the two obvious fathers as well as a third in the unfortunate and improbable Uncle George. G. Thomas Tanselle sees the Indian father as the central character. His cut foot suggests an unconscious desire for castration deriving from his guilt for his wife's suffering, and his pipe his refusal to accept the white man's conventional role of the "proud father," played by George. Tanselle's more interesting suggestion is that the story may be read as analogous to the "gradual supplanting of one culture by another" (Item 53).

Joseph DeFalco places the story's conflict between the "primitive," "dark," "intrusive," and "irrational" side of life represented in the Indian camp, and the "civilized," "scientific," "secure," and "rational" side represented by the doctor (28, 30). His charges against the doctor—arriving improperly prepared, ignoring his patient's pain, belatedly considering the husband's suffering—have been answered as they deserved to be. The doctor's professional and personal behavior may be faulted, but hardly by citing Uncle George's gift of cigars as evidence of a "unity and harmony" with the dark

Indian forces. George's obvious dramatic function in the story is to offer comic relief, as does the mere mention of him in the final dialogue.

Kenneth Bernard followed Tanselle to suggest that George was the father of the Indian boy, that the birth of this half-breed is "symbolic of the violent way in which the older culture is . . . fused into the newer," and that the mother's "screams are the screams of the death of a civilization" to which the white doctor is impervious as he performs a "cultural Caesarian" (291).

This heavy burden of social guilt seems to press the meaning out of several details, not the least of which is that the doctor, however ineptly and for whatever reason, did save two Indian lives. Although Gerry Brenner is convinced that Uncle George's paternity explains George's presence in the story and the Indian's suicide, he also questions the burdensome symbolism of this reading (239 n. 15). Finally, this pressing issue weighed on the conscience of Hemingway criticism itself until Philip Young, who fathered the field, was forced to confess that *he,* not Uncle George, fathered the Indian boy (ii–iii).

With that the partial exoneration of the doctor and his brother began. George Monteiro drew on the work of the sociologist Talcott Parsons to describe the necessary role of the physician as "affective neutrality . . . enabling one's medical training and objectively learned technique to control one's behavior" (147). The Indian father, he argues, is the only character without a "role . . . or life-sustaining function." His wound confines him to the painful scene, but his wife's agony removes him from its center, and so contributes to his suicide (147, 153–54). The doctor's relaxation after the delivery into a trite phrase about the proud fathers who are "usually the worst sufferers in these little affairs" predicts a terrible truth.

This restitution of the white men in the story continued in Penner's article with some simple and logical reasons for their behavior—courtesy with the cigars, necessity with the operation—and traced the change in the relationship between Nick and his father. At first unable or unwilling to communicate, the doctor gives oblique and unnecessary answers to Nick's questions. But after the suicide, the doctor no longer maintains "the pose of infallibility"; and in the dialogue returning in the boat he takes his natural role as a father, and a father who loves his son (199).

The later commentaries have the virtue of considering the significance of the story's narrative structure and its juxtaposition of an unnatural birth and death. These two events at the boundaries of life are linked by the two wounds, the inappropriate fishing knife and razor, and the last dialogue between the father and son. Nick's simple questions are profound; his father's honest answers are as much as one can say in the presence of either event and surely of both. For Monteiro, Nick first discovers death in life at the camp and then life in the warm water of the lake in the "sharp chill of

the morning" (155). For Penner, this makes the story "one of the very few
. . . in which Hemingway allowed himself to explore the hopeful paradox,
'out of ugliness comes beauty,' or 'out of death, life' " (201). And Joseph
Flora, drawing on archetypal patterns, implies that this night journey into a
"primitive" world initiates not only Nick but his father. As Indian fathers
traditionally instruct their sons in their initiation into manhood, so the doctor,
at first unwittingly, and at last with "real wisdom and convincing humanity,"
tells his son about birth and suffering and death. And about love, too: for
if we consider that the Indian father dies "in his wife's place" (30–31) to
silently silence her agonized screams and to bring his son into life, then what
remains, like an afterimage, between the lines of Nick's questions and his
father's answers suggests the final human cost of loving.

To review at some distance the critical commentary on "Indian Camp"
is to recognize the story's remarkable achievement. Hemingway's fourth story,
written under some duress on his return to Paris in 1924 and published
almost immediately, has never been seriously challenged as the profound and
original work of fiction it is. It has appealed to all the critical schools and
survived them all with something left unanswered, perhaps unanswerable. It
has invited and evaded psychoanalytic and archetypal analyses. Sociological
interpretations seem dated confessions of the 1960s; and neither they nor the
literary historians have drawn on the traditions and history of the Indians in
Michigan as they retreated before the white farmers and vacationers.

And, finally, the story, as we all know, cast a long shadow, which
Hemingway witnessed four years later and at the end of his life.

Works Cited

PRIMARY

Dateline: Toronto. Ed. William White. New York: Scribner's, 1985.

Ernest Hemingway: Selected Letters, 1917–1961. Ed. Carlos Baker. New York: Scribner's, 1981.

A Moveable Feast. New York: Scribner's, 1964.

The Nick Adams Stories. New York: Scribner's, 1972.

The Short Stories of Ernest Hemingway. New York: Scribner's, 1938, 91–95.

SECONDARY

Bernard, Kenneth. "Hemingway's 'Indian Camp.' " *Studies in Short Fiction* 2 (Spring 1965): 291.

Brenner, Gerry. *Concealments in Hemingway's Works*. Columbus: Ohio State UP, 1963.

DeFalco, Joseph. *The Hero in Hemingway's Short Stories*. Pittsburgh: U of Pittsburgh P, 1963.

Flora, Joseph M. *Hemingway's Nick Adams*. Baton Rouge: Louisiana State UP, 1982.

Grimes, Larry. "Night Terror and Morning Calm: A Reading of Hemingway's 'Indian Camp' as Sequel to 'Three Shots.'" *Studies in Short Fiction* 12 (1975): 413–15.

Monteiro, George. "The Limits of Professionalism: A Sociological Approach to Faulkner, Fitzgerald and Hemingway." *Criticism* 15 (Spring 1973): 145–55.

Montgomery, Constance. *Hemingway in Michigan*. Waitsfield: Vermont Crossroads, 1977.

Oldsey, Bernard. "Hemingway's Beginnings and Endings." *College Literature* 7 (Fall 1980): 213–38.

Penner, Dick. "The First Nick Adams Story." *Fitzgerald/Hemingway Annual* (1975): 195–202.

Smith, Paul. "Hemingway's Early Manuscripts: The Theory and Practice of Omission." *Journal of Modern Literature* 10 (July 1983): 268–88.

———. "The Tenth Indian and the Thing Left Out." *Ernest Hemingway: The Writer in Context*. Ed. James Nagel. Madison: U of Wisconsin P, 1984.

Tanselle, G. Thomas. "Hemingway's 'Indian Camp.'" *Explicator* 20 (Feb. 1962), Item 53.

Waldhorn, Arthur. *A Reader's Guide to Ernest Hemingway*. New York: Farrar, 1972.

Young, Philip. "Letter to the Editor." *Studies in Short Fiction* 3 (1966): ii–iii.

7

Cat in the Rain

Composition History (February 1923–March 1924)

Hemingway's earliest notes for "Cat in the Rain" were sketched in late February 1923 at Rapallo, the setting for the story. He and Hadley had finally accepted Ezra Pound's invitation—the rains in Chamby-sur-Montreux, and the promise of the Mediterranean sun were compelling. Hemingway's mood was close to equivocal and is reflected in these early notes. He wrote, "Cats love in the garden. On green tea tables to be exact. The big cat gets on the small cat. Sweeney gets on Mrs. Porter. Ezra gets nowhere except artistically of course." He gently ridiculed Mike Strater's art and fell into a reverie of his nights with Hadley. "Hadley and I are happy sometimes. We are happiest in bed. . . . Now I lay me down to sleep in bed. There are no prayers in bed. If the beds [sic] wide enough we will be bride enough. . . . Sleeping is good. I used to lie awake all night. That was before. This is after. . . . You cannot tell about the tide" (KL/EH 670.4).

Then or soon after he completed four pages of a manuscript, gave that up, and later marked it "False start Rapallo story possible Fascisto story" (KL/EH 321). That false start identifies the hotel, describes the train trip from Genoa, and gives the wife's nickname, Kitty. Two rich fragments: the reference to T. S. Eliot, the suggestion that Pound was getting "nowhere except artistically," the name "Kitty," and the curious notes on his connubial life with Hadley, all suggest a story ready to be written, but it was postponed.

A year later he returned to the story with another manuscript of ten pages (KL/EH 319) and identified it as a "First Draft Original Manuscript/ March 1924/E.M.H." This was followed by a nineteen-page titled manuscript with another rejected title, "The Poor Kitty" (KL/EH 320). Then came the typescript, titled "Cat in the Rain" and bearing his Paris address (KL/EH 322).

Hadley's letter to Grace Hemingway in February mentions two stories finished and another begun (KL/EH, Hadley Hemingway to Grace Hemingway, 20 February 1924). Various combinations of stories are possible; most probably the two completed stories were "Indian Camp" and "Cat in the Rain," and the third he was beginning was "The End of Something" or "The Three-Day Blow," but having had a beginning for the story in hand since 1923 and a similar story published that summer ("Out of Season"), it would make sense to return to "Cat in the Rain."

Publication History (October 1925)

If it is likely that the story was completed in March 1924 with a professional typescript titled and addressed, one may wonder why there is no immediate evidence of Hemingway's submitting it for journal publication. Perhaps its setting and subject were still too close to his own experience; perhaps the story's partial indebtedness to Eliot was more than he wished to display in a journal, like the *Transatlantic Review,* with a commitment to recognizing original work. When he wrote to Pound on 17 March that Ford had accepted "Indian Camp," he added, "Several others he cant publish" (*Letters* 112). If "Cat in the Rain" was among those several, those reasons for not publishing it remain. Or it might be, simply, that Hemingway had his eye on "the Boni Liveright book" he first mentioned to Edward O'Brien in November 1923 and was saving the story for it (*Letters* 112).

Whatever the reasons, "Cat in the Rain" joined two other stories from this period, "The End of Something" and "The Three-Day Blow," along with "The Battler" from the following winter, to be the four first published in the Boni and Liveright *In Our Time* of October 1925.

Sources and Influences

Although over a year passed between the story's first sketch and the final typescript, it retained the traces of Hemingway's experiences of February 1923 in Rapallo. Sometime early in February Hadley might have known she was pregnant, and that news would have offered another reason to join the Pounds in a warmer climate. Hemingway had been postponing the journey with letters to Pound not too discretely inquiring whether he would be in Rapallo or "running down the road," as they said then, to Calabria with Nancy Cunard (*Letters,* 29 January 1923, 78). As it was, the Pounds stayed only five days after the Hemingways arrived on 7 February. If, as Carlos Baker states, Hemingway stopped sleeping with Hadley to stay in shape for boxing or tennis with Strater, who had a sprained ankle (105), the "Rapallo" sketch seems a curious celebration of the joy of continence. Of Rapallo itself, he told Gertrude Stein, "The place aint much" (*Letters* 79).

In his letter to Scott Fitzgerald (ca. 24 December 1925) Hemingway denied any biographical source for the story: "Cat in the Rain wasn't about Hadley. . . . When I wrote that we were at Rapallo but Hadley was 4 months pregnant with Bumby. The Inn Keeper was the one at Cortina D'Ampezzo and the man and the girl were a harvard kid and his wife that

I'd met at Genoa. Hadley never made a speech in her life about wanting a baby because she had been told various things by her doctor and I'd— no use going into all that" (*Letters* 180). The letter confirms more with its denials than it asserts, even without the accompanying misinformation on the occasion of "Out of Season." Hadley was only one month along, for certain, at Rapallo, although she was four months pregnant at Cortina. No one has yet tracked down the Harvard kid and his wife, a bookish fellow no doubt and like Hubert of "Mr. and Mrs. Elliot." What is most interesting is Hemingway's remark that the wife's speech is about "wanting a baby," and his sentence that breaks off just *after* it implies, as Jeffrey Meyers claims, that a doctor had told Hadley not to have a child or to abort the one she was carrying (120). If that implication is false, it is perfectly consonant with the rest of the letter and doubly revealing that Hemingway remembered it that way.

Sometime during those five days in mid-February Ezra Pound lent Hemingway a copy of "The Waste Land," the poem of Eliot's that most profoundly influenced Hemingway's fiction. Hemingway's contempt for "Major Elliot"—as he called him—and the "heavy, uncut pages" of his *Criterion*, where the poem had been published in October 1922, reveals as always his attempts to outmatch the poet in prose. And with "Out of Season," written two months after the first sketch for this story, "Cat in the Rain" shares a lineage from that poem. The opening sentences of the sketch compare two cats copulating with Eliot's low and lusty Sweeney on Mrs. Porter and then contrast them with his and Eliot's mentor, Pound, who "gets nowhere except artistically of course." An odd beginning but not altogether a false start, for the lines he alludes to come from Eliot's "The Fire Sermon" and in turn allude to Andrew Marvell's "To His Coy Mistress": "But at my back I always hear/Time's wingèd chariot hurrying near." Hemingway, restive in a dry season, may have watched the cats and read of Sweeney with some envy. Perhaps a bit of that emotion underlies the description of the wife's sensual response to the hotel-keeper (*Stories* 168, 169).

But it was the previous section of "The Waste Land," "A Game of Chess," that he drew on for the private confrontation between the husband and wife, similar to, but more dramatic than, the Concordia scene in "Out of Season." A woman before her mirror, thinking of her hair and threatening some impulsive act to bestir her supine and cynical companion and finally driven to a neurotic outburst, all derive from Eliot's poem. So much so, that when he tells her to "Shut up and get something to read," we almost expect him to hand her the poem or say, "I think we are in rats' alley/Where the dead men lost their bones" ("The Waste Land," ll. 115–16).

The concluding part of "A Game of Chess," the monologue in the pub on Lil and Albert, offers some ancillary evidence that here and perhaps in "Out of Season" the issue underlying the conflict between the husband

and wife is an abortion. But, as in the earlier story, it seems to make little difference.

Finally, the story still has traces of the workshop. The first paragraph seems at times to overwork repetition: the war monument "glistened in the rain. It was raining. The rain dripped from the palm trees." And the passage beginning "The wife liked him . . ." suggests a set-piece Hemingway found effective in "Up in Michigan" and was trying out again, not all that successfully (*Stories* 167, 168). But he had learned a good deal from writing "Out of Season." Here, too, he juxtaposes contrasting inner and outer scenes, a foreign couple and those who wait upon them in an Italian resort, a dry and sterile relationship and an unregenerative rain, ending with the ironic gift of a tortoise-shell cat, like the earlier story's fishing that came to nothing.

Critical Studies

The earliest studies of "Cat in the Rain" considered the story's scenic structure, although none remarked its almost exact analogue in "Out of Season." John Hagopian described the "five symmetrically arranged scenes" enclosed by an introductory descriptive paragraph and the concluding scene marked by the maid's knock upon the door: the hotel room, the lobby, the square, then the lobby and the room again. He noted some of the thematic changes through these scenes in the terms for the wife and her terms for the cat, to which we should add the terms for the husband and note the scenes in which there is no reference to the cat (221–22). In the first scene she is "the American wife," he is "the husband," and she refers to the cat as "the poor kitty," a rejected title for the story (KL/EH 320). In her passage through the lobby past the hotel-keeper she is "the wife" and there is no reference to the cat. Out in the square she becomes "the American girl," and speaks of the cat, the kitty, and *il gatto*. Returning through the lobby she is "the American girl" or "the girl," and the cat is not mentioned. And back in the room, the husband is named George, she becomes "his wife," and as her anxiety approaches hysteria the "poor kitty" becomes a "cat."

That pattern is clear, although it may only support what is apparent in the rest of the story. The shift from "wife" to "girl" to "wife" concomitant with that from "kitty" to "cat" to "kitty"—and at last in desperation to "cat"—counterpoints two diminutives or terms for the young with their opposites, aligning "kitty" with "wife" and "girl" with "cat." That complex of images, for Hagopian, "points to a crisis involving the lack of fertility" and reveals the woman's desire for the cat as a barely sublimated wish to have a child. She is aroused by the figure of the hotel-keeper who, unlike her supine husband, rises when she passes. Her visceral reaction to the padrone is cast in language that "might be appropriately used to describe a woman who is pregnant." If that is so, however, one wonders how Hagopian arrives at the conclusion that their marriage is "strictly companionate" (221).

John Magee added the darkening progression from natural daylight, when the wife first looks out at the square, to the artificial light she sees at last to argue that her ultimate fate is an "artificial and sterile fulfillment" (Item 8). How sterile that fulfillment might be was demonstrated by Warren Bennett's consideration of the padrone's gift of a tortoise-shell cat: that cat is no kitty, has not been in the rain, is probably a male given its size, and like almost all tortoise-shell males is sterile.

Gertrude White's article reaches for a larger perspective, questions some strained readings, and concludes that the story should be read as a "paradigm of man's plight" rather than as the "drama of a particular crisis in a particular relationship" (244). She questions Hagopian's rather shy intimation that the "man in the rubber cape" is a sort of ambulatory phallus with a condom for protection against the fertilizing rain—a rather odd notion, by the way, of a prophylactic's function. Nor would she admit Horst Kruse's contrary suggestion that the man constitutes an allusion to the ubiquitous "man in the macintosh" in *Ulysses* and to Leopold Bloom's fancy that as the thirteenth at Dignam's funeral he must be Death (29). For White, that man walking through the square, now emptied of artists, is simply "a man going about his business in the world in any weather"; he suggests "the normal routine of things: neither the neurotic world of the wife's 'I want' nor the husband's indifference and absorption in the secondary world of books" (243).

Her essay raises the important question of what meanings we may ascribe to the rain in this story, which follows "The Waste Land" in several ways and prefigures something of *A Farewell to Arms*. In Eliot's poem the archetypal associations with rain, from the divine to the demonic, the generative to the destructive, are perhaps less important than the dramatic ways in which his characters respond to this element of life. Some devoutly pray for it, others fear its challenge to waken to life. In "Cat in the Rain," White would suggest, the rain falls less profoundly on the characters: "men must live in a world in which climate and weather are not calculated to their desires and their dreams" (242). Nor does the rain carry the portentous meaning Catherine sees so prophetically and Frederic later comes to understand in *A Farewell to Arms*.

The conclusion that follows from this argument will not draw every reader with it. For White, the cat in the rain is symbolic "not only of the child [the wife] wants but of the child she is; the child in her which her husband refuses to indulge . . . in a world that takes no account of one's nature, one's comforts, one's desires" (243). This may be the world the story presents, but it does not necessarily follow that the authorial tone is "aloof and ironic with a languid hint of cruel laughter," persuading us that since this is way the world is we are not asked to "pity this woman, despise this man" (245). For we can both accept such a world and also pity the woman and despise the man, or better, pity them both.

David Lodge's essay of 1980 is the most perceptive and reasoned of all those on this story and one of the most challenging for all of Hemingway criticism. The first section reviews three contemporary general theories and their methodologies under the categories of narratology and narrative grammar, the poetics of fiction, and rhetorical analysis—no mean task but brilliantly accomplished. His purpose is to determine whether it is "possible, or useful, to bring the whole battery of modern formalism and structuralism to bear upon a single text," here, "Cat in the Rain" (6).

He considers several problems of interpretation, beginning with the meanings attributed to the tortoise-shell cat, first by Carlos Baker who thought it to be the first cat in the rain, and then by John Hagopian who suspected it was not. An inauspicious beginning, perhaps, for, as Warren Bennett has noted, the two are clearly not one. That raises the question, however, of whether the wife's failure to get the first cat she saw ("I want that kitty.") is compensated with the gift from the hotel-keeper after her appeals for *a* cat, possibly any cat. This in turn leads to the meaning of the reversal in the last scene: either a happy one (Baker) or an ironic twist (Hagopian). Lodge finally finds Baker's assumption unwarranted and Hagopian's preferable. But in the process he effectively demonstrates how some of the structural methodologies he introduced in the first section can resolve some of the crucial differences among readers of the story. He corrects Hagopian's easy identification of the rain as a symbol of fertility, incidentally affirming White, and argues that the wife's sensations as she passes the hotel-keeper and her other cravings are more those of a woman who is pregnant than one who wants to be and cannot (16–17).

The essay is informed with a variety of contemporary theories of narrative structure, voice, and perspective, all brought into play with critical virtuosity. It ends with an analysis of the way the story's first paragraph "establishes the thematic core of the story through oppositions between nature and culture, joy and ennui. Joy is associated with a harmonious union of culture and nature, ennui as the result of some dissociation or discontinuity between culture and nature" (18).

Finally, the essay represents something of a challenge to Hemingway scholarship, for it demonstrates that, indeed, contemporary critical theories are both possible and useful for understanding Hemingway's fiction. That David Lodge's essay rests in a lonely eminence offers a comment on recent Hemingway criticism and, happily, an opportunity for that criticism in the future.

Works Cited

PRIMARY

Ernest Hemingway: Selected Letters, 1917–1961. Ed. Carlos Baker. New York: Scribner's, 1981.

The Short Stories of Ernest Hemingway. New York: Scribner's, 1938, 167–70.

SECONDARY

Bennett, Warren. "Marriage Failure and the Tortoise-Shell Cat In 'Cat in the Rain.'" Unpublished paper.

Eliot, T. S. *The Waste Land and Other Poems*. New York: Harcourt, 1934.

Hagopian, John V. "Symmetry in 'Cat in the Rain.'" *College English* 24 (Dec. 1962): 220–22

Kruse, Horst. "Hemingway's 'Cat in the Rain' and Joyce's *Ulysses*." *Literatur in Wissenschaft und Unterricht* 3 (1970): 28–30.

Lodge, David. "Analysis and Interpretation of the Realist Text: A Pluralistic Approach to Ernest Hemingway's 'Cat in the Rain.'" *Poetics Today* 1 (1980): 5–19.

Magee, John D. "Hemingway's 'Cat in the Rain,'" *Explicator* 26 (September 1967), Item 8.

Meyers, Jeffrey. *Hemingway: A Biography*. New York: Harper, 1985.

White, Gertrude M. "We're All 'Cats in the Rain.'" *Fitzgerald/Hemingway Annual* (1978): 241–46.

8

The End of Something

Composition History (March 1924)

"The End of Something" might have been one of the "two dandy stories" Hadley mentioned in her letter to her mother-in-law on 20 February 1924 (KL/EH, Hadley Hemingway to Grace Hemingway), but it seems more likely that she was referring to "Indian Camp"—with or without "Three Shots"—and "Cat in the Rain." It could well have been the third she mentioned he was at work on in that letter; for it, like the manuscript of "Cat in the Rain" (KL/EH 319), is marked in his hand, "Original Manuscript/March 1924 (First Draft) Paris E.M.H." (KL/EH 373; cp., KL/EH 319).

Like the manuscript for "Indian Camp," however, this one for "The End of Something" (KL/EH 373) shows some evidence of an earlier start. The first four manuscript pages of the narrative (to *Stories* 109, 1. 32, ". . . Hortons Creek.") are on one style paper (with the watermark "Basseau") and pages 5-10 on another (with no watermark). The date of composition of this story is further complicated by its association with "The Three-Day Blow." In *A Moveable Feast* Hemingway remembered writing that sequel to "The End of Something" in January 1922 (5). Either his memory failed him and he confused two periods of writing—not unusual when someone recalls events from thirty years ago—or it did not. It is conceivable that "The Three-Day Blow" *was* begun in early 1922 and lost with those stolen in December; there is only a two-page fragment of a manuscript paragraph in the Hemingway Collection (KL/EH 762).

But the typescript submitted for publication (KL/EH 96) is similar to that for "The End of Something," and it is reasonable to assume that both stories were finished sometime in late March of 1924. The different kinds of paper used for the manuscript suggest, however, that, as with "Indian Camp" and "Cat in the Rain," Hemingway might have had beginnings or sketches for these stories in hand when he turned to fiction again in the early months of 1924.

Publication History (October 1925)

Like "Cat in the Rain," which probably preceded it, and its companion story, "The Three-Day Blow," which followed it, "The End of Something" was a story Hemingway was holding for the imminent publication of his first major collection. He might well have seen by this time that a sequence of Nick Adams stories was in the making and that they would be better understood in one volume. Whatever his reasons, "The End of Something" was first published in the first edition of *In Our Time* in October 1925.

Sources and Influences

Scott Fitzgerald reviewed *In Our Time* in the May 1926 *Bookman,* and cited "The End of Something" as an instance of those early stories that make us "immediately aware of something temperamentally new" (Stephens 18); and since then no critic has demonstrated any substantial literary influence on the story. If the opening description of Horton Bay in its decline serves to foreshadow the end of Nick's affair with Marjorie, that strategy was a common one Hemingway might have learned from any author. It is the rest of the story that strikes the original note.

Again, as with "Indian Camp," some of that originality may derive from the remembered landscape of Michigan, the people he knew, and the end of his adolescence. Constance Montgomery has described the original details of the town and the bay and reproduced an old tintype of the village with a lumber schooner docked at the mill. The villagers, of course, differ in their recollections of how serious Ernest's affair with Marjorie Bump may have been (132–34); but Carlos Baker's informants remember her as "much enamored" of him (64). In an interview with Donald St. John, William B. Smith saw himself as the model for Bill and suggested that he might have opposed the romance in 1919 since two years later he thought Hadley "too old" for Hemingway (St. John 10–11; Johnston 21–22). In fact, both manuscripts identify the character as Bill Smith.

That last recollection may well be the most relevant of the biographical details behind the story, for "The End of Something" was a harbinger of fiction to come. Joseph Flora has noted that this is the first of the Nick Adams stories to "portray Nick away from the family" and the only one (before "Summer People") in which he shares "an extended scene with a female companion" (54–55). Even with that curious slight on the Indian girl Trudy in "Fathers and Sons," the point is worth noting. More important, however, is that the story and its sequel introduce a dramatic triangle in which one man chooses a companionship with another over that with a woman. So it is that "The End of Something" is a prototype for the marriage tales, as "The Three-Day Blow" is the first of the stories of men without women.

Critical Studies

Of the several critical issues the story has raised, the first and perhaps least interesting concerns the function of the two introductory descriptive paragraphs on the day a decade before when the lumber schooners made the last trip to take away "everything that had made the mill a mill and Hortons Bay a town" (*Stories* 107). Philip Young began with the suggestion that the story "is like a chapter in a novel," requiring the following chapter, "The Three-Day Blow," to explain Nick's reasons for jilting Marjorie (34–35). Horst Kruse responded with the argument that the introductory paragraphs offer the moral—"all things run their natural course, and submission and acceptance are the only sensible responses" (156)—and therein rests the integrity and unity of the story. Kruse's quest for analogy finds Nick allegorized as the schooner and Marjorie as the deserted landscape around the bay, but goes hopelessly awry in the anatomy of a perch when he associates its ventral fin with her hymen (161). Harry Barba drew on Aristotle and the story's literal, dramatic, and symbolic levels of meaning to suggest that not only does the end of lumbering "shadow forth" the end of the lovers' romance, but that the dissolution of their love is a "commentary" on the fate of the mill (77)—but how, we are left to wonder. Others, like Joseph Whitt, associate Marge with the schooner when she leaves in the boat and Nick in his desolation with the landscape and the town.

Joseph DeFalco has characterized the passage as a "correlative parable of exploitation and waste that . . . foreshadows the whole of the coming story." Nick and Marjorie figure in a pattern of images of "second growth" and become "participants in the great cycle of existence"; but while Nick grows in awareness of the emblematic nature of the scene, implying "death and waste . . . before a renewal may occur," Marjorie sees the landscape as "indicative of the romance of life". This argument is strained at times—the loss of the "vital machinery" of the mill "symbolizes Nick's loss of belief in the ordered machinations of his childish universe"—but it attempts a connection between the introduction and the central drama of the story (41–43).

If one feels restive with any of these analogies, the reason may be suggested when DeFalco describes the introductory paragraphs as an "appended parable" (42). That the paragraphs *do* seem appended may account for the attempts to give them some relevance to the rest of the story. But no parable with some immutable maxim can capture the dramatic development of the following story. Both Nick and Marjorie are, as in any good fiction, changed characters by the last line; nothing that may describe them at the beginning of the story can adequately describe them at its end.

To question the controversy over who is the schooner, who is the bay, and what of the machinery removed by the men, let alone the perch's ventral fin, is not to deny the rich extensions of meaning with which Hemingway invests the landscape of his stories or the gestures of the characters who live in it. Rather it is to ask a prior question, rarely considered, about the idiosyncratic nature of Hemingway's metaphors and how they seem to come to rest somewhere beyond the literal but always this side of the allegorical.

With that question answered, we might then ask whether the rather ponderous association between the decline of the lumbering industry and the end of an adolescent romance adds to our understanding of either event. If it does not, then we might conclude that Hemingway could have legitimately consigned these two paragraphs to the limbo of things left out, however heretical that suggestion may seem.

Once the introductory paragraphs are out of the way, most of the commentators agree upon the meaning of the dramatic conflict at the story's center. Marjorie's romantic affection for "our old ruin" that "seems more like a castle" and her innocent display of skill at fishing, which Nick claims he taught her, condemns her in his view: she is romantic, possessive, and—most important—she knows too much about feeding trout and the rising moon, and knows it "happily." She also knows that for Nick that is not what is "really the matter" and that he is talking "silly." With her direct questions and his halting responses, she becomes the tutor and he the tyro, when he matches her earlier romanticism with his puerility by admitting that love "isn't fun any more." Then, as Joseph Flora notes, Marjorie "proves her worth by behaving with great dignity" (56), and, one would add, with a telling last shot. She takes the boat, and when Nick offers to push it off, she tells him, "You don't need to." She is last seen "in the boat on the water with the moonlight on it" (*Stories* 110–11). She instinctively knows of the waxing and waning moon, not simply as a romantic image, but as a symbol of the cycles of life, from long before Horton Bay lost its mill.

The story's conclusion, with the departure of Marjorie and the arrival of Bill, has elicited comments on both its formal and thematic implications. It is something of a "surprise ending," though neither of the O. Henry sort nor dissimilar from the endings of other stories like "Indian Camp" and "Ten Indians" (Flora 57). Indeed, Bill's arrival and his obvious complicity in jilting Marjorie, is appropriate if one of Nick's unspoken reasons for ending the affair is that she knows too much of the male domain.

One question raised by the ending may be framed in the terms one chooses for the relationship between Nick and Bill: it may represent the "safer world of male camaraderie" (Flora 58) or offer partial "proof of Hemingway's latent homoeroticism" (Brenner 20–21, 242 n. 38). Or both. Joseph Whitt was the first to argue that the curious sentence, "Bill didn't touch him, either," referring to the earlier one, "They [Nick and Marjorie] sat on the blanket without touching each other" (*Stories* 110, 111), reveals the story's "undefined tension" in the conflict of "a man torn by the contradictions of unexpressed homosexual tendencies" (Item 58). Alice Parker's objection that Nick will find little "comfort for his miserable feeling of inadequacy within himself" (Item 36) in his relationship with Bill may be true but does not deny the latent nature of that relationship.

Certainly the two sentences set Marjorie and Bill in opposition. The story's manuscripts show that Hemingway added the two sentences as he was working through revisions of the moment of Bill's appearance. The first manuscript does not include the phrase "without touching each other" in the sentence describing Nick and Marjorie sitting on the blanket; and when Bill arrives he wrote, "He lay there until he felt Bill's arm on his shoulder. He felt Bill coming before he felt his touch." In the second manuscript that is revised to "He lay there while he |felt| heard Bill come into the clearing walking around through the woods. He felt Bill coming up to the fire. |He felt Bill's hand on his shoulder.|" Then to the description of Nick and Marjorie he added the phrase "without touching each other" and to this scene the sentence "Bill didn't touch him, either."

Hemingway seems to have been aware that Bill's arm, even his hand, on Nick's shoulder might have been too revealing a gesture. Moreover, he was attempting to convey how Nick felt and perceived—not only or even primarily with his senses—his girl's departure and his friend's arrival. Neither one touches him; yet with his face buried in the blanket, it is as if he senses them as disembodied representations of a conflict within his mind.

In the story's first manuscript, Nick dismisses Bill as finally as he did Marjorie, "Oh go. Go away," and then softened it to "Go away for a while." Bill does, for a while, and then returns in "The Three-Day Blow." And so does Marjorie, or at least the thought of her, for the conflict in that story is still unresolved. As his friend served as an alternative to his girl in "The End of Something," so she in the sequel remains as an alternative to his friend. Nick's sense in the later story that "there was always a way out" (*Stories* 125) is a vain and youthful thought. Anyone with a smattering of tragedy in mind would read this as a fateful remark, almost inviting the kinds of encompassing circumstances that will not so easily be put off but will hold Nick to hard decisions.

Works Cited

PRIMARY

A Moveable Feast. New York: Scribner's, 1964.
The Short Stories of Ernest Hemingway. New York: Scribner's, 1938, 107–11.

SECONDARY

Baker, Carlos, *Ernest Hemingway: A Life Story.* 1969. New York: Scribner's, 1988.

Barba, Harry. "The Three Levels of 'The End of Something.'" *Philological Papers* 17 (June 1970): 76–80.

Brenner, Gerry. *Concealments in Hemingway's Works.* Columbus: Ohio State UP, 1983.

DeFalco, Joseph. *The Hero in Hemingway's Short Stories* Pittsburgh: The U of Pittsburgh P, 1963.

Flora, Joseph M. *Hemingway's Nick Adams.* Baton Rouge: Louisiana State UP, 1982.

Johnston, Kenneth G. " 'The Three-Day Blow': Tragicomic Aftermath of a Summer Romance." *Hemingway Review* 2 (Fall 1982): 21–25.

Kruse, Horst H. "Ernest Hemingway's 'The End of Something': Its Independence as a Short Story and Its Place in the 'Education of Nick Adams.' " *Studies in Short Fiction* 5 (Winter 1967): 152–66.

Montgomery, Constance. *Hemingway in Michigan.* Waitsfield: Vermont Crossroads, 1977.

Parker, Alice. "Hemingway's 'The End of Something.' " *Explicator* 10 (Mar. 1952), Item 36.

Stephens, Robert O., ed. *Ernest Hemingway: The Critical Reception.* N.p.: Burt Franklin, 1977.

St. John, Donald. "Interview with Hemingway's 'Bill Gorton.' " *Connecticut Review* 1 (April 1968): 6–11.

Whitt, Joseph. "Hemingway's 'The End of Something.' " *Explicator* 9 (June 1951), Item 58.

Young, Philip. *Ernest Hemingway: A Reconsideration.* 1952. New York: Harcourt, 1966.

9

The Three-Day Blow

Composition History (March 1924)

Although the composition history of "The End of Something" is fairly certain, some questions still surround the composition of its sequel, "The Three-Day Blow." Hemingway rather vividly recalled writing it in January 1922 (*Moveable Feast* 5), two years before the evidential date of its companion piece. Nor is there the usual manuscript version preceding his own typescript (KL/EH 96) as there is for "The End of Something."

Which story was written first may seem an idle question: as Philip Young argued, we read the stories as if they were two related chapters, one a dramatic act and the other a dialogue revealing something of that act's motive and response (34–35). But if "The Three-Day Blow" was written first, that offers some evidence for the study of Hemingway's practice as a writer; for at times he began in the middle of a narrative and then returned to its beginning.

But with no more than the extant manuscripts for evidence, it is probable that "The Three-Day Blow" was written soon after "The End of Something" in late March 1924.

Publication History (October 1925)

With "The End of Something" and "Cat in the Rain," this story makes the third of those Hemingway apparently did not submit for publication but saved for the Boni and Liveright book he had had in mind since November 1923 (*Letters* 104). And with them it was first published in October 1925 in *In Our Time*.

Sources and Influences

If there are few literary sources for its companion story, there are fewer still for "The Three-Day Blow." The two boys' drunken pontifications on matters of great moment in life, literature, and baseball have something of the tone of the dialogues in James Joyce's "Ivy Day in the Committee Room" and "Grace" (*Dubliners* 118, 150). Robert Gajdusek finds that its placement in *In Our Time*—fifth like "After the Race" in *Dubliners*—supports some analogies between the two stories (54–55). But all this falls short of precise and demonstrable evidence of Joyce's influence. So, too, do the "interesting links" Kenneth Johnston cites between *Romeo and Juliet* and the story—one begins and the other ends in an orchard, and Bill plays Benvolio to Nick's Romeo—tenuous connections given the differences between the two works (22).

Some critics have argued that the books Nick and Bill discuss reveal literary influences on the story itself: George Meredith's *The Ordeal of Richard Feverel* offers the analogies of father protecting a son from "the temptations of the flesh . . . ('the Apple-disease')" (Johnston 23); a hero whose "distrust of the female" stems from his mother's conduct and his father's incomprehension of "the realities of the world"; and an ending with "unfaithfulness to a devoted, lovely, and unsophisticated girl" (Flora 61–62). Maurice Hewlett's *The Forest Lovers: A Romance* is a chivalric tale in which the hero "marries a dirty, ragged girl only to save her from hanging"; she withholds herself until he truly loves her, and he gallantly places the bundling sword between them (Johnston 23). Finally, Hugh Walpole's *Fortitude* describes the conflict of a young writer who believes his calling demands that he be ruthless in his relationships with others, and G. K. Chesterton's *The Flying Inn* provides the boys with satiric lines to ridicule abstention and justify their drinking (Johnston 23).

Only two of these authors, Meredith and Walpole, suggest thematic parallels with the story's delayed subject, the end of Nick's affair with Marjorie; but Nick "couldn't get into" the first and remembers the second for the behavior of the hero's father (*Stories* 118).

This and the sophomoric tone of the boys' literary discussion imply that the books they mention serve less as informing sources and more as elements in a comedy of adolescence. Finally, these literary works have been cited for analogies with Nick Adams's experience beyond this story: *Richard Feverel* for some "striking parallels" with Nick's family experience (Flora 61), and *Fortitude* for Nick's "identification" with the novel's hero, a young writer (Johnston 23).

If Hemingway drew on his boyhood friend William B. Smith for the character of Bill, then the differences between the model and the fictional portrait may be more interesting than their similarities. William Smith spent summers with his aunt and uncle, Dr. and Mrs. J. W. Charles, at their Horton Bay cottage close by an orchard. But there the similarity ends: his father, a professor of mathematics, was unwelcome there since Mrs. Charles blamed him for her sister's early death (Baker 569). Bill's father in the story is an artist, a drinker, and a hunter in contrast to Nick's father, the abstinent doctor. So the Charles's cottage has been remodeled into an ideal retreat for boys to play at being men without women.

Critical Studies

Jackson Benson, often quick to the critical scene, was the first to consider at length Hemingway's humor and the irony of its "dark laughter." With his lead others have taken up the "humorous applicability of the novel titles" in the story and the "bookish melodrama of Nick's thoughts" (67). Kenneth Johnston sees Bill as the tutor and Nick as the tyro in an almost Jamesian dialogue. When Nick, with an uneaten apple in his pocket, dismisses *Richard Feverel* and the paternal warning against "the Apple-disease," Bill then teases him by "recommending *Forest Lovers* and *The Dark Forest*" and alluding to the lovers' parting on the wooded point. When Nick judges *The Forest Lovers* to be a "swell book" but questions the practicality of the naked sword, the "gallant idealist has been shouldered aside by the ignoble realist." When he later sees his strange and unrecognizable face in the mirror, we know that he is not only drunk but has been "radically changed by his disillusioning experience" (23).

Through all that inebriated literary talk we come to discover what much of the story is about: in simple and tentative terms, it concerns the conflicts of maturation between an ennobling idealism and a practical realism. This, of course, is the stuff of comedy; but when that conflict remains unresolved, as it does in Nick's mind at the end of the story, the comedy approaches its darker versions. So Kenneth Johnston's conception of the story as a form of tragicomedy is appropriate.

In the course of a controversy over the dating of the events of "The Three-Day Blow," largely with the boys' conversation on baseball, that dialogue was shown to support the story's pattern of disillusionment. The argument over the dating of the baseball season went on for some ten years with claims for 1916 (Monteiro, "Hemingway's Pleiade"), for 1917 (Burns; Monteiro, "Dating the Events"), and for 1919 (Johnston): the best evidence from baseball history and the luckless tale of Heinie Zim (Henry Zimmerman) supports George Monteiro's claim for 1917. The counter-evidence for 1919 is largely biographical: Nick's statement that he and Marjorie were planning to marry and go to Italy is read as reflecting Hemingway's postwar familiarity with Italy and his early plans to go to Italy with Hadley. And that date would link Nick's disillusionment with the corruption of the sacred game to the Black Sox scandal of 1919. But all the literary evidence in the story, especially in the characterization of Nick as a naif with wine, women, and books, argues for a date before Nick's war experiences. As Stuart Burns notes, after such an experience perhaps "Candide or Don Quixote could have retained this kind of innocence; but not Hemingway *or* his fictional self" (135).

The question is of primary importance for literary biographers who have their own reasons for dating the story closer to Hemingway's association with

Marjorie Bump and for those anthologists concerned with the sequence of the Nick Adams stories. Again, the best response to those concerns is in George Monteiro's "Dating the Events," where he concludes that although Hemingway may have conflated later events with those of 1917, it is the most probable date (210), and in Stuart Burns's arrangement of the stories in a sequence of Nick Adams's experience (138–39).

Although there are exceptions, it is often the rule that the more biographical criticism one finds for a Hemingway story the less interesting it is for those who look for formal, thematic, or archetypal patterns to invoke general summaries of its meanings—another way of saying that "The Three-Day Blow" is not one that engages critical interest. Kenneth Johnston, with his notion of the tragicomic structure of the tale, explains the lack of attention to the story by the divided response it evokes. We may "sigh with the disenchanted Nick, to take seriously the tragedy of the heart, and, at the same time . . . smile at the resiliency of heart-broken youth, to laugh at the humorless lad who . . . stalks out into the storm to enjoy the hunt" (25).

Hemingway may have recognized that the story needed another version. Between 1925 and 1927 he returned to its themes with the drafts of "Ten Indians" and reconsidered the drama of a lost love, boyhood friends, and two fathers.

Works Cited

PRIMARY

Ernest Hemingway: Selected Letters, 1917–1961. Ed. Carlos Baker. New York: Scribner's, 1981.

A Moveable Feast. New York: Scribner's, 1964.

The Short Stories of Ernest Hemingway. New York: Scribner's, 1938, 115–25.

SECONDARY

Baker, Carlos. *Ernest Hemingway: A Life Story.* 1969. New York: Scribner's 1988.

Benson, Jackson J. *Hemingway: The Writer's Arts as Self-Defense.* Minneapolis: U of Minnesota P, 1969.

Burns, Stuart L. "Scrambling the Unscrambleable: *The Nick Adams Stories.*" *Arizona Quarterly* 33 (Summer 1977): 133–40.

Flora, Joseph M. *Hemingway's Nick Adams.* Baton Rouge: Louisiana State UP, 1982.

Gajdusek, Robert E. "Joyce's Presence in Hemingway's *In Our Time.*" *Hemingway Review* 2 (Fall 1982): 48–61.

Johnston, Kenneth G. " 'The Three-Day Blow': Tragicomic Aftermath of a Summer Romance." *Hemingway Review* 2 (Fall 1982): 21–25.

Joyce, James. *Dubliners.* 1916. New York: Viking, 1962.

Monteiro, George. "Dating the Events of 'The Three-Day Blow.' " *Fitzgerald/Hemingway Annual* (1977): 207–10.

———. "Hemingway's Pleiade Ball Players." *Fitzgerald/Hemingway Annual* (1973): 299–301.

Young, Philip. *Ernest Hemingway: A Reconsideration.* 1952. New York: Harcourt, 1966.

10
The Doctor and the Doctor's Wife

Composition History (March–April 1924)

The manuscripts for "The Doctor and the Doctor's Wife" follow the typical sequence for Hemingway's early stories. First, there is a heavily revised, untitled ink manuscript (KL/EH 367) of eleven pages; then a titled and addressed ink manuscript incorporating the revisions of the first (KL/EH 368); and finally a version typed by Hemingway and another by someone else (KL/EH 96, 97). Further, as is often the case, the most interesting revisions occur on the first draft, which Hemingway began as a rather quick sketch of the narrative, then added details of the characters and slightly revised its ending. From first to last, Hemingway seems to have had this story well in mind and waiting to be written, and its biographical origins may tell us why.

The first manuscript is somewhat unusual in that the date Hemingway assigned it is more precise than any others given to the manuscripts of this period: He wrote on its first page, "Original manuscript—First Draft, April 7, 1924, Paris, E.M.H." Moreover, the verso of its last page bears an odd note in his hand: "When you look back on it you always find a place where you think, well, if I hadn't done that I'd have been all right. Don't feel disgraced if you're a cuckold. Even a bull has horns" (KL/EH 367). Whether the dating and the comment were both written at the same time; what made him recall, if he inscribed it later, the *date* on which he completed the manuscript; to whom he addressed his consolations on cuckoldry or whom he quoted, and why?—these questions are, like Thomas Browne's on what songs the sirens sang, puzzling but within conjecture.

But not here, for it is enough to say that the story was written sometime in the last week of March and the first week of April and intermittently revised through the spring and summer of 1924.

Publication History (December 1924; October 1925)

"The Doctor and the Doctor's Wife" might have been submitted to the *Transatlantic Review* that spring, but accepted for later publication on the grounds that "Indian Camp" had just appeared in April and the immediate appearance of another story by the journal's subeditor would be unseemly. On 2 May Hemingway wrote to Edward J. O'Brien asking that he send two stories to an agent, but they were probably "The End of Something" and "The Three-Day Blow" (*Letters* 117). With the death of John Quinn, the journal's angel, in late July, the fate of the review was momentarily bleak; but by early August, when Krebs Friend agreed to support it, Hemingway could tell Gertrude Stein that "the transatlantic is going on" (*Letters* 120).

Hemingway wrote again to O'Brien on 12 September that "I've been so busy writing I haven't been able to work to get stuff published—just that one story in the April Transatlantic ["Indian Camp"] and one coming out next month" (*Letters* 124). Carlos Baker believes the second story was "Mr. and Mrs. Elliot," which appeared in the Autumn-Winter issue of the *Little Review;* but since Hemingway had sent O'Brien a version of that story in May with doubts that it would be published, one would expect him to make some reference to that fact in this second letter. Finally, that Hemingway offered to send O'Brien proofs of the story he mentions in September argues that he had not sent him a draft of it in May.

That evidence is rather more delicate than one would like, but until more is found it seems likely that "The Doctor and the Doctor's Wife" was submitted to the *Transatlantic Review* in the late summer or early fall and accepted for publication in December 1924. By then Hemingway was well along in preparing the *in our time* chapters, the three stories from his first collection and those written in this miraculous year for submission to Boni and Liveright and their publication in October 1925.

Sources and Influences

Hemingway needed few literary models for "The Doctor and the Doctor's Wife" with his recollections of his boyhood experiences at Walloon Lake, the family cottage "Windemere," and the Indians who sawed driftwood logs for his father. The relationship he imagined between the doctor, Henry, and his wife seems close to that portrayed in unpublished drafts of "Fathers and Sons" and the best of the recent biographies, Michael Reynolds's *The Young Hemingway*. Dick Boulton was a half-breed Indian, his eldest son was named Eddy and reappears in "Fathers and Sons"; he was related to Billy Tabeshaw through marriage; was a rough drinker who, according to one village recollection, was saved from alcohol poisoning by Dr. Hemingway only to accomplish that death soon after (Montgomery 69–70) or, in another recollection, got drunk and drowned or was dismembered by a train (St. John 82). (His most enduring contribution to Hemingway's boyhood and fiction was, of course, his daughter Prudence, who figures in "Ten Indians," "Fathers and Sons," and "The Last Good Country.")

One of the more curious items in Hemingway's correspondence is a letter to him from his father dated 8 March 1925 in which he recognized the story's origin and placed it in the summer of 1911. He "got out the Old Bear Lake book and showed Carol and Leicester the photo of Nic Boulton & Billy Tabeshaw . . . on the beach. . . . That was when you were 12 yrs. old & Carol was born that summer. It was by accident I was shown this article. Wish, dear boy, you would send me some of your work often" (KL/EH; *Richard* Boulton is so identified in county records.) Doctor Hemingway either did not read the story carefully or saw little connection between him or his wife and the characters of the doctor and his wife. If he had and kept it to himself, Hemingway reassured him in his reply: "I put in Dick Boulton and Billy Tabeshaw as real people with their real names because it was pretty sure they would never read the Transatlantic Review. I've written a number of stories about the Michigan country—the country is always true—what happens in the stories is fiction." And then, as if he knew his father *had* been offended and concealed that emotion, he added, "So when you see anything of mine that you don't like remember that I'm sincere in doing it and that I'm working toward something. If I write an ugly story that might be hateful to you or to Mother the next one might be one that you would like exceedingly" (*Letters,* 20 March 1925, 153).

In the light of the story, there is something terribly pathetic about those two letters. The father, deliberately it seems, grasped at details from 1911— the last year in which he and his eldest son were close—and found in his photograph album a picture to fix the events in those happy years and so deny what the story must have recalled, his estrangement from his wife. To read Reynolds's *Young Hemingway,* especially chapters 3–5, along with this story is to see how close it comes to an explicit presentation of his parents' characters, the dissolution of their once happy family and their marriage. With the family correspondence in the collections at the Kennedy Library and the University of Texas, Reynolds has found strong analogues between Clarence Hemingway's and the doctor's erratic and impulsive behavior, his depression—even his reaching out for a lost comradeship with his son—and between Grace Hemingway's and the doctor's wife's religiosity, her retreat to her darkened bedroom—even her Christian Science, the closest analogy he could find for Grace's interest in spiritualism (132).

At the end of the story Nick looks up from his book and knows intuitively that his father needs him desperately, and like two boyhood companions they leave for the healing woods. The story, for Hemingway, may well have been like Nick's intuition, at long last a gesture of understanding for his father's predicament and a silent offer of his love. Perhaps, after all,

Dr. Hemingway read the story better than anyone else could have and with better reasons for liking it.

Critical Studies

The dangers that await the critic who insists on the biographical sources of "The Doctor and the Doctor's Wife" are clear and, perhaps, present in the preceding section. Richard Fulkerson cites six earlier studies (Baker; Burhans; Gurko; Montgomery; Rovit; and Young) for stating or implying that Nick "witnesses" the events in the story; and he argues that they have been misled by the autobiographical incident into the "standard, incorrect, reading" that finds Nick as the "focus of the story" (61–62). He is right: Nick does not "watch" nor is he "shocked to see" his father's humiliation before Boulton and his wife (Baker 129; Rovit 56). For most of these critics, however, the misleading impulse, if it is one, was not so much the biographical sources of the story as their interest in finding a unity in either the Nick Adams stories or those in *In Our Time*. Carlos Baker and Earl Rovit err in passages summarizing, in Baker's phrase, "The Education of Nicholas Adams" (Baker 128). And, of course, Philip Young has long held that the individual stories are more like chapters in a novel. Clinton Burhans, seeking the "complex unity of *In Our Time*," notes that it is "uncertain" whether Nick witnessed his father's quarrel"—which it is not—in order to link the story with "other accounts of Nick's deepening understanding and insight" (320).

To agree that Nick does not witness the story's first two scenes is to raise the more interesting question of whether the end of the story implies that he did not need to see it to know what had probably happened. One can understand why a youngster would prefer to read a book rather than to hear his parents' conversation echo in the emotional distance between them; but would a boy of twelve read a book in the woods when the Indians had come to hook the logs from the sand and saw them up, unless something else has kept him away?

The story's conclusion and its manuscript revisions suggest that Nick immediately understands the implication of his father's first words "Your mother wants you to come and see her"; that is, "I have come to see you." In the first draft, Hemingway wrote, "Nick was sitting with his back against a tree" (KL/EH 367), and revised it later to his father "found Nick sitting with his back against a tree. . . ." Once he had established that Nick's father was seeking him, he could revise the dramatic exchange after Nick's decision to go with his father from Nick's looking *up* at his father to his father looking *down* at him. Finally, after ending the story with Nick's placing the book in his shirt and his father's first "All right. Come on," he added the ending in which the father places the book in *his* pocket, and Nick suggests a place "where there's black squirrels" (*Stories* 103).

If we can allow that the first two scenes are dramatic representations of conflicts that Nick has not witnessed but imagined, and which he recognizes when he meets his father in the third, then such psychological interpretations of the narrative as Joseph DeFalco's have a point. For him the story is enacted on a border between the wilderness and civilization, a "meeting place of two opposing forces . . ., the light and the dark, the known and the unknown," and the half-breed Boulton, who knows both realms, is "an exemplar . . . in rebellion against the authority of Nick's father" (33–34). Challenging him with the white man's morality on the question of the ownership of the logs, Boulton denigrates both Nick's father and the morality of the society he represents (35). In the second scene the mother lying in her darkened room suggests not only her ineffectuality as a wife but, for DeFalco, a "terrible mother figure who would lure her son back to the womb to be smothered by her protective nature" (36). In the final scene, Nick rejects the return to the womb and journeys toward experience, leading "the fallible father figure in order to restore him" (36).

Such a reading accounts for the sexual allusions in the story: "Dick" taunts the doctor with the familiar short form "Doc," puts his "axes down on the little dock," tells him not to "go off at half cock," and spits on his log. Dick uses his axe outdoors, the doctor "fondles his gun . . . indoors" (Grebstein 7–8) in a "fantasy of violence" that is "sexual and even onanistic" (Davis, Item 1), and so on. But others, like Jackson Benson, may account for the same conflicts, the doctor's restraint before Dick Boulton, and his wife's reduction of him to a "misguided child" in need of her benign view of humanity and an occasional proverb, by recalling the sentimental Victorian "spiritualization of love" and the norms of nicety that were standard in Hemingway's family in his youth (8–9).

To question the truth of the doctor's explanation of Boulton's motive on the grounds that he lies to his wife about losing his temper, and that although she may not know the truth, she somehow "knows a lie when she hears one" (Arnold, Item 36), is to resurrect those Victorian attitudes, and incidentally, to ignore the fact that the Indian had cut the doctor's driftwood without comment in the past (Fulkerson 64; see also Davis, Item 1). Stephen Fox passes over that point in his construction of the story as a "portrait of civilized half-truths" (23). They are the "rationalizations" the doctor uses in his argument with Boulton, who is portrayed as an almost noble savage, in the account he offers his wife, and in her responses. He concludes with a discussion of the story's central position in the *In Our Time* collection and its "chapters," and sees its ending as a harbinger of the resolution and renewal in a natural setting of "Big Two-Hearted River" (25).

Commentary on the story's final scene, only eight lines of dialogue and two of narrative, has sometimes been wasted on the question of whether this is Nick's or his father's story, as if it had to be one or the other. Hemingway could have ended the story with the final line "It was cool in the woods even on such a hot day." He had used a similar one for "Up in Michigan," and this one would recall the ending of "Indian Camp." But the mother's request to tell Nick that—in her curious use of the third person—"his mother wants to see him" (*Stories* 102) predicts the conclusion, as do the three references to "Nick's father" before the opening dialogue. His dialogue tags through the two scenes and into the last when he reports her request are "the doctor"; but at the end, where the dialogue incidentally needs no tags, he is referred to—again three times—as "his father," creating, as Joseph Flora notes, "a sense of benediction" (42). This suggests that from the outset Hemingway intended to portray the conflicts between "The Doctor and the Doctor's Wife" in order to present "the important choice (in a story full of choices) that Nick must make" (Flora 42).

There is an almost even division among critics over whether the final scene represents the father's "regression" from the adult world of moral decisions to the world of nature with a child "too young to see his weakness" (Arnold; Davis), or a brief and touching moment in the life of a father who "has been severely beaten, . . . needs something, [and] finds it in his son" (Flora 42). But Nick's father is not finally defeated. He leaves with his son, if only for a while; and whether to spite his wife or to save himself, he assents to Nick's choice and so confirms its significance not only for Nick but for himself.

The consequences of this momentary union of father and son are threaded through the later Nick Adams stories. Flora has called attention to the fact that in none of them do we see "Nick in the presence of his mother" (43), although she rises with a vengeance in his memory to dominate his father once again in "Now I Lay Me"; and in "The Last Good Country" she is still in bed with a sick headache. Nick's father appears in only three other stories and in each he is associated with Indians, "Indian Camp," "Ten Indians," and "Fathers and Sons." In the last story, Nicholas Adams remembers his father after his suicide: "He had died in a trap that he had helped only a little to set, and they had all betrayed him in their various ways before he died. All sentimental people are betrayed so many times" (*Stories* 489–90).

And in that story in which he both pardons his father for his suicide and assumes his share of the guilt, he wreaked a son's imaginary revenge on Dick Boulton. In his recollection of making love with Trudy Gilby (Prudence Boulton), he is driven wild by the thought of her brother Eddie's lust for his sister Dorothy; and there in the place where they hunt black squirrels, he imagines himself shooting and scalping "the half-breed" son of Dick Boulton (*Stories* 494).

Works Cited

PRIMARY

Ernest Hemingway: Selected Letters, 1917-1961. Ed. Carlos Baker. New York: Scribner's, 1981.

The Short Stories of Ernest Hemingway. New York: Scribner's, 1938, 99-103.

SECONDARY

Arnold, Aerol. "Hemingway's 'The Doctor and the Doctor's Wife.'" *Explicator* 18 (Mar. 1960), Item 36.

Baker, Carlos. *Hemingway: The Writer as Artist.* 1952. Princeton: Princeton UP, 1972.

Benson, Jackson J. *Hemingway: The Writer's Art of Self-Defense.* Minneapolis: U of Minnesota P, 1969.

Burhans, Clinton S., Jr. "The Complex Unity of *In Our Time.*" *Modern Fiction Studies* 14 (Fall 1968): 313-28.

Davis, Robert Murray. "Hemingway's 'The Doctor and the Doctor's Wife.'" *Explicator* 23 (Sept. 1966), Item 1.

DeFalco, Joseph. *The Hero in Hemingway's Short Stories.* Pittsburgh: U of Pittsburgh P, 1963.

Flora, Joseph M. *Hemingway's Nick Adams.* Baton Rouge: Louisiana State UP, 1982.

Fox, Stephen. "Hemingway's 'The Doctor and the Doctor's Wife.'" *Arizona Quarterly* 29 (Spring, 1973): 19-25.

Fulkerson, Richard. "The Biographical Fallacy and 'The Doctor and the Doctor's Wife.'" *Studies in Short Fiction* 16 (Winter 1971): 61-65.

Grebstein, Sheldon N. *Hemingway's Craft.* Carbondale: Southern Illinois UP, 1973.

Gurko, Leo. *Ernest Hemingway and the Pursuit of Heroism.* New York: Crowell, 1968.

Montgomery, Constance. *Hemingway in Michigan.* Waitsfield: Vermont Crossroads, 1977.

Reynolds, Michael. *The Young Hemingway.* Oxford: Blackwell, 1986.

Rovit, Earl. *Ernest Hemingway.* New York: Twayne, 1963.

St. John, Donald. "Hemingway and Prudence." *Connecticut Review* 5 (Apr. 1972): 78-84.

Young, Philip. *Ernest Hemingway: A Reconsideration.* 1952. New York: Harcourt, 1966.

11
Soldier's Home

Composition History (April 1924)

On 2 May 1924 Hemingway wrote two letters, one to Ezra Pound in which he told him that he "had 10 stories done," and a second to Edward O'Brien with the same tally and enclosing a draft of "Mr. and Mrs. Smith" (*Letters* 115, 117). With the three from *Three Stories* (1923), the five between "Indian Camp" and "The Doctor and the Doctor's Wife," and one that was to become "Mr. and Mrs. Elliot," "Soldier's Home" makes the tenth story. In the letter to O'Brien he asked about "this Harper's Short Story Contest," and since the typescript of "Soldier's Home" (KL/EH 710) was returned to him in a Harper and Brothers' envelope with a self-addressed attachment and was postmarked 13 October, Hemingway must have completed the story in early May and submitted it soon after that.

The two other extant manuscripts are a two-page false start and an ink and pencil manuscript, fairly heavily revised and close to the submitted typescript, of some twenty-nine half- and full-pages (KL/EH 708, 709).

One other letter suggests a relatively early date of composition and might even mark the occasion that led him to begin the story. He wrote to Pound on 17 March 1924 and mentioned that he was at work on some "damn good stories" and wished Pound were there to confirm or correct his judgment. He only had Ford Madox Ford to advise him, but Ford had "never recovered in a literary way from the mirricle [sic] . . . of his having been a soldier." Unlike de Maupassant, Balzac, Stendhal, and, by implication, Hemingway, who "just learned" from the war, Ford was always going on "under the social spell of it." The comment ends with the unlikely decision "to start denying I was in the war for fear I will get like Ford to myself about it" (*Letters* 113). It may be no more than coincidental that when Krebs later turns to reading histories of the engagements he had been in, he imagines that "now he was really *learning* about the war. He had been a good soldier" (*Stories* 148), but the line repeats the sentiment in the letter to Pound and adds a phrase that recalls Ford's *The Good Soldier*.

If anyone had been "under the social spell" of war, it was Ernest Hemingway in January 1919, and this letter to Pound in Rapallo may have recalled his own war experiences and the heroic tales he told at home. The letter ends with a remark on Mussolini's recent honoring of Gabriele D'Annunzio as Prince of Monte Nevoso and a note that after "renouncing all of Italy and its works I've gotten all nostalgique about it" (*Letters* 114). Thus the confessional note in "Soldier's Home" could have been elicited by the news of D'Annunzio reminding him of how he had drawn on some of the exploits of that flamboyant Italian in his own inventions for the home folks in 1919.

Publication History (June, October 1925)

Hemingway's first try at publication for "Soldier's Home" in the late spring of 1924 was unsuccessful. Harper and Brothers returned it on 13 October—and, incidentally, followed it a week later with the second story he submitted, "Cross-Country Snow." Both stories were apparently submitted with self-addressed return envelopes; the Harper and Brothers' envelopes in which they were finally returned were addressed with a section cut from the original envelopes, still bearing part of a postal mark "RETURNED . . ."— presumably for insufficient return postage (KL/EH 710, 346).

This minor but familiar postal problem may account for the fact that when Hemingway wrote to Robert McAlmon on 20 November in response to an invitation to submit for the *Contact Collection of Contemporary Writers*, he told him that he had "only two new stories *on hand*" and both were too long (*Letters* 135, italics added; Carlos Baker is probably correct in identifying them as "A Lack of Passion" and "The Undefeated," 135 n.) But by 10 December Hemingway did have a story in hand and told McAlmon that it "is the best short story I ever wrote so am sending it. It's short enough anyway" (*Letters* 139). So it was published in June 1925 in the *Contact Collection of Contemporary Writers*. Whatever rejection he felt from Harper's must have been solaced by his publication in a collection with Djuna Barnes, Norman Douglas, Havelock Ellis, F. M. Ford, and H.D.; and if not with them, then with Joyce, Pound, and Stein, who were also in the volume. And four months later the story was included in the Boni and Liveright edition of *In Our Time*.

Sources and Influences

The most compelling biographical source for "Soldier's Home" is Hemingway's own experience when he returned from Italy in early 1919 with the trappings of a hero, a few real but most of them secondhand souvenirs. The two biographers who have concentrated on this period, Peter Griffin and Michael Reynolds, have in different ways demonstrated the discrepancies between Hemingway's experience in the war and the various stories he told to civic clubs, high school audiences, and his own friends. Like returning veterans from any war, particularly those who have not been engaged in combat or only accidentaly so, he made up for it, as does Krebs, with "quite unimportant lies [that] consisted in attributing to himself things other men had seen, done or heard of, and stating as facts certain apocryphal incidents familiar to all soldiers" (*Stories* 146). And like Krebs, Hemingway had a younger tomboy sister (Madelaine or "Sunny"), a Civil War veteran for a grandfather, and a sometimes sanctimonious mother who insisted he make something of himself.

Finally, there is the name Harold Krebs, compounded perhaps, as Carlos Baker suggested, from the first names of Harold Stearns and Krebs Friend (585). That Krebs Friend worked along with Hemingway on the *Cooperative Commonwealth* in 1920-21 and rescued the *Transatlantic Review* in the spring of 1924 with his wife's money, is probably much less important than that he was a victim of severe shell shock. Hemingway's Harold Krebs shows no physical wounds—which, for a marine who saw action from Belleau Wood to the Argonne in the summer of 1918, was very good luck—but with other men who were true veterans he "fell into the easy pose of the old soldier among other soldiers: that he had been badly, sickeningly frightened all the time" (*Stories* 146). The legitimacy of that pose can be left for later; for the moment, however, it does seem to allude to a symptom of shell shock. Hemingway's daily acquaintance with this veteran whose wounds would not heal at the time he was writing swashbuckling stories like "The Woppian Way," might well have been recalled—and, in a way, been acknowledged—when Krebs Friend agreed to finance the journal for which Hemingway was serving as a subeditor.

Following that suggestion, Peter Hays has argued that the story's most striking image, "Krebs looked at the bacon fat hardening on his plate" (*Stories* 151), echoes another from Ford Madox Ford's *Some Do Not . . .* in which Tietjens mocks the sentimental sham of the Pre-Raphaelites—particularly Rossetti—"gazing into a mirror that reflects their fetid selves . . . and plates sickening with cold bacon fat and gurgling about passion" (Ford 17). Hays cites two similarly unappetizing images—from Joyce's "A Painful Case" (1914) and his *Portrait of the Artist as a Young Man* (1916)—and all three, he argues, coagulate about issues of hypocritical sexual morality (21-22). Although the similarities among the issues in "Soldier's Home" and the three earlier works is tenuous, the image of hardening grease seems to have taken on in those years an almost iconic association with a stultifying, normal, and homey morality. As Hays notes, the best evidence for the influence from Ford's novel is that it had begun serialization in the *Transatlantic Review* in January and was published in April of 1924.

No one writing in 1924 about the disillusionment of a returned veteran would have lacked for other literary precedents—there were the War Poets, Pound with the "Mauberley" poems, and D. H. Lawrence with "England,

My England." Postwar disillusionment had been in the air long enough to become so stale it could sour the attitudes of veterans like Krebs not only toward the mercantile and religious values of the homefolks but toward their own sense of what the war and true heroism had been like.

The prose style of the story, however, seems to regress to the styles of Gertrude Stein and Sherwood Anderson—almost as if he had not yet written "Indian Camp." Twice in the story he repeats a sequence of sentences with variations on the verb *to like* similar to the third paragraph of "Up in Michigan" and reminiscent of Stein. Other syntactical patterns in the story are close to those he used to parody Anderson a year later in *The Torrents of Spring*. Finally, the complexity of Harold Krebs's memories and emotions, the convoluted and sometimes erratic attitudes he takes toward his sister, his mother, and the girls of the town—somehow even his name—suggest that he could be just as unhappily at home in *Winesburg, Ohio*.

Critical Studies

The earliest of the critical studies of "Soldier's Home" is one of the most extensive. Joseph DeFalco places the story after his analyses of the war stories "Now I Lay Me," "A Way You'll Never Be," and "In Another Country" to dramatize the conflicts of the veteran for whom the experience of war prohibits his ever returning to the familial, social, and religious "home" he left. The title is clearly ironic both in that Krebs no longer has a real home and in that it cannot serve, as Soldiers' Homes are meant to, as "a place of comfort and security where a battle veteran may live out his life under the care of some benevolent agency" (137). DeFalco describes the three-part structure of the story—authorial portrait, the dialogue with his sister and mother, and the concluding decision to leave for Kansas City— and finds its conflict and resolution foreshadowed in the two photographs described in the first two paragraphs (138–39). The first suggests "the strict and stolid environment surrounding" fraternity brothers with their uniform collars; the second a more informal view of an awkward world in which uniforms never fit, the girls are not beautiful, and the Rhine does not appear in the picture—a picture that corrects any "romantic notion of soldiers-of fortune . . . in an idyllic European setting" (139–40).

The conflict implied in the two photographs becomes for DeFalco a preview of Krebs's having to live through, once again, the experience of individuation between a domineering—his term, of course, is "devouring"— mother and an absent and emasculated father. Krebs's insistence on the harsh truth, as he sees it, in his dialogue with his mother is a necessary act of rebellion preliminary to a more decisive departure than that at his enlistment. Thus the story is a variation on the usual pattern in its depiction of "a character who has already gone through . . . the formidable task of maturation . . . in war" (143).

Arthur Waldhorn sees Krebs quite differently as Nick Adams's double, "an extreme version of the apprentice who . . . yields to *nada* to assure that his life will run smoothly, and accepts oblivion without dignity." His lying to "meet the expectations of society" leaves him "blank and barren, desiring neither factitious nor authentic experience" (67). This reading of Krebs bears some weight, for Hemingway is explicit in his description of the motives and consequences of those lies but curiously reticent on the details of Krebs's war experience.

The omniscient narrator does tell us that Krebs enlisted in the Marine Corps in 1917 and returned with the Second Division in the summer of 1919. (In the manuscript Hemingway dated his return 1920 and probably had that date in mind when he wrote that Krebs returned "years after the war was over" [KL/EH 709; *Stories* 145]. See the discussion of this discrepancy in Boyd, Jones, and Monteiro.) He had been with the marines attached to the army's Second Division from Belleau Wood in June to the Battle of the Argonne in September 1918 and, as the second photo shows, with them on the Rhine after the Armistice. He suffered no obvious wounds, apparently acted bravely at those times "when he had done the one thing, the only thing for a man to do, easily and naturally, when he might have done something else"—an odd locution suggesting that even in Krebs's silent reveries he will not use words like *bravery* or *cowardice*.

Although the two photographs seem at first to contrast a conventional home life, starched with hypocrisy like the college boys' collars, and the rumpled but authentic experience of the war; Krebs's inner conflict emerges when in order "to be listened to at all he had to lie." With that the "actualities" of his war experience become as distasteful as his exaggerations of them; and so his moral disgust, his nausea broadens to *all* "experience" until he adopts "the easy pose of an old soldier among other soldiers: that he had been badly, sickeningly frightened all the time. In this way he lost everything" (*Stories* 145–46).

And the narrative insists that "he lost everything." Having betrayed whatever actualities may have been represented by his war experience, his attention is caught only long enough to notice the "patterns" of the girls in their "sweaters and shirt waists with round Dutch collars," recalling the conventionality of the first photograph of the fraternity brothers. But there his interest in the girls ends; "he would not go through all the talking." So, too, he turns to histories of the engagements he was in and wishes "there were more maps . . . [,] good detail maps"—which, one might argue, are to his actual deeds in the war as the patterns he sees in the girls' dresses are to the girls themselves. When, in his reading, he senses that "he was really learning about the war . . . [and] had been a good soldier" (*Stories*

147–48), legitimate questions might be asked about what he *had* learned on the battlefields of 1918 and whether the lies he told were not so much exaggerations of actualities but substitutes for nothing. This complex and ambivalent part of the story resonates, of course, all through the later war fiction and especially *A Farewell to Arms,* as it so obviously casts a light on Hemingway's grandiloquent behavior in the early months of 1919.

For the interpretation of the story, however, this reading supports Arthur Waldhorn's characterization of Krebs as a latter-day Bartleby the Scrivener—not a farfetched analogy, by the way—who denies complications and consequences, which is to say, life. John Roberts's response to Waldhorn not so much denies his position as it argues that Krebs's decision finally saves him from this morally catatonic condition. Roberts's conclusion—that since Krebs was once a fraternity brother, went to a Methodist college, enlisted in the marines, and still thinks about girls, there is the possibility for change—may be a doubtful induction; but he seems to agree with Waldhorn when he writes that what disorients Krebs "is not the truth of war but the lies of the Midwestern view of war, not the truth of death but the lie of life" (517). That appealing parallelism does not quite fit Krebs's behavior: he accepts the midwestern—which we might more charitably read as an almost universal—view of war, and he denies the "truth of death," whatever that is, until he is authorized by a history book. For Roberts, Krebs's agony arises when he cannot reconcile truth and falsehood; but it is more likely that it arises when he can and does.

This leaves the question of the ending: Roberts, and before him DeFalco, argue that the ending of this story, like that of "Big Two-Hearted River" in which the protagonist finds solace "in the ritual of sports," predicts the beginning of another stage in the "continuation of his psychic and spiritual journey" (DeFalco 144; Roberts 517–18). That is reasonable but not inconsistent with Waldhorn's interpretation—but for the question raised by the story's last line, "He would go over to the schoolyard and watch Helen play indoor baseball" (*Stories* 153).

In a study that contemplates the meaning of that apparently innocent last line and the larger significance of sport in Hemingway, Robert Lewis wrote the most detailed analysis of "Soldier's Home" and its place in the Hemingway canon. That article offers a model for scholarship on the stories, and its depth and range cannot be adequately acknowledged here.

His analysis of Krebs's passion for patterns, like those suggested in the fraternity brothers' and the town girls' collars, is directed toward the central question of the story, a question he phrases with Amy Lowell's line "Christ! What are patterns for?" With that question Lewis rescues the story from the slough of autobiography and offers an interpretation of the story's last sentence. His argument is that Krebs, whether he knows it or not, finds that his sister's tomboy accomplishments in "indoor baseball" offer him a momentary respite with the pattern that sports provide "of an uncomplicated world without hypocrisy." Thus Krebs's final decision marks his reaching out, as other Hemingway characters do, to a "game" that demands rules, but only those rules that are "purely arbitrary and gratuitous and without pretense to meaning or significance outside themselves" (24–25).

This interpretation confirms Waldhorn's skepticism by noting that in Hemingway "even sport, the last refuge of the fanatic, can be corrupted and destroyed just as faith, love, and even language had been" (27).

With this reading of the story, the last line questions whether Krebs will ever leave the "soldier's home" where he finds the desperate solace of a world ordered but with no more meaning than a game. If he does not, he might as well stay in Oklahoma as leave for Kansas City.

Works Cited

PRIMARY

Ernest Hemingway: Selected Letters, 1917–1961. Ed. Carlos Baker. New York: Scribner's, 1981.

The Short Stories of Ernest Hemingway. New York: Scribner's, 1938, 145–53.

SECONDARY

Baker, Carlos. *Ernest Hemingway: A Life Story.* 1969. New York: Scribner's, 1988.

Boyd, John D. "Hemingway's 'Soldier's Home.'" *Explicator* 40 (Fall 1981): 51–53.

DeFalco, Joseph. *The Hero in Hemingway's Short Stories.* Pittsburgh: U of Pittsburgh P, 1963.

Ford, Ford Madox. *Parade's End.* New York: Knopf, 1961.

Griffin, Peter. *Along with Youth: Hemingway, The Early Years.* New York: Oxford UP, 1985.

Hays, Peter L. "'Soldier's Home' and Ford Madox Ford." *Hemingway Notes* 1 (Fall 1971): 21–22.

Jones, Horace P. "Hemingway's 'Soldier's Home.'" *Explicator* 37 (Fall 1978): 27.

Lewis, Robert W., Jr. "Hemingway's Concept of Sport and 'Soldier's Home.'" *Rendezvous* 5 (Winter 1970): 19–27.

Monteiro, George. "Hemingway's 'Soldier's Home.'" *Explicator* 40 (Fall 1981): 50–51.

Reynolds, Michael S. *The Young Hemingway.* New York: Blackwell, 1986.

Roberts, John J. "In Defense of Krebs." *Studies in Short Fiction* 13 (Fall 1976): 515–18.

Waldhorn, Arthur. *A Reader's Guide to Ernest Hemingway.* New York: Farrar, 1972.

12

Mr. and Mrs. Elliot

Composition History (April 1924)

"Mr. and Mrs. Elliot" has been both more and less neglected than it deserves to be. One might wish that those biographers who found in it yet another instance of Hemingway's bad taste, callous contempt, and occasional stylistic infelicity had neglected the story altogether; while one might also wish for a larger company of critics who thought of it as, possibly, a short story. Never one to attract much critical notice, once the object of the story's satire was revealed, there was little more to say except to regret its triviality.

Now, of course, readers of Carlos Baker's biography know that it was originally titled "Mr. and Mrs. Smith," that Hemingway had Chard Powers Smith in his sights, and that the two exchanged angry and characteristic letters in 1927, two years after the story's publication—Smith called Hemingway "a worm who attempted a cad's trick, . . . a contemptible shadow," and Hemingway threatened to knock him down (KL/EH, Smith to Hemingway, 2 January; *Letters* 242).

Most biographers have followed Carlos Baker in dismissing the satire as a "malicious gossip-story" ridiculing the Smiths' "alleged sexual ineptitudes" (133). We are not told who, other than Hemingway, made that allegation, or with what evidence. But for Hemingway, Chard Powers Smith was an easy mark and natural enemy: he was independently wealthy, had degrees from *both* Harvard and Yale, lingered in Latin Quarter cafés, rented châteaux along the Loire, and wrote poetry in perfect classical meters with perfect Petrarchan emotions—Yale published his first volume in 1925.

Although by the spring of 1924, Hemingway was writing at an astounding pace, nearly half his titles had been published and *re*-published—six poems, six *in our time* chapters, and "My Old Man"—so he turned again to Edward O'Brien. He wrote that he had "quit newspaper work," was "about broke," and needed an agent to "peddle" the ten stories he had written. He enclosed three, one of which he was sure would not sell but which O'Brien could keep "as a souvenir"—it was titled "Mr. and Mrs. Smith" (*Letters* 117, 2 May 1924).

Hemingway sent the story partly as an appreciative memento to the publisher who first accepted one of his stories ("My Old Man") and partly to pass on literary gossip. But not for him to publish, for soon after Hemingway sent a typescript to Jane Heap for publication in the *Little Review*'s Winter issue (1924–25) with the name Smith crossed out and Elliot inserted (Jane Heap Collection, University of Wisconsin Library at Milwaukee).

Hemingway's motive for changing the names from Smith to Elliot might have arisen from his often inordinate fear of a libel suit. Or perhaps sometime in the late spring of 1924, his original satiric intent was deflected by the news that Mr. and Mrs. Smith's "alleged sexual ineptitudes" had been resolved, tragically—Mrs. Smith had died in Naples on 11 March 1924 in childbirth, a month before Hemingway wrote his story and sent it as a souvenir. Perhaps, finally, with its submission to the very literary *Little Review*, Hemingway decided to direct his satire toward another poet, one with more fame than Chard Powers Smith, for T. S. Eliot had been published in that journal since 1917 and by Hemingway's lights was even more deserving of contempt.

Of the five extant manuscript items, only two are complete. There is a holograph fragment of the story's first three sentences using the names Mr. and Mrs. Smith (KL/EH 586). The first complete version is a holograph manuscript entitled "Mr. and Mrs. Smith" (KL/EH 585). Another fragment, two pages of typescript (KL/EH 587) is related to the second complete version, the typescript submitted to Jane Heap (University of Wisconsin-Milwaukee). (The last fragment appears on the verso of page 189 of the University of Texas manuscript of *Death in the Afternoon*, and is of more relevance to the composition of that book than the story [Lewis 36–37]).

Publication History (October 1924; October 1925; October 1930)

"Mr. and Mrs. Elliot" was first published in October 1924 in the *Little Review*'s Autumn–Winter 1924–25 issue. When Boni and Liveright received the manuscripts submitted for *In Our Time*, this story's fate became part of that for "Up in Michigan." They rejected that story out of hand, and Hemingway wrote "The Battler" as a substitute. Their contractual agreement also objected to obscenities and insisted on excisions. Hemingway deferred to Liveright's "on the spot"—that is to say, American—notion of what is "unpublishably obscene," one suspects, in order to save "Mr. and Mrs. Elliot" from the rejection suffered by "Up in Michigan" (*Letters* 154–55, 31 March 1925).

Allen Shepherd noted some of the changes in the Liveright edition of what in 1925 might have been construed as obscenities: instead of the Elliots *trying* to have a baby they are allowed to *think* about it. For example, compare the sentences following the first in the original:

> They tried as often as Mrs. Elliot could stand it. They tried in Boston after they were married and they tried coming over on the boat. They did not try very often on the boat because Mrs. Elliot was very sick. (*Stories* 161)

with those in the Liveright text:

> They were married in Boston and sailed for Europe on a boat. It was a very expensive boat and was supposed to get to Europe in six days. But on the boat Mrs. Elliot was quite sick. (*In Our Time* 109)

Moreover, Hemingway added two paragraphs, one describing the transatlantic passage and another—the more important—describing the Elliots' response to Paris:

> Paris was quite disappointing and very rainy. It became increasingly important to them that they should have a baby, and even though someone had pointed out Ezra Pound to them in a café and they had watched James Joyce eating in the Trianon and almost been introduced to a man named Leo Stein, it was to be explained to them who he was later. (*In Our Time* 112)

These added passages and the accepted excisions suggest that, as with of "Up in Michigan," Hemingway was willing to submit to his publisher's sense of the proper at almost any cost. He did so here only after dropping some famous names he could claim as acquaintances, which would put these literary poseurs, as Shepherd says, "beyond the pale" (16).

However much he bowed to his publisher's sense of propriety in 1925, Hemingway must have felt some belated pleasure five years later when, with *The Sun Also Rises* and *A Farewell to Arms* behind him, he could demand of Maxwell Perkins that the 1930 edition of Scribner's *In Our Time* would include "the original Mr. and Mrs. Elliot" (*Letters* 327, 12 August 1930). And the version we have now is restored to its original published form.

Sources and Influences

Hubert and Cornelia Elliot of Hemingway's story are so like the deracinated figures of Eliot's "The Waste Land" that they would have been unnoticed along the shores of the Starnbergersee or chatting in the Hofgarten with those who "read, much of the night, and go south in the winter" (29). And, like the neurotic and sickly women and their indifferent companions in the poem, the Elliots' union is as barren and rootless as the landscape through which they aimlessly drift. So if one adds the characters of Eliot's poem to those of the Chard Powers Smiths, the gossip in Hemingway's story may be redeemed by the story's evident literary origins: it is to Eliot's "The Burial of the Dead" what "Cat in the Rain" is to his "A Game of Chess."

But nothing in the lives of the Smiths or Eliot's characters accounts for all of the story's details, so one might add Mr. and Mrs. Hemingway to this composite portrait. Like Hubert and Cornelia Elliot, the Hemingways sailed to Europe soon after their marriage; for all Hemingway's claims of poverty, he was living on Hadley's not insubstantial trust fund; Ernest, like Hubert, was twenty-five in 1924, and, although no virgin, had married an older woman. The passage on the Elliots' arrival in Paris added to the 1925 version of the story—"Paris was quite disappointing and very rainy. . . . [E]ven though someone had pointed out Ezra Pound to them in a café and they had watched James Joyce eating in the Trianon and almost been introduced to Leo Stein . . . , they decided to go to Dijon" (112)—recalls that the Hemingways arrived in a rain-swept Paris, did not deliver their letters of introduction, and left almost immediately. And this passage on the Parisian cafés—"So they all sat around the Café du Dome, avoiding the Rotonde across the street because it is always so full of foreigners, . . . and then the Elliots rented a chateau in Touraine" (*Stories* 163)—echoes one of Hemingway's earliest *Toronto Star* articles of 1922 that condemns the Rotonde as a "showplace for tourists in search of atmosphere" (*Dateline* 114). While the Elliots fled to a château on the Loire, the Hemingways left for a chalet in Chamby.

Critical Studies

The critics who do not mention this story are almost as rare as those who do more than that. There are only two of the latter, Allen Shepherd (noted above) and Joseph DeFalco. Two others spend little more than a page to draw on the story for evidence supporting another point. Richard Peterson used the characterization of Hubie Elliot to mark the general point of Hemingway's portrait of Robert Cohn in *The Sun Also Rises*. Like Cohn, Elliot is a "tourist-writer," unforgivably rich, and insensitive to landscape (Touraine is too much like Kansas). He agreed that the story may be humorous if one takes the position of the narrator, but found that it is "too much tinged with the superiority of the [Hemingway] hero looking out or down on those unfortunates 'not in the know' " (174–75). Sheldon Grebstein argued that the passage on chronically sick southern women is a "particularly blatant authorial intrusion" that prefigures "the bad Hemingway of the 1930s"; but he noted in passing that the only other instance occurs in the opening of "Soldier's Home"—which here may support the contemporaneous dating of the two stories' composition (81–82).

Joseph DeFalco's analysis is alone in saying nothing about the story's biographical origins, although they clearly served to support his sense that the stories often center on classic psychological or archetypal conflicts, and by implication, Hemingway's. He noted that the story is unusual in that its narrative mode differs from the "conventional mode of structuring" in the other stories (155). A good point—Hemingway here chose a strategy that depends little upon the conjunction of scenes and much upon a narrative voice that parodies the language of his subjects in seeming to recount an unhappy story simply from then to now.

The issue about which the rest of the story gathers is, for DeFalco, the metaphorical suggestion of the story's first line, "Mr. and Mrs. Elliot tried very hard to have a baby." Mrs. Elliot's sickness is more than physical. Mr. Elliot's marriage to a woman fifteen years older, his "outsized mother complex," and his fixation on sexual purity, all eventuate in an ironic resolution. His "poetry has become his substitute mate"; Mrs. Elliot's "girl friend has become a surrogate husband"; for now she has fulfilled her maternal role and he has realized his maternal fixation: the Elliots have had their baby, and it is Mr. Elliot (157–58).

One may question DeFalco's emphasis on a maternal fixation or his rather dated notions of the "abnormal," but his analysis stands alone as a reading of the story as a work of fiction. So it is a bit of a shame that later critics and biographers have too quickly assumed that Hemingway was attacking Chard Powers Smith when, at the same moment, he might have been inadvertently dramatizing emerging issues in his own life: if not his ambiguous feelings toward his mother, then at least his identification of the physical and literary creative acts.

With a longer view of Hemingway's career and the literary history of his times, "Mr. and Mrs. Elliot" deserves another reading. It is one of his best and most sophisticated satires, in that it transcends its seminal gossip to reveal the pretensions of the elite expatriates of Hemingway's generation, those who knew enough to frequent the Café du Dome rather than the Rotonde, but not much more.

Works Cited

PRIMARY

Dateline: Toronto. Ed. William White. New York: Scribner's, 1985.

Ernest Hemingway: Selected Letters, 1917–1961. Ed. Carlos Baker. New York: Scribner's, 1981.

In Our Time. New York: Boni and Liveright, 1925.

The Short Stories of Ernest Hemingway. New York: Scribner's, 1938, 161–64.

SECONDARY

Baker, Carlos. *Ernest Hemingway: A Life Story.* 1969. New York: Scribner's, 1988.

DeFalco, Joseph. *The Hero in Hemingway's Short Stories.* Pittsburgh: U of Pittsburgh P, 1963.

Eliot, T. S. *The Waste Land and Other Poems.* New York: Harcourt, 1934.

Grebstein, Sheldon N. *Hemingway's Craft.* Carbondale: Southern Illinois UP, 1973.

Lewis, Robert W. Jr. "The Making of *Death in the Afternoon.*" *Ernest Hemingway: The Writer in Context.* Ed. James Nagel. Madison: U of Wisconsin P, 1984.

Peterson, Richard K. *Hemingway: Direct and Oblique.* The Hague: Mouton, 1969.

Shepherd, Allen. "Taking Apart 'Mr. and Mrs. Elliot.' " *Markham Review* 2 (Sept. 1969): 15–16.

13

Cross-Country Snow

Composition History (April 1924)

The evidence for the composition of "Cross-Country Snow" in April 1924 is more circumstantial than one would wish. The first reference to the story occurs in a letter to Edward O'Brien of 12 September 1924 in which Hemingway explained the structure of his projected collection: the stories would return to the Michigan setting with "Big Two-Hearted River" after "a ski-ing story and My Old Man" (*Letters* 123). In May he had told O'Brien that he had ten stories completed, and with the tally of fourteen in this September letter, "Cross-Country Snow" must have been among them. Moreover, the signed and addressed typescript of the story (KL/EH 346) was, like that of "The Doctor and the Doctor's Wife," apparently submitted to a Harper and Brothers' fiction contest and returned, like that other submission after being held up in the mail, on 20 October 1924.

The earliest manuscript item appears to be a twelve-page typescript with a holograph conclusion, a word count, and an insert on the verso of page 2, "It's a shame Hellen couldn't come" (KL/EH 344). That insert indicates Hemingway's tentative decision to introduce Nick's approaching fatherhood before the pregnant waitress appears.

The second and third items are a three-page pencil fragment numbered 6–8 intended as an insert for Item 344 (KL/EH 345) and a three-page ink fragment marked on the verso of page 3 "Continuation Skiing Story" (KL/EH 696). In each of these tentative inserts in the dialogue (*Stories* 187) Hemingway introduces the subject of George's father. With a second bottle of wine, George turns silent and his "face had that dreaming look that in his father had become vacuity" (KL/EH 345). In the second, to Nick's question about what is troubling him, George replies, "I wish my father wasn't such a damn fool," and Nick comforts him with the observation that "Everybody's father is a damn fool" (KL/EH 696). That last may reflect something of the mood in which Hemingway wrote "The Doctor and the Doctor's Wife"; but his long-standing private contempt for David O'Neil was mirrored as well in "Mr. and Mrs. Elliot," for O'Neil was also an independently rich and vacuous poet touring Europe (see *Letters* 72–74, 77–78, 114–16). These rejected inserts were probably composed sometime in the spring of 1924 when Hemingway, in one of his darker moods, contemplated fatherhood, the literary scene, and the lives of the rich.

The final typescript (KL/EH 346) and the typescript made up but not used for the 1925 edition should settle some contradictions in the characters' names. Hemingway changed the name Adams to Nick through the first page of the text, but missed the first reference to Mike (*Stories* 183); changed Mike to Nick throughout except for a second instance (186) and a third where someone caught it for him (188). Such instances of editorial carelessness should temper such comments as Joseph Flora's on the significance of Mike as a nickname (!) for Nick (191) or as a "code name" like Gidge for George (196).

Publication History (January 1925; October 1925)

The only point to make of the publication of "Cross-Country Snow" is that either it was submitted to two publishers simultaneously (Harper and Brothers for their contest and the *Transatlantic Review*), or that Hemingway was by this time so well thought of by Ford Madox Ford that when the story was returned to Hemingway in November 1924, he could submit it to Ford's journal and be assured of publication three months later.

Whatever the case, the story was published in the January 1925 issue of the *Transatlantic Review,* and in October the story entered the canon with the publication of *In Our Time.*

Sources and Influences

"Cross-Country Snow" reflects a time in Hemingway's life, as the biographies tell us, when on vacation at Chamby-sur-Montreux he and Hadley spent some days with the David O'Neils and their teenage son George, nicknamed Gidge, at the end of the skiing season in the winter of 1922–23. By then, according to Carlos Baker, Hadley had told Ernest she was pregnant, and they had decided to return to Toronto for the birth (104). With that much evidence the story has been associated with the other marriage tales— "Out of Season," "Cat in the Rain," and "A Canary for One"—to provide another chapter in that sequence of stories chronicling the dissolution of Hemingway's first marriage.

Of the few critics who do more than note the story, none has found in it any interesting evidence of literary influence. Arthur Waldhorn, in his discussion of Hemingway's style, cites one of the four early paragraphs describing Nick's and George's downhill runs to exemplify how the dramatic rhythm of the descent is caught in the syntax of linked participial phrases and an occasional image (35–36). Such sentences look back to the "Paris

1922" sentences (Baker 90–91) and some of the *In Our Time* chapters, as they look ahead to others in later stories and novels. But neither Hemingway nor any other writer could claim exclusive rights to this mimetic device.

Waldhorn observed a similarity between these passages and the characters' dialogue in which "their unemphatic language communicates feeling without having to define it" (36); yet some of the differences between the two styles are more interesting. The skiing passages are more than occasionally metaphoric: "The funicular car bucked . . . , the gale scouring . . . had swept . . . a wind-board crust . . . , the snow driving like a sand-storm . . . , he went over . . . feeling like a shot rabbit" (*Stories* 183). Once inside, the two boys' brief and colloquial language does express their feelings for the last run, but awkwardly, because as George says, "It's too swell to talk about" (*Stories* 185).

The story's structure—a significant scene or event, a dialogue between two friends drinking, an implicit subject rather abruptly introduced and then not quite dismissed with a variety of vinous wit—is one Hemingway had recently followed in greater detail in "The Three-Day Blow" and used again in the Burguete fishing scene in *The Sun Also Rises*.

Critical Studies

Placing the story in the sequence of marriage tales has led its few commentators to consider it the first of those episodes in which marriage and parenthood are set in contrast with "the period of youth and irresponsibility," here represented by skiing in Europe (DeFalco 173; Flora 195). Hemingway's model in "The Three-Day Blow" may account for that perception: here Nick and George are "the boys"; both use boyish language, *Gee, swell, wait a sec,* and so on; and Nick's role as tutor to George's tyro is uncertain. As Flora notes, Nick is more sophisticated with wine than he is in "The Three-Day Blow" and can hold it better than George (192); but Flora misses the fact that Nick is no better or worse a skier than his friend: both skiers have fallen once; and when Nick makes a Christy turn (with both legs together) at George's suggestion, both boys know that he does so to protect a bad leg, and both know that there is a risk, for a telemark is a safer turn in soft and drifted snow.

Nick is clearly more familiar with Switzerland—he knows the local wine, speaks German to the waitress, and has fished the Austrian Schwarzwald. For all that, his notion that Swiss women—whether from the cantons in the north, where German is spoken and Catholicism practiced, or from the south, a day's ride from Calvin's Geneva, never get married "until they're knocked up" (*Stories* 186) is clearly his own invention, and hardly evidence that the Swiss "culture puts a major value on fertility, having children" (Flora 194).

As a cultural generalization it is equivalent to the notion that all Swiss "have goiter" (*Stories* 188), a remark the boys both recognize as ludicrous.

However adolescently pretentious his statement, the question Nick asks himself when he notices the waitress's pregnant condition remains, "I wonder why I didn't see that when she first came in" (185). The answer to that question is implied when George, now thoughtful with the wine, abruptly asks, "Is Helen going to have a baby?" Nick tells him that she will "later *next* summer," not later *this* summer, which would date the story in December. Nick, however, seems reconciled to the fact: he is glad, now, and although both he and Helen would rather not return to the States, it is "not exactly" hell (187).

Here the story demands a critical decision. Read with the other marriage tales and the biography, we assume that Nick and Helen are married. But nothing in the story itself asserts that; in fact, Nick's failure to notice the waitress who is both unmarried and pregnant, may argue that Nick, too, is unmarried, and that the story is more an epilogue to "Hills Like White Elephants" than a prologue to the marriage tales.

Whether one feels an editor's discomfiture over Hemingway's carelessness with the names in the first and all subsequent editions or a critic's sense that he had not quite come to terms with the relationship between the characters of Nick and George, it is difficult to argue against those critics who find the story trivial, for it does seem manifestly offhand. At times it reads like an unfinished exercise—the mimetic sentences on the downhill run, the dialogue that equates "the boys" when Hemingway was clearly about to differentiate between their different experiences, and the introduction of the Swiss woodcutters with an unrealized literary purpose—all these features suggest a hastily written story, sent off to a fiction contest and belatedly returned, quickly submitted to the *Transatlantic Review* where it could not be turned down, and then ignored in later publications by Hemingway, his editors, and—with some reason—his critics.

Works Cited

PRIMARY

Ernest Hemingway: Selected Letters, 1917–1961. Ed. Carlos Baker. New York: Scribner's, 1981.

The Short Stories of Ernest Hemingway. New York: Scribner's, 1938, 183–88.

SECONDARY

Baker, Carlos. *Ernest Hemingway: A Life Story.* 1969. New York: Scribner's, 1988.

DeFalco, Joseph. *The Hero in Hemingway's Fiction.* Pittsburgh: U of Pittsburgh P, 1963.

Flora, Joseph M. *Hemingway's Nick Adams.* Baton Rouge: Louisiana State UP, 1982.

Waldhorn, Arthur. *A Reader's Guide to Ernest Hemingway.* New York: Farrar, 1972.

14

Big Two-Hearted River

Composition History (May–November 1924)

The history of the writing of "Big Two-Hearted River" and its circulation among prospective publishers seems a biography in little of Hemingway's experience of the year between the late spring of 1924 and May 1925. After an early false start, the writing was interrupted by editorial work for Ford's *Transatlantic Review* and then by the obligatory trip to Pamplona, from which he drew a good deal of material for its original but inappropriate ending. Then submitted with the rest of the prospective *In Our Time* stories, its ending was revised after a sharp remark from Gertrude Stein and a very fortunate moment of self-criticism. Like the other stories of 1924, it waited for book publication for several months and at the last moment was submitted to a journal. But all through that year of writing and revision, Hemingway knew that the last story in his proposed collection would have to be, like James Joyce's "The Dead," a long story that would constitute his claim to originality—and, at last, it did.

There are eight manuscript items in the Hemingway Collection of the Kennedy Library (KL/EH 274–81), of which six are of interest here for dating the story's composition.

The first is a three-page ink manuscript fragment (KL/EH 279) which is clearly a false start: begun in the first-person, with two companions—Al (Walker) and Jock (John Pentecost), Hemingway's high school friends on a 1919 fishing trip in the Upper Peninsula—then shifted to an omniscient point of view, it described the burned out remains of the town (Oldsey 218–19). This fragment could well have been left over from the winter of 1923 when Hemingway had begun several stories but left them unfinished (*Letters* 144).

The biography and correspondence suggest that he began the story sometime in mid-May 1924 (on 2 May he had only ten stories written [*Letters* 115]). Ford Madox Ford left for the United States in late May, leaving Hemingway with the editing of the July issue and the gathering of materials for the August issue of the *Transatlantic Review*. Hemingway managed to get that done by late June, but that work held up his writing of "Big Two-Hearted River" to some point between the beginning of Part II and the passage at which the original ending begins (*Stories* 221–28; see

"On Writing," *Nick Adams Stories* 233–41). Although there is no immediately apparent break in the first complete manuscript (KL/EH 274), the references in the original ending date that part of it in late July or early August, after his "Sun Also Rises" sojourn in Pamplona and Burguete from late June to the end of July.

So the latter third of the original story was written between the end of June and the middle of August and then typed (KL/EH 274; and 275, a Hemingway typescript). At that time he admitted to Gertrude Stein that the story was "swell about the fish, but isn't writing a hard job though?" (*Letters* 122, 15 August 1924). Indeed it was, and she told him so; as she reported later in her *Autobiography of Alice B. Toklas,* she noted that he "had added to his stories a little story of meditations and in these he said that The Enormous Room was the greatest book he had ever read. It was then that Gertrude Stein had said, Hemingway, remarks are not literature" (219). She was right and Hemingway knew it (although he objected in the manuscript of *The Sun Also Rises* [Svoboda 38]).

By then he had sent one copy off to Donald Ogden Stewart with typescripts of the other *In Our Time* stories to offer to New York publishers, first to George Doran (KL/EH 96). But he knew that "all that mental conversation in the long fishing story is the shit and have cut it all out. The last nine pages. The story was interrupted you know just when I was going good and I could never get back into it and finish it. I got a hell of a shock when I realized how bad it was and that shocked me back to the river again and I've finished it off the way it ought to have been all along. Just the straight fishing" (*Letters* 133, 15 November 1924).

That shock of recognition that returned him to the river, however late in the composition of the story, may have been recorded in the original manuscript (274) when he saw "how Cezanne would do the stretch of river and the swamp . . . and [h]e waded across the stream, moving in the picture." Twice in that manuscript Nick is described as "holding something in his head" (*Nick Adams Stories* 240–41), and it is probable that what he had in his head was what Hemingway knew then was the right ending for his story, "the straight fishing" up to the swamp and what it might be like in there.

So sometime in late November, when Hemingway realized that he had to give Don Stewart "the change in the Big Two Hearted River now" to avoid the irony of their publishing it "because of the stuff I've got to cut" (*Letters* 134), he sent him a typescript of his manuscript revision of the ending (KL/EH 278, 277). And there the story rested until January 1925 when he decided to submit it to *This Quarter.*

Publication History (May 1925; October 1925)

"Big Two-Hearted River" was submitted for publication to Ernest Walsh for his new journal *This Quarter* in January 1925, although Hemingway had sent it to him earlier (*Letters* 144); and it was published in the May 1925 issue. The only relevant document between that publication and its inclusion in *In Our Time* (October 1925) is a curious set of the first eight pages of the *This Quarter* proofs with proofreader's marks and several suggested revisions—all of them insensitive to Hemingway's style and all ignored. They are identified as Hadley Hemingway's, even though the handwriting differs significantly from that in her letters of the period (KL/EH 280).

So by the grace of Gertrude Stein's quick remark and the laggardly reading at George Doran's, the story achieved its rightful form and its intended place concluding *In Our Time* in October 1925. Hemingway's luck was still with him.

Sources and Influences

The story originated in a fishing trip in the late summer of 1919 with Al Walker and Jock Pentecost to the Fox River in the Upper Peninsula, enthusiastically described in a letter to Howell Jenkins (*Letters* 28–29, 15 September 1919). Sheridan Baker was the first to identify the river, the town of Seney, and the terrain the three must have walked to have fished, as Hemingway reported, the two branches of the Fox some fifteen miles south of the Pictured Rocks on Lake Superior (150–52, 157–59). The discrepancies Baker noted between the lay of the land, the history of Seney and its devastating fires, the character of the river, and the fictional details of Nick's experience have provided evidence, of course, for the interpretation of the story as an imaginary venture.

But Hemingway had done a good deal of fishing before and after that trip to most of the streams in the Upper and Lower Peninsulas *except* the Two-Hearted, and his letters of the early 1920s to his boyhood friends are filled with exuberantly colloquial versions of the more muted appreciations of streams and campsites and the thrill of fishing in the story. He had drawn on much of that early experience in his fishing articles for the *Toronto Star* in April–November 1920 (*Dateline* 14, 22, 44, 48, 50, 62); and the passages in the story on pitching the tent, cooking breakfast, catching and rigging bait, and the exhilaration of hooking a large trout still retain some of the textbook details and procedures of those articles.

Once Hemingway admitted in *A Moveable Feast* that the "story was about coming back from the war but there was no mention of the war in it" (76), substantiating Philip Young's intuition, that "thing left out" was restored to the story. Now few read it without drawing on some explanatory reference to the later war stories, "In Another Country," "Now I Lay Me," "A Way You'll Never Be," the Burguete scene in *The Sun Also Rises* and the wounding in *A Farewell to Arms*. Others have considered its formal and thematic similarities with the story written just before it, "Soldier's Home," and the one written after it, "The Battler" (See *Critical Studies* below). All of which argues that the story is not only a culmination of the fiction of *In Our Time* but also central to the other stories of the late 1920s and early 1930s.

On the issue of literary influences, two contradictory facts seem, curiously enough, to argue for the story's originality: first, that it has no obvious earlier model; and second, that it seems to allude to a legion of them. Jeffrey Meyers finds a similarity between Hemingway and Kipling—the story's omission of the war is similar to Kipling's directives in *Something of Myself* (Hemingway's copy of which was published in 1937); and the use of fishing gear in Hemingway is like the "operation of locomotives in '.007' " (114). Earl Rovit finds in the Fox River a locale for Nick Adams like Spencer Brydon's "jolly corner" in Henry James's story. There is something of Jack London's wilderness tales that is more palpable in the story; and with Hemingway's admiration for Joseph Conrad, several have suggested that the river, unnamed in the story, is two-hearted in being both the "stream of life" and Conrad's necessary "destructive element."

Joseph Flora's recent study exemplifies the paradox of an original story with a long literary history: in his interpretation he finds parallels with Thoreau, Frost (both "Directive" and "Stopping by Woods"), Twain, Descartes, Bunyan, Housman, Crane, and both the Old and New Testaments—some of the analogues are simply descriptive but all are interesting. He begins this list, however, by suggesting that in Joyce's "The Dead" Hemingway found what his collection needed: "the longest story by far . . . and a masterpiece." Not so much a model as a mark to be met, Joyce's story challenged Hemingway to end his collection with "something uniquely his [that] would not remind readers of anyone but Hemingway" (146).

Critical Studies

The long and varied record of critical responses to "Big Two-Hearted River" began in the summer of 1925 soon after its publication in *This Quarter*. Carlos Baker reports that Dean Gauss and Scott Fitzgerald in a partly witty and partly serious conversation with Hemingway said he "had written a story in which nothing happened" and so it lacked "human interest"; and Hemingway replied that as "ordinary book reviewers [they] hadn't taken the trouble to find out what he had been trying to do" (*Writer as Artist* 125). They were right in the sense that nothing happens between characters, nor could it with Nick alone, but wrong in that the narrative is filled with significant gestures, acts, and events that range from a simple reflex to a complex ritual.

In 1945 Malcolm Cowley first took the trouble to find out what Hemingway was trying to do. His introduction to *The Portable Hemingway*, one of the earliest and most influential studies, placed him along those "haunted and nocturnal writers" in the tradition of Poe, Hawthorne, and Melville. And the gestures and acts in those stories in which nothing seems to happen, serve in fact as rituals, incantations, or spells "to banish evil spirits" and, for Nick in this story, as ways to keep in abeyance whatever needs he has left behind, whatever thoughts he must choke off (40, 48).

In 1952 Carlos Baker listed nearly every one of Nick's actions as a ritual and found underlying those in fishing a set of "codes of fair play" and a "carefully determined order of virtue and simplicity which goes far towards explaining from below the oddly satisfying effect of the surface story." But these rituals, he noted, fall between two "atmospheric symbols": the burned land, which Nick must pass through and the swamp, which, for now, he must avoid. He allows the "legitimate guess" that both the movement to the river and away from the swamp suggest that Nick is a returned veteran seeking some natural therapy (125–27).

In the same year Philip Young's *Ernest Hemingway* set a benchmark in Hemingway criticism with two general arguments: first, that *In Our Time* is "subtly, even obscurely, organized and . . . is in large part devoted to a scrupulously planned account of [Nick's] character and the reasons for it" (30); and second, that from chapter 6, in which Nick is wounded in the spine and declares his "separate peace," "the Hemingway hero is to be a wounded man, wounded not only physically but—as soon becomes clear—psychically as well" (41). For Young the memory of a traumatic wound has pervasive complications that are manifested in the formal and stylistic features of the fiction. In this story a "terrible panic is barely under control, and the style—this is the 'Hemingway style' at its most extreme—is the perfect expression of the content of the story"; with its fixation on detail and repetitive, almost mechanical, movement, it resembles the behavior a "badly shell-shocked veteran" who can control himself only by "performing simple jobs over and over in a factory: this, and then that. And then that and this" (46).

When Hemingway heard of Young's thesis he was furious, and the tale Young tells in his 1966 foreword of his efforts to publish read like the scholar's version of Nick Adams's "nightmares at noonday." But once published, the profound influence of his book, at least on the critics who consider "Big Two-Hearted River," is marked by the fact that few contest his interpretation of the story in the light of the later war stories and the wound. The majority of the studies cited here from Sheridan Baker (1959) to Howard Hannum (1984) agree with or slightly modify Young's analysis: Sheridan Baker noted the discrepancies between the Nick Adams and the river setting in this story and in the later war stories (154–56); and others, like Arthur Waldhorn, have suggested that Nick is well on his way toward recovery from the hallucinations of "A Way You'll Never Be" and has become a " 'master apprentice,' putting to use all he has wrenched from his violent education" (65). Most of those who deny or subordinate the traumatic wound, find other fears for Nick elsewhere—from a sense of preternatural evil to sexual psychosis—and even Keith Carabine's counter-argument that the story celebrates the twofold euphoria of Nick's return to the river and Hemingway's repossession of the country, admits that one definition of euphoria is an "unfounded feeling of optimism" (40, 44). So as Young himself said in an interview, "I have the feeling that the business of the wound has stuck in a lot of minds" (Morton 4).

Another critical issue was raised in Cowley's 1945 introduction when he noticed "the waking-dreamlike quality" of the story (41). With Young's insistence upon collating it with the other Nick Adams stories, and Sheridan Baker's demonstration of the discrepancies among them and, less significantly, others between the rivers and landscapes of Michigan and those Hemingway described, some readers inevitably questioned the nature of the narrative and its position on a continuum from a literal account of actions and thoughts to an account of a series of imagined events in Nick's waking dream. In 1927 Hemingway seemed almost to have invited this speculation by repeating the details of this story in the first two pages of "Now I Lay Me," which end with "Some nights too I made up streams, and some of them were very exciting, and it was like being awake and dreaming. Some of those streams I still remember and think that I have fished in them, and they are confused with streams I really know. I gave them all names and went to them on the train and sometimes walked for miles to get to them" (*Stories* 363–64).

Although that passage from "Now I Lay Me" should dispel any reading of "Big Two-Hearted River" as a reportorial account—if the story itself does not—it may tempt some to conceive of the narrative as only a waking dream or so shaped by Nick's imagination that he might as well be in bed. Young's insight into the scene in which Nick watches the trout from the bridge, like Nick's vision itself, has been distorted or misconstrued. He wrote that the "whole trip is seen as these first fish are seen. Nick goes about his business of fishing as if he were a trout keeping himself steady in the current. The whole affair is seen sharply but is slightly distorted . . ." (44). It is fair to say, as does Robert Gibb, that Young has found in the scene both "a world and a point of view," but not that the scene "gives us a world *as* a point of view," nor that Young fuses "the perceptor with the perception, making the trout extensions of Nick's consciousness," nor, finally, that it "is only a matter of degree to suggest that the entire landscape of the story is a mental one" (23). It is through such slight shifts of "degree" that one finds oneself in another quadrant. Young did not "fuse the perceptor with the perception," nor did Hemingway or, more precisely, the seldom noticed narrator of the story. The several manuscripts for the scene demonstrate Hemingway's decision to deny that Nick creates a world out there and to affirm that he discovers in that world an emblematic and usable present—and those two acts of perception are literally worlds apart (Smith 280–81).

A second reading of the story as a projection of Nick's consciousness is William Adair's. His argument rests on the assertions that Hemingway's landscapes are "often interior"; that they share images from the "dreaming part of Hemingway's mind . . . where they have accrued a subjective intensity and value"; that "we frequently get the 'same' landscape from work to work [with] essentially the same emotive and symbolic value" (144). With the liberties allowed by those critical adverbs, he finds every major event in the story echoed later in "A Way You'll Never Be" (1932), *A Farewell to Arms* (1929), and *Across the River and Into the Trees* (1950). This apparently anachronistic reading is "not much of a problem," for "the important image 'waist-deep in swamp water' " in the two stories and the last novel occurs in Hemingway's *Toronto Star* article of 1922 "A Veteran Visits the Old Front" (150).

The first assumption for this sort of reading, of course, is that by 1924 Hemingway had in mind a set of images or actions that he could arrange in a variety of patterns about the central experience of his wounding: the return to a burned-out or shelled town by a river ("A Way You'll Never Be"), a trip over hills or mountains to a camp or dugout *(A Farewell to Arms)*; remembering dead trout or human corpses *(Across the River and Into the Trees)*; the experience of hooking a large trout or nearly dying *(A Farewell to Arms)*; and soldiers wading to death at Porto Grande *(Across the River)*. One crucial question, however, which may have less to do with the assumption's validity than with its usefulness, is whether it limits or extends our understanding of the story. One might well ask whether one can conceive of the setting of "Big Two-Hearted River" as a mental landscape and still hold that Nick's fishing or the story itself is more than an exercise in solipsism. And one should consider whether the diminution of what is distinctive, original, and palpably there in the story is worth the distant allegorical representations of Hemingway's wounding. Although these readings assume as their warrant Hemingway's latter-day remark in *A Moveable Feast,* "The story was about coming back from the war but there was no mention of the war in it" (76), one could just as well take that as a suggestion to leave the story as he did, still with no mention of the war.

Perhaps in response to Hemingway's remark critical studies of "Big Two-Hearted River" burgeoned in number and variety in the following decade (1965–75), wilted a bit, and then returned with the opening of the Kennedy Library's manuscript collection in the early 1980s. And critics in that later period, reviewing their predecessors, tended to categorize that earlier work by critical disciplines or, in less kindly terms, by "preconceived theories"— psychological or mythic, Freudian or Christian, even symbolic (Carabine;

Hannum). Few of those earlier works, at least the more persuasive ones, are limited to a single theory, nor does a category like "psychological" admit the differences between, say, Philip Young's book of 1952 and Gerry Brenner's thirty years later.

It is an interesting if rather general observation, however, that those who focus on Nick's character, his "inward terrain," the concluding vision of the swamp, and the analogues in the other stories find the story ending in failure; while those who place more emphasis on the narrative, the day's fishing on the river, and the story largely in itself, see its conclusion as at least a qualified success. If, for example, the swamp exists only in Nick's imagination and is distorted by his recollected wounding and some deeper sexual fears, then he is no closer to recovery than the Nick of "A Way You'll Never Be" (Twitchell 276); if, however, the swamp with all its menacing aspects is "there"—like the rest of the river—then his decision not to fish it but to return to camp assumes the deliberate and conscious qualities of his other actions in the narrative and affirms "a sense of miracle, or recovery of the wounded Nick" (Flora 175).

Philip Young is often cited as the first of the critics to bring the insights and terms of psychology to the study of Hemingway; but today his suggestions that Nick's traumatic wound originated in Hemingway's experience and that we should read all the Nick Adams stories as chapters in a novel seem no more than any New Critic of the 1950s would have uttered from his armchair, especially now that so many more detailed psychological analyses have been written. The first major work in that discipline that considered "Big Two-Hearted River" was Richard Hovey's *Hemingway: The Inward Terrain* (1968). With the assumption that the events in the story are acts in a psychic drama, Nick's reluctance to fish certain spots along the river and ultimately in the swamp argue for some deeper fear. After his first trout, Nick looks for "deep holes" along the banks, finds one covered with branches, hooks and loses a trout as his line is fouled. Then he drifts his bait into a hollow log, hooks and lands his last trout. That these places have "certain analogies to the female organs" may be a fact, but whether the swamp, "with its dank overgrowth and yielding, fertile softness *symbolizes* femaleness" is a matter of interpretation (35–36, italics added). James Twitchell has extended Hovey's analysis to argue that at the end of the story "there is no swamp . . . outside the imagination or memory of Nick Adams" for topographical reasons: streams that feed swamps in Michigan or elsewhere are neither pebbled or bouldered nor do they run fast and deep within them. Thus the projected description of the swamp has a "hallucinatory quality" that distorts it into something "more 'female' and dangerous" (275–76). Once the terrain is cast inward, it is irrelevant that, as Sheridan Baker noted, the actual Fox River is sandy and the Two-Hearted rocky (157). So, too, are the interests of other readers in the narrative: they would argue that on that fictional river Nick looks for the deep holes because that is where the fish are when the sun is high; and even though he may be reluctant to fish the swamp, he deliberately tests himself with the overhanging branches, knowing he will fail, and with the hollow log where he brilliantly succeeds.

In Gerry Brenner's recent and more rigorous psychoanalytic study of Hemingway's fiction centering on the novels, he mentions "Big Two-Hearted River" in a footnote that others would have made an article. For his study the story is more a reflection of the wounding, Hemingway's fear of amputation (castration), and through his childhood experiences fishing with his father, in which "the only deeply disturbing event would be the moment his father takes his knife to the fish and cleans them" (242 n.). Others would argue that Nick—or Hemingway, for that matter—was never so squeamish; and that the moment when Nick guts the two fish is perhaps the most simple, clear, and clean act in his long and often complicated day. That day begins with Nick's watching a mink cross the logs over the river into the swamp; as the day ends in his contemplation of the swamp, he understands why such animals "that lived in swamps were built the way they were," and he tosses "the offal ashore for the minks to find" (*Stories* 231). This interpretation of the story finds the meaning of that moment in its foreshadowing, its association with the swamp, and its similarity with a primitive ritual offering.

Those critics who are more concerned with the implications of the narrative and less with those of Nick's psychological condition, seek the meaning of Nick's experiences in some recurrent archetypal pattern, and their readings are variously characterized by others as mythic or Christian. All, however, admit that Nick has suffered some wound, most likely in the war, and that the story is a set of trials in the quest for restoration. Joseph DeFalco finds a parallel in the story with "Soldier's Home" in that each follows "some great psychic shock," but here there is a partial but significant recovery from the "complete irrationality" of "A Way You'll Never Be." Nick's journey rests "upon the 'return to familiar ground' motif," and is motivated by his compulsion "to reaffirm the existence of order in the world [in] a place where the need had been satisfied before the full knowledge" of that world's irrationality (144–46). With the "traditional references to myths of rebirth," Nick has left behind all other needs—particularly the need for thinking, which recalls "past experiences . . . too destructive to normality"—except the burden of his pack, which "quite literally . . . pertains to the need for the return." Once he arrives at the river, all his actions and gestures are significant by virtue of their "form, not the content, which is their saving grace" (148–49). To have fished the river well as far as he did and then to realize his own physical and emotional limits is to discover "the possibility of complete reconciliation and final emergence as a man who has attained selfhood" (149, 151).

After some twenty years of other interpretations, DeFalco's seems almost reticent in its settling for the least and the most literal meaning of Nick's experience; but his remark, almost in passing, that we should consider the form and not the content of that experience was well taken then and is still to be fully understood.

For those who find a mythic pattern in "Big Two-Hearted River," the first issue is whether or not, as Cowley argued, Hemingway's rituals are "pre-Christian and pre-logical" (49). William Stein's article in 1960 might have resolved the issue, for he finds analogues between Nick and both the Fisher King and Christ as redeemers of the waste land, an interpretation similar to some of those of *The Sun Also Rises*. For others the crucial passage is, inevitably, the description of Nick's evening meal, with his recollection of an earlier trip on the Black River and whether to make the "coffee according to Hopkins" (*Stories* 216–18).

The more literal reading of the passage and its seeming origin in Hemingway's biography lend it a lighthearted, almost offhand, tone. Charles Hopkins, an assignment editor on the *Kansas City Star* and, as Hemingway wrote in a letter to James Gamble, a friend who "takes his fishing seriously" (Griffin 119), fished twice with Hemingway: once in early May 1918 at Horton Bay just before Hemingway was called to duty with the Red Cross, and again on the Sturgeon River, and probably the Black, in the last few days of August 1921, just before his marriage to Hadley. (The Black River, incidentally, is the only one mentioned in the story, first in this episode, and then introducing the original conclusion reprinted as "On Writing"; and on a page of notes for the story Hemingway considered it as a possible title [KL/EH 281].) There may be evidence for the rest of the details of Hopkins's story, or they may have been transposed and conflated from Hemingway's own experience.

The recollection of Hopkins begins with Nick's decision to follow his friend's gospel and bring the water *and* coffee to a boil, and it ends after one bitter cup that somehow makes a "good ending to the story." With his mind "starting to work" but knowing "he could choke it because he was tired enough," Nick returns to his tent and falls asleep. Jack Stewart responded to both William Stein, who sees Nick's meal as a sacrament intended to recover a "holistic" past with Hopkins at its center as an "exemplary model," and Robert Evans, for whom "the bitter cup . . . is nothing less than the age-old draught of loss, betrayal, and a broken promise" (166–67). Stewart agrees that the "symbolic communion [is] a celebration and revival of Hopkins' virtues." Stewart is, in the familiar critical phrase, one of those "reminded of the Last Supper and Christ's words" as well as, by implication, of a "departed" Master who received a "message from a distance" and let a bitter cup pass from him to remind others of their own "Gethsemane," and so on. Once those allusions are suggested, however, Stewart concludes that Nick rejects "his communion with Hopkins as sentimental dependence" even though it has pointed him toward "the self-sufficiency he must strive to attain" (194–96).

Joseph Flora's analysis of the narrative ranges more widely—as is suggested by the cited analogues from Genesis on—and the pattern he infers is the more abstract "religious quest" similar to that in Frost's "Directive." He assumes the prior experience of Nick's wounding, and considers him a latter-day version of the wounded Fisher King and fisher of men. As he moves from the burned land to the restorative river, Nick is returning, as did Descartes to a first and "undeniable assertion" with this difference: Nick seems to begin with "I feel, therefore I am." With this Flora underlines the importance of Nick's discovery of "all the old feeling" as he watches the trout at the bridge, and of his subsequent discovery that he "*felt* he had left everything behind, the need for thinking, the need to write, other needs" (*Stories* 210, italics added). However un-Cartesian, Nick begins where Descartes did, "with what he could absolutely trust . . . to find—perhaps—what he cannot lose, maybe even God" (Flora 153).

From there on Flora gathers a variety of literary parallels about the central events of Nick's burdened and up-hill journey to the river. Nick speaks three times: to the blackened grasshopper "for the first time"—and for Flora "the biblical and religious overtones are insistent" in recalling Adam's first words (157); again to justify his eating what he was willing to carry—and his voice sounded strange; and finally to exclaim over his first meal, " 'Geezus Chrise,' he said happily." Little is made of any sacral meanings of the meal itself or the coffee and with little loss. But not enough is made of the insight that when the coffee proves bitter, Nick "laughs—viewing the ending with ironic amusement, *seeing it as part of a story and himself as writer*" (164, italics added). There, in a throwaway line, Flora turns our attention for a moment away from Nick as one who must leave behind the "need for thinking" and "other needs," all unspecified, to Nick as one who must choke off the quite precise "need to write."

Although Part II begins with the "exhilaration of the aubade" and Nick's fishing is associated with the reverence for life and even the life one must take, as in *The Old Man and the Sea,* the end of the story and the vision of the swamp is, in Flora's view, not so much threatening as it is enticing. The river is two-hearted in that it is both the river of life and of death; and like the woods of Frost's poem, the swamp is in some ways lovely and certainly dark and deep. Nick's decision then becomes a triumphant affirmation of life or, at least, "the affirmation that the artist needs, a belief that the future matters, a belief that he will have a chance to create work that will have a life beyond life" (174–75). If that is so, and both his persuasive reading and other evidence argues that it is, then he seems to have underbid a strong hand. In any case, his reading is variously the most restrained and the most daring of recent studies of the story.

Other than the interpretations that seem to gather about the poles of character—conceived more or less in terms of psychology—and narrative—more or less in terms of myth—there are several from the 1970s that are more traditionally formalist or more concerned with particular matters of technique. Of the latter, there is Elizabeth Wells's statistical analysis of the story's prose style, a useful exploratory study of the style this story, more than any other, established as quintessentially Hemingway's. On the experimental use of point of view, Carl Ficken demonstrates how it serves to suggest a penetration of Nick's mind (106–07), and Sheldon Grebstein how it suggests both Nick's "geographical isolation . . . and his emotional insularity" (83–84).

In one of the early formalist analyses, Paul Anderson begins by establishing Hopkins's character as a standard of self-sufficiency with which we must judge Nick's behavior, as he himself does when he justifies carrying the canned food (565). (Anderson does not mention, however, Nick's hidden motive for not only the heavy pack but the longer than necessary hike: to tire himself so that sleep will come quickly.) Once that standard is set, Nick either insulates himself from endangering experiences or sets himself those simple graduated tasks he knows he can accomplish. The story records his initial failure and later qualified success as he moves through a concentric series of figurative (the pine plain) and actual bodies of water (the river) to confront the deepest Dantesque circle (the swamp) (567).

Frank Kyle's comparative analysis places Nick's initiation into the evils of society in "The Battler" against this story's introduction to an awareness of evils more universal and, so, potentially his own. Keith Carabine's bristling essay counters with a demonstration of the euphoria that pervades Nick's fishing but admits there may be a less happy reason for it. Although both essays clearly contradict one another, each offers persuasive and reconcilable interpretations of discrete passages.

Finally, Howard Hannum's article joins, somewhat uncomfortably, the practice of "immersion therapy" from Conrad and some psychiatrists (who, we are told in a note, "use it only as a last resort" [2 n.]), and a conventional notion of the "lyric story" to argue that the "lyric" features of "Big Two-Hearted River" are similar to those of the "irregular ode." Parts I and II are structurally related as are the strophe and antistrophe of the ode: the latter repeating "with some variation and in inverted order, the thematic elements, actions, emotions, even the prose rhythms" of the former. That "pattern includes joy, steadying work, hiking or fishing, and the *heart-tightening* or *heart-stopping* observation of the trout" (9). Beyond that the analogy with the Romantic ode fades, and the article adumbrates some of the earlier psychological studies and some more interesting similarities between this and other narratives.

With the publication of *The Nick Adams Stories* in 1972, the original conclusion was titled "On Writing" and included as the second "story" in the section "Company of Two" (233-41). The conclusion is taken from the typescript KL/EH 275, written in August 1924 and replaced in November with the published text (*Stories* 228 ["It was getting hot . . ."]-32). Clearly never intended as a story or to be published—recall Hemingway's letter to McAlmon and Gertrude Stein's aphorism "remarks are not literature"—it is "on" more than writing but deserves that essayistic title. Since its publication, many have alluded to the rejected conclusion, and three critics have drawn on it for more extensive studies of the story's composition and meaning.

Hemingway had mentioned Paul Cézanne as his master in *A Moveable Feast* (13, 69) and occasioned some general considerations of the painter's influence (Watts; Grebstein). But in "On Writing" he mentions several individual paintings in the Luxembourg, the Bernheim Gallery, and Gertrude Stein's collection that Meyly Chin Hagemann has been able to identify. With those paintings as evidence and Erle Loran's analysis of Cézanne's composition, she draws a variety of analogies between the painter's aesthetic principles and techniques and Hemingway's ironic vision and style. Her research is invaluable, but her conclusions rest on some insecure comparisons between the visual and verbal arts (Smith 283-85).

Few would disagree that Hemingway's rejection of this conclusion was a wise decision, however late and, as he himself said, lucky it was. Yet its model in miniature is the reverie on Hopkins in Part I: both are associated with fishing on the Black River; both set in opposition male camaraderie in fishing and men with women, their girls or their wives; and both end as Nick senses a completed "story": Nick's bitter coffee "made a good ending" and when he saw "how Cezanne would do the stretch of river and the swamp" he returns to camp "holding something in his head" (*Nick Adams Stories* 240, 241). No one, however, has argued for the excision of the Hopkins episode.

Bernard Oldsey, in one of the first and most perceptive studies of the manuscripts, found the rejected conclusion a "rambling interior monologue"—which, of course, it was intended to be—and a "tricky piece of self-portraiture" fortunately excised (220-21). It is all of that, but the monologue is patterned and was carefully revised between manuscript and typescript. All the remembered experiences—which, but for the recollections of Michigan, occurred or were on Hemingway's mind from late June to August 1924—are structured with dichotomies: books versus experience, knowledge versus ignorance, marriage versus bachelorhood, and literary invention versus realistic description. Finally, with Cézanne as his model of a truly original artist set against almost all the derivative writers he knew, the last dichotomy emerges as art versus literature itself: "Nick, seeing how Cezanne would do the stretch of country, stood up. The water was cold and actual. He waded across the stream, moving in the picture" (*Nick Adams Stories* 240).

Oldsey objects to this passage as a "kind of *trompe l'oeil* trickery" Nick and Hemingway must forgo in order to write the way Cézanne painted (223). That is true if it is simply a trick, but the passage has a curious analogue in *A Moveable Feast* when Hemingway recalled writing the scene that begins the story: "When I stopped writing I did not want to leave the river where I could see the trout in the pool. . . . But in the morning the river would be there and I must make it and the country and all that would happen" (76–77). Nick's movement from the actual river into a painting in the rejected conclusion is reversed in the recollection when the act of writing creates a river that "would be there." One suspects that for Hemingway neither moment was a trick, but rather a metaphor expressing his simple conviction of the reciprocal acts of the artist's creation and the reader's recreation.

Joseph Flora's consideration of "On Writing" turns away from his earlier perception that Nick sees the Hopkins reverie as "a story and himself as a writer" to the argument that the story's placement after "Cross-Country Snow" and the four marriage tales in *In Our Time* is justified now that we know from "On Writing" that Nick is married. He has, "like Hopkins, . . . made some choices, and a major one was a commitment to a woman" (181). Although his conception that "the pristine quality of the aubade experience"— and the story is only momentarily an aubade and then not wholly pristine— could not accomodate the inclusion of "On Writing" is correct, the inappropriateness of that earlier conclusion does not rest in the fact that it is about writing but in the fact that it is so trivial.

If only with its unintended title, "On Writing" does return us to various comments from the last twenty years of criticism. At the outset Sheridan Baker sensed that it was almost as if "the Nick of this story, not Ernest Hemingway, had written 'Big Two-Hearted River' " (156) and nearly every later critic has repeated that impression. Both the critics who are concerned with the story's psychology and those with its archetypal patterns admit the informing power of Nick's imagination; Joseph DeFalco recognized that Nick's actions find their "saving grace" in their "form, not their content"—and that content, we might add, is at the end not much more than two fish, while the form is everything. If Joseph Flora is right in reading the Hopkins episode as a story and Nick as its writer and Bernard Oldsey is right in suggesting its similarity, albeit a "lapse," with "On Writing," then more attention might be given to what the *story* tells us of what Nick has left behind after the vision of the trout at the bridge.

On Philip Young's intelligent speculation in 1952, confirmed by Hemingway's word in 1964, it was the war—and only the war. But what if it was not that, or not primarily that? We are told that Nick had "left everything behind, the need for thinking, the need to write, other needs." In the original manuscript he wrote first, "the |necessity|/need/for thinking, the |necessity|/need/to write, |the need to talk|/other needs/" (KL/EH 274). Certainly neither Hemingway nor Nick Adams had any need to think or talk about the war. But from the spring of 1924 through the following summer, Hemingway felt most acutely the need to write the last and definitive story for the projected *In Our Time,* matching Joyce's "The Dead." Whatever his "other needs"—and they must have been many—those he felt he must leave behind were those he associated in his first draft, to *think* and to *talk* about rather than to *do* the one thing he had to, write. His decision to reject the original conclusion, which recalled his summer filled with bullfights and talk and letters to Gertrude Stein, was, in effect, to ask the questions he recalled in *A Moveable Feast,* "What did I know best that I had not written about and lost? What did I know about truly and care for the most?" (76).

Looking back over these representative commentaries on "Big Two-Hearted River," one might wonder what is left to say were it not for the sense that, as with precious few stories in the language, one suspects that there will always be something left undiscovered. Hemingway knew that this story was his best and told Fitzgerald so two months after *In Our Time* was published (*Letters* 180). In the late 1950s, unsure of the lasting strength of his talent, he began to insist on the undiscovered dimensions of his fiction and mentioned the war as one for "Big Two-Hearted River." In June 1959 he elevated his theory of omission to a general rule for fiction in "The Art of the Short Story." There he suggested another thing left out: "there were many Indians in the story, just as the war was in the story, and none of the Indians nor the war appeared. As you see, it is very simple and easy to explain" (88).

Works Cited

PRIMARY

"The Art of the Short Story." *Paris Review* 23 (1981): 85–102.

Dateline: Toronto. Ed. William White. New York: Scribner's, 1985.

Ernest Hemingway: Selected Letters, 1917–1961. Ed. Carlos Baker. New York: Scribner's, 1981.

The Nick Adams Stories. New York: Scribner's, 1972.

A Moveable Feast. New York: Scribner's, 1964.

The Short Stories of Ernest Hemingway. New York: Scribner's, 1938, 209–32.

SECONDARY

Adair, William. "Landscapes of the Mind: 'Big Two-Hearted River.'" *College Literature* 4 (1977): 144–51.

Anderson, Paul Victor. "Nick's Story in Hemingway's 'Big Two-Hearted River.'" *Studies in Short Fiction* 7 (Fall 1970): 564–72.

Baker, Carlos. *Ernest Hemingway: A Life Story.* 1969. New York: Scribner's, 1988.

———. *Hemingway: The Writer as Artist.* 1952. Princeton: Princeton UP, 1972.

Baker, Sheridan. "Hemingway's Two-Hearted River." *Michigan Alumnus Quarterly Review* 65 (Winter 1959): 142–49; rpt. in *The Short Stories of Ernest Hemingway: Critical Essays.* Ed. Jackson Benson. Durham: Duke UP, 1975, 150–59.

Brenner, Gerry. *Concealments in Hemingway's Works.* Columbus: Ohio State UP, 1983.

Carabine, Keith. "'Big Two-Hearted River': A Reinterpretation." *Hemingway Review* 1 (Spring 1982): 39–44.

Cowley, Malcolm. Introduction *The Portable Hemingway.* New York: Viking, 1945; rpt. in *Hemingway: A Collection of Critical Essays.* Ed. Robert P. Weeks. Englewood Cliffs: Prentice–Hall, 1962.

DeFalco, Joseph. *The Hero in Hemingway's Short Stories.* Pittsburgh: U of Pittsburgh P, 1963.

Evans, Robert. "Hemingway and the Pale Cast of Thought." *American Literature* 38 (May 1966): 161–76.

Ficken, Carl. "Point of View in the Nick Adams Stories." *Fitzgerald/Hemingway Annual.* (1971): 212–35; rpt. in *The Short Stories of Ernest Hemingway: Critical Essays.* Ed. Jackson J. Benson. Durham: Duke UP, 1975, 93–112.

Flora, Joseph M. *Hemingway's Nick Adams.* Baton Rouge: Louisiana State UP, 1982.

Gibb, Robert. "He Made Him Up: 'Big Two-Hearted River' as Doppleganger." *Hemingway Notes* 5 (Fall 1979): 20–24.

Grebstein, Sheldon N. *Hemingway's Craft.* Carbondale: Southern Illinois UP, 1973.

Griffin, Peter. *Along with Youth: Hemingway, The Early Years.* New York: Oxford UP, 1985.

Hagemann, Meyly Chin. "Hemingway's Secret: From Visual to Verbal Art." *Journal of Modern Literature* 7 (Feb. 1979): 87–112.

Hannum, Howard L. "Soldier's Home: Immersion Therapy and Lyric Pattern in 'Big Two-Hearted River.'" *Hemingway Review* 3 (Spring 1984): 2–13.

Hovey, Richard B. *Hemingway: The Inward Terrain.* Seattle: U of Washington P, 1968.

Kyle, Frank B. "Parallel and Complementary Themes in Hemingway's 'Big Two-Hearted River' and 'The Battler.'" *Studies in Short Fiction* 16 (1979): 295–300.

Meyers, Jeffrey. *Hemingway: A Biography.* New York: Harper, 1985.

Morton, Bruce. "An Interview with Philip Young." *Hemingway Notes* 6 (1980): 2–13.

Oldsey, Bernard. "Hemingway's Beginnings and Endings." *College Literature* 7 (1980): 213–38.

Rovit, Earl. *Ernest Hemingway*. Boston: Twayne, 1963.

Smith, Paul. "Hemingway's Early Manuscripts: The Theory and Practice of Omission." *Journal of Modern Literature* 10 (July 1983): 268–88.

Stein, Gertrude. *The Autobiography of Alice B. Toklas*. New York: Harcourt, 1933.

Stein, William B. "Ritual in Hemingway's 'Big Two-Hearted River.'" *Texas Studies in Literature and Language* 1 (Winter 1960): 555–61.

Stewart, Jack F. "Christian Allusions in 'Big Two-Hearted River.'" *Studies in Short Fiction* 15 (1978): 194–96.

Svoboda, Frederic Joseph. *Hemingway and "The Sun Also Rises": The Crafting of a Style*. Lawrence: UP of Kansas, 1983.

Twitchell, James. "The Swamp in Hemingway's 'Big Two-Hearted River.'" *Studies in Short Fiction* 9 (1972): 275–76.

Waldhorn, Arthur. *A Reader's Guide to Ernest Hemingway*. New York: Farrar, 1972.

Watts, Emily Stipes. *Ernest Hemingway and the Arts*. Urbana: U of Illinois P, 1971.

Wells, Elizabeth J. "A Statistical Analysis of the Prose Style of Ernest Hemingway: 'Big Two-Hearted River.'" *Fitzgerald/Hemingway Annual* (1969): 47–69.

Young, Philip. *Ernest Hemingway: A Reconsideration*. 1952. New York: Harcourt, 1966.

15

The Undefeated

Composition History (September–November 1924)

"The Undefeated" links Hemingway's first two major volumes of short stories, *In Our Time* and *Men Without Women:* it was written in the months between the first ending of "Big Two-Hearted River" in August 1924 and the revised ending in November. In the letter to Robert McAlmon of 15 November 1924 in which he writes that he has revised its last nine pages to just "the straight fishing," he adds that he has also "finished a long 45 page story I think you will like (*Letters* 133). Those dates are corroborated in a letter to Ernest Walsh of 27 March 1925 in which he remarked that "I wrote my guts out into it" (153 n.; KL/EH, Hemingway to Ernest Walsh).

He had this story in hand then before *In Our Time* was accepted for publication, and but for its length at least, might have submitted it to Boni and Liveright as a substitute for "Up in Michigan." He was clearly saving it for his second volume of stories; and after some later rearrangements of the sequence of stories for that volume, "The Undefeated" was placed first.

Hemingway wrote again to McAlmon on 20 November to tell him he only had "two stories in hand. One is unpublishable I'm afraid as well as too long. [This one, Carlos Baker speculates correctly, was "A Lack of Passion."] The other is a hell of a good one, by far the best I've written but about 10,000 words" (*Letters* 135). By this time he had likely completed the KL/EH manuscripts 790–92 and 794. The first (790) is a sequence of four booklets and added pages in manuscript that begins the story late in the narrative (*Stories* 254, "Zurito leaned forward on the barrera . . .") during the gypsy Fuentes's placing of the banderillas and before Manuel's wounding and the killing of the bull. Hemingway might have intended the story to begin just before this climax, but it is more probable that this manuscript is incomplete. The second (KL/EH 791) is a Hemingway typescript titled "The Bullfighters," addressed, and revised in pencil for a professional typist. (KL/EH 792 and 794 are fragments.)

Some time in late November and December Hemingway had a professional typist's version done (KL/EH 793), which he later marked as the "first typewritten mss." This was most likely the version sent on 21 January 1925 to G. H. Lorimer, editor of the *Saturday Evening Post;* for Hemingway, knowing the *Post*'s scruples, noted on page 38 of the typescript, "Change the word bastards to bums wherever it is offensive" (See *Letters* 148).

Other than all the preliminaries missing from the first manuscript version, there are two remarkable and major differences among the various early and the published versions. Through them all Manuel's dedication of the bull to the president is more fatalistic than the formula in the final version (*Stories* 257); it reads, " 'I promise that I will fight faithfully and loyally and that I will kill the bull or he will kill me,' was what Manuel was saying" (KL/EH 790, 791, 793). Hemingway probably recognized this as too melodramatic and predictive, and between these versions and publication he revised Manuel's dedication to the more formulaic one.

The second set of variations among the manuscripts concerns, as is often the case, the ending (*Stories* 266). In the first manuscript version, he ended it with "He felt very tired" (KL/EH 790). In the first typescript, he ended it with the next sentence, "He felt very, very tired" (KL/EH 791). In the typescript sent to Lorimer (KL/EH 793) and the final version, he added the action that distinguished between Retana's and Zurito's attitudes toward the doomed bullfighter, when Retana leaves with a shrug and Zurito stays to watch his friend die. The first, and especially the second, would have come too close to the sentimental and pathetic. The final ending recalls the story's first two episodes and its two opposed choric characters, Retana and Zurito, and it turns us away from the inevitable death of Manuel to the question of how one, recognizing its inevitability, should act in response to that recognition.

Publication History (Fall 1925; October 1927)

In February 1926, Hemingway told Walsh he had "re-discovered that The Undefeated *is* a grand story and I'm very proud I wrote it" (*Letters* 192). His shifting evaluations of the story, although partly depending on whether he was writing to Walsh or Fitzgerald, may well say something of his sense of the most remunerative market for fiction. With no contract for the *In Our Time* stories in the fall of 1925, he could have decided to break into the American market. In the letter to Lorimer, he noted that he tried to write "The Undefeated" "to show it the way it actually is, as Charles E. Van Loan used to write fight stories" (*Letters* 148). The allusion was ingratiating: Van Loan (1876–1919), a former editor at the *Post*, had written eight volumes of stories on boxing, racing, baseball, and golf and one on "the moving-picture game" for which Lorimer had provided an appreciative introduction. Hemingway could have felt that in that league his *was* a "great story"; but when it appeared in *This Quarter* (Autumn–Winter 1925–26) along with a Callaghan story Hemingway thought was "as good as Dubliners"

(*Letters* 187), he raised his standards as he had done when he wrote to Fitzgerald. In that letter to his friend and competitor, which placed "My Old Man" with "the bull fight story and 50 Grand" among the "kind that are easy for me to write" (*Letters* 180), that is to say, stories that Lorimer might accept for the *Post,* he was, early on in their relationship, implying something about Fitzgerald's success with the editors and readers of the *Saturday Evening Post*—and it was not kind.

After some indecision about its placement in the collection, "The Undefeated" finally took its place as the first of the stories in *Men Without Women* in October 1927.

Sources and Influences

The inception of "The Undefeated" began in the late spring and early summer of 1923 with Hemingway's introduction to bullfighting, first with Robert McAlmon and William Bird in Madrid and through Andalusia, and then with Hadley in July at Pamplona. An instant aficionado, he wrote two of his better *Toronto Star* articles, celebrating the excitement of his discovery, his admiration for the toreros Chicuelo and Nicanor Villalta, and his first sense of the ritual as a tragedy (*Dateline,* 20, 27 October 1923, 340, 347). His second article, "Pamplona in July," described the fight in which Manuel Garcia, Maera, failed several times at the kill, hitting bone and spraining his wrist (*Dateline* 352–53). Maera and that occasion were later celebrated in *Death in the Afternoon* (77–83), and Hemingway drew in part on that bullfight for the narrative of "The Undefeated."

In late July and August he wrote the five bullfight chapters, 10–14 of *In Our Time* (12–16 of *in our time*), the last two of which center on Maera. Elements of "The Undefeated" recall the goring of a picador's horse (chap. 10), an angry cushion-throwing crowd that cuts off the torero's pigtail (11), Villalta's classic and dramatic killing of a bull (12), Maera's contempt for a drunken bullfighter (13), and finally his first version of the death of Maera (14), who was alive and well at the time.

In July 1924 Hemingway made his third trip to Spain, this time with the "Sun" set, saw Maera again, and on his return wrote the original conclusion for "Big Two-Hearted River." In that rejected ending, Nick's recollection of his friendship with Maera is introduced in an *ubi sunt* passage that turns on the discrepancy between the real experience of the bullfight and the rhetoric of the bullfight journalists, much as the books on fishing cloud the experience of a trout stream (*Nick Adams Stories* 236–37). In "The Undefeated" Hemingway dramatically contrasts the action in the bullring with the jargon of "the substitute bull-fight critic of *El Heraldo,*" who leaves early since he can get the details from the morning papers (*Stories* 248–51, 253, 256).

When he had finished "The Undefeated," Hemingway returned to correct his *In Our Time* version of the death of Maera in "Banal Story," written in early 1925, with an account of his actual death from tuberculosis, not a bull, and his funeral. Finally, in one of the most dramatic passages in *Death in the Afternoon,* he refashioned the story of the first fight of Maera's he had seen in which, as in Manuel Garcia's, he hits bone, is painfully hurt, and kills the bull at last on the sixth attempt.

Whatever the similarities between Manuel Garcia and Maera, Scott MacDonald observed that "in *Death in the Afternoon* alone (260–62, 251–52), two other matadors have at least as much in common with [Hemingway's] protagonist . . . as does Maera": Manolo Martinez and Manolo Bienvenida (MacDonald 15). Susan Beegel's recent article on the relationship between the story and *Death in the Afternoon* offers an even earlier model. With a rejected eight-page manuscript for *Death in the Afternoon,* which includes a brief account of the life and death of a nineteenth-century bullfighter, Manuel Garcia, Espartero, she demonstrates that although the story's narrative may have been suggested by Maera's fight in 1923, the career and character of the story's Manuel Garcia is closer to Espartero's (13–17). She discovered in Hemingway's collection of bullfight newspapers three issues of *La Lidia* from 1889 and 1892 that describe events in Espartero's career close to Manuel Garcia's: he had "lost work during a season due to at least one serious goring." In a corrida in Madrid, he required "seven thrusts to kill a bull in one fight," and fell and was knocked down in a second. Finally, he was criticized as lacking "sufficient skill to kill bulls 'recibiendo' " (receiving the bull's charge at the kill) (18). Finally, she notes some "25 works on bullfighting published prior to the completion of 'The Undefeated' " in Michael Reynolds's inventory of Hemingway's reading (18).

Although Beegel's survey of all the Spanish sources is incomplete—as Hemingway's very likely was—her discovery of Espartero as a more probable model for Manuel Garcia may well explain the differences Hemingway drew between Garcia's reputation as a torero and Maera's, and why he chose to have his character killed in the ring as was Espartero.

If "The Undefeated" connects Hemingway's second series of *In Our Time* chapters and his *Toronto Star* articles with *Death in the Afternoon,* it is also related to the two versions of the conclusion of "Big Two-Hearted River." It was written between his completion of the first ending in August 1924 and his decision to revise that ending with Nick's recognition of the potential tragedy of fishing the swamp. "The Undefeated" is Hemingway's attempt to dramatize his perception that the bullfight gathered in a single ritual the elements of tragedy. The writing of that story could well have contributed to the effect of Gertrude Stein's reading of, and his own dissatisfaction with, the original manuscript of "Big Two-Hearted River." If so, then all the recollections of Maera in the original conclusion, cast in dramatic form in "The Undefeated," would have offered the obvious lesson for the completion of "Big Two-Hearted River" and led him to the perception of fishing the swamp as a metaphor of a "tragic adventure" in its final version.

Critical Studies

There are three studies of the stylistic and formal elements of "The Undefeated." Francis Christensen drew a lesson from Hemingway on descriptive-narrative writing to demonstrate, with sometimes overwhelming statistics, that Hemingway's narrative style here and in other stories depends more upon the sequence and positioning of modifiers than upon nominals, as we have become accustomed to believe—an insight that later studies of the manuscripts have confirmed. Sheldon Grebstein considered the story's instance of Hemingway's recurrent patterning of "inner and outer" scenes, with the introductory dialogue in Retana's office and the concluding dialogue in the infirmary enclosing the narrative of the corrida, itself counterpointed with the idioms of the bullfighter and the reporter. Scott MacDonald used the shifting narrative perspective from Manuel's to the narrator's to those of a variety of "judges" (Zurito, the reporter, and the crowd) to contest the torero's stature and significance as a tragic figure (see below).

Nearly every writer on Hemingway has mentioned "The Undefeated"; but relatively few have offered extended analyses and—with the exception of MacDonald, whose notes offer a fair review of others to 1972—there is little disagreement among them. From Philip Young on, Manuel Garcia was cited as an exemplar of the code hero and associated with Santiago in *The Old Man and the Sea* (Young 65, 124; see also Waldhorn 26). Keneth Kinnamon associated him with Maera and Hemingway's celebrated "catalog of virtues" and valor in *Death in the Afternoon* (Kinnamon 63). Earl Rovit found in Manuel Garcia an early instance of the way in which the "tutor" figures in Hemingway first define themselves ("I am a bull-fighter" [*Stories* 236]); then "tend to transcend the fixed coordinates of their temporal lives and become *types*," (The Bullfighter); and finally, "refined" of that typicality, become archetypes in a myth (84).

Commentaries such as these may suggest some of the reasons for the unusual critical unanimity on this story. "The Undefeated" had from the first the ring of an authoritative story on an exotic subject and seven years later took on a further validity from *Death in the Afternoon*. The ancient and archetypal aura of the corrida and the romantic associations with the torero impel us toward a clear and conventional reading of the narrative. Moreover, the story draws on the familiar design of tragedy, and so it gathers about it not only the prestige but also the classic interpretations of that venerable tradition.

Nearly every study of the story states or implies the critical and evaluative terms of tragedy. Joseph DeFalco read Manuel Garcia's return to bullfighting as a "redemptive ordeal," presided over by Zurito, the retired picador, serving as the archetypal figure of the "wise old man" (198–99). When he belatedly kills the bull, his contempt for both its corrupt carcass and the jeering crowd marks his "fierce individuality which his victory has brought to the surface." And with the completion of the ritual, the story "approximates the motif of crucifixion and redemption in the Christ story" (201).

Wirt Williams's comprehensive study of the varieties of tragedy in Hemingway's fiction examines the story's narrative as examples of Northrop Frye's distinctions between tragedies of fate and moral flaw. Williams argues that "The Undefeated" has "not only the demanded magnitude, statement, and impact of authentic tragedy, but it offers also one of the noblest tragic conditions: the fatal flaw of the aging matador is also the elevating character that gives him redemption, transcendence, and heroic identity" (90–91). Manuel Garcia's downfall is the result of a tragedy of both circumstance and character, and Williams places it within the tradition of those two conceptions from Aristotle through Hegel to Frye.

To return to Scott MacDonald: his essay examines the changes in narrative point of view to consider the ways in which the separate voices in the story present a sequence of value judgments on Manuel Garcia's perception of events, his decision to return to the ring, and his performance as a torero. Although he seems to misconstrue Manuel's reaction to the bull's head on the wall of Retana's office and the intended effect of the reporter's offhand and general notes on the corrida, he demonstrates the way in which the reporter's commentary and the crowd's reaction support each other in an evaluation of Manuel Garcia's first set of "acceptable veronicas" and Zurito's pic-ing (*Stories* 249, 250). With those two "judges" established, he explains why the second set of veronicas, in which the torero sidestepped, was met by the crowd's silence and the reporter's term "vulgar." After the first two acts of the corrida in which the talents of the old picador Zurito and the young banderillero Fuentes are established, the final act of the corrida is presented through the point of view of Manuel Garcia; but the "judges" are variously critical: Zurito is nowhere to be seen, Retana's man tells him to wipe his face, and finally the crowd litters the ring with cushions and the reporter presumably tosses in his champagne bottle.

The final act of the corrida, the killing of the bull, is a disaster, certainly, but MacDonald errs in stating that it "receives the reaction it deserves, the reaction any competent bullfight crowd would give a mediocre performance that ended artlessly" (8). MacDonald argues that in the infirmary Manuel "is allowed to keep his *coleta* [the torero's pigtail] not because of any virtue in his performance, but because of Zurito's desire to . . . prevent Manuel from sitting up on the operating table" (10).

MacDonald's judgment of Manuel's final performance as a torero seems harsh because it ignores elements that Williams characterizes as "universe-inflicted" and Frye would consider as aspects of a fated tragedy (91). Manuel was at the mercy of a mediocre bull, as Retana said, and he is gored after tripping over a cushion thrown from the crowd—as if their judgment of his performance fatally condemned him.

So it seems that somewhere between the conventional reading of the story and MacDonald's, perhaps at some point moderated by Williams's sense of the varieties of the tragic narrative, one could reconcile the minor differences in the story's interpretation. It is one of the variants of classical tragedy, and one of the stories in which Hemingway used a pattern that served him well in later fiction.

Works Cited

PRIMARY

Dateline: Toronto. Ed. William White. New York: Scribner's, 1985.

Death in the Afternoon. New York: Scribner's, 1932.

Ernest Hemingway: Selected Letters, 1917–1961. Ed. Carlos Baker. New York: Scribner's, 1981.

The Nick Adams Stories. New York: Scribner's, 1972.

The Short Stories of Ernest Hemingway. New York: Scribner's, 1938, 235–66.

SECONDARY

Beegel, Susan F. "The Death of El Espartero: An Historic Matador Links 'The Undefeated' and *Death in the Afternoon*." *Hemingway Review* 5 (Spring 1986): 12–23.

Christensen, Francis. "A Lesson from Hemingway." *College English* 25 (October 1963): 12–18.

DeFalco, Joseph. *The Hero in Hemingway's Short Stories*. Pittsburgh: U of Pittsburgh P, 1963.

Grebstein, Sheldon N. *Hemingway's Craft*. Carbondale: Southern Illinois UP, 1973.

Kinnamon, Keneth. "Hemingway, The *Corrida,* and Spain." *Texas Studies in Language and Literature* 1 (Spring 1959): 44–61; rpt. in *Ernest Hemingway: Five Decades of Criticism*. Ed. Linda Wagner. East Lansing: Michigan State UP, 1974. 57–74.

MacDonald, Scott. "Implications of Narrative Perspective in Hemingway's 'The Undefeated.'" *Journal of Narrative Technique* 2 (January 1972): 1–15.

Rovit, Earl. *Ernest Hemingway*. Boston: Twayne, 1963.

Waldhorn, Arthur. *A Reader's Guide to Ernest Hemingway*. New York: Farrar, 1972.

Williams, Wirt. *The Tragic Art of Ernest Hemingway*. Baton Rouge: Louisiana State UP, 1981.

Young, Philip. *Ernest Hemingway: A Reconsideration*. 1952. New York: Harcourt, 1966.

16

Banal Story

Composition History (January–February 1925)

Philip Yanella's study of what is apparently the only extant manuscript of "Banal Story" dates the composition of the story between the Danny Frush-Edouard Mascart fight on 27 January 1925 and 30 January, the date (without the year) on a letter to Jane Heap included with or written soon after the manuscript. Both the manuscript and the letter are in the Jane Heap Collection at the University of Wisconsin-Milwaukee. The Frush-Mascart fight is referred to both in the story (*Stories* 360) and the letter. Other remarks in the letter and notes for possible deletions confirm that date, as does a letter of 1938 in which Hemingway wrote that the story "was written in Schruns at least a year" (in fact, a year-and-a-half) before "The Killers" in May 1926 (*Letters* 470). Finally, several of the sentences parodying *The Forum* come close to those in the December 1924 and January 1925 issues of that journal; and the directive to "Think of these things in 1925" (*Stories* 361) suggests that is the year to come.

But this raises a question: for even if Hemingway had a January 1925 issue of *The Forum* at the Hotel Taube in Schruns in time to parody it in a manuscript written at the end of that month, how can we explain what seem to be the references Wayne Kvam has found to issues of *The Forum* from February through July 1925 (184–87)? He cites about ten allusions: several might have been found in issues before January 1925, but there are two from February, and three from May through June. Some are distant, but a few are very close: Hemingway wrote, "Do we want big men—or do we want them cultured?" (*Stories* 360), clearly alluding to a Yale student's article of February 1925 on a question that was troubling his campus, "Big Men—Or Cultured?" (Kvam 185, 191 n. 17). Neither this nor other articles of the winter and spring of 1925 were announced in earlier issues of *The Forum,* but Hemingway would have needed little more than a flyer or advertisement with forthcoming titles to include their topics in his parody of the editor's style. It is possible, as Michael Reynolds suggested in conversation, that Hemingway received news of literary issues in the offing from Dorothy "Dossie" Johnston, who was staying at Schruns and was the daughter of the librarian of the American Library in Paris (Baker 587; *Letters* 148).

With the letter to Jane Heap and the manuscript, Yanella is able to note the differences between the manuscript and the *Little Review* version. Hemingway added a note in the letter's margin that "if the word farts or fart isnt allowed by post office leave it out and let it go blank." She went further and deleted the three sentences in which the story's character farts "silently" or "unvoluntarily" before and during some moving moments of reading *The Forum* (Yanella 175–76). The delicacy of her decision did not mask Hemingway's sense that *The Forum* deserved no less than a flatulent response, if only to underscore, as Yanella remarked, "the connection between banality and anality" (176).

Publication History (Summer 1926; October 1927)

For all those decorous revisions, the story lay in the *Little Review*'s offices for well over a year before it was published in their Spring–Summer 1926 issue. Hemingway, too, seemed to have lost interest in it. It does not appear in his preliminary tables of contents for *Men Without Women* until January 1927 (KL/EH 120 B) and only there in parentheses and last place. In May he offered it rather apologetically to Max Perkins: he wrote that he had forgotten it and that it "wasn't much but I remember Edmund Wilson writing that he liked it so it might be worth getting hold of" (*Letters* 251; 4, 27 May 1927).

Wayne Kvam continues the publication history of the story by noting the variants between the *Little Review* version and that in *Men Without Women* of October 1927.

Sources and Influences

The two principal sources for "Banal Story," the editorial comments and articles from *The Forum* (1924–25) and Hemingway's "revised" version of the death of Maera in chapter 14 of *In Our Time,* provide the story's ironic structure (Kvam 182–88). Celebrating its fortieth year in January 1925, *The Forum* was proclaimed a "magazine of controversy" and, by no less an authority than Carl Sandburg, "the barometer of American intelligence" (Kvam 183). (Whether that barometer was forecasting a high or a low is not indicated, but Hemingway had no doubts.) Under its current editor, Henry G. Leach, the editorial commentaries took on the ebullient quizzicality that Hemingway so happily parodies: "Our children's children—what of them? Who of them? . . . Are you a girl of eighteen? Take the case of Joan of Arc. Take the case of Bernard Shaw" (*Stories* 360–61).

But *The Forum* rankled Hemingway most with its certitude on the rules for fiction and the sentimental slop it published. Hemingway's two sentences on Arthur Hamilton Gibbs's serialized romance *Soundings* misses its heady mix of deep thoughts and heavy petting; nor does it match the unintended humor of a summary of the story in the January 1925 issue: "Nancy Hawthorne, a charming young English girl, has been spending a year of freedom in Paris. . . . Nancy Hawthorne has felt herself attracted to Bob. But she is not sure of herself. Her single previous contact with sex has been only an incident; a boy, 'Curly,' in the little village of Brimble, England, . . . kissed her one night, but she felt no reciprocal emotion" (*The Forum* 122–23, 116).

Hemingway's parodic style (paragraphs 3–8 and 10–18) is one he could call up in a moment—his letters, particularly to Fitzgerald, often fall into this mode—and he used it again in *The Torrents of Spring* and the Burguete chapters of *The Sun Also Rises*.

The final paragraph on the death and burial of Manuel Garcia Maera serves not only to contrast its style with the vacuous queries and inflated abstractions of the parody but also to dramatize in itself the story's ironic point that when the mourners buy the memorial lithographs of Maera they lose "the pictures they had of him in their memories" (*Stories* 361).

Except for that rather explicit point, this final paragraph might well have substituted for Hemingway's first, and premature, description of the torero's death in chapter 14. That he took this occasion in a satire of a journal's romantic vision of life to rewrite his 1923 version of Maera's death by goring now that the torero had in December 1924 "drown[ed] with the pneumonia" (*Stories* 361) raises an interesting critical question.

Critical Studies

Before the articles by Philip Yanella and Wayne Kvam in 1974, there had been only three brief references to "Banal Story." Joseph DeFalco considered the story a demonstration of "the addiction of the people to unimportant tabloid romances while a singular event is taking place: the death of a hero," and cited it in support of his archetypal analysis of "The Capital of the World" (95); Nicholas Joost saw it simply as a dramatic contrast between the American and Spanish cultures, which misses the analogy suggested in the final paragraph (150–51); and Carlos Baker passed by the story as a "final tribute to Maera," which it is (184).

Philip Yanella concluded his study of the story's manuscript and text with the argument that the issue of the story rests in the "distinction between reality and romance, good art and bad art," and finally between the "romance of the unusual" proclaimed by *The Forum* and the last paragraph's presentation of the real "as a matter of unadorned facticity" (178).

Wayne Kvam's close reading of the story's structure and its text extends Yanella's conclusion toward statements of Hemingway's "aesthetic" in *Death in the Afternoon, Green Hills of Africa,* and *For Whom the Bell Tolls.* Here he is persuasive; but when he reads paragraphs 1, 2, and 9 as the "writer's definition of life [that] also includes romance" rather than part of the parody of the "romance of the unusual," he misses the broad humor of "cricketers . . . sharpening up their wickets" and the sound "in the far-off dripping jungles of Yucatan . . . of the axes of the gum-choppers" (*Stories* 360; Kvam 188). Had he known that Hemingway's manuscript originally read: "How good it felt. | He farted silently into the warm depths. | Here, at last, was life" and *"There* was Romance. | He farted unvoluntarily |" (Yanella 175), one suspects that Kvam would have revised his interpretation of those passages.

Although between them the articles of Yanella and Kvam are unusual in their thorough consideration of the story's manuscript, its sources, analogues, structure, and the intent of its parody—which for two articles on a brief story is a great deal—there is more to be said.

There is the question of what part Hemingway's reading of *The Forum* may have played in his decision to record the real circumstances of the death of Maera; or, to complicate the matter, how his reading of the death of Maera may have contributed to his creation of a persona who at times—as Kvam's analysis may suggest—seems to come close to accepting the assumptions of *The Forum*. If these questions are still open, then the importance of this story in the development of Hemingway's aesthetic principles deserves reconsideration.

Perhaps all of these issues rest in the intention of the title: Which part or aspect of this work is a "Banal Story"? Certainly, for Hemingway, the parodied sources in *The Forum;* but it is more likely that banality is an honorific term for the account of the death of Maera, especially so if its antonym is the "romance of the unusual" in the words of America's "intellectual periodical" (Kvam 183).

Hemingway's antipathy to *The Forum* and what it represented lasted for years. Twice in 1929 and 1930 he received letters from Henry G. Leach requesting a story and prescribing its form; and in one manuscript he considered publishing "Three Love Stories," including "The Sea Change," introduced with a laconic statement of that journal's prescriptions for fiction (KL/EH, Henry G. Leach to Hemingway 28 June 1929, 2 May 1930; KL/EH 681). And probably about that time he wrote out a sketch that began with *The Forum*'s description of its audience, its requirements for a "narrative or at least plot" and no more than three thousand words. Then he wrote a sketch of the death of a bullfighter, Angel Carralta, "which occurred yesterday morning at 10:15 in the infirmary of the Plaza de Toros in the town of Inca in the Island of Mallorca"—a sketch that would not meet those requirements for it "was completely without plot" (KL/EH 681 A).

Works Cited

PRIMARY

Ernest Hemingway: Selected Letters, 1917-961. Ed. Carlos Baker. New York: Scribner's, 1981.

The Short Stories of Ernest Hemingway. New York: Scribner's, 1938, 360-62.

SECONDARY

Baker, Carlos. *Ernest Hemingway: A Life Story.* 1969. New York: Scribner's, 1988.

DeFalco, Joseph. *The Hero in Hemingway's Short Stories.* Pittsburgh: U of Pittsburgh P, 1963.

Joost, Nicholas. *Ernest Hemingway and the Little Magazines.* Barre, MA: Barre Publishers, 1968.

Kvam, Wayne. "Hemingway's 'Banal Story.' " *Fitzgerald/Hemingway Annual* (1974): 181-91.

Yanella, Philip Y. "Notes on the Manuscript, Date, and Sources of Hemingway's 'Banal Story.' " *Fitzgerald/Hemingway Annual* (1974): 175-79.

17

The Battler

Composition History (December 1924–March 1925)

Among all the letters of February and March 1925 and the two surviving manuscripts of "The Battler" there is some confusing evidence for dating the story's composition. Carlos Baker's account in the biography places its revision after Hemingway first learned that Boni and Liveright had accepted *In Our Time* with two cables from Harold Loeb and Donald Ogden Stewart sent on 22 and 23 February, received on the 26th, and ecstatically answered in a letter to Loeb on the 27th. Liveright's confirming cable arrived on 5 March, but a letter in mid-March objected to a passage in "Mr. and Mrs. Elliot" and all of "Up in Michigan."

But then Baker has Hemingway revising the story "through the night of February 12th and finishing it on the morning of Friday the 13th" (140–41). His evidence is a letter from Hemingway to Ernest Walsh dated "Friday–Feb 13–1925" in which he wrote that "Liveright is making me cut a story ["Up in Michigan"] and I've had to finish—revise and type another" (Barrett Library, University of Virginia; see Baker 586–87). The second story Hemingway had to finish, in the sense of having to "revise and type," might have been the carbon of the "Mr. and Mrs. Elliot" typescript he had submitted to the *Little Review,* which was about to appear. Nothing in this letter, whenever it was written, clearly identifies "The Battler."

That letter is in answer to two from Walsh of 4–5 February and would have been received just as Hemingway was on his way up to the Madlenerhaus for more than two weeks of skiing. It opens with an apology and notes that "we've just now come down." It seems likely that the letter was misdated: none of his other letters from 14–17 February to William B. Smith now in the Princeton Library Collection notes Liveright's acceptance; his letter to Walsh of 9 March proudly announces the news of the forthcoming volume but says nothing of their objections to "Up in Michigan" (*Letters* 152); and incidentally *March* 13 fell on a Friday, too.

The first manuscript (KL/EH 269), however, supports Baker's suggestion that the story was begun in mid-December 1924. The first four pages were written in ink and the remaining fifteen typed with holograph revisions. All through the following January Hemingway wrote to friends that he had done nothing "beyond starting 3 or 4 stories and not being able to go on with them" and that "as usual in the country I have an awful time writing" (*Letters* 144, 147). Hemingway spent most of February skiing in the mountains east of Schruns and returned to Paris on 13 March. It would have made sense for him to postpone the revision of his first draft (KL/EH 269) and to complete his typescript (KL/EH 270) on his return to Paris where he had written so well a year ago. If so, "The Battler" was completed sometime between early March, when he knew he had to replace "Up in Michigan," and the 31st, when he returned the "signed contract and a new story to replace the one you are eliminating as censorable" (*Letters* 154).

Liveright must have received a typescript close to Hemingway's (KL/EH 270): in that letter of 31 March Hemingway noted rather ingenuously, "that it is no longer necessary to eliminate that fine old word son of a bitch," and his typescript uses it several times; but Liveright preferred another fine old word and substituted *bastard*. So, too, almost consistent references to Bugs as *nigger* in the typescript become *negro* in the text. Finally, Hemingway's titles changed from "The Great Man" (KL/EH 269) to a title in the letter of 31 March, "The Great Little Fighting Machine," rejected for the one it now bears, "The Battler."

Publication History (October 1925)

Hemingway waited over a month to hear from Liveright. In the meantime he wrote to John Dos Passos that "this Battler . . . is a hell of a swell new Nick story and better than Up in Mich" (*Letters* 157). Finally they replied with the contract, a check for two hundred dollars, and some objections about the "fine old word," for Hemingway almost apologetically noted he had seen the word in proofs of Harold Loeb's book and Scott Fitzgerald's *The Great Gatsby* (*Letters* 160). On 22 May he returned the galley proofs and it took the fifth position following "The Three-Day Blow" in the sequence of *In Our Time* stories.

Sources and Influences

Two aspects of "The Battler"—its setting and the original or originals for the punch-drunk Ad Francis—have been identified. Carlos Baker first summarized a Hemingway notebook recording a fishing trip with Lewis Clarahan on 10–17 June 1916 (24–25). Frederic Svoboda has retraced the route from Kalkaska to Mancelona and noted the differences between the actual and literary landscapes: Hemingway extended the tamarack swamp by many miles, widened the river, and placed a bridge where there was only an embankment (41–44). Svoboda's suggestion that the swamp and the bridge might have been reflected in those in "Big Two-Hearted River" may have some point, for he had completed the revision of that story sometime in November 1924. None of the events of the story, however, has much to do with Hemingway's experience on the trip—he bought a ticket from Kalkaska to Mancelona for twenty-seven cents (Svoboda 44).

Philip Young suspected that Ad Wolgast, "The Michigan Wildcat," was the model for Ad Francis: he was the "lightweight champion of the world in 1910 but lost most of his mind in the process, spent away a fortune and was declared legally incompetent in 1917" (37 n.). In a letter to Carlos Baker, Hemingway identified Francis as a composite of Wolgast and Oscar "Battling" Nelson and Bugs as Wolgast's trainer "in the period of his decline" (141, 587). Nicholas Gerogiannis finds the model for "Ad Francis' stamina" in Nelson's "almost inhuman capacity for taking punishment" and the cause of his "simple-mindedness and confused memory" in Wolgast's career of fighting "with his face."

Georgiannis's article is more interesting in noting the elements that Hemingway invented: Wolgast was cared for by Jack Doyle, a white man, and neither Wolgast nor Nelson "was ever managed by his sister (or any woman) . . ., ever married his sister, or was ever involved in a scandal that resembles what happened to Ad Francis" (187–88 n.).

For the story's literary sources, Philip Young drew on "The Battler" in his claims for the more pervasive influence of Mark Twain's *The Adventures of Huckleberry Finn*. Hemingway substituted the railroad for Twain's river and "significantly intensified Huck's misadventures for a later generation," in particular Huck's meeting with the Duke and the Dauphin. "While the two river tramps were only moderately—and often amusingly—sinister, the railroad tramps are intensely so, and they are not funny." And when Bugs takes over Jim's role as obsequious servant to the Dauphin, "what was innocent play in Twain has become something else in Hemingway, just as what was innocent affection in Jim is something else again in Bugs" (236–37; see also Glen Singer, Item 9).

Gerogiannis later cited two disparate literary analogues: Henry Fielding's "The Man on the Hill" episodes in *Tom Jones* (bk. 5, chaps. 10–15; bk. 9, chap. 2) and Jack London's articles on his life as a tramp in *Cosmopolitan* (May 1907–March 1908) and *The Road* (1907). The influence of Jack London on Hemingway's writing began early in his unpublished fiction of 1919–21; and if this story was written as a last minute substitute, he might well have turned to a formula he had used before—an innocent narrator who hears an insider's story in a confrontation with an experienced veteran or boxer (Smith 576).

The analogy with Fielding's "Man on the Hill" story rests largely on a perceived relationship between this story and Hemingway's later story "The Last Good Country": that is, in Fielding the episode leads into a "mock-incestuous" involvement between Tom and his mother Jenny Jones; Ad

Francis's relationship with his "sister" is, as far as we know, a rumored one; and the relationship between Nick and his sister "Littless" in "The Last Good Country" is largely her fantasy, although there are some cuddly moments that make one wince for Nick. Moreover, "The Last Good Country," was written in the 1950s, although it does precede "The Battler" in the chronology of Nick Adams's career.

Finally, "The Battler" should be read within the sequence of stories of past and present boxers from the early Chicago fiction through "Fifty Grand" and "The Killers" and, as Joseph DeFalco and Joseph Flora have done, with the other story set on the rail line to Petoskey, "The Light of the World."

Critical Studies

However likely it is that Hemingway reverted, in a sense, to a variety of formula fiction he had experimented with years before in Chicago, it is apparent that writing the *In Our Time* stories in 1924, especially "Big Two-Hearted River," informed his sense of what sort of story would be appropriate in the collection that brought Nick Adams through his adolescence with "The Three-Day Blow" and then returned to him, or someone like him, after the war with "Soldier's Home" and "Cross-Country Snow." Some "threshold experience," as Joseph DeFalco terms it, or some initiatory conflict beyond the boyhood region of Walloon Lake, in Joseph Flora's study, could well have seemed appropriate for the collection. It is relevant, too, that in an early arrangement of the stories (probably in September 1924), Hemingway considered switching the places of "The Three-Day Blow" and "My Old Man" (KL/EH 97A), which at the cost of breaking the unity of "The End of Something" and "The Three-Day Blow," would have offered something of an initiation into the adult world that is shared by "My Old Man" and "The Battler."

In any case, this story seems to benefit from what he had learned with "Indian Camp"—a sudden introduction to a dark wilderness, a bewildering and violent experience in the firelight, a protective figure, and a departure with a concluding sentence that comes close to that in "Indian Camp" with its moment of discovery and the cadence of its introductory phrases: "He found he had a ham sandwich in his hand and put it in his pocket. Looking back from the mounting grade before the track curved into the hills he could see the firelight in the clearing" (*Stories* 138).

Yet it is the elements of the story that are unaccounted for by Hemingway's boyhood fishing trips, the history of boxing, or its placement in the collection that mark "The Battler" as a mature work. For example, it may be that Hemingway had nothing more in mind than the shuffling gentility of the stereotypical black in the character of Bugs; but a blackjack at the base of the skull—"I'm afraid I hit him just a little hard." (*Stories* 136)—seems excessive. Philip Young (39), Arthur Waldhorn (58–59), and Joseph DeFalco (77) all suggest that the relationship between the fighter and his black companion is homosexual, almost sadistic, and for Hemingway sinister at the least.

Others may take a more benign view. William Bache held that the function of the campsite scene is to disabuse Nick of the "easy dichotomy" that divides the world into "kid things—naiveté, friendliness, candor—and adult things—cruelty, deception, hypocrisy." The episode at the camp blurs those distinctions when Ad assumes the role of a child but is clearly "crazy," and when Bugs takes the role of a "mammy," a sentimental figure from childhood, but with a brutal blackjack (Item 4). And recently Joseph Flora argued that Bugs is a "true professional . . . who cares about quality" in campsite cooking and in the conversational amenities (93).

But those polite conversational counters take on a surreal, almost terrifying, absurdity in those violent circumstances, as when Bugs says "I wish we could ask you to stay the night but it's just out of the question" (*Stories* 138). Such remarks remind us of Philip Young's sense that "we have heard before [that] unctuousness [and] obsequious servility" in Twain and, he might have added, even earlier in Melville's "Benito Cereno."

Moreover, the story still awaits some explanation of the motive for placing at its center Bugs's revelation of what, after all the beatings, finally drove Ad Francis crazy, the "unpleasantness" over the reported fact that he had married his sister—something that Nick remembers (*Stories* 136–37). Some later history of boxing may reveal an incestuous pugilist, but the question will remain: of all the possible revelations in fact or fiction, why did Hemingway settle on this one?

Other than on these contested or unanswered questions—the role of Bugs, which some see as threatening and others as both paternal and ogreish (DeFalco 77), and the apparently inexplicable concern with rumored or actual incest—the critical commentaries on this story are in unusual agreement. The more persuasive interpretations view the story as Nick Adams's initiation into a world where men are beaten and deformed and finally driven crazy. Nick still has the adolescent bravado to claim he is from Chicago and has "got to be tough" (*Stories* 131, 133), but his swaggering is as empty here as it is in "The Killers"—he is embarrassed and sickened by the sight of the fighter's beaten head.

When Ad Francis asks Nick if he's "ever been crazy," Nick says "No," and asks, "How does it get you?" (*Stories* 132). That question clearly places the story before the action of "Big Two-Hearted River," for in the latter story Nick knows its answer.

Frank Kyle's comparative study of "The Battler" and "Big Two-Hearted River" distinguishes between the narratives of a younger Nick Adams that "portray a pre-initiatory period of innocence" ("Indian Camp," "The Doctor and The Doctor's Wife," and "Ten Indians") and those in which Nick has passed beyond "formal initiation rites [to] learn life himself, through experience" (295). He notes the similar and contrasting elements of "The Battler" and "Big Two-Hearted River": the railroads, the vicious brakeman and the solicitous baggageman, the two campsites and their campfires against the "gloomy obscurity of the dark and misty swamps" (296–99). To associate the two stories as parts of one complex initiation, Kyle reads "The Battler" as Nick's first journey alone into an adult world and his "first personally painful encounter with society." But he has yet to ascribe "social evil" to the "general nature of mankind" and to comprehend the significance of security and order maintained in the outcasts' campsite (298). To connect the two stories, Kyle argues that Nick has been to the war in the interim and, in the former story, learns to control his own suffering with the ordered rituals of his own campsite, confronts the swamp, and returns to society (300).

Such a reading places some strain on both stories and obscures clear differences in vasty phrases—like "irrational evil"—but it serves to demonstrate that when Hemingway was pressed for another story in early 1925, he had in mind that interval between Nick's adolescence in "The Three-Day Blow" and his maturity in the postwar narratives. The episodic chronicle of Nick Adams needed a predictive moment when the callow kid who claims he is tough can catch a portentous glimpse of someone who has been so beaten his memory goes awry.

Works Cited

PRIMARY

Ernest Hemingway: Selected Letters, 1917–1961. Ed. Carlos Baker. New York: Scribner's, 1981.

The Short Stories of Ernest Hemingway. New York: Scribner's, 1938, 129–38.

SECONDARY

Bache, William. "Hemingway's 'The Battler.'" *Explicator* 13 (Oct. 1954), Item 4.

Baker, Carlos. *Ernest Hemingway: A Life Story.* 1969. New York: Scribner's, 1988.

DeFalco, Joseph. *The Hero in Hemingway's Fiction.* Pittsburgh: U of Pittsburgh P, 1963.

Flora, Joseph M. *Hemingway's Nick Adams.* Baton Rouge: Louisiana State UP, 1982.

Gerogiannis, Nicholas. "Nick Adams on the Road: 'The Battler' as Hemingway's Man on the Hill." *Critical Essays on Ernest Hemingway's "In Our Time."* Ed. Michael Reynolds. Boston: Hall, 1983.

Kyle, Frank B. "Parallel and Complementary Themes in Hemingway's Big Two-Hearted River Stories and 'The Battler.'" *Studies in Short Fiction* 16 (1979): 295–300.

Singer, Glen W. "Huck, Ad, Jim, and Bugs: A Reconsideration, *Huckleberry Finn* and Hemingway's 'The Battler.'" *Notes on Modern American Literature* 3 (1978), Item 9.

Smith, Paul. "Hemingway's Apprentice Fiction: 1919–1921." *American Literature* 58 (Dec. 1986): 574–88.

Svoboda, Frederic Joseph. "Inventing from Experience in 'The Battler.'" *Up in Michigan: Proceedings of the First National Conference of the Hemingway Society.* Ed. Joseph J. Waldmeir. East Lansing: Michigan State UP, 1983.

Waldhorn, Arthur. *A Reader's Guide to Ernest Hemingway.* New York: Farrar, 1972.

Young, Philip. *Ernest Hemingway: A Reconsideration.* 1952. New York: Harcourt, 1966.

Men Without Women
(October 1927)

18

Fifty Grand

Composition History (January 1924–November 1925)

Carlos Baker's dating of the composition of "Fifty Grand" in October or November 1925 (157) is supported by a manuscript fragment that includes three pages of a bullfight story and a one-page "Outline of 2nd Book of Short Stories" (KL/EH 596). Among the stories Hemingway marked "To Write" are an "Indian Story (Started in Chartres)" and a "Boxing Story—Fifty Grand." The first version of "Ten Indians" was written in a notebook dated in Chartres, 27 September 1925 (KL/EH 202 C); and in a 24 December letter Hemingway referred to the boxing story as familiar to Scott Fitzgerald (*Letters* 180).

The idea for the story—or what he thought was its idea—had been in his mind for some time. Three related manuscript fragments suggest that on his return from Toronto to Paris in January 1924, he sketched out some introductory sentences for stories about his experiences in Chicago and notes for "Fifty Grand" (KL/EH 386, 605, 387). The first (386) includes notes on a fighter, some "Wicked New Yorkers," and comments of a "Jerry" on women and Jews in a hotel lobby, all on letterhead from the R.M.S. *Antonia* on which Hemingway returned to France. The second (605) lists some beginning sentences on Nick Neroni, Krebs, a typist, and Paul Dallas Rust (all Chicago acquaintances); and the third (387) continues these and ends with what Hemingway recalled as "that lovely revelation of the metaphysics of boxing" that began the original version of the story. Fitzgerald recommended deleting that introduction; Hemingway did and never forgave him for it. It reads: " 'Say, Jack,' I said, 'how did you happen to beat . . . Leonard?' 'Well,' Jack said, 'Benny's a pretty smart boxer. All the time he's in there, he's thinking, and all the time he's thinking, I'm hitting him' " (KL/EH 387; "Art of the Short Story" 89).

The one remaining typescript in the Kennedy Collection (388) includes only the first three and the last page of the story, bears a rejected title, "Jack," and Hemingway's note, "1st 3 pages of story mutilated by Scott Fitzgerald with his [illegible] unaltered" as well as Fitzgerald's note to cut on page three—"do yourself" (Beegel 15). In 1959 Hemingway recalled writing the story with that "metaphysical" beginning and deleting it in deference to Scott to point up a lesson on "how dangerous that attractive virtue, humility, can be" ("Art of the Short Story" 89); but all three pages of the typescript deserved to be cut; and however lovely the revelation seemed in retrospect, it had less to do with the story than Hemingway imagined.

Later manuscripts may well turn up: Hemingway sent the story to a variety of journals, gave it to Manuel Komsoff to shorten, and sent a typescript to Maxwell Perkins at *Scribner's Magazine* with the cuts marked *stet* on 4 May 1927 for publication in *Men Without Women*. (See Scott Donaldson and Susan Beegel for detailed studies of the story's composition.)

Publication History (July, October 1927)

From the outset Hemingway considered "Fifty Grand," like "My Old Man" and "The Undefeated," to be in a far less important category, "not the thing I'm shooting for . . . , [t]he kind that are easy for me to write" (*Letters* 180, Hemingway to Fitzgerald, 24 December 1925). By mid-March 1926 it had gone to *Colliers,* the *Saturday Evening Post,* and *Liberty* and was turned down; then even *Scribner's Magazine* rejected it as too long. In May he expected it to be translated for the summer issue of *Nouvelle Review Française,* but had to wait a year. By September he had given it to Manuel Komsoff to cut, and later wrote to Perkins that he hoped it would be published "before boxing is abolished" and suggested sending it to *College Humor.* In January 1927 he told Perkins to send it to the *Atlantic Monthly,* then in February hoped they would reject it.

Once reconciled to its first publication in his second volume of short stories, he sent Perkins the manuscript he had given to Komroff to cut with the deletions restored; whereupon the *Atlantic Monthly* published it in July 1927, and *Nouvelle Revue Française* followed in August with "Cinquante mille dollars" (*Letters* 197, 205, 219, 225, 230, 241, 247).

This complex history of the publication of "Fifty Grand" seems to reflect Hemingway's sometime attraction to a popular market when his accounts were low and his submission of stories that were perhaps too "easy" for him to write. But his luck was with him when the *Atlantic Monthly* offered him $350—the most he "had yet been paid for a short story" (Carlos Baker 182)—and with that honor the story entered the canon in the fall of that year with the publication of *Men Without Women.*

Sources and Influences

As with "The Undefeated," for which speculation began with one torero's career and ended with several, so commentary on *the* original prizefight behind "Fifty Grand" has ended with evidence that Hemingway drew on at least two for this narrative. Phillips and Rosemary Davies draw on the *New*

York Times and *New York Herald* accounts of the Jack Britton-Mickey Walker fight in New York's Madison Square Garden 1 November 1922, the similarities of their names to those of the fictional characters (Jack Brennan, Jimmy Walcott), their careers, and some questions raised about the fight itself, to argue that Hemingway's reliance upon these details forced him to "resort to what verges on melodrama" to reconcile Britton's real courage and Brennan's final throwing of the fight (258).

Carlos Baker, with the original introductory remark in hand, associated the fight with the Jack Britton-Benny Leonard contest in New York's Hippodrome 26 June 1922. Citing the manuscripts of the story and "The Art of the Short Story," Baker considered Dan Daniel's account in *The Ring* of "Leonard's Foul Punch" evidence for the earlier fight (590).

Finally, James Martine questioned both single sources. The Davies's argument for the Britton-Walker fight is suspect since there were no foul punches; and Baker's is improbable since "a fighter does not go to camp to prepare for a bout he has already fought"—that is, if the initial anecdote from the Britton-Leonard fight is a matter of history, why are the two fighting again? Martine offers a third and celebrated fight that Hemingway witnessed (as he had not the other two) between Battling Siki and George Carpentier on 24 September 1922 in the Mont Rouge arena in Paris. Siki, a flamboyant character Hemingway could not have missed in the Parisian cafés, was—on his own admission—to throw the fight; he "fairly battered Carpentier into oblivion"; then the referee "stopped the fight, awarding it to Carpentier on a foul." But the crowd, including Hemingway, objected so strongly, "the fight officials . . . awarded the bout to Siki" (124). Martine concludes that the fictional prizefight was "an amalgamation of at least two real-life bouts" (125). And a good deal more, one would add. None of the fights cited, for all the similarities in names or the suggestions of foul blows, offers an original for the story's "counter double-cross"—not a doubling of the double-cross, as Baker suggests (157). So it comes as no surprise that Hemingway drew on some familiar names and the recent history of boxing he had so avidly followed, and then complicated those materials in a fictional twist of his own invention.

Perhaps in recalling those fights of 1922 Hemingway was impelled even further into his past to his earliest fiction. His second high school story, "A Matter of Colour," published in the *Tabula* of April 1916, has some of the rudimentary elements of "Fifty Grand": narrated by a boxer's manager, Bob Armstrong, it tells of a fighter with a bad hand, if not at the end of his career, and depends for the twist in the plot on an improbable trick that fails and for its humor on ethnic stereotypes (Sheridan Baker 62). Hemingway repeated this formula, learned from Lardner, O. Henry, and Kipling, in two of his Chicago stories of 1919–21, "The Woppian Way" and "The Current"; and in them he developed a narrative voice—mixing the periphrastic and colloquial in the sports writer's style (Smith 576–79). The mannerisms of that style were discarded, happily, when he began to see boxing as more than an occasion for a tricky plot, an ethnic joke, or an exuberant metaphor—and "Fifty Grand" marks that change.

"Fifty Grand" should be read in the sequence of four other stories from 1922 to 1926: three that preceded it, "My Old Man" (1922), "The Undefeated" (1924), and "The Battler" (1925); and, of course, the one that perfects them all, "The Killers" (1926). With "My Old Man" Hemingway drew again on the first-person narrator intimate with the protagonist who wins in defeat—although the roles of the tutor and tyro are reversed—and a plot in which a fixed game is spoiled, the cheaters cheated. Like Manuel Garcia in "The Undefeated," Jack Brennan endures the punishment of his last fight to lose on his own terms; and "The Battler" suggests a dark final chapter for the fighter that went too many rounds and now lives in the past with the brutal mercies of his trainer. Finally, "Fifty Grand" may be read as part of what Hemingway claimed he left out of "The Killers" along with "all Chicago" ("Art of the Short Story" 100). Ole Andreson could have been guilty of double-crossing a syndicate as was Brennan, but by May 1926 Hemingway had learned to leave that as a suggestion and turn to the larger questions of how one faces, not a syndicate but an immutable fate.

Critical Studies

When Wirt Williams admitted that in "Fifty Grand" "irony and reversal are followed so swiftly by counter-irony and counter-reversal [and] catastrophe and transcendence displace each other so rapidly that one has a problem telling which is which" (96), he marked the source of radical disagreement among the story's critical readers. Jack Brennan is either a "homebody, worrywart, tightwad fighter" (Sheridan Baker 61) or "the consummate professional, . . . like the king of old, [with] *hybris*" (Martine 127); and the story is either "supremely comical (Rovit 61) or a "meaningful *agon* . . . with the forces of immorality" (DeFalco 212). Some part of the controversy depends on differing conceptions of what is meant by "professional," or more general constructs like the "code-hero," the "tutor," and the "tyro," or even whether one low blow deserves another—or two.

Once again Philip Young raised the issue when he argued that Jack Brennan, like Manuel in "The Undefeated" and Harry Morgan in *To Have and Have Not*, are code-heroes in facing "the conditions of life, which is a highly compromising affair, . . . making a deal with it, and then sticking to his bargain if it kills him" (65). This assumes, of course, that more conventional moral positions on murder, as with Harry Morgan, for example, or on betting against oneself, as with Jack Brennan—are irrelevant.

With this much forgiven, one can invoke archetypal associations, as did DeFalco, in order to see Brennan's suffering a low blow as an "ordeal that transcends the moral quality of the wager" and also, by analogy with Faustus and Mephistopheles, as an act that "defeats the forces of immorality upon their own grounds" (211–12). Arthur Waldhorn, too, found "Fifty Grand" a "nasty story of an attempted double-cross" and still pardoned Brennan as one impelled by the code to "honor even a dishonorable agreement," since that code "asks of a man that he try to impose meaning where none seems possible, that he try in every gesture to impress his will on the raw material of life" (27). And however perplexing the story, Wirt Williams found that Brennan's "real enemy is time" and that he achieves an ironic "triumph-in-loss" (97). For all these critics the story represents an approximation of tragedy.

But for others it is a comic story. For Earl Rovit, Brennan is a parsimonious lout—he does avoid the tip and play a mean game of cribbage—so that when he must choose between the championship and fifty grand, his choice and his remarks are predictable " 'It's funny how fast you can think when it means that much money' " (*Stories* 326). But conceding this, Rovit also had to admit that the story is an "exposure in venality to the non-committed first-person narrator (the tyro), and an indication that the professionals (tutors) can be trusted only within their special areas of mastery" (44–45). Sheridan Baker argued that "Fifty Grand" is a comic version of "The Undefeated," that Jerry Doyle's "limited intelligence turns all the tawdry details comic and frank," and that we are given "the wisdom of the ring as if it were the wisdom of the world" (61–62). And that is the issue: if it is not, the story approaches comedy; if it is, it approaches tragedy.

Phillips and Rosemary Davies suggested that the discrepancy between the earlier parts of the story and the ending was the result of a "less than perfect joining of factual and imaginative elements" that "verges on melodrama in order to link the unsavory aura of illegal gambling with the real courage of Jack Britton" (257–58). James Martine met them and others on their own grounds by partially discounting the Britton-Walker fight except for the names of the fighters and some others. Citing the Siki-Carpentier fight, he argued that the story is more important as a recreation of the decade from 1919 to 1929 of "swindling managers and fouls aplenty and referees of dubious credentials," of Prohibition and a time when "prizefighters were more important (and better known) than presidents" (125).

So it was—perhaps still is—but the question remains: is Jack Brennan a lout or a hero? Martine admitted there is something loutish about him but held that "heroism exists especially in, and in spite of, the 'sordid, everyday world.' " Citing Doyle, he noted, " 'Everybody's got to get it sometime.' Everyone loses, of course; it is *how* that matters." The code is invoked again: "If life must beat you, . . . there is nothing 'unethical' about getting some small consideration for participating in the game . . . which can only go against you" (125–27).

Any review of the critical commentary on "Fifty Grand" must note that it is unusually extensive for a relatively slight though long story. Much of it is spent identifying one or several of its sources, and most commentators find themselves impelled to the limits of comedy by the story's inconsistencies or to the limits of tragedy by its associations with other stories and characters who more clearly act within the confines of the code-hero, the tutor, or the tyro. Those that find the story comic offer a nice corrective for the story's more ponderous readings, as does Earl Rovit when he suggests a variation on the concept of the tutor and tyro. And Martine, who tends toward a more tragic reading, notes that the narrator, Jerry Doyle, is no innocent tyro, while Jack Brennan is hardly a tutor (126).

All that criticism leaves at least two comments to make, one practical and the other theoretical. Jack Brennan's bet on Walcott is a bet *for* himself, and he knows very well what Jerry Doyle presumes to tell him, that "Everybody's got to get it sometime" (*Stories* 304). For him the fight is not fixed but inevitable, and so he advises Jerry to put money on Walcott even after he has spent a half hour with the fixers, Steinfelt and Morgan (*Stories* 308–09, 313). So Brennan's bet on himself is more a recognition of his prospects, an honest bet, not a fix. If he fails, morally or otherwise, it is when he realizes in the twelfth round that the fight has been fixed for him to win on Walcott's foul. So he fouls Walcott twice, once to set things even, and a second time to win not only the way the syndicate would have but also the only way he could.

Finally, there is a way to reconcile the controversy between those who read "Fifty Grand" as a comedy and those who read it as a tragedy. Both may be right, if the story is conceived as an ironic narrative, one that intermingles the narratives and juxtaposes the expectations of both the comic and tragic to arrive at the sort of dead center with which the story ends: " 'No,' Jack says, 'It was nothing' " (*Stories* 326). If Brennan is too much a parsimonious lout to be tragic, or one who has seen and suffered too much to be comic, then neither critical term may suit him or the story. We might resolve that conflict by conceiving of Jack as a typically ironic character in a typically ironic narrative balanced between the dispensations of both tragedy and comedy.

Works Cited

PRIMARY

"The Art of the Short Story." *Paris Review* 23 (Spring 1981): 85–102.

Ernest Hemingway: Selected Letters, 1917–1961. Ed. Carlos Baker. New York: Scribner's, 1981.

The Short Stories of Ernest Hemingway. New York: Scribner's, 1938, 300–26.

SECONDARY

Baker, Carlos. *Ernest Hemingway: A Life Story.* 1969. Scribner's, 1988.

Baker, Sheridan. *Ernest Hemingway.* New York: Holt, 1967.

Beegel, Susan F. *Hemingway's Craft of Omission: Four Manuscript Examples.* Ann Arbor: UMI Research, 1988.

Davies, Phillips G., and Rosemary R. Davies. "Hemingway's 'Fifty Grand' and the Jack Britton-Mickey Walker Prize-Fight." *American Literature* 37 (Nov. 1965): 251–58.

DeFalco, Joseph. *The Hero in Hemingway's Short Stories.* Pittsburgh: U of Pittsburgh P, 1963.

Donaldson, Scott. "The Wooing of Ernest Hemingway." *American Literature* 53 (Jan. 1982): 691–710.

Martine, James J. "Hemingway's 'Fifty Grand': The Other Fight(s)." *Journal of Modern Literature* 2 (Sept. 1971): 123–27.

Rovit, Earl. *Ernest Hemingway.* Boston: Twayne, 1963.

Smith, Paul. "Hemingway's Apprentice Fiction: 1919–1921." *American Literature* 58 (Dec. 1986): 574–88.

Waldhorn, Arthur. *A Reader's Guide to Ernest Hemingway.* New York: Farrar, 1972.

Williams, Wirt. *The Tragic Art of Ernest Hemingway.* Baton Rouge: Louisiana State UP, 1981.

Young, Philip. *Ernest Hemingway: A Reconsideration.* 1952. New York: Harcourt, 1966.

19

An Alpine Idyll

Composition History (April 1926)

Carlos Baker's chapter, "The Year of the Avalanches," recounting the second winter in Schruns from early December 1925 to late January, Hemingway's February trip to New York to sign with Scribner's, and the revision of *The Sun Also Rises* in March 1926, leaves little time for the completion of "An Alpine Idyll" before his return to Paris in early April. Certainly the experiences of those dark winter months, beginning with deadly avalanches, the tales they must have occasioned of death in the snow, and ending with his infidelity in Paris hotel rooms, the lies and the remorse, and always "the need to write, other needs," provided a perfect scene for the story (Baker, *Ernest Hemingway: A Life Story* 160–68).

There are four manuscripts of the story (KL/EH 244–47). The earliest is a titled pencil manuscript that may have been written some months earlier (244); the second, untitled and in pencil, is identified in another hand as "First or Early Draft" and is closer to the final version (245); the third is a Hemingway typescript carbon with the Paris address of the Guaranty Trust Co. of New York, his "regular" address during the dissolution of his marriage (*Letters* 206). On 4 May 1926 he wrote to Fitzgerald he had "finished a story—short—and am sending it to Scribners tomorrow" and noted when he signed it Ernest, "(Christ what a name)" (*Letters* 203). A month later, with no word from *Scribner's Magazine,* he wrote to Perkins asking whether they had ever received it and noting he had another copy, probably the professional typescript (KL/EH 247) (*Letters* 209, 5 June 1926).

The first manuscript has some of the marks of an early sketch. He set in place elements on which he might build toward several implications he could leave out later as he did with the manuscripts of "Ten Indians" and "The Killers." In this manuscript the skiers have returned from the "Madlenerhaus" to find their mail; in the published version they have returned from the "Wiesbadenerhutte." (The year before, Hemingway had returned from the Madlenerhaus to Schruns to find cables accepting *In Our Time.*) Galtur and "the other side of Paznaun" where the peasant lives (*Stories* 347) are some fifty kilometers east of Schruns, as Baker notes, so Hemingway may have deliberately moved the setting east to set the story apart from both the skiing of 1924–25 and from his likely sources among the townspeople of Schruns in the winter of 1925–26.

In this first try Hemingway also makes clear the general sense that the peasant Olz is crazy: He forces the sexton to drink schnapps, "if you drink with me," and orders a liter of it. "You're crazy," says the sexton. "No, I don't think so," Olz replies. Later the waitress winks knowingly at the two Americans and the sexton taps his forehead.

Other elements of this manuscript are more revealing. First, John thinks of the narrator as a writer. He says, "That's a good story for you. It's a good thing I've got a good appetite." And the narrator replies, "It's no good. Nobody would believe it." And at the end the two skiers wonder whether Olz may have killed his wife. In this manuscript, then, Hemingway not only establishes the possibilities that the peasant is insane and murdered his wife; but also that the narrator is a writer considering both the peasant's motives and the story's credibility as fiction. All this seems to support Joseph Flora's interpretation of the story as a central episode in the development of Nick Adams as a writer.

But this manuscript offers a radically different version of the narration, if not the narrative. Here the two Americans are invited to join the sexton and the peasant to share the liter of schnapps; and the sexton, with leading questions, elicits the story directly from Olz, while in the final version the story is told by the sexton with some inaccurate and biased interpolations from the innkeeper after the peasant leaves. The critical question is whether the story is meant to be believed because it was originally told firsthand, or is suspect because it is finally retold secondhand soon after its original telling.

It was the revised version, however, that Hemingway sent to Perkins on 5 May 1926 (KL/EH 246 or more likely 247) for publication in *Scribner's Magazine*. It was shorter than "The Undefeated" but "too terrible, like certain stories by Chekhov and Gorky," for Scribner's readers (Baker, *Ernest Hemingway: A Life Story* 171).

Publication History (September, October 1927)

Scribner's rejection of "An Alpine Idyll" must have struck Hemingway as appropriate for the summer of 1926, for he wrote to Fitzgerald, "[o]ur life is all gone to hell which seems to be the one thing you can count on a good life to do." With little hope he submitted it to *New Masses*—in his mind "a puerile . . . house organ"—and they too rejected it (*Letters* 216–17). But Paul Rosenfeld, one of the editors of *The American Caravan*, had requested a story that summer; Hemingway considered sending "A Lack of Passion" and then could not finish it. When Rosenfeld asked again in January 1927, Hemingway asked Perkins to submit the story *Scribner's Magazine* had held so long and then rejected, for *The American Caravan* "is not only a book but a worthy American adventure" (*Letters* 241). Whatever the note of irony in the remark, he would have found some satisfaction in seeing the story appear in the September 1927 issue of *The American Caravan: A Yearbook of the American Short Story,* just one month before it was published in *Men Without Women.*

Sources and Influences

Both the story's macabre anecdote and the narrator's questioning its truth, have led some to assume that its sources may be found in a tradition of "Tyrolean 'tall tales' " of frozen and lantern-jawed corpses (Hattam 261). Carlos Baker suspected that Hemingway could have heard the tale from Fräulein Glaser, a young ski instructor in Schruns, "whose taste for the macabre" and stories of death and suicide he had sampled in March 1926 (*Ernest Hemingway: A Life Story* 168). But the fact of the tall-tale tradition has nothing to do with the fictional "facts" of the story, which, true or not, are less important than the narrator's response to them.

The structure of the narrative of the story was at hand. In his Chicago fiction of 1919–21, Hemingway had used a formula in which a knowledgeable narrator and an innocent companion enter a bar and hear an "inside" narrative from one or more "locals" and wonder over its meaning and validity—"The Mercenaries" and "The Woppian Way" are examples (Smith 576–77).

Finally, that the story draws on the macabre, the bizarre, or at least the unnatural—as the moralists have it—is hardly surprising: Hemingway's high school stories were adolescent revels in such incidents; his first work in the American Red Cross in Italy was to collect the human fragments after a munitions factory explosion in Milan; and from his wounding in 1918 on he was gathering materials for "A Natural History of the Dead." This much would suggest that he and his narrator would be less interested in whether the tale was true or false than in how one responds to its telling.

Critical Studies

That point was made early on when Philip Young compared "An Alpine Idyll" with "The Killers," another story of the spring of 1926, in which the focus "centers on the responses of the listeners" and not on the central incident itself (60). Even when Edward Hattam raised the question of the story's source in a tall tale, he noted that since it showed no "sign of levity," and that none of the minor characters—the innkeeper, the sexton, or priest—seems aware of such tales, Hemingway "chose to ignore the folk stories" of which he was quite aware (262–65).

But Myra Armistead argued otherwise. She noted that the peasant left after the innkeeper insulted him with a remark to the sexton in dialect. Thus the sexton had little time "to digest the incident into the story he now tells in such measured words," and when the innkeeper remarks, " 'This is where it's good,' " (*Stories* 348) it is as if he is contributing to a familiar story he has somehow convinced the sexton to tell in order to confirm his feeling that peasants, like Olz, are beasts (Armistead 257). This might explain why the narrator asks the innkeeper rather than the sexton, whom he suspects, if the story is true. Her analysis also bears on the innkeeper's last remark, " 'He didn't want to drink with me, after *he* [the sexton] knew about his wife,' " (*Stories* 349) in order to lend credibility to a tall tale (258). But however complex the story it is neither Nabokov's nor James's. And to read it as such, as does Armistead, is to reduce it to a Tyrolean joke on tourists and to gather its meaning in a condemnation of the Austrians who have "become insensitive to the feelings of their fellow man" (258).

Armistead drew on Carlos Baker's first analysis of the story in *Hemingway: The Writer as Artist*. There he associated the contrast between the "unnatural" skiing in the harsh sun of the mountains and the natural spring in the valley with that between the peasant's "sense of human dignity and decency" that had atrophied in the winter and that of the village once things had thawed into sensitivity (120). A nice parallel, but one could argue that the peasant is not brought "to judgment before the priest and sexton" (121); rather, their springtime morality is seriously questioned by the peasant's harsh mountain realism. Joseph DeFalco, for example, suggested that those who fail to understand the peasant's act miss his "absolute coming to terms with death" (216).

Until recently, critics have taken stern positions on the story's presentations of acts of "moral outrage" (Rovit 83), and the concluding decision to dine as the moral equivalent of some undergraduate's "goldfish eating" (Benson 55). But lately two more considered opinions counter those readings.

Wirt Williams has identified this story, as he did "The Undefeated," as an ironic tragedy, offering other terms like black comedy and even gallows humor as a fish to the uncritical. He sees the narrator's descent from "the 'unnatural' heat of the mountain sun . . . as an attempt to flee the life force." Williams might have found a better term, yet he was right to argue that "the impulse of life is not simply to continue in the face of, but even to obliterate, death, not so much by rejecting it as by absorbing it totally and dismissing it" (95–96). If that is the case—and Hemingway's refusal to offer this story as a tall tale and a trick on the innocent observers suggests it is—then, again, the story asks us to consider the drama of those who witness it.

Joseph Flora's extended analysis does just that, assuming that the story, as the manuscripts suggest, is told by Nick Adams, the writer. Although

Flora spent more energy than is needed to relate this story to "Cross-Country Snow" and its place in the Nick Adams chronology, his reading of the story lifts it out of the trivial concerns with its origins in Tyrolean tall tales or dead questions of morality. What Flora did so persuasively is to enter the mind and imagination of the narrator to reenact the story's drama of perception. He noticed why the priest does not return the customary greeting, "Gruss Gott," establishing that the priest and, one might presume, the sexton have learned something to make them "puzzle again over the nature of man" (200). "He notices, too, that the peasant spreads "the earth evenly as a man spreading manure in a garden" (*Stories* 343), the first and controlling metaphor of the story. That act, as Flora noted, is of a kind with the bereaved husband's telling remark in Frost's "Home Burial"—"Three foggy mornings and one rainy day/Will rot the best birch fence a man can build"—a recognition that all things, perhaps especially the best things, *are* things and so must rot, while those who are left must go on. Finally, the most compelling part of his reading is in those passages that interpret the descriptive and narrative paragraphs as moments in the narrator's or Nick Adams's developing awareness of the scene surrounding this anecdote, its narrator and audience, and his own responses to it.

Although Flora was as much concerned to place the story in a crucial position in the Nick Adams sequence, and he argued that point well, his sensitive and careful reading of the story would be as interesting if the narrator were anonymous.

Works Cited

PRIMARY

Ernest Hemingway: Selected Letters, 1917–1961. Ed. Carlos Baker. New York: Scribner's, 1981.

The Short Stories of Ernest Hemingway. New York: Scribner's, 1938, 343–49.

SECONDARY

Armistead, Myra. "Hemingway's 'An Alpine Idyll.'" *Studies in Short Fiction* 14 (1977): 255–58.

Baker, Carlos. *Ernest Hemingway: A Life Story.* 1969. Scribner's, 1988.

———. *Hemingway: The Writer as Artist.* 1952. Princeton: Princeton UP, 1972.

Benson, Jackson J. *Hemingway: The Writer's Art of Self-Defense.* Minneapolis: U of Minnesota P, 1969.

DeFalco, Joseph. *The Hero in Hemingway's Short Stories.* Pittsburgh: U of Pittsburgh P, 1963.

Flora, Joseph M. *Hemingway's Nick Adams.* Baton Rouge: Louisiana State UP, 1982.

Hattam, Edward. "Hemingway's 'An Alpine Idyll.'" *Modern Fiction Studies* 12 (Summer 1966): 261–65.

Rovit, Earl. *Ernest Hemingway*. Boston: Twayne, 1963.

Smith, Paul. "Hemingway's Apprentice Fiction: 1919–1921." *American Literature* 58 (Dec. 1986): 574–86.

Williams, Wirt. *The Tragic Art of Ernest Hemingway*. Baton Rouge: Louisiana State UP, 1981.

Young, Philip. *Ernest Hemingway: A Reconsideration*. 1952. New York: Harcourt, 1966.

20

The Killers

Composition History (September 1925–May 1926)

The story Hemingway told of the composition on 16 May 1926 of "The Killers," "Today Is Friday," and "Ten Indians" has assumed over the years the character of a legend like that of the accounts of his wounding in 1918 and the loss of the manuscripts in 1922. But when he first mentioned this marathon of writing in a letter to Max Perkins on 5 June 1926, he noted only that "in Madrid I wrote three stories ranging from 1400 to 3000 words" and held out the prospect that he would have them "re-typed and sent on" (*Letters* 209). (He held "Ten Indians" for revision for a year, sent "Today Is Friday" to another publisher and "The Killers" to Perkins in late August.)

The more legendary account of his writing the story, however, came very late, some thirty years after the event during the years of writing *A Moveable Feast* and, like that memoir, itself as much a fiction as a history of the writing of fiction. George Plimpton had sent him a list of questions for one of the series of *Paris Review* "interviews" in February 1957, and by early March Hemingway had written out answers for "21 of the 32 pages sent" (*Letters* 874). Plimpton returned his version of the interview with Hemingway's original manuscript on 3 July; and the first version was published in the following spring (Smith, "Hemingway's Early Manuscripts," 274). It was a fine story:

> The stories you mention I wrote one day in Madrid on May 16 when it snowed out the San Isidro bullfights. First I wrote "The Killers" which I'd tried to write before and failed. Then after lunch I got in bed to keep warm and wrote "Today is Friday." I had so much juice I thought maybe I was going crazy and I had about six other stories to write. So I got dressed and walked to Fornos, the old bullfighter's café, and drank coffee and then came back and wrote "Ten Indians." This made me very sad and I drank some brandy and went to sleep. ("Interview" 33)

It was so fine a story he repeated it word for word in "The Art of the Short Story" of 1959 (97–98).

But on the face of it the account is suspect—even if he had finished half of "The Killers," his word count for the day would have exceeded five thousand (close to ten times his usual stint)—and in bed with a typewriter in a cold room and time out for a visit to a bullfighters' cafe. The manuscripts of two of the stories belie that memory as well: he had a rough draft of "Ten Indians" that he revised in Madrid and then again the following spring; he had nearly half "The Killers" in a manuscript he cut and completed then or shortly afterward. So only "Today Is Friday," the least of his accomplishments, could have been started and finished on that day. But if it was not a day of original writing, it was still one of that remarkable revision so characteristic of his craft.

Of the three manuscripts of "The Killers" (KL/EH 535-36A), the first was the one he returned to on that cold Sunday in Madrid. It is a manuscript of seven pages (the first typed) with an introduction he later rejected. It follows the story through to the moment Max takes the ham and eggs Al ordered and Al takes Max's bacon and eggs. If, as it seems, that introductory part of the story represents what Hemingway remembered having "tried to write before and failed" at, then it should give evidence of both his sense of a false start and his discovery of the story's true course.

This first manuscript differs markedly from the second in two ways: It opens on a cold, wintry day in Petoskey, Michigan—reminiscent of Hemingway's 1919-20 stay there—with Nick Adams leaving the pool hall, stopping off for the *Chicago Tribune* at the station, and going into the Parker House, where George O'Neal and he share some Prohibition liquor; and Nick says there is "not a thing" in the Chicago papers. With this much he might have had in mind the structure of one his "Chicago" stories in which a question is planted early on and harvested with a later revelation in which, after the killers leave, Nick and George might look at the Chicago papers, learn about a fighter's double-cross, and so on. This is not to suggest that this manuscript derives from Hemingway's Chicago period; but it may argue for a date of composition in the fall of 1925, for it seems close to the recollections of Michigan in the first version of "Ten Indians" written then.

With the emphasis of this introductory scene on Nick in Petoskey reading the *Chicago Tribune* during Prohibition, Hemingway did not concern himself here with establishing Nick as an observer; the passage in which he watches the two men who have just entered does not appear (*Stories* 279, ll. 8-10).

But this manuscript does include the first of a series of images he extended in the later manuscript, images that suggest an ironic dislocation in which one object or person serves as an agent for another—here, the time on the clock, twenty minutes fast, for real time. If that sequence of images is as crucial as most critics have agreed, then the moment in the narrative at which Hemingway felt he had failed before is precisely that at which Al and Max's orders are reversed, the second of the images in that pattern. It seems more than a coincidence that Hemingway left the first manuscript at a point when the narrative, like the apparently trivial question of who ordered what, was becoming confused—"Don't you remember?" Al asks George (*Stories* 281). But when he finally returned to it, he might well have seen that the true direction of his story was toward and through that significant confusion in which so many elements serve as agents for something or someone else: from simple orders in a diner and the clock on the wall, through George for Henry, Mrs. Bell for Mrs. Hirsch, to Al and Max for some sinister other and, finally, Nick Adams for Ole Andreson.

The second manuscript is a typed and written draft with pencil corrections. It bears the inscription "Madrid—May 1926/For Uncle Gus [Pfeiffer—Pauline's uncle]/written between 2:15 and 8 p.m." (KL/EH 536). That inscription could not have been added much before Hemingway's marriage to Pauline in May 1927 when Uncle Gus became a likely patron. The note that it was written in some six hours in the afternoon of one day and the rejected title "The Matadors"—Spanish for "killers" and suggested perhaps by his visit to the bullfighters' café—argue that this was the manuscript completed on that marathon day of 16 May.

There is a curious break in the text of this manuscript. The typescript pages (1-9) delete the Petoskey introduction, set the scene in Summit, and turn the story's focus more toward Nick's witnessing the events. The last typescript page is torn and the remaining ten holograph pages carry the narrative from the killers' departure and George's release of Sam and Nick (*Stories* 286) to the conclusion. The first page of the holograph conclusion is marked "Add the Killers" and contains a passage of some infelicitous and repetitive dialogue later deleted: Sam repeats his line "I don't like it" or "I don't want it" four times; George tries to calm him down; Nick seems to delight in the fact that "It's a tough place all right," and Hemingway adds, "He was very excited about it all." Then they ask Sam to make a couple of ham and egg sandwiches. That Hemingway lost the drift of his story for a moment is a more likely explanation for this temporary lapse than that this moment marks his return to the manuscript he had begun earlier.

But the story still needed more than simple retyping. Beyond the lapse after the killers leave, there are some improbable moments of dialogue. When Max tells George, "You'd make some girl a nice wife, bright boy," George replies, "Yes? . . . Your *boyfriend* isn't going to come." Had that remark remained, the story, one suspects, would have ended differently—at least for George. And, finally, in this version the "landlady," although not named, is apparently Mrs. Hirsch, for the parting exchange with Mrs. Bell was added with the third manuscript.

This last manuscript is an uncorrected carbon of a Hemingway typescript that was sent to Archibald MacLeish in the late summer of 1926 (the carbon is in the Houghton Library of Harvard University; KL/EH 536 A is a photocopy.) It is very close to the published version of the story; apparently its original was the one Hemingway sent to Perkins on 21 August (*Letters* 214).

Publication History (March, October 1927)

Between June and August of 1926 Hemingway's estimate of his prospects for publishing his stories began in despondency and ended in jubilation. When he wrote to Perkins on 5 June, he had heard nothing of *Scribner's Magazine*'s response to "An Alpine Idyll," which he had submitted in early May. When he mentioned that he had written "three stories ranging from 1400 to 3000 words" but had not had them "re-typed and sent on as I was waiting word on Alpine Idyll" (*Letters* 209), it is as if he was presenting the prospect of a variety of stories of assorted lengths as a quid pro quo for some favorable answer on the earlier story, even though only "Today Is Friday" was ready for submission.

When that strategy—if that is what it was—failed, he finally sent his own typescript (KL/EH 536 A) to Perkins on 21 August. But not without irony and some self-pity, for he remarked that he had received a request from a Sears Roebuck radio station to broadcast *The Torrents of Spring* with his own commentary, because they felt "it gives common people a real thrill . . . to hear the voice of a well known, admired author." Since the typescript of "The Killers" was "typed by the well known, admired author himself on a six year old Corona," Perkins might send it on to Sears Roebuck "to show to a lot of common people" if *Scribner's Magazine* rejected it, as he thought they would—for he told Fitzgerald, he sent it to Scribner's "just to see what the alibi would be" (*Letters* 213-14, 216).

But Perkins's response was favorable and quick, for by 7 September Hemingway wrote to Fitzgerald that they had accepted it by cable and "even cynical little boys like Ernest get pleasant surprises" (*Letters* 216). Scribner's published it in their March 1927 *Magazine* and then in *Men without Women* that October.

Sources and Influences

"The Killers"—like the earlier "Indian Camp" and other later stories recognized as Hemingway's best—seems both original and familiar: original in that there is no one fiction that could have served as its model; familiar in that like so many stories of a young boy's initiation it gathers together recognizable strands of that archetypal event (DeFalco 63-71). Thus, although critics have noted partial similarities between it and other fictions, few have suggested substantive literary sources.

Not for want of trying, of course. Lowry Wimberly, as early as 1936, found an odd similarity between the scene in which Al and Max place their orders and one in Horatio Alger's *Jed, The Poor House Boy,* but there it ends. John Hagopian and Martin Dolch noted the similarity between the story and O. Henry's "The Ransom of Red Chief": both take place in a town called Summit; both the kidnappers and the killers act in a theatrical manner and say they have "to keep the boy [or bright boy] amused" (99). (Later critics in search of witty literary allusions in Hemingway might argue that here lies the motive for naming the lunchroom [O.] Henry's.) And as Philip Young noted and J. A. Ward agreed, there may be similarities—other than the two victimized Swedes—between "The Killers" and Stephen Crane's "The Blue Hotel," which Hemingway praised in *Green Hills of Africa* (Young 194–95; Ward 7–8)).

A more interesting analogy is the one Arthur Waldhorn drew between this story and Kafka's fiction—the killers are like the "undertakers" of *The Trial:* both are as "ridiculous and unreal" as their purposes are "serious and sinister" (61). Moreover, Hemingway is like Kafka in creating a scene as if it were reflected in a cracked mirror with all the objects, events, and characters inexplicably anomalous and awry.

The story shares some of the simpler elements of Hemingway's fiction written in Chicago in 1919 to 1921, but its complete inversion of that earlier formula is testimony to how far he had come in five years. "The Ash Heel's Tendon" (Griffin 174–80) has a killer with a contract, one of a class who usually like "to work in pairs and to work close"; a barroom setting with the usual mirror the killer watches; an uneasy bartender, two marked victims, and an impending gun battle that does not occur—all narrated by an insider with Hemingway's periphrastic Chicago style (Smith, "Hemingway's Apprentice Fiction," 576–77). Not only does Hemingway invert these elements from his Chicago fiction, he subverts the stereotypes by both exaggerating them and bringing them to terrifying life.

Several critics have commented on the elements the story shares with those written close to its date of composition like "Today Is Friday," those that describe fighters like Ad Francis in "The Battler" and Jack Brennan in "Fifty Grand" (Fenton), or those that see Nick through an initiation as does "The Light of the World" (DeFalco, Flora). But just as there is no one earlier model for "The Killers," none of the later stories that may serve as its prologue or reflect its consequences returns to reconsider the events in Henry's lunchroom.

Few of the suggestions of historical places and persons that Hemingway might have drawn on do more than raise questions about why Hemingway might have obscured or ignored them. Moreover, many of them are founded on suspect sources—Leicester Hemingway's biography and A. E. Hotchner's sycophantic memoir. Edward Stone questioned Hemingway's purpose in moving the action from the "Kitsos" restaurant on Chicago's North Side, where he and Bill Horne ate in 1920, to suburban Summit (14–15); and Kenneth Johnston found an answer in a letter from Summit's mayor in 1978—the village's many rooming houses served as a "refuge . . . [w]hen the 'heat' was on in Chicago" (250).

Although there was a fighter named Andre Anderson, he never "threw a fight or ever got involved with big-time gamblers" (Johnston 250); and we are left with Phillips and Rosemary Davies's source for the story in the murder of William James Brennan on 16 June 1924. Brennan—whose name Hemingway used in "Fifty Grand"—was, like Ole, a relatively young and "retired" heavyweight, and well liked. He was shot down by two murderers, but in his own café in New York. With these "relatively obvious" parallels and circumstances "roughly alike," they argued that the change from New York to Summit and from an accomplished to an aborted murder serve the same purpose: if the code-hero is to be motivated purely by that code, he must be "isolated and inactive" (36–38). Others have argued that it is precisely Ole's isolation and inactivity that denies him the status of a code-hero; so the validity of this source, not surprisingly, depends on the relevance the notion of the code-hero has to the story.

Critical Studies

Among all the early and influential works, from Malcolm Cowley's "Nightmare and Ritual" article in 1945, to Philip Young's *Ernest Hemingway* and Carlos Baker's *Writer as Artist* in 1952, probably no single study has had more influence on Hemingway criticism than Cleanth Brooks and Robert Penn Warren's analysis of "The Killers" in their short story anthology, *Understanding Fiction* (1943). Now, after nearly a half-century of Hemingway scholarship, it seems as if the meanings they found have become embedded in the story itself, so that in arguing with them it is as if one is arguing with Hemingway. The reason for this impression is obvious—almost every Hemingway critic since then was taught, or taught others, or at the least had to respond to, that reading in their learning or teaching careers.

One should recall that Brooks and Warren were addressing teachers and, through them, their students, citing other stories in their anthology and other Hemingway fictions, in a blithe violation of the principles later critics have assumed were sacrosanct in New Criticism. In any case, they turned their attention to a question the story raised—"Whose story is it?" Dismissing the notion that the story might be the killers' or even Ole Andreson's, they turned to the last scene to argue that it is Nick's—the one character on whom a significant "impression has been made," an impression that was no less than the "discovery of evil" (316–17).

That notion of Nick's discovery may have been a bit emphatic. Although the killers *are* evil in anyone's book, the evidence they drew on to substantiate their point was critically more important than the point itself. They underlined the significance of the narrator's offhand remark: Nick "had *never* had a towel in his mouth *before*" (*Stories* 286). From there they went on to demonstrate that the "towel is sanctified in the thriller as the gag" as the real intent of the killers is in their vaudevillian appearance and their dialogue, a "stereotyped banter that is always *a priori* to the situation and overrides the situation" (317–18). Their last and nicest point is that Mrs. Bell and her perceptions of Ole are as ironically sanctified versions of his impending death as the gag is of what Nick felt in his mouth and the movies are of what has happened and what will. At the end of their essay they note that just as the killers act and Ole reacts to a code—not the "code" of the Hemingway hero, as some have thought—so George accepts the morality of that code, but not Nick (319).

Brooks and Warren's analysis has convinced most critics since then, if not in its general conclusions at least in its method. Some twenty-five years later, however, R. S. Crane published his objections to that reading in a letter he had written a decade earlier to one of his students; and it is the most persuasive of the readings that counter Brooks and Warren's. He began with the assumption that the "technical question of how the characters, actions, and speeches of the boys in the lunchroom are related to the situation involving the killers and Ole Andreson." Citing Henry James, Crane argued that anything having to do with the boys is a matter of "treatment" and that having to do with Ole and the killers is of a Jamesian "essence"—the true subject. In support of that assumption he offered four arguments.

First, the subject, Ole's conflict with the killers, "is quite independent, in its structure of probabilities and events, of the boys in the lunchroom. You can forget about the occurrences in the lunchroom and still have a coherent situation that would have worked itself out precisely as it does had these occurrences never been invented" (303–04).

Second, the story's "peculiar moral and emotional quality . . . is undoubtedly clarified and vivified for us by the boy's reaction, . . . they in no sense create it" (304–05). However shocking to the boys, Ole's plight is his own, that of a "once active man . . . who has finally given up," and is all the more awful "because of the disproportion between this deliberate inactivity in the face of death" (306–07).

Third—and this is a summary of a complex argument—all the "action involving the boys is thus primarily a sequence, expertly contrived, of expository and choric devices" (311).

And fourth, Crane agreed that Nick may have passed "from ignorance to knowledge," but that discovery was only "something peculiar to a very special situation." Thus Nick is only an "impersonal messenger" to Ole; a "utility character in Hemingway's rendering of an action with which Nick has nothing essential to do"; and, in his concluding dialogue with George, he serves only an "expository function" (312–13).

Crane's argument is closely reasoned, as is Brooks and Warren's; and, more than theirs, it assiduously ignores extratextual evidence. But it depends on a distinction between the story's "subject" or "essence," Ole's plight, and its "form" or "treatment," the boy's reaction and especially Nick's, a distinction between form and content that Brooks and Warren might well question.

In the two decades between Brooks and Warren's analysis and Crane's article, most commentaries turned to specific issues of setting, character, and plot and most often were drawn to one or the other of those influential critics' conclusions and, in the story, to either Nick or Ole.

One of the earliest (1952) was a one-page note by Edward Sampson that extended the list of discrepancies in the story like that between Mrs. Hirsch and Mrs. Bell: "Henry's," once a saloon, is now a lunchroom run by George; the clock is twenty minutes fast; the killers, in coats that do not fit, take each other's order, look like vaudevillians, and act for "a friend." All these patterned details support Brooks and Warren's sense of the story's world as one in which "individuality has been lost, people have accepted their positions as agents of other people, many things are not what they seem, and even murder has become like everything else, mechanized, routine, efficient" (Item 2).

Edward Stone turned from those to other discrepancies between the story's scene and what one assumes about a village, albeit a suburb of Chicago. He questioned, for example, George's relationship with the last customer, one of only four in an hour; Nick's ignorance of Mrs. Bell, unless he is an outsider; the killers' knowledge of Ole's habits; why no one calls the police; and so on (12–15). Although Stone wondered about the liberties Hemingway took with "factual authenticity," he admitted at last that however improbable some of the details of the small-town setting, it is essential to one of his effects: "the shock to a young, impressionable stranger at the surrealistic appearance and the pervasiveness of crime in Chicago" (15). Nick's ignorance of where Ole lives and of Mrs. Bell hardly marks him as a stranger, of course, and it is not the pervasiveness of Chicago crime that so shocks him; but Stone's allusion to the killers' "surrealistic appearance" should answer the questions he raised over details of the setting and Hemingway's seeming disregard for authenticity. Had Hemingway been authentic, whatever the term means, George would have been the story's spokesman. Like Crane, Stone read "The Killers" as Ole's story, with an irony compounded by a "modern protagonist" who surrenders to those "nominal, half-hearted" figures of Nemesis, Al and Max (16–17).

One of the apparently realistic details that creates the sense of a surreal setting is the clock on the wall in Henry's lunchroom. William Morris first linked the inaccurate clock with Brooks and Warren's comment on Nick's dialogue with Mrs. Bell, who had noted that she serves as does the Porter in *Macbeth*. He pointed out that the clock time, "which not only the characters but also the reader must correct through mental effort to real time . . . five times within . . . three hundred climactic words, . . . slows the reading to fit the suspense [and makes] the reader one of the group waiting for Ole" (Item 1).

Charles Owen watched that clock and noted that at "the very moment when the suspense is greatest"—at six o'clock when Ole is expected— Hemingway "disrupts the time sequence," and moves the action ahead to six thirty-five. In the story's longest paragraph and a "unique intervention by the narrator," we are told what *had* happened in that half-hour while another five minutes passes. With that, Owen argued, "both violence and suspense are canceled," and we are led with a new awareness from that experience to the larger significance of the story enacted in the last of its three hours. For Owen, it is more than Nick's story and more than a confrontation with evil: it is our story and it questions Nick's and our response founded on a "faith in expedients, a faith that makes him representative of a whole tradition in American culture," a faith, one would add, which some readers invoke when they wonder why no one called the police (45–46). Owen concluded, therefore, that both Nick's frustration and his decision to "get out of this town" represent a futile "transfer of flight," a flight "that in a real sense he catches from Ole and ironically for the reason that Ole ceases to flee, . . . will be no more successful" (46). However brief, Owen's article is important for its direction of a formalist analysis toward issues of cultural history at an early moment (1960) in contemporary Hemingway criticism.

That Brooks and Warren first read this story as a discovery of evil may have encouraged later critics to see its cast of characters as types, almost as allegorical figures in a universal drama: Hagopian and Dolch suggested that Max is a Catholic, Al a Jew (though both eat pork); noted that Sam is a black, the rest whites, and that all are Americans except Ole the Swede (103). Howard Livingston went on to suggest that in their dialogue, Al, who mentions "girl friends in a convent," and Max, who says Al could only know a "kosher convent" (*Stories* 284), display an "empty sectarian ethnocentrism" they "evidently learned from their respective Sunday schools" (43). Then Lawrence Walz found a motif of "confused sexuality" in that dialogue and Max's jibe that George would "make some girl a nice wife" (Item 38). Most of these remarks are offhand and like those one might expect from vaudevillians or murderers killing time. When Edward Sampson gave us his short list of discrepant details, he remarked that although there are "other details that fit into this pattern, it would be silly to say that they all did" (Item 2).

The question whether it is Nick's or Ole's story might be resolved, albeit in a textbook fashion, by determining which character in the story changes or develops or which one, at the end, enacts or expresses the most comprehensive and complex understanding of the story's events. Crane's argument for Ole is not vitiated by his inaction (for the decision not to act *is* an act), but because it was antecedent to the story's events and, in any case, is most dramatically realized in Nick's responses.

Oliver Evans, nearly a decade before Crane's article, held that Mrs. Bell's remarks increase our sympathy for Ole, and that Nick, with "no particular reality," is simply an instrument to record "the emotions of pity and terror inspired by the sight of a strong man lying helpless on a bed" (591). Evans might have been more persuasive had he not remarked that never having "been gagged does not necessarily argue for [Nick's] excessive innocence," that Brooks and Warren's "recondite reasons" for the reference to the *towel* rather than a *gag* ignores the fact that "the gagging takes place in a kitchen" (591).

For many, the story's true import rests in its final dialogue. The attitude of Sam, the black cook, reflects the role his society has imposed on him: everyone calls him a nigger, let those white folks kill each other; and in a way his is the most intelligent response. Philip Young might agree with this, for early on he characterized Nick's response as "abnormally sensitive" and "roughly as excessive as the cook's is deficient," that is, if one takes as the "average" George's reaction (48–49). And that is the point, for George is so comfortably average, typical, and "sleazy": that last term is taken from Brooks and Warren, for their sense of the killers' dialogue as "sleazy . . . , inflexible and stereotyped banter that is always *a priori* to the situation" (318) is just as appropriate to George's dismissal of the fact that someone is going to kill someone else: "He must have got mixed up in something in Chicago. . . . Double-crossed somebody. That's what they kill them for" (*Stories* 289). And what does he reach for to wipe the counter? A towel. Despite the fact that Hagopian and Dolch may have felt that George, though "no self-sacrificing hero [is] far more responsible and humane than . . . the cook," it most certainly does not follow that his "is the prudent wisdom that Nick must learn to acquire" (100–01; see also Davis 320). If that were the case, Hemingway would have changed Nick's decisive line to "I'm going to get a job in this town as a short-order cook."

Perhaps Brooks and Warren's original question was the wrong one in that it assumed that the story is *either* Ole's *or* Nick's, when in fact it is *both* theirs. When they noticed that Mrs. Bell looks after Mrs. Hirsch's place, and when Edward Sampson went on to remark that nearly every object in the scene and every character serves as an "agent" for something or someone else, the obvious conclusion would be that Nick Adams is serving as an agent for Ole Andreson, as Charles Owen argued, and that the two characters, the only ones with full names, must be seen as one, or at least as functions of one another.

Those critics who conceived of Nick Adams's education as the story of a young "tyro" learning the constraining terms of the code-hero, as did Philip Young and Arthur Waldhorn, saw the two figures as critically inseparable. Two other critics who commented briefly on the irrepressible Mrs. Bell have argued that her function in the story is not, as Brooks and Warren suggested, primarily to establish the "world of normality," but ironically to convince Nick that there is no such world and so unite him with Ole in a vision of the "horror of the killer's nonchalance" (Weeks, Item 53; Moore 428).

A good deal of the commentary on the story has been drawn together in Joseph Flora's analysis of "The Killers" as if it were a chapter in a novel of Nick Adams's life, one that closes the period of his adolescence and introduces his experience as a soldier in war and at home. Following Nick's experiences in "The Battler" and "The Light of the World," which may accustom us to seeing Nick as an observer, this story seems at first to be "atypical" in that Nick is "almost hidden as a character" until he is singled out when the killers ask him his name. From then on it is Nick's story even when he is tied and gagged "offstage." Although reading the story as a "drama" makes something of Nick's absence in much of the first scene, he could not have missed what happened or was said (" 'I can hear you, all right,' Al said from the kitchen" [*Stories* 283].) With that experience Nick is "markedly changed from the young man he was at the beginning of the story. . . . Nick has previously learned something about the precariousness of all life, but he had never comprehended the potential for total evil in human nature, the potential for impersonal destruction—sometimes released in war" (103). That last insight is persuasive, for none of the stories of Nick's earlier experience engages him in the anonymous killing of war. In 1926 Hemingway gave the story the tentative title "The Matadors"; a more appropriate one might have been "The Soldiers."

In the last twenty years of commentary on "The Killers," at least three identifiable critical approaches or theories have emerged: variants of archetypal theory, literary history, and generic criticism.

Joseph DeFalco had earlier considered the stories as parts of a single archetypal narrative. "The Killers" was, for him, an initiation ritual reflecting the "nursery drama" presided over by two adult figures: the "dark hermaphroditic mother-guide figure of the cook," who would restrain Nick and keep him from the necessary acquisition of knowledge of the world; and the "arbiter guide figure," George, who impels him toward further experience.

DeFalco drew on analogies with the "waste land myth" for the archetypal dimensions of that experience, including the young hero's attempt to restore and redeem the "traditional wounded hero-king" of the Grail stories. That in these fallen times that ideal is "an illusion," marks this story as an ironic narrative; and with both the abstract similarities with the Grail legend and their inversions, DeFalco was led to locate the story in our own times, for Ole Andreson is the "athlete-hero . . . who summarizes the aims and attitudes of the whole culture" (69), as James Martine demonstrated with "Fifty Grand."

Those resonant archetypal features of the story lend authority to those who find in it elements of tragedy. Earl Rovit found in "The Killers" one of those situations of "moral outrage" that demands some appropriate response (83); and John Reardon associated the killers with that "destructive force" against which the Hemingway hero must "measure his stature as a man" (134). Both comments, however, suggest that the tragedy centers in Ole's experience and character. Jackson Benson, however, noted that although the killers, like "some natural disaster, . . . move in for the kill without any concern for retribution or arrest," only "Nick's reaction gives Ole's victimization intellectual distance" and so places the story "within the sphere of tragedy" (143–44). Wirt Williams identified the story's specific position within the tragic sphere with the argument that when Ole accepts the "old tragic postulate of nemesis" and Nick is "forced to understand that there is evil in the universe that cannot be explained or conquered or evaded, . . . the tragic spirit is invoked but then shrouded; the tragic impact is not there, nor is it meant to be" (95). It is not meant to be tragic in any classic sense of the term, as Williams suggests in his introduction, since it is a perfect instance of Northrop Frye's definition of ironic tragedy—narratives that evoke and then deliberately deny the expectations of the tragic conventions.

In a latter-day response to Brooks and Warren's interpretation, W. J. Stuckey has argued that "the experience created by 'The Killers' moves at depths inaccessible to rational conception" (133); but, undeterred, he conceived of the story's effect in terms of literary history, particularly that notion of American literature that centers on the conflicting traditions of Realism and Romance. Although he imputed to Brooks and Warren later conceptions of the code-hero, like Arthur Waldhorn's, and therefore found Nick's response a "refusal of initiation" (129), when he arrived at his point, he suggested that the story is about the "sudden appearance in the rational world of the terrifyingly irrational," and that Hemingway has brought into the "tradition of realism that element of romance, danger, that the conventions of realism have banished or forced into exile" (131). Thus Hemingway's introduction of the killers with their images of theatricality is a strategy to circumvent "middle class conceptions of reality." For one who "writes out of such a tradition [of realism] is forced to take the attitudes inculcated by that tradition seriously—if only to find a way around them" either by an escape into the past or the exotic or, as Hemingway does, by domesticating danger as "something that might be encountered on an ordinary afternoon" (132). Insofar as that issue of American literary history was articulated in the essays and fiction of William Dean Howells and Henry James, Hemingway is on the right side with James and thereby an inheritor of the antiromantic tradition in Melville and Hawthorne (133).

Something of this argument, one of the few that considers Hemingway in nineteenth-century American literary history, draws some support from the more recent biographies that find him rebelling against the "smiling aspects of life" (Howells's phrase)—at least as they appeared in Oak Park. But it does not confront the fact that Hemingway's literary education by 1925 included few early American writers other than Sherwood Anderson, whose mark is on this story, and a good many European writers, Joseph Conrad among them.

Finally, the variety of commentaries that have noted "The Killers" dramatic elements—the domination of dialogue, the narrative passages that read like stage directions, the four-part scenic structure with its divisions marked as if by lighting cues to the "arc-light" (*Stories* 285, 286, 288)— and, of course, those that have remarked on its proximity to tragedy, have been realized in two studies informed by concepts of generic criticism. Earlier critics, like Sheridan Baker, had noted that the story, "for all its power, is a hybrid, an observation of the tough world that shifts to a revelation of Nick's inner agony" (58). And Arthur Waldhorn remarked that "a comic spirit informs 'The Killers' as it does 'The Light of the World' but dwells here in the precincts of death rather than life," that Al and Max "pop out of the imaginary screen intent upon actual murder," so that along "the length of this razor's edge between the comic and the tragic Nick is painfully stretched" (61).

Of the two major interpretations of the story's dramatic dimensions, Joseph Flora's is the most recent and, in some ways, the most conventional, for his analysis of the story's structure draws on parallels with earlier and more traditional examples in the history of drama. In an earlier article, Wolfgang Schlepper returned to Hemingway's story to discover one of the sources of absurdist drama and the plays of Harold Pinter and, almost in passing, offered an original reading of the story's dramatic structure. He cited Pinter's fascination in so many plays with "two people in a room . . . as a very potential question: What is going to happen to these people in the room? Is someone going to open the door and come in?" And we recall that Hemingway in his room in Madrid in 1926 cut the original manuscript to begin with "The door of Henry's lunch-room opened and two men came in" (*Stories* 279). Pinter's near obsession with rooms casts a new light upon Henry's lunchroom and other settings that recur in Hemingway—the café, the railroad station, even the firelit clearing—and in which the archetypal constituents of food and shelter are sometimes perverted or violated (105). Schlepper cataloged a variety of enlightening similarities between "The Killers" and Pinter's *The Birthday Party*—and there are others in *The Dumb-Waiter*—and then he returned to Nick. He is "the modern playwright's ideal audience, . . . he alone is left without a function in the realistic framework of the story." But, like others of us in an "ideal audience" of absurdist drama, he will not accept the words of others like George, and the "room is not the same any more" (111).

In 1982, in a fortuitous confirmation of this argument, Tom Stoppard reflected on his indebtedness to Hemingway. He remarked on "the inadequate truism that Hemingway is a writer who leaves things out. My own memory of reading Hemingway for the first time is that of being often intrigued by what he had put in and left in." He cited Nick's conversation with Mrs. Bell, and asked, "What on earth is this about?" (22) Of course, Stoppard knew what that scene was about, just as he knew what the apparently irrelevant scenes in his own plays were about. What he was acknowledging was his indebtedness to that scene and to others in Hemingway that suggested his sense of a world in which the question "What on earth is this about?" is the first and only one.

The indebtedness of playwrights like Harold Pinter and Tom Stoppard to Hemingway and his indebtedness to them reminds us of T. S. Eliot's perception "No poet, no artist of any art, has his complete meaning alone. . . . What happens when a new work of art is created is something that happens to all the works of art that preceded it" (4–5).

Works Cited

PRIMARY

"The Art of the Short Story." *Paris Review* 23 (Spring 1981): 85–102.

Ernest Hemingway: Selected Letters, 1917–1961. Ed. Carlos Baker. New York: Scribner's, 1981.

"An Interview with Ernest Hemingway." *Paris Review* 18 (1958): 60–89; rpt. in *Ernest Hemingway: Five Decades of Criticism*. Ed. Linda W. Wagner. East Lansing: Michigan State UP, 1974, 21–38.

The Short Stories of Ernest Hemingway. New York: Scribner's, 1938, 279–89.

SECONDARY

Baker, Carlos. *Hemingway: The Writer as Artist*. 1952. Princeton: Princeton UP, 1972.

Baker, Sheridan. *Ernest Hemingway*. New York: Holt, 1967.

Benson, Jackson J. *Hemingway: The Writer's Art of Self-Defense*. Minneapolis: U of Minnesota P, 1969.

Brooks, Cleanth, and Robert Penn Warren. *Understanding Fiction*. New York: Crofts, 1943.

Cowley, Malcolm. Introduction. *The Portable Hemingway*. New York: Viking, 1945; rpt. in *Hemingway: A Collection of Critical Essays*. Ed. Robert P. Weeks. Englewood Cliffs: Prentice, 1962.

Crane, R. S. *The Idea of the Humanities and Other Essays Critical and Historical*. Chicago: U of Chicago P, 1967.

Davies, Phillips G., and Rosemary R. Davies. " 'A Killer Who Would Shoot You for the Fun of It': A Possible Source for Hemingway's 'The Killers.' " *Iowa English Yearbook* 15 (1970): 36-38.

Davis, William V. " 'The Fell of Dark': The Loss of Time in Hemingway's 'The Killers.' " *Studies in Short Fiction* 15 (1978): 319-20.

DeFalco, Joseph. *The Hero in Hemingway's Short Stories*. Pittsburgh: U of Pittsburgh P, 1963.

Eliot, T. S. *Selected Essays*. New York: Harcourt, 1932.

Evans, Oliver. "The Protagonist of Hemingway's 'The Killers.' " *Modern Language Notes* 73 (1958): 589-91.

Fenton, Charles A. *The Apprenticeship of Ernest Hemingway: The Early Years*. New York: Farrar, 1954.

Flora, Joseph M. *Hemingway's Nick Adams*. Baton Rouge: Louisiana State UP, 1982.

Griffin, Peter. *Along with Youth: Hemingway, The Early Years*. New York: Oxford UP, 1985.

Hagopian, John V., and Martin Dolch, eds. *Insight I: Analyses of American Literature*. Frankfurt-am-Main: Hirschgraben, 1962.

Hemingway, Leicester. *My Brother, Ernest Hemingway*. Cleveland: World, 1961.

Hotchner, A. E. *Papa Hemingway: A Personal Memoir*. New York: Random, 1966.

Johnston, Kenneth G. " 'The Killers': The Background and the Manuscripts." *Studies in Short Fiction* 19 (1982): 247-51.

Livingston, Howard. "Religious Intrusion in Hemingway's 'The Killers.' " *English Record* 21 (1971): 42-45.

Martine, James J. "Hemingway's 'Fifty Grand': The Other Fight(s)." *Journal of Modern Literature* 2 (1971): 123-27.

Moore, L. Hugh, Jr. "Mrs. Hirsch and Mrs. Bell in Hemingway's 'The Killers.' " *Modern Fiction Studies* 11 (1965-66): 427-28.

Morris, William E. "Hemingway's 'The Killers.' " *Explicator* 18 (Oct. 1959), Item 1.

Owen, Charles A., Jr. "Time and the Contagion of Flight in 'The Killers.'" *Forum* 3 (1960): 45–46.

Reardon, John. "Hemingway's Esthetic and Ethical Sportsmen." *University Review* 34 (1967): 13–23; rpt. in *Ernest Hemingway: Five Decades of Criticism*. Ed. Linda W. Wagner. East Lansing: Michigan State UP, 1974, 131–44.

Rovit, Earl. *Ernest Hemingway*. Boston: Twayne, 1963.

Sampson, Edward C. "Hemingway's 'The Killers.'" *Explicator* 11 (1952), Item 2.

Schlepper, Wolfgang. "Hemingway's 'The Killers': An Absurd Happening." *Literatur in Wissenschaft und Unterricht* 10 (1977): 104–14.

Smith, Paul. "Hemingway's Apprentice Fiction: 1919–1921." *American Literature* 58 (1986): 574–88.

———. "Hemingway's Early Manuscripts: The Theory and Practice of Omission." *Journal of Modern Literature* 10 (1983): 268–88.

Stone, Edward. "Some Questions about Hemingway's 'The Killers.'" *Studies in Short Fiction* 5 (1967): 12–17.

Stoppard, Tom. "Reflections on Ernest Hemingway." *Ernest Hemingway: The Writer in Context*. Ed. James Nagel. Madison: U of Wisconsin P, 1984.

Stuckey, W. J. "'The Killers' as Experience." *Journal of Narrative Technique* 5 (1975): 128–35.

Waldhorn, Arthur. *A Reader's Guide to Ernest Hemingway*. New York: Farrar, 1972.

Ward, J. A. "'The Blue Hotel' and 'The Killers.'" *CEA Critic* 21 (1959): 7–8.

Walz, Lawrence A. "Hemingway's 'The Killers'" *Explicator* 25 (1967), Item 38.

Weeks, Robert P. "Hemingway's 'The Killers.'" *Explicator* 15 (1957), Item 53.

Williams, Wirt. *The Tragic Art of Ernest Hemingway*. Baton Rouge: Louisiana State UP, 1981.

Wimberly, Lowry Charles. "Hemingway and Horatio Alger." *Prairie Schooner* 10 (1936): 208–11.

Young, Philip. *Ernest Hemingway: A Reconsideration*. 1952. New York: Harcourt, 1966.

21

Today Is Friday

Composition History (May 1926)

Of the three stories Hemingway claimed to have written on 16 May 1926, "Today Is Friday" is the only one with manuscript evidence to suggest that it might have been begun and, but for minor revisions, completed on that day. (For an account of that day in which Hemingway claimed to have written this story, "The Killers" and "Ten Indians," see Chapters 20 and 29.) But, as is often the case, even those manuscripts question some of the more dramatic details of the story.

Two are extant: the first (KL/EH 769) is his five-page typescript with pencil and ink corrections and two rejected titles: "One More for the Nazarene" and "Today is Friday, or The Seed of the Church." His recollection that "after lunch I got in bed to keep warm and wrote 'Today is Friday'" ("Interview" 33) is questioned by his earlier note on the manuscript of "The Killers" that it was "written between 2:15 and 8 p.m." (KL/EH 536) and, perhaps, that KL/EH 769 is typed. The second manuscript is in Yale University's Beinecke Library; another of his own typescripts, it incorporates corrections made on KL/EH 769. This was the version he sent to Edith Finch of *The As Stable Pamphlets* on 18 August 1926 indicating that it was "the only mss . . . I have and would like to have it back" (Yale, Beinecke Library).

The first typescript, then, probably was written on that Sunday in May 1926, in or out of bed; and the second, sometime between then and mid-August in response to Finch's request. The revisions on both typescripts are minor, suggesting that Hemingway had somewhat less than his ordinary interest in realizing the potential of earlier drafts, as he did with the two other stories he worked on that day, "The Killers" and "Ten Indians."

Publication History (Fall 1926; Fall 1927)

It is likely that "Today Is Friday" remained in its original version of May 1926 until Hemingway returned to Paris in early August. On 14 August Edith Finch wrote him from Paris to inquire whether he "might possibly do, for a series of pamphlets which two young Americans are putting out, an essay." *The As Stable Pamphlets* she represented were intended to alternate the work of unrecognized writers with that of the more famous; Finch also noted that Hemingway had been recommended by Gertrude Stein and included a copy of her "Descriptions of Literature," which they had just published. Hemingway could hardly ignore this request to support such a worthwhile publishing venture—except for the fact that he had no "essay" at hand and was hardly in the mood to write one (KL/EH, Edith Finch to Hemingway, 14 August 1926).

Mere notions of genre, however, were no constraint in those days when he had decided to "give away all [his] stories" (*Letters* 216), and so he sent her the second typescript of the "story" he had titled a "play" in response to her request for an "essay" on 18 August (Yale University, Beinecke Library Collection). Two months later George Platt Lynes, the editor of the pamphlet series wrote him that "your play, 'Today is Friday.' is to be published November tenth [1926]" and that a small honorarium would follow with several copies of the pamphlet in lieu of the manuscript Hemingway had requested to be returned (KL/EH, Lynes to Hemingway, 28 October 1926).

Sources and Influences

Most of the details Hemingway selected for this ironic epilogue to the Crucifixion were drawn from the Synoptic Gospels: Matthew, Mark, and Luke all record the Roman soldiers, the nailing to the cross, the presence of the women and Mary Magdalene, the disciples' absence, and the mocking of Christ—the second soldier's question "Why didn't he come down off the cross?" echoes the taunt in Matthew 27:40 "If thou be the Son of God, come down from the cross." (One curiosity of the story is that a Roman soldier, indeed the most skeptical of the three, would assume Christ might have been able to save himself.) But only in John 19:34 does a Roman soldier pierce the body of Christ with a spear to insure his death—which Hemingway interprets as the least act of mercy the first soldier could do. This act and its motive sets the first soldier apart and invests him with a moral authority over the second soldier.

The scene and dialogue are reminiscent of Hemingway's Chicago stories of 1919–21 with the speakeasy banter—"You've been drinking water"—and the call for some hair-of-the-dog. And the story's low burlesque derives from the conversation that treats the "main event" of Christianity as if it were just that, a prizefight in which the champion either showed guts or perhaps took a fall.

Of those critics who mention the story—and few do more than that—most note that it is Hemingway's first use of the Christ story in his fiction. What has not been noticed is that with this story Hemingway seems to have anticipated later critics who might object to his version of the Crucifixion. The ironic strategy of casting the ancient in contemporary language is hardly unusual. Moreover, one might argue that if the life of the bullfighter in the story he had recently written, "The Undefeated," can be read as an *imitatio Christi*, it is hardly less logical that those who crucified Christ might have thought of him as a boxer. If the story of Christ is an instance of the eternal manifested in the temporal, nothing about it can be anachronistic. Joseph DeFalco drew the parallel with the earlier stories of 1924–25 (197, 211); as did Earl Rovit with the major in "In Another Country" (64); and as nearly everyone else has done with Santiago of *The Old Man and the Sea* (Young, Sheridan Baker).

If not a source, "The Killers" is a close companion, in both circumstances of composition and structure, of "Today Is Friday" (Sheridan Baker 59, Waldhorn 89). If after writing "The Killers" in the morning of 16 May 1926, he turned to this story, then details of the first seem to recur as in an ironic epilogue. In both there are the hired killers, a waiter of sorts named George in a diner or restaurant; each story opens with ordering food or drinks and is concerned primarily with the varying responses to the manner in which the victims—both "prize" fighters—faced or will face their deaths. Those responses in "The Killers" and "Today Is Friday" range from denial and a politic lack of interest (Sam the cook and George, a black and a Jew, both victims of racial and ethnic slurs) through cynical, simplistic, and conventional explanations (George and the second soldier) to admiration and sympathetic concern for the victim (Nick and the first soldier). Lest these similarities lead us to find Mrs. Bell an avatar of Mary Magdalene, the differences between the two stories deserve critical attention.

Critical Studies

It is hardly surprising that differences among critics on the meaning and value of "Today Is Friday" depend in large part upon their reactions to the discrepancy between the divine event at Calvary and its dramatic translation to Chicago. Carlos Baker admitted he disliked the story in his 1952 study and later dismissed it for dialogue that resembles "a locker-room discussion among high-school sophomore football players" (*Ernest Hemingway: A Life Story* 169). Nonetheless, Joseph DeFalco, drew extensively on Carl Jung to argue that Hemingway dramatizes the ways in which "Christ, by His crucifixion, represents a conscious assimilation" and thus a victory over "the Caesarean madness that afflicted" his world (187–88). The first Roman soldier's comments suggest some awareness of that meaning—and one might add that Hemingway had in mind the biblical "centurion" who is convinced of Christ's divinity at the Crucifixion (Matt. 27:54). The pitfall Hemingway faced in the story is its potential for sentimentality, which he avoided "by approaching his subject obliquely"—or, as Baker suggested, with the other pitfall of tough locker-room talk. DeFalco, however, is the only critic who considered the story's title and its implied question: Which day is Friday? If "today" is not only the day of the Crucifixion but *this* day, then one might recognize the "complicity of contemporary man in [its] events" (189). Whether this explains or explains away the disparity between the story's subject and its style is still at issue.

Sheridan Baker argued for the story's "positive Christianity . . . empowered by its rough inarticulateness" (59). Sheldon Grebstein used the story to demonstrate a bravura display of Hemingway's dialogue skills but concluded that the "method verges on self-parody" (114–15). Similarly, Wirt Williams found the style a self-parody even though he agreed that it approached the concept of tragedy (96).

Finally, Arthur Waldhorn raised the most intriguing critical question when he contrasted the use of clichéd dialogue in "The Killers" and "Today Is Friday." He noted that the "clichés that become remarkably pertinent in 'The Killers' stubbornly remain . . . as stereotypic as the dialogue is anachronistic" in "Today Is Friday," and that the problem several have had with the story is "not one of irreverence but of irrelevance" (89). Indeed, a crucial critical issue; for although it may explain the success of "The Killers" and the failure of "Today Is Friday," it suggests that irrelevance is as much a moral term as irreverence. If Santiago can be conceived of as imitating the passion of Christ, with both reverence and relevance, who is to deny relevance *and* reverence to the conception of Christ as a prizefighter? Especially if today is Friday.

Works Cited

PRIMARY

"An Interview with Ernest Hemingway." *Paris Review* 18 (1958): 60–89; rpt. in *Ernest Hemingway: Five Decades of Criticism*. Ed. Linda W. Wagner. East Lansing: Michigan State UP, 1974, 21–38.

Ernest Hemingway: Selected Letters, 1917–1961. Ed. Carlos Baker. New York: Scribner's, 1981.

The Short Stories of Ernest Hemingway. New York: Scribner's, 1938, 356–59.

SECONDARY

Baker, Carlos. *Ernest Hemingway: A Life Story*. 1969. New York: Scribner's, 1988.

———. *Hemingway: The Writer as Artist*. 1952. Princeton: Prineton UP, 1972.

Baker, Sheridan. *Ernest Hemingway*. New York: Holt, 1967.

DeFalco, Joseph. *The Hero in Hemingway's Short Stories*. Pittsburgh: U of Pittsburgh P, 1963.

Grebstein, Sheldon N. *Hemingway's Craft*. Carbondale: Southern Illinois UP, 1973.

Rovit, Earl. *Ernest Hemingway*. Boston: Twayne, 1963.

Waldhorn, Arthur. *A Reader's Guide to Ernest Hemingway*. New York: Farrar, 1972.

Williams, Wirt. *The Tragic Art of Ernest Hemingway*. Baton Rouge: Louisiana State UP, 1981.

Young, Philip. *Ernest Hemingway: A Reconsideration*. 1952. New York: Harcourt, 1966.

22

A Canary for One

Composition History (August–September 1926)

When Ernest and Hadley returned from the Riviera in August 1926 to "set up separate residences," he accepted Gerald Murphy's invitation to use his studio at 69, rue Froidevaux, where, years later, he remembered writing "A Canary for One" (Baker 173; *Letters* 470). By the 21st he was well along with the proofs of *The Sun Also Rises*, and on 7 September he wrote to Fitzgerald that he had sent off "Today Is Friday" and "The Killers," and had "completed a new story, yest. and am starting another one" (*Letters* 216). The first was likely a late version of "A Canary for One" (the second was "In Another Country"), for by 23 November the story had been typed and mailed, and Scribner's had reviewed it and mailed their acceptance (*Letters* 230).

There are three manuscripts of the story (KL/EH 307–09): the first is a pencil manuscript with the title "Give Her a Canary"; the other two are Hemingway typescripts, the second of which (309) is more carefully revised and corresponds closely to the *Scribner's Magazine* version.

Scott Donaldson's perceptive study of Hemingway's revisions in these manuscripts as evidence of his craftsmanship is an exemplary work of criticism. Donaldson leaves little to add, except that the absence of some revisions one looks for reading through these manuscripts raises some, perhaps presumptuous, questions about Hemingway's care, or even interest, in revising its first few pages. Donaldson remarked that given the story's occasion—the train trip with Hadley to Paris in mid-August—"it is remarkable that Hemingway was able to tell the story at all as soon as he did" (210).

But however remarkable that may be, here it is interesting that his major revisions begin when the narrator reveals himself as the husband (*Stories*, 339, l. 14). At that point, through both the first manuscript and the next typescript Hemingway introduced him with the curious sentences "My wife and I are not characters in this story. It was just that the American lady was talking to my wife" (KL/EH 307, 308). From that moment on in the last typescript (309), the story is brilliantly revised, as Donaldson has shown. But before that moment there are few revisions. Some of the unrevised lines may seem intentional; and although Donaldson justified some, like the unidiomatic use of the verb "to be" in the first three paragraphs, he admitted that others, like the description of the Negro soldiers as "too tall to stare" and "Nothing had eaten any breakfast" (*Stories* 338, 340)—are "curious" (206).

Although it is a heresy to suggest that Hemingway might well have blotted a line, these manuscripts seem to suggest that once he had arrived at the American lady's dialogue and twice insisted that the narrator and his wife were only witnesses, not characters implicated in the drama, he turned his attention to the story of her daughter's tragic and Jamesian damnation, and simply ignored some infelicities in the earlier pages of his manuscript.

But the narrator and his wife *are* actors in this drama of separation; and Hemingway not only faced that fact but, as Donaldson demonstrated, he worked hard through five different versions to meet "the hazard he ran with his ending" (209-10). Donaldson's tracing of the revisions through those variant endings is a persuasive demonstration of Hemingway's attention to the details of his art. But with that so nicely proved, one wonders why Hemingway was so apparently inattentive in revising the earlier pages of his story.

Publication History (April, October 1927)

Hemingway was assured of publication for "A Canary for One" with a letter from Scribner's of late November 1926. Through that fall he read proofs and in December applauded the suggestion that it, "The Killers," and "In Another Country" be published together: he wrote Max Perkins that "all 3 complement one another and would make a fine group" (*Letters* 240, 21 December 1926). Precisely how they might have complemented one another is a question, but "A Canary for One" did appear in the April 1927 issue of *Scribner's Magazine* with "In Another Country"—"The Killers" had been published in the March issue.

During the early months of 1927, Hemingway wavered briefly over including the story in his next collection. He included it in a list of stories for his next book in January. In February, however, he had decided on a title, *Men Without Women,* and something of a theme: "In all of these, almost, the softening feminine influence through training, discipline, death or other causes, [is] absent," and the list did not include "A Canary for One" (*Letters* 245, 14 February). But by May he was on his honeymoon with Pauline, and he included the story as well as "Hills Like White Elephants"— both of which belie his sense of his title's implication.

Sources and Influences

The origin of "A Canary for One" in the last train trip Ernest and Hadley took together in August 1926 was apparently confirmed in a letter from Hadley to Carlos Baker almost forty years later (Baker 592), although one may wonder whether her reading of the story provided some of the details of what must have been a harrowing trip. In any case, the story's biographical provenance seems to have inhibited questions concerning its literary sources.

Philip Young rather obliquely suggested some similarity with F. Scott Fitzgerald's stories of broken marriages, but the resemblances are faint. Julian Smith found more pervasive influences in T. S. Eliot's "The Waste Land"; and certainly some of the story's prophetic images, its atmosphere of sterility and psychic imprisonment, the aimless chatter of the American lady, the hopeless memories of the American wife, and the embittered silence of the narrator broken only to remark upon disaster, are all characteristics of Eliot's influential poem. And if that poem lies behind the other marriage tales, "Out of Season" and "Cat in the Rain," then one might expect it here in the last of the group.

More recently, Lois Rudnick has noted an analogue between the American lady's story of prohibiting her daughter's marriage and Henry James's "Daisy Miller" (12-19). But aside from the shared setting in Vevey the anecdote has more dissimilarities than similarities with James's story: the daughter has none of Daisy's spirit; the Swiss suitor is a most un-Jamesian engineer; and although the American lady is as dithery as Mrs. Miller, she is of tougher stock. One could argue that the anecdote is as much a reversal of James's *The American,* with the American lady in the role of Madame de Bellegarde.

"A Canary for One" brings the marriage tales of 1923 and 1924— "Out of Season," "Cat in the Rain," and "Cross-Country Snow"—to the conclusion they had predicted. They, and "Hills Like White Elephants" of 1927, portray a rootless, wandering couple miserably mismatched, who in this story have finally, mercifully it seems, come to terms with silence and separation. The wife, with her memory of their once lovely days in Vevey, has the sensitivity of the girl in "Hills Like White Elephants." The husband has some of the cynical detachment of the one in "Cat in the Rain"; but here, if we imagine that the scenes of destruction he witnesses and the irony of the American lady's story are meant to reveal his shame and suffering, then we can take solace in his deserving it.

Critical Studies

The relatively few critical studies of "A Canary for One" as an independent story center on two related critical issues: first, whether or not the story is flawed by what seems a shift from an objective third-person to a subjective first-person narrative point of view midway in the action with the revelation delayed to its last line (Dolch, Hagopian, and Cunliffe 96-99);

and second, whether or not elements of the scene and action are functions of the narrator's selective perception and thus indicative of his mood, if not his impending separation from his wife—for example, whether or not the American lady's worry over missing "signals of departure" is an ironic reference to other such signals of which he is acutely aware.

If the second question is answered affirmatively, then of course the first is resolved: if the couple's separation is prefigured in the images of the burning farmhouse and the wrecked train, then the revelation is no more an O. Henry or "wow" ending than, say, the last lines of "Indian Camp." (The issue of "wow" endings that Hemingway raised later in *Death in the Afternoon,* incidentally, is sometimes taken too seriously; for in the dialogue with the Old Lady the writer does not abjure those endings altogether, only those that are "too hearty a wow" [182].)

So it was the strategy of Joseph DeFalco, Julian Smith, Scott Donaldson, and Trisha Ingman to demonstrate in various ways how the preceding elements of the story not only predict but demand its last line. DeFalco was the first to argue that the "accumulation of detail up to the ending in itself reveals a meaning which parallels the final resolution"; moreover, the "narrator's concern for minute details . . . , his close account of the woman and her daughter, and his apparent dispassionate attitude . . . function . . . as does Nick's attention to the details of fishing in 'Big Two-Hearted River' " (174–75). Julian Smith's meticulous reading of the text discovered a variety of instances to prove the point; and Scott Donaldson's consideration of the manuscripts made evident Hemingway's late but decisive intention "not to mislead his audience but to guide it toward understanding without erecting obvious signposts" (205).

With such detailed studies as these only a few questions remain. Jackson Benson raised one in suggesting that the story follows a pattern evident in others in which the conflict centers on a discrepancy between two observers, one (the narrator) aware, and the second (the American lady) unaware of the tragedy of a "courageous protagonist," here the American lady's daughter, caged by her mother's insouciant cruelty (148). Another is the question that rests in some of the inexplicable, seemingly careless, lines in the early pages of the story before Hemingway introduced his narrator and, as it were, admitted his own engagement in the narrative.

It may be that both questions are resolved into one: the dramatization of the American lady's blithe cruelty toward her daughter offered the narrator some momentary surcease from a deep sense of guilt that troubles the early pages of his story and is admitted only in the last line. Joseph Flora suggested that this story, with the marriage tales and other fictions, displays one of Hemingway's pervasive themes—in simple terms, the perplexing evidence of "how people can treat those they love in the frightful ways they sometimes do" (210).

Works Cited

PRIMARY

Death in the Afternoon. New York: Scribner's, 1932.

Ernest Hemingway: Selected Letters, 1917–1961. Ed. Carlos Baker. New York: Scribner's, 1981.

The Short Stories of Ernest Hemingway. New York: Scribner's, 1938, 337–42.

SECONDARY

Baker, Carlos. *Ernest Hemingway: A Life Story.* 1969. Scribner's, 1988.

Benson, Jackson J. *Hemingway: The Writer's Art of Self-Defense.* Minneapolis: U of Minnesota P, 1969.

DeFalco, Joseph. *The Hero in Hemingway's Short Stories.* Pittsburgh: U of Pittsburgh P, 1963.

Dolch, Martin, John V. Hagopian, and W. Gordon Cunliffe. "A Canary for One." *Insight I: Analyses of American Literature.* Ed. John V. Hagopian and Martin Dolch. Frankfurt-am-Main: Hirschgraben, 1962.

Donaldson, Scott. "Preparing for the End: Hemingway's Revisions of 'A Canary for One.'" *Studies in American Fiction* 6 (Autumn 1978): 203–11.

Flora, Joseph M. *Hemingway's Nick Adams.* Baton Rouge: Louisiana State UP, 1982.

Ingman, Trisha. "Symbolic Motifs in 'A Canary for One.'" *Linguistics in Literature* 1 (1976): 35–41.

Rudnick, Lois P. "Daisy Miller Revisited: Ernest Hemingway's 'A Canary for One.'" *Massachusetts Studies in English* 7 (1978): 12–19.

Smith, Julian. "'A Canary for One': Hemingway in the Wasteland." *Studies in Short Fiction* 5 (Summer 1968): 355–61.

Young, Philip. *Ernest Hemingway: A Reconsideration.* 1952. New York: Harcourt, 1966.

23

In Another Country

Composition History (September-November 1926)

Two of Hemingway's letters to Scott Fitzgerald during the fall of 1926 say something of the relationship between the life of the man and the life of the writer. Early in September he wrote that "Our life has gone to hell which seems to be the one thing you can count on a good life to do." He and Hadley had separated, Pauline had returned to the States, and Ernest was, in his own words, "wallowing in bathos." But by the end of November he wrote to his friend that he had had "a grand spell of working." And he had: Scribner's accepted "The Killers" in September and "A Canary for One" in November; by which time he had finished "In Another Country," was at work on "Now I Lay Me," and, as he told Fitzgerald, had "two other stories" he could not send out but which would "go well in a book"—probably "A Pursuit Race" and "A Simple Enquiry" (*Letters* 217, 222, 231). No mean achievement for anyone suffering through the early months of a separation; but Hemingway often worked well when he was alone.

When he wrote to Fitzgerald on 7 September that he had "completed a new story, yest. and am starting another one," he was referring to "A Canary for One" and "In Another Country" (*Letters* 216). For the latter, he probably recalled the revised typescript fragment that takes the story to the second passage on the Italian major (KL/EH 492 A ends at *Stories* 270 [". . . I had the grammar straight in my mind"]). On 23 November he wrote Max Perkins that he "was writing on another Italian story," and the next day he assured Fitzgerald that what he had sent them was "a hell of a good story about Milan during the war" and that he had just "finished a better one I should be typing now" (*Letters* 230–31).

So by 23 November he had worked through his second version, titled and with pencil corrections (KL/EH 492), and sent to Scribner's a professional typescript. This chronology is particularly interesting in that it demonstrates that Hemingway's first war story—if we except the *In Our Time* chapters and "Soldier's Home"—was written directly after "A Canary for One" and led immediately into "Now I Lay Me," the penultimate version of which was titled "In Another Country—Two" (KL/EH 622). And that chronology lends some support to those critics from Richard Hovey to Millicent Bell who argue that "In Another Country" and its sometime sequel are as much or more about the consequences of commitment in marriage as they are about effects of a wounding.

Publication History (April, October 1927)

Scribner's accepted "In Another Country" soon after they received it in November 1926, for by 21 December Hemingway eagerly approved their plan to publish it in the same issue of *Scribner's Magazine* with "A Canary for One" and, he assumed, "The Killers": "All 3 complement one another and would make a fine group," he wrote to Max Perkins (*Letters* 239).

As the number of stories ready for his next collection grew, he began listing them in various sequences through the winter and spring of 1927. In January he noted it was "pretty good," placed it second and then seventh in a list of ten stories; then in March it came fifth in a list of twelve titles. Each of these unpublished lists (KL/EH 120 B, 120 C) also included "In Another Country—Two" ("Now I Lay Me"), but neither of his letters to Max Perkins so much as mentioned that second story (*Letters* 245, 14 February; 250, 4 May).

"In Another Country" was published with "A Canary for One" in the April 1927 issue of *Scribner's Magazine* and then, although second to "The Undefeated," introduced those stories that are significantly about "men without women" in the October volume. Julian Smith has speculated that "The Undefeated" was placed first to capitalize on the recent success of *The Sun Also Rises*.

Sources and Influences

Although no critic has cited any specific literary source for "In Another Country," few have neglected to associate the story with Hemingway's own recuperation from his wounding in the summer of 1918 and with the later stories and novels that drew on that experience. Like Hemingway, the narrator was wounded severely in the knee—and his wounding was somewhat more of an accident than others' (*Stories* 270)—recuperated in Milan with mechanical therapy, and was decorated and cited in language similar to that quoted in the story (Lewis 224). The descriptions of the streets of Milan and their shops, the "patriotic" café girls at the Cova, and the details of hospitals and doctors, all have the character of remembered experience.

The relationship of this story to others is a debated one. Those who assume that the narrator is the unnamed Nick Adams find the occasion for his wound in the earlier chapter 6 of *In Our Time* and other versions of its aftermath in the later stories "Now I Lay Me" and "A Way You'll Never Be." Others, like Julian Smith, argue that the story itself could have formed a chapter in *A Farewell to Arms,* although it would have been a rather obvious foreshadowing of the novel's ending. Finally, the note of discomfort the narrator feels over the language of his citation and his habit of imagining he had done the heroic deeds of the wounded "hawks" he knew recalls Krebs's lies in "Soldier's Home."

With the controversy over whether "In Another Country" is better understood as a Nick Adams story, a possible chapter in *A Farewell to Arms,* or even evidence with "Now I Lay Me" offering a darker reading for the "marriage tales," questions are raised that are, of course, matters of critical interpretation.

Critical Studies

Some commentaries, however, manage to avoid the issue of the place and meaning of "In Another Country" in the Hemingway canon. One of the first was Rosemary Stephens's enumeration of the narrative's elements that occur in three's: beginning with the dead carcasses hanging outside the shops—for her a controlling metaphor—on to bridges, wounded soldiers (ignoring the major as a fourth), photographs the major views after his three days away from the hospital, and including some rather distant triads, like Barabas's three sins from the epigraph's source, which are somehow translated into the three issues of the story—death, society, and sex—and countered by the three elements of a "code" embracing duty, courage, and stoicism. The function of these triplets—some interesting, some not—is to suggest some archetypal, mystical, or Christian ideal of "perfection" or "ultimate basis of experience" (82), with which we are meant to interpret the story.

Jackson Benson raised a critical issue contrasting the source of the story's effect with that of "The Killers." He recognized that the story's larger concern is the definition of courage and that the major's behavior, in a different but as persuasive way, demonstrates it, as does Nick's reaction in the first story and the narrator's inability to react in the second (144–45).

One of the most perceptive of the recent readings of the story is Colin Cass's. He elaborated on the definitions of "another country" in which the narrator finds himself: he is in the country of another language, a country of civilians, of genuine heroes, and through the major a country in which "love, despair, and death" are foreign to him (309). Cass made literary arithmetic persuasive when he noted that the verb "to look" appears nine times in the story—a significant statistic, since in "A Way You'll Never Be," where one would expect it to exceed that number proportionally, it is half that (311). And more important, after the story's opening paragraph in which the narrator is the subject of the verb, it is the major who "looks" in all remaining eight instances. This insight might have convinced others of the story's unity and its modernity: for from its celebrated first paragraph on it is a story of perception, and one complicated as we witness, through the narrator, the major, a perceiver perceiving. One might amend Arthur Waldhorn's statement (69) to read, "What the reader perceives is what Nick learns to perceive from the major."

The issue of whether or not one may read this story with evidence drawn from the other Nick Adams stories is still with us, and largely because the differing assumptions of both parties have not been admitted or settled. There is no question that the narrator of "In Another Country" is not in every detail the Nick Adams of "Now I Lay Me," "A Way You'll Never Be," or Frederic Henry or Krebs or Colonel Cantwell. But this is not to deny that they share certain traits of character and similar experiences that allow, if they do not demand, something of a "synoptic view" (Julian Smith) or the notion of a "generic Nick" (DeFalco).

Philip Young was the first to hold that the narrator of "In Another Country" was an avatar of Nick Adams, and that his conflicts were related to those of Jake Barnes and Frederic Henry (58-59); so, too—with fewer claims—did Earl Rovit (97), Arthur Waldhorn (97), and Joseph Flora (135). Over against them are Joseph DeFalco (135), Julian Smith (137), and James Steinke (33 ff.), who argued for a narrator distinct from Nick Adams. The crucial questions are complex ones of intention and, finally, of what counts as interpretive evidence. Both those who consider "In Another Country" isolated or within the canon of Nick Adams stories have discovered new and interesting aspects of the story. Perhaps the test of their critical assumptions rests in the degree to which their analyses illuminate the story's dimensions and even challenge and expand those critical axioms.

Joseph DeFalco began his analysis with the generalization that it is about "the effect of war upon individuals who really have no control over its machinations"—thus, the story's controlling image is the machine. The narrator, for DeFalco, is in "suspension between faith and unfaith" (130-31); and his dilemma is that he is confronted with the choice between the position of the major, "a weak and disillusioned man" who admits the "failings of his philosophical pessimism," and "the forces represented by the machines," both of which are inhumane (135-36).

Julian Smith, in search of the "thing left out," argued that so much has been omitted from "In Another Country" that the "young American narrator, . . . the secret center of the story, has frequently been ignored or relegated to a minor position" below that of the Italian major, as did Carlos Baker, Philip Young, and Leo Gurko. What has been left out of the story is the "dead wench alluded to in the story's title taken from Marlowe's *The Jew of Malta* by way of [the epigraph to] T. S. Eliot's 'Portrait of a Lady':

> Thou hast committed—
> Fornication: but that was in another country,
> And besides, the wench is dead" (137-38).

The major did not fornicate with a wench, but, according to Smith, Frederic Henry did; moreover he and the narrator of this story are "young Americans attached to the Italian army, are both equally interested in medals, both wounded in the leg, and afflicted by a knee that won't bend. Both walk across Milan from their hospital quarters to another hospital for mechanical therapy—and both stop to drink at the same place before returning" (138). These similarities suggest that the story could have become part of the novel, following either chapters 18 or 22. Smith concluded that it is a "more impressive story" if one imagines the narrator has also lost his wife or fiancée— in spite of the fact that he tells the major he hopes to marry—and that the major, a "tutor" figure, teaches him "*not* that one should not marry, but how one should accept the loss of one's wife: one returns to what one has been doing, even if it is something as ridiculous and futile as mechanotherapy for a ruined hand" (140). This argument, that "the story needs the novel if it is to be read with any understanding of the narrator's reason for telling it" (138), is not simply intended to interpret the story within the novel, as it were, but also to suggest, through its association with "A Canary for One," its origins in Hemingway's experience and *his* reason for telling the story, recalling it as "a usable truth following the loss" of Hadley (140).

James Steinke dissociated the story from both the novel and its companion "Now I Lay Me" by distinguishing between the narrator and Nick on the evidence of their dissimilar wounds, their psychological effects, and the two characters' relative maturity (34). In a detailed reading of the story he further discriminated between what the narrator as a much younger man perceived and what he understands in the present narration ("[T]his was a long time ago" [*Stories* 269].) In this analysis the older narrator's "control is unobtrusive in the introductory section and his brief entrances seem casual" until the final episode. Until then we are led to assume that the narrator at the time of the story's events was perceptive not only of the details in the scene but also of "a whole range of complications in [its] social life," and therefore capable of understanding the implications of the major's tragedy. Steinke argued, however, that this is not the case, and that the full impact of the "final episode . . . , told with great force of sympathy by the older narrator, [leaves] the young American rather bewildered" (35). Some of that apparent bewilderment may be indicated by the younger man's halting and repeated reaction to the major's revelation that his wife had just died; but, as Jackson Benson noted, that inadequate reaction is essential to the story's impact (144–45). Steinke concluded by citing as evidence of the younger narrator's bewilderment the remark "I do not know where the doctor got [the photographs of restored hands]. I always understood that we were the first to use the machines" (*Stories* 272). But such photographs had been shown before and the narrator had remarked that "none of us believed in the machines . . . and it was we who were to prove them" (*Stories* 271).

That the narration, like Frederic Henry's, takes place long after the events is worth consideration; unfortunately, the narration does not display those disparate kinds of diction one finds in, say, Joyce's "Araby," that allow one to discriminate between the narrator as a younger and older man. Little in the text proves that the younger narrator does not realize the implications of the story's powerful ending then or soon after. Colin Cass's analysis of the nine occurrences of the act of looking noted that seven occur in the last two climactic pages. The narrator notices as a young man and recalls as an older one that in those seven last acts of perception the major looks three times "at the wall," "straight ahead," and, again, "at the wall" with its deluding photographs; once "down at the machine" in contempt; and then three times "through the window," "at nothing," and finally "out of the window" (*Stories* 271–72). That Hemingway sensed the importance of that symmetrical sequence of acts of desperate perception is clear in the manuscripts: the last of them was added in pencil to the second typescript (KL/EH 492).

Earl Rovit, Arthur Waldhorn, and Joseph Flora are typical of those critics who have followed Philip Young's lead in reading "In Another Country" as a "generic" Nick Adams story; and Flora, the latest, offers the most detailed and persuasive argument.

Earl Rovit drew on the story to demonstrate and extend the recurrent dramatic relationship between the tutor and tyro figures. The major's outburst "A man must not marry. . . . He should find things he cannot lose" (*Stories* 271) is only a momentary and natural "cry of outrage," and "does not preclude his exposure to the risks of the incalculable" (63). The major does not believe in bravery, but he does "believe in grammar, in punctuation, in courtesy, and in following the line of duty." As "an exemplar . . . of dignified resolution in meeting disaster," he teaches Nick that "bravery is merely another illusion" and that there is " 'another country' . . . , in which unillusioned courage is a more valuable quality" (97). The story ends with "the irony of the unsaid": although Nick has not gathered his impressions into a "conceptual form"—indeed, had he done so, the story would have failed—the "selection of every detail is controlled by Nick's mind" (97).

Arthur Waldhorn followed Rovit's interpretation, agreeing that although "Nick admits nothing of the Major's impact on him, . . . [i]ts power emerges . . . in the significant details Nick records. What the reader perceives is what Nick learns—that displayed feelings need not signify weakness and that bravery is not measured only on the battlefield." In fact, the major's outcry is "a critique of the limitations of the 'code,' for the Major knows that settling for what cannot be lost excludes love" (69).

Joseph Flora's consideration of the story ranged as far back as Nick's experiences in "Indian Camp" and "The End of Something" and forward through the war stories to "A Way You'll Never Be." He traced the strategies of distancing in the earlier sections, away from the war, away from the past, and away from that other country, that establish Nick as a "reliable observer of others . . . and a keen observer of himself" (135–37). But once Nick is established as a reliable narrator, the unique shift to indirect discourse (*Stories* 270) suggests Nick's "stunned reaction to the major's outburst" at his easy assumptions about the Italian language (140–41). As James Steinke remarked later, the major's insistence on learning the grammar of the language is equivalent to learning those rules that constrain our experience. And we may assume that from then on Nick not only speaks grammatically but he also understands the "grammar" that informs the final scene. In Flora's analysis, this is an important moment in Nick's career, for he conceives of the Nick Adams stories as "an artist's progress," and this one "bodes well for Nick's future . . . aspirations to be a writer" (143). And also, of course, for Hemingway's.

Works Cited

PRIMARY

Ernest Hemingway: Selected Letters, 1917–1961. Ed. Carlos Baker. New York: Scribner's, 1981.

The Short Stories of Ernest Hemingway. New York: Scribner's, 1938, 267–72.

SECONDARY

Baker, Carlos. *Hemingway: The Writer as Artist.* 1952. Princeton: Princeton UP, 1972.

Benson, Jackson J. *Hemingway: The Writer's Art of Self-Defense.* Minneapolis: U of Minnesota P, 1969.

Bell, Millicent. "*A Farewell to Arms:* Pseudoautobiography and Personal Metaphor." *Ernest Hemingway: The Writer in Context.* Ed. James Nagel. Madison: U of Wisconsin P, 1984.

Cass, Colin S. "The Look of Hemingway's 'In Another Country.'" *Studies in Short Fiction* 18 (1981): 309–13.

DeFalco, Joseph. *The Hero in Hemingway's Short Stories.* Pittsburgh: U of Pittsburgh P, 1963.

Flora, Joseph M. *Hemingway's Nick Adams.* Baton Rouge: Louisiana State UP, 1982.

Gurko, Leo. *Ernest Hemingway and the Pursuit of Heroism.* New York: Crowell, 1968.

Hovey, Richard B. *Hemingway: The Inward Terrain.* Seattle: U of Washington P, 1968.

Lewis, Robert W. Jr. "Hemingway in Italy: Making it Up." *Journal of Modern Literature* 9 (1981): 209–36.

Rovit, Earl. *Ernest Hemingway.* Boston: Twayne, 1963.

Smith, Julian. "Hemingway and the Thing Left Out." *Journal of Modern Literature* 1 (1970): 169–72; rpt. in *The Short Stories of Ernest Hemingway: Critical Essays.* Ed. Jackson J. Benson. Durham: Duke UP, 1975, 135–47.

Steinke, James. "Hemingway's 'In Another Country' and 'Now I Lay Me.'" *Hemingway Review* 5 (1985): 32–39.

Stephens, Rosemary. "'In Another Country': Three as Symbol." *University of Mississippi Studies in English* 7 (1966): 77–83.

Waldhorn, Arthur. *A Reader's Guide to Ernest Hemingway*. New York: Farrar, 1972.

Young, Philip. *Ernest Hemingway: A Reconsideration*. 1952. New York: Harcourt, 1966.

24

Now I Lay Me

Composition History (November–December 1926)

Hemingway's letters of the fall of 1926 show a curious disparity between his pride in "Now I Lay Me" and his reticence to discuss it with Max Perkins for publication. On 23 November 1926 he wrote to Perkins that he was "writing on another Italian story"; and on the following day he told Fitzgerald he had "just finished a better one [than "In Another Country"] that I should be typing now" (*Letters* 230–31). On this evidence, it seems that he had completed at least the first full version of the story (KL/EH 619) by late November.

Then or shortly after that date the typescript was titled in pencil "Now I Lay Me." His next typescript (KL/EH 622) bore the title used in his tentative lists of stories of the early months of 1927, "In Another Country—Two/A Story" (KL/EH 120 B and C). The carbon of a professional typescript (KL/EH 621) is titled in ink "Now I Lay Me," the original of which was probably sent to Scribner's for the *Men Without Women* volume later that spring.

But between the end of November 1926 and nearly six months later, Hemingway did not mention the story to Perkins, at least in the published correspondence.

By the winter of 1926–27, Hemingway seems to have realized that if he could write and publish six or so stories in *Scribner's Magazine* or elsewhere, he could then fill out the volume with others less attractive to journal editors, and Max Perkins. In his letter to Fitzgerald on 24 November 1926, he said as much: "Have two other stories [probably "A Pursuit Race" and "A Simple Enquiry"] that I know can't sell so am not sending them out—but will go well in a book" (*Letters* 231).

But why, if he felt that "Now I Lay Me" was even better than "In Another Country," did he not submit it to Scribner's in the full year before his next volume would be published? The sequence of manuscripts before the first typescript may suggest an answer. They were written in four stages:

I. KL/EH 618, p. 1: two brief false starts, in the first, "Three of us lay on the floor . . . and listened to the silk worms"; the second looks forward to the first paragraph of *A Farewell to Arms*.

II. KL/EH 619, pp. 1–2 and KL/EH 620, originally numbered 3–7 and renumbered 5–9. This first typescript does not include the scene in which Nick's mother burns his father's specimens and artifacts.

III. KL/EH 618, pp. 2–3. This manuscript is a draft of the burning scenes.

IV. KL/EH 620, pp. 1–4, is a revision of 619, pp. 1–2; incorporates 618, pp. 2–3; and renumbers 619, pp. 3–7, as 5–9.

This determination of the order of composition of the manuscripts is of some significance, particularly for those interpretations of the story that assume the sequence of events in the final version represents the author's pattern of associating one event with the next.

Finally, the manuscript (618, pp. 2–3) and the typescript (620, pp. 1–4) are remarkable for two features. First, the typescript includes the first instance of the image of "a red silk handkerchief being pulled out of your pocket if your pocket was your body" (KL/EH 620) representing the loss of consciousness at the wounding. According to Malcolm Cowley's 1949 portrait of Hemingway, he repeated that image to his friend Guy Hickok (47); and another version of the experience appears in the manuscripts of *A Farewell to Arms* (Reynolds, *Hemingway's First War* 30).

Second, both the manuscript and the typescript reveal a crucial and obvious fact that few have noticed. The final version of the story implies that Nick was at most an observer of his mother's burning of his father's treasured artifacts. But in the manuscript there is a telling line and revision as the smiling wife meets her returning husband: "I've been cleaning out the basement, dear," my mother called from the porch, "and |Ernie's|/Nicky's/helped me burn the things" (KL/EH 618).

I can recall no other Hemingway manuscript in which he inadvertently has Nick's mother call him Ernie.

Publication History (October 1927)

If the most interesting fact of the publication history of "Now I Lay Me" is that Hemingway did not submit it to a journal, speculation on his reasons is inevitable. Perhaps he felt that, like "A Pursuit Race" and "A Simple Enquiry," it would not appeal to the tastes of the journal readers—but he quickly published "Hills Like White Elephants" in *transition* that summer. Perhaps, at a later reading in January, he thought less of it or no more than he did of those other two stories, which he marked as "maybe good" (KL/EH 120 B). Or finally, he may have thought that it was too revealing, too obviously autobiographical to be published separately, or without the defining title and other stories of men without women.

Whatever his reasons for withholding the story through the winter and spring of 1927, he had by then decided on its position, serving as a second part of his imaginative return to the aftermath of the war and his wounding. And finally it took its place, a place of honor and significance, as had "Big Two-Hearted River" earlier, concluding his second collection of stories, *Men Without Women,* in October 1927.

Sources and Influences

As with other stories, it seems that the apparently autobiographical nature of "Now I Lay Me" has chilled any interest in its literary sources; and if so, there is an irony in the fact that so little of its narrative can be corroborated as personal history. Hemingway was wounded (once, not twice as was Nick); suffered from insomnia; slept one night on a visit with two friends in a silk "factory" (before, not after he was wounded, as Nick was [Baker 43]); he loved trout fishing and cherished his recollections of the sport; and when he was six, his grandfather died, his family moved from the grandfather's house in which Ernest was born to "a new house designed and built" (*Stories* 365) by his mother when he was seven (Baker 7). If the rest of the story is not fiction, it is still, in varying degrees, unsubstantiated "fact."

All the more important elements of the story, all those so precisely and dramatically realized, have been taken by one biographer after another as personal experience and then read by later critics, in turn, as biographical evidence to support an interpretation—most often a psychological one—of the story. There are four major remembered episodes in the story that are central to any interpretation: the wounding, the fishing, and the two scenes in which Nick's mother burns his father's biology specimens and his Indian artifacts.

The evidence for the effects of the wounding has some support from not altogether reliable occasions. His recollection that when he had been struck unconscious and felt his soul "go out of me and go off and then come back" and his fear that that might recur "at the moment of going off to sleep" (*Stories* 363) find some dubious support in his bravura performances in school assemblies and social groups in January 1919, "[I]t seemed as if I were moving off somewhere in a red din. I said to myself, 'Gee! Stein, you're dead,' and then I began to feel myself pulling back to earth"—his brother Leicester (who was four at the time) cites this in his memoir (47). Malcolm Cowley, in 1949, cited Hemingway's account of the experience to Guy Hickok, whom he knew in the 1920s: "I died then. . . . I felt my soul or something coming right out of my body, like you'd pull a silk handkerchief out of a pocket by one corner. It flew around and then came back and went in again and I wasn't dead anymore" (47). And finally there is the manuscript of *A Farewell to Arms* that records "myself" or the "me that was gone" sliding away and back on "a long thin wire through the center of my soul" and then is revised to the simple account in the novel (Reynolds *Hemingway's First War* 30; *A Farewell to Arms* 54).

Whether Hemingway was dramatically extenuating the almost instantaneous experience of unconsciousness—the mortar shell landed a yard away— for high school classes only two years behind him, then later for Guy Hickok, and finally muting the experience in his novel ten years later; or whether this was a "traumatic" event, as Philip Young argued, or an "out-of-body" experience with as profound consequences, as Allen Josephs has it, are questions that depend upon fictional accounts and later recollections for proof. But whether through fact or fiction, the story is intimately related to the other accounts of the wounding in *A Farewell To Arms* and "A Way You'll Never Be."

So, too, with the memories of fishing, particularly those in "Big Two-Hearted River" that are alluded to in this story (*Stories* 363–64), one must decide whether the recurrence of an event in fiction makes it fact.

Finally, there are the burnings of Nick's father's specimens and artifacts, two events that, if they occurred, must have been separated by three or four years (1905 and 1908) when Hemingway was six and nine. The details of the story are so perfectly realized that biographers, like Peter Griffin, place Hemingway at "the pantry window" watching the event (12); but without the story, there would have been no bonfire, no charred snakes or arrowheads, and precious little kindling for psychoanalytic readings of the marriage of Ed and Grace Hemingway. Michael Reynolds is alone in refusing to draw on that fiction, in spite of the impression that Nick's vivid recollection is beyond even Hemingway's powers of invention.

Critical Studies

For thirty years after Philip Young's exploratory study in 1952, criticism of "Now I Lay Me" has been dominated by a variety of psychoanalytic interpretations, some so bold that they make Young's original assertions seem mild and obvious. Following Nick Adams through the earlier stories to those after his wound, Young noted the "remarkable resemblance between a psychiatrist's description of how a man acts who has been badly hit" and Nick Adams's behavior in the stories after "Big Two-Hearted River" (20).

Even those critics who found the story less impressive for the seeming disunity between its subjective and objective sections, recognized the "restrained terrors" beneath Nick's memories (Rovit 79) and his insomnia as "not only a symptom of psychic illness but also a form of therapy" (Waldhorn 62).

Joseph DeFalco was the first of those following Young to find a unity in the story through an analysis that begins with psychoanalytic and ends in archetypal terms. Nick's "willful precipitation of regressive infantile reveries marks him as suffering from some acute mental disorder"; but "what might have been a mere account of a battle-traumatized veteran . . . achieves . . . universal implications" (105). DeFalco noted the ironic discord between the second line of the prayer alluded to in the title, "I pray the Lord my soul to keep," and Nick's fear for "the flight of his soul" that may not return (106). This fear is grounded in the "fear of the loss of God as a symbol of authority" and so is related to the boy's memory of the first god that failed, his father (107). For the memories of fishing, DeFalco moved into archetypal and religious dimensions: Nick, the fisherman, "in the role of the authoritarian law-giver, . . . cannot bear the vision of the salamander and cricket wriggling on a hook because their behavior is analogous to his own crucified state of hyper-sensibility" (109).

DeFalco accepted the Freudian reading of the two scenes of burning, in fact he nearly dismissed them as "hardly worth mentioning," to return to Nick's next dreamlike move, "to recreate his own identity by recreating the world of his own experience" (112). This reverie is interrupted by the recurrence of the sound of the silkworms eating, which, for this analysis, is associated with the classical Fates, spinning, measuring, and cutting the thread of life, for Nick makes the "telling comment: 'but the silkworms were not frightened by any noise we made and ate on steadily' " (113).

This interpretation has the virtue of uniting the passages of reverie with the concluding dialogue. The conversation with John, for whom the universal anodyne is marriage, points up the ironic fact that Nick is "now at one with the ineffectual and emasculated father figure"; Nick cannot marry, for to do so would be to usurp "the power of the father, a circumstance which is precluded because of the trauma that had its origins in the nursery intrigue" (114).

Two years later, Richard Hovey offered the more classical Freudian analysis of the story. He suggested that the structure of the story displayed a striking analogy with the free association of "psychiatric treatment" and, as in other stories, "wounding is linked with rejection of marriage" (181). He, too, noticed an ambiguity in the allusive title, relating not only to a fear associating death and sleep but also implying a "longing to return to the imagined security of early childhood" (182).

The story begins, as do some psychoanalytic sessions, with the "observation of some external fact"—here, the silkworms feeding—which by association suggests the theme of one's mortality and so connects with Nick's wounding but also leads into the next recollection of fishing with other worms and, of course, the burned snakes later. But the reverie of fishing, a way to pass the night hours, is also a way to "screen away awareness [of] the painful contents of Nick's psyche" that indicates a tenacity that is somehow "compulsive, sickly" (183). Thus, when Nick turns to "the earliest thing," the "fishing fantasies are marked as "analogous to 'resistance' in the psychoanalyst's patient" (184). What has been repressed until Nick is "cold-awake" is, of course, the recollection of the two objects in the attic: the tin box with the wedding cake and the jars of snakes, clear symbols of the female and male genitalia (185). Hovey's analysis united, as a psychiatrist's would, the two wounds: "the first 'wound'—the child's feared wound of emasculation . . . operates in both halves of the story: a wound that cripples the ability to love" (186).

Hovey's 1965 article established something of a psychoanalytic model for later interpretations. Two critics since then have extended or modified his reading. First, Julian Smith asserted that Nick's "memory of his father's symbolic castration is selective, not random, highly personal, not removed"; and with that assumption argued that the Nick of this story is, in fact, closer to Jake Barnes of *The Sun Also Rises* than he is to the other manifestations of Nick Adams (143-45). And more recently, Gerry Brenner's extended psychoanalytic study of Hemingway's works confirmed aspects of Hovey's analysis but argued that he overlooked "a more crucial issue, Nick's shock at his father's response to Mrs. Adams' deed." Brenner agreed that the "shelling at Fossalta remobilized repressed castration anxieties" but he held that those anxieties originated first in the boy's fears of his father (241, n. 29; 242, n. 38).

This summary of those variously psychoanalytic critics—DeFalco, Hovey, Smith, and Brenner—does not fully or fairly represent their complex arguments; each of them should be read carefully—certainly not with the tone of Julian Smith's petulant response to a critic he misread, "That kind of talk gives us all a bad name" (142).

In recent years other critics have helped Nick Adams up from the psychiatrist's couch and placed him at the writer's desk. Earlier critics had noticed but not given much importance to the fact that Nick is the narrator telling this story well after the event in which he, as a younger man, was the principal actor; and if he was in therapy, it has kept him sane at least until now. Joseph Flora began his interpretation with the remark that we are reading a memory within a memory—as in so much of Hemingway's fiction—one of the past and one of the narration (114). Nick, in fact, has served as his own "good psychiatrist, uncovering just the sorts of things he needs to uncover," at least until he faces the prospect of the "black swamp" of the war and again of the "Big Two-Hearted River" (117). Flora's reading of the story is the best account of its relationship to all the other Nick Adams stories, establishing it as a crucial one in Nick's development as a writer (122).

Others have followed Flora's lead, sometimes encouraged by the image of the silkworm, sometimes not. Kenneth Johnston used the life-cycle of the silkworm as an analogy to Nick's experience: emerging "from the cocoon of adolescence" with the "threads of memories he attempts to weave a kind of protective shield"; but the analogy, burdened with details "not unlike" those of the history of the silkworm, breaks down (7-9). Frank Scafella, in two articles, reads the silkworm image as one referring to "imagination at work: . . . symbolic of the soul poised in creative action, . . . achieved through imaginative transmutation of experience into art" ("Imagistic Landscape" 7). Most of this argument is founded on a transcendental conception of the soul that is persuasive in Emerson but less so in Hemingway (" 'I and the Abyss' " 4). James Steinke, in a less philosophical reading, finds in Nick's reveries "a pragmatic and sophisticated kind of self-awareness" (34).

The issue—and one hopes there are others—seems so far to be one of whether the story is to be read as a record of Nick's, or even Hemingway's, unresolved problems; or to be read as Hemingway's or his persona's transmutation of a troubling past into a, at least temporary, resolution in artistic form. Some time ago, Lionel Trilling said that writers are distinctive in their talents to turn maladies into art.

Works Cited

PRIMARY

Ernest Hemingway: Selected Letters, 1917-1961. Ed. Carlos Baker. New York: Scribner's, 1981.

A Farewell to Arms. New York: Scribner's, 1929.

The Short Stories of Ernest Hemingway. New York: Scribner's, 1938, 363-71.

SECONDARY

Baker, Carlos. *Ernest Hemingway: A Life Story.* 1969. Scribner's, 1988.

Brenner, Gerry. *Concealments in Hemingway's Works.* Columbus: Ohio State UP, 1983.

Cowley, Malcolm. "A Portrait of Mister Papa." *Life* 10 Jan. 1949; rpt. in *Ernest Hemingway: The Man and His Work.* Ed. John K. McCaffery. Cleveland: World, 1950, 34-56.

DeFalco, Joseph. *The Hero in Hemingway's Short Stories.* Pittsburgh: U of Pittsburgh P, 1963.

Flora, Joseph M. *Hemingway's Nick Adams.* Baton Rouge: Louisiana State UP, 1982.

Griffin, Peter. *Along with Youth: Hemingway, The Early Years.* New York: Oxford, 1985.

Hemingway, Leicester. *My Brother, Ernest Hemingway.* New York: Fawcett, 1963.

Hovey, Richard B. "Hemingway's 'Now I Lay Me': A Psychological Interpretation." *Literature and Psychology* 15 (1965): 70-78; rpt. in *The Short Stories of Ernest Hemingway: Critical Essays.* Ed. Jackson J. Benson. Durham: Duke UP, 1975, 180-87.

Johnston, Kenneth G. "The Great Awakening: Nick Adams and the Silkworms in 'Now I Lay Me.'" *Hemingway Notes* 1 (1971): 7–9.

Josephs, Allen. "Hemingway's Out of Body Experience." *Hemingway Review* 2 (1983): 11–17.

Reynolds, Michael S. *Hemingway's First War: The Making of A Farewell to Arms.* Princeton: Princeton, UP, 1976.

———. *The Young Hemingway.* Oxford: Blackwell, 1986.

Rovit, Earl. *Ernest Hemingway.* New York: Twayne, 1963.

Scafella, Frank. "'I and the Abyss,' Emerson, Hemingway, and the Modern Vision of Death." *Hemingway Review* 4 (1985): 2–6.

———. "Imagistic Landscape of a Psyche: Hemingway's Nick Adams." *Hemingway Review* 2 (1983): 2–10.

Smith, Julian. "Hemingway and the Thing Left Out." *Journal of Modern Literature* 1 (1970–71): 169–72; rpt. in *The Short Stories of Ernest Hemingway: Critical Essays.* Ed. Jackson J. Benson. Durham: Duke UP, 1975, 135–47.

Steinke, James. "Hemingway's 'In Another Country' and 'Now I Lay Me.'" *Hemingway Review* 5 (1985): 32–39.

Waldhorn, Arthur. *A Reader's Guide to Ernest Hemingway.* New York: Farrar, 1972.

Young, Philip. *Ernest Hemingway: A Reconsideration.* 1952. New York: Harcourt, 1966.

25

A Pursuit Race

Composition History (November 1926–February 1927)

The earliest allusion to both "A Pursuit Race" and "A Simple Enquiry" in Hemingway's correspondence is in a letter to Scott Fitzgerald of 24 November 1926. He wrote that he had sent off "In Another Country," had finished a "better one that I should be typing now"—almost certainly "Now I Lay Me"—and had "two other stories that I know can't sell so am not sending them out—but that will go well in a book" (*Letters* 231). That he had not mentioned the two stories the day before in a letter to Max Perkins, did not refer to them again until 14 February 1927, and then described them as two he had "just done," the first "about the advance man for a burlesque show who is caught up by the show in Kansas City" and the second as "a little story about the war in Italy," confirms his sense of the two stories' chances for journal publication and his plan to finesse them in *Men Without Women* (*Letters* 245).

The first extant version of each story is his typescript (on a typewriter with a red ribbon, no less) and bearing some penciled revisions (KL/EH 667 and 694). Until that typewriter is identified, it seems probable that these versions are the ones he referred to in late November. Knowing they would not sell, Hemingway probably put them aside until the following February, by which time he had a list of stories with word counts for his next volume to send to Perkins (*Letters* 245; see also KL/EH 120 B). The second and final versions of the two stories are his revised typescripts (KL/EH 668 and 695, carbons of the originals sent to Scribner's).

Hemingway's revision of "A Pursuit Race" between the first and second version are of critical interest. The story's brilliant first paragraph originally began with its second sentence ("In a pursuit race . . ."), leaving the reference of the metaphor until its last sentence. Later, Hemingway moved the first sentence of the original second paragraph ("William Campbell had been in a pursuit race . . .") to open the story and to make the metaphor immediately explicit (KL/EH 667; *Stories* 350).

Other revisions between the two versions may or may not be minor: in the first version William Turner is named Watson; the passage on the light burning all night ("He turned off the electric light . . . in the morning" [*Stories* 351]) was added later; the pun on "sheet/shit" is made explicit seven lines later ("You're talking through shit you mean" [KL/EH 667]); and Hemingway tentatively considered deleting much of the dialogue about the "wolf" Campbell wards off with whiskey, a wolf he had named "Horace" in a marginal note (*Stories* 352, KL/EH 667).

Publication History (October 1927)

"A Pursuit Race" was ready for publication with revisions in the fall of 1926, and Hemingway was considering its place in the next collection from February 1927 on—like "A Simple Enquiry" he thought it was "maybe good" (KL/EH 120 B). It was first published in *Men Without Women* in October 1927.

Sources and Influences

Although the title and central metaphor of "A Pursuit Race" probably derive from Hemingway's early interest in the bicycle races in Paris, Charles Fenton has noted that Hemingway's brief but intense experiences reporting for the *Kansas City Star* in 1917–18 sowed the seeds for both "A Pursuit Race" and "God Rest You Merry, Gentlemen,"—"a memorable harvest of his *Star* assignments" (49). And if there are no traces of his meeting burlesque show managers like Campbell and Turner, he certainly could have while covering the police beat, the railroad station, and the hospital in that city.

Other than that possible source in Hemingway's early experience, most critics have associated the story with "The Killers," which he had completed in the late summer of 1926, and "A Clean Well-Lighted Place" of the early 1930s. And that consideration leads to critical questions.

Critical Studies

It seems likely that, as Hemingway may have suspected, "A Pursuit Race" would not have attracted what little critical notice it did, had it not been published in a collection with "The Killers" and followed some six years later by "A Clean Well-Lighted Place."

Edmund Wilson, in a review of 1927, cited the story for evidence contradicting contemporary reviews of Hemingway, to argue that the story is about "a man who has just lost a desperately prolonged moral struggle" (114), and to turn our attention away from Campbell's agony to Turner's reaction to his desperate situation. And it is true that Turner was "a man who knew what things in life were very valuable," and so did not awaken the sleeping Campbell (*Stories* 355). This act of Turner's may be associated with Nick's in "The Killers," and is very close to the older waiter's response in "A Clean Well-Lighted Place."

But Turner's role as a sympathetic witness, like Nick's or the older waiter's in the other stories, leads most critics to assume that what William Campbell faces is the ineluctable fate of Ole Andreson or the *nada* of the old man in "A Clean Well-Lighted Place." For Carlos Baker, Campbell is engaged in the "whole widespread human predicament, deep in the grain of human affairs," facing the "ultimate horror" (*Writer as Artist* 123). For Sheldon Grebstein, whatever humor there is in Campbell's childlike manipulation of Turner, beneath it lies "the stark recognition of life's terror by those exhausted souls who stop running" (187). Wirt Williams found the pursuit race a metaphor for Campbell's situation and the "mortal predicament" of us all, while Turner—an ominous name—is both Campbell's brother and "a transient figure of catastrophe" (94).

Two critics seemed to disagree over the story's mood. Grebstein found a potential for humor and satire in the "contrast between the businesslike, sober, and well-adjusted Mr. Turner . . . and the collapsed, drunken, drug-addicted wreck William Campbell. . . . [B]ut no satire is forthcoming because the narrative sympathy extends almost equally to both" (186). Larry Grimes, on the other hand, assumed a rather stern moral position, arguing that the story, like others, "presents bizarre behavior as an alternative to socialization." He contended that, unlike Nick Adams who turns back from the swamp in "Big Two-Hearted River," Campbell has entered it and now manifests "behavior patterns that are as irrational as those exhibited by the most insane" (75). Turner's concern for Campbell is reasonable; he "speaks for society (the show) and places great faith in its protective and restorative powers. Campbell, the lone advance man, has voted no confidence in society's way of making meaning" (76). Grimes concluded, however, that the game metaphor of the story suggests that Campbell has options other than "sliding" like Turner, he "can either be a graceful loser or a pathetic failure," and he clearly fails gracelessly (77). That is a rather harsh reading that rests on the judgment that this is a "grotesque tale of heroin addiction and slow drug death" (75) and that there is a real difference between Turner's accomodation to society and being a graceful loser.

For some recent critics William Campbell has been overtaken by more than alcohol and heroin. Richard Hovey, in 1968, suggested that he is afflicted with some unidentified venereal disease (17). In 1983 Gerry Brenner, in a passing remark, noted that both "A Simple Enquiry" and "A Pursuit Race" openly display "homoerotic situations" and left it at that (22). A year later Ernest Fontana argued that for Campbell the "ultimate horror is his homosexuality and his relationship with his 'wolf' or older lover [from whom] he has contracted his venereal disease." He cited two dictionaries of slang and one of prison language based on "linguistic research in the greater Kansas

City area in 1916–1917" (44) that identify *wolf* as a term for an aggressive pederast. Twice in his last rambling discourse Campbell pauses over the word *horses:* " 'Keep away from women and horses, and, and—' he stopped" and " 'If you love women you'll get a dose,' William Campbell said. 'If you love horses—' " (*Stories* 354). Fontana used the second instance to argue that "the slang context implies that he has contracted from his male lover not only a venereal infection but the emotional desolation that drives him both to drink and heroin" (44). He might have added that *horse* is a slang term for heroin and a narcotic addict; and it may be of moment that in Hemingway's first manuscript, Campbell says of his wolf, "I call him Horace" (KL/EH 667). One questionable feature of this interpretation of the slang word is that Campbell seems pleased that he has got his "lovely wolf" back (*Stories* 352). That, however, does not vitiate Fontana's conclusion that the irony "underlying this stark text is that the advance man for a gaudy heterosexual burlesque show becomes the main act of Hemingway's own understated study of homosexual self-hatred" (45).

"A Pursuit Race" is a complex and, in some ways, a provocative story that has not been afforded the critical study it deserves. Tom Stoppard, in a recent address, acknowledged his indebtedness to Hemingway and singled out the first paragraph of the story as "one of the greatest paragraphs written in English." He called it a "piece of writing that mimics its subject matter. It is a paragraph in which the burlesque show is in a pursuit race with a metaphor. And what happens is that the burlesque show catches up on the metaphor and the metaphor has to get down from its bicycle and leave the page" (24).

Works Cited

PRIMARY

Ernest Hemingway: Selected Letters, 1917–1961. Ed. Carlos Baker. New York: Scribner's, 1981.

The Short Stories of Ernest Hemingway. New York: Scribner's, 1938, 350–55.

SECONDARY

Baker, Carlos. *Hemingway: The Writer as Artist.* 1952. Princeton: Princeton UP, 1972.

Brenner, Gerry. *Concealments in Hemingway's Works.* Columbus: Ohio State UP, 1983.

Fenton, Charles A. *The Apprenticeship of Ernest Hemingway: The Early Years.* New York: Farrar, 1954.

Fontana, Ernest. "A Pursuit Race." *Explicator* 42 (1984): 43–45.

Grebstein, Sheldon N. *Hemingway's Craft.* Carbondale: Southern Illinois UP, 1973.

Grimes, Larry E. *The Religious Design of Hemingway's Early Fiction*. Ann Arbor: UMI Research, 1985.

Hovey, Richard. *Hemingway: The Inward Terrain*. Seattle: U of Washington P, 1968.

Stoppard, Tom. "Reflections on Ernest Hemingway." *Ernest Hemingway: The Writer in Context*. Ed. James Nagel. Madison: U of Wisconsin P, 1984.

Williams, Wirt. *The Tragic Art of Ernest Hemingway*. Baton Rouge: Louisiana State UP, 1981.

Wilson, Edmund. "The Sportsman's Tragedy." *New Republic* 14 Dec. 1927: 102–03; rpt. in *Hemingway: The Critical Heritage*. Ed. Jeffrey Meyers. London: Routledge, 1982, 113–17.

26

A Simple Enquiry

Composition History (November 1926–February 1927)

"A Simple Enquiry" is closely related to "A Pursuit Race" (see Chap. 25): its first version (KL/EH 694), typed in red as was that for "A Pursuit Race," was one of two Hemingway referred to on 24 November 1926 as those that "can't sell . . . but will go well in a book" (*Letters* 231, Hemingway to Scott Fitzgerald); and its second version (KL/EH 695), close to the first, is a professional typescript he told Max Perkins was one of two he had "just done" on 14 February 1927—"a little story about the war in Italy" (*Letters* 245). Neither the first nor second typescript bears substantive revisions.

Publication History (October 1927)

Again, like "A Pursuit Race," this story was ready for publication in the fall of 1926; and by February 1927 Hemingway was considering its placement in his next collection of stories. It was first published in *Men Without Women* in October 1927.

Sources and Influences

When Hemingway wrote to his editor that "A Simple Enquiry" was a "little story about the war in Italy," he might have intended it as a modest allusion to his own experience in 1918; but, of course, his brief venture at the front was in the summer and not with alpine troops, as these Italian soldiers seem to be. It is also possible that his reticence just before publication was intended to divert attention not only from the homosexual major but also from the story's partial indebtedness to D. H. Lawrence's "The Prussian Officer" (1914).

Some thirty years later when he was writing *A Moveable Feast,* he seemed to hint at the indebtedness. His second chapter ("Miss Stein Instructs") ends with a discussion of his attitudes toward homosexuals—"I thought that I had lived in a world as it was and there were all kinds of people in it and I tried to understand them, although some of them I could not like and some I still hated." The dialogue then turns to "an old man with beautiful manners and a great name who came to the hospital in Italy" and to whether one should pity those who—in Stein's phrase—attempt to "corrupt" younger men (*Moveable Feast* 19–20). At the outset of the third chapter ("Une Génération Perdue"), Hemingway—as if recollecting their last conversation—tells Stein of his current reading, especially D. H. Lawrence, who "wrote some very good short stories, one called 'The Prussian Officer' "— clearly not one of Stein's favorites (26).

Sheridan Baker noticed the similarity between the two stories and found that Hemingway's sketch suffers by comparison with Lawrence's longer work (58). Although the two stories share a homosexual officer attracted to his heterosexual orderly, and a scene in which the officer questions his servant about his love for a girl, the differences between the two sets of characters and the two stories' resolutions are large and significant. Lawrence's officer is brutal and sadistic; Hemingway's is gentle and sympathetic. "The Prussian Officer" ends in tragedy; Hemingway's ends with an ironic question evoking a reconsideration of the story's brief incident.

Critical Studies

Few critics have noticed the story and then only briefly; and all of them either cite the tale to exemplify one or another of Hemingway's attitudes toward homosexuality or find in the major's behavior a disturbing metaphor of war's demoralization.

Carlos Baker found that Hemingway's depiction of homosexuality ranged from "the artist's simple acceptance of the fact" through "outright scorn full of . . . disgust" to "amused raillery at the expense of the afflicted" (*Writer as Artist* 139–40). (That last term of Baker's is typical of most of the attitudes toward homosexuality assumed by earlier critics.) Baker placed the story "near the area of simple acceptance" and verging on the humorous. Arthur Waldhorn thought the major is the object of Hemingway's less tolerant attitude: he "has too much unguent on his sunburned face and too much unction in his manner" (228–29).

In an early review Edmund Wilson was the first to read the story as verging on an allegory that displays "that strange demoralization of army life which is scarcely distinguishable from stoicism"; but then Wilson went on to note that "the value of the incident lies entirely in the fact that the major refrains from dismissing the boy," in an act of sympathy like William Turner's decision not to wake Campbell at the end of "A Pursuit Race" (114). Joseph DeFalco was more explicit in his interpretation of the major's attempt to seduce the orderly: it is a "metaphor for the absolute danger inherent in the war itself. Sexual aberration becomes symbolic and symptomatic of the unnaturalness of war" (131–32).

Finally, both Richard Hovey and—more recently—Gerry Brenner have cited the story in their psychoanalytic studies of latent homoeroticism in Hemingway's fiction. For Hovey the homoerotic theme originates in Hemingway's antipathy toward his mother; for Brenner, it is marked more importantly by a fixation on his father. Both this story and its companion, "A Pursuit Race," "openly display homoeroticism and the accompanying affiliative wish" represented by "father figures" (William Turner and the major) and their final gestures of benediction (Brenner 18–22).

For all these brief notices, "A Simple Enquiry" still awaits a full and formal interpretation. Both its central similarity with Lawrence's story and its brevity suggest that Hemingway accepted the challenge of "The Prussian Officer" and attempted to suggest a less dramatic and less discursive resolution of the conflict with which both stories begin. Hemingway's major has been misread; neither is he unctuous nor is his sexuality an aberration symbolic of the unnaturalness or demoralization of war—he is far from Melville's Claggart. His adjutant Tonani knows what is going on, smiles when Pinin leaves; but he respects his officer and protects his deserved rest.

There are at least two unnoticed ironies in the story. The first begins with the title: the major's enquiry is anything but a simple one; in fact he cannot even finish the sentences that begin it when the orderly seems to misunderstand the question "[Y]ou are not corrupt?" And when the orderly looks at the floor twice, the major "smiled. He was really relieved: life in the army was too complicated." Then he offers the orderly the chance to return to his platoon or to remain where there is "less chance of being killed" (*Stories* 329). The second irony, not unusual in Hemingway, resides in the story's last sentence. "The little devil, he thought, I wonder if he lied to me" (*Stories* 330). And we wonder, too, whether Pinin was lying. Has he invented the girl he is in love with? Does he know, as the adjutant does, of the major's homosexuality? Does he know that the officer's attraction to him will insure him a safer place than his platoon's position? And if so, which of them is the more corrupt? Life in the army is, indeed, too complicated for the major's simple enquiry.

Works Cited

PRIMARY

Ernest Hemingway: Selected Letters, 1917–1961. Ed. Carlos Baker. New York: Scribner's, 1981.

A Moveable Feast. New York: Scribner's, 1964.

The Short Stories of Ernest Hemingway. New York: Scribner's, 1938, 327–30.

SECONDARY

Baker, Carlos. *Hemingway: The Writer as Artist.* 1952. Princeton: Princeton, UP, 1972.

Baker, Sheridan. *Ernest Hemingway.* New York: Holt, 1967.

Brenner, Gerry. *Concealments in Hemingway Works.* Columbus: Ohio State UP, 1983.

DeFalco, Joseph. *The Hero in Hemingway's Short Stories.* Pittsburgh: U of Pittsburgh P, 1963.

Hovey, Richard B. *Hemingway: The Inward Terrain.* Seattle: U of Washington P, 1968.

Waldhorn, Arthur. *A Reader's Guide to Ernest Hemingway.* New York: Farrar, 1972.

Wilson, Edmund. "The Sportsman's Tragedy." *New Republic,* 14 Dec. 1927: 102–03; rpt. in *Hemingway: The Critical Heritage.* Ed. Jeffrey Meyers. London: Routledge, 1982, 113–17.

27

On the Quai at Smyrna

Composition History (Winter 1926–1927)

In early August of 1930 with some forty thousand words written for *Death in the Afternoon,* Hemingway received a request from Max Perkins for an introduction to the Scribner's reissue of *In Our Time*—they had recently acquired the rights from Boni and Liveright—and, if he could manage it, some "new material" for this edition. On 12 August he replied with some rancor: he refused to "jazz it up with anything of another period . . . to make it sell as a new book," and he was "too busy, too disinterested, too proud or too stupid" to write an introduction for it. He urged Perkins to enlist Edmund Wilson for that task and promised that he would "return the book to you with a few corrections, the original Mr. and Mrs. Elliot, and with or without a couple of short pieces of the same period depending on how these seem in the book between now and then—not later than the first week in September" (*Letters* 327).

Hemingway was adamant: he did not write an introduction for the 1930 *In Our Time* nor did he send any new material; but he did find at least one short piece, if not "of the same period," closer to 1925 than to 1930. Any reader familiar with the chapters of *In Our Time* recognizes their affinity with the "On the Quai at Smyrna," especially chapter 2 ("Minarets stuck up in the rain out of Adrianople" [*Stories* 97]).

Although Hemingway was in Paris when Smyrna fell to the Turks, he had been reading the newspaper accounts of that tragedy just before he left for Constantinople at the end of September. And, if he could draw on news stories for chapter 6 of *In Our Time,* as Michael Reynolds has shown (31–37), it is likely that he sketched out a manuscript in the early 1920s for what became "On the Quai at Smyrna."

If he did not write a draft manuscript then for the 1924 or 1925 chapters, he must have done so soon after, for the one typescript of the story (KL/EH 641) was typed in late 1926 or early 1927 on the same borrowed typewriter with the same red ribbon he used for the typescripts of "A Pursuit Race" and "A Simple Enquiry" in that period (KL/EH 667 and 694).

Although Hemingway had been in Wyoming since mid-July 1930 and probably traveling with few old manuscripts, he had been at work for some time on both *Death in the Afternoon* and "A Natural History of the Dead."

He had several manuscript fragments from an earlier time at hand for the composition of both the story and the bullfight book and could very well have brought the "On the Quai" typescript along for reference.

He begins *Death in the Afternoon* expecting to be "horrified and perhaps sickened by what I had been told would happen to the horses," because "I had just come from the Near East, where the Greeks broke the legs of their baggage and transport animals and drove and shoved them off the quay into the shallow water when they abandoned the city of Smyrna" (*Death* 1-2).

Later, close to the passage in his manuscript of *Death in the Afternoon* completed by mid-August 1930, he tells the Old Lady that the scenes at Smyrna "called for a Goya to depict them." The Old Lady objects: "You wrote about those mules before," and the Author apologizes, "I know and I'm sorry." Hemingway had written of them at the outset of this book, but the Old Lady had been invoked after that; so hers is a projected "recollection" of the imminent publication of "On the Quai at Smyrna," which Hemingway knew would be published well before *Death in the Afternoon*.

So it seems that Hemingway might well have sketched out this story or chapter in the early 1920s; then typed it in the winter of 1926-27. At that time he might have considered the penciled titles "On the Quai" and "On the Quai at Smyrna." With the typescript at hand and Perkins's request for an "introduction," Hemingway rejected those titles and added "INTRODUCTION BY THE AUTHOR," and by the first week of September had it typed again and sent to Scribner's.

On that surviving typescript Hemingway inserted two brief sentences in pencil, and tried another ending that would turn the narrator's recollection away from the last to the first scene. Before the last two sentences he wrote: "They were nice people too. Didn't they didn't [*sic*] want the animals to be us[ed ?] I wish L. G. [?] could have seen them. But the strange thing of the whole show was the way they'd all start screaming. But the strange thing of the whole show was how they'd scream each night at midnight" (KL/EH 641). This was all deleted, and he concluded the story with the narrator's remarks on this "most pleasant business" (*Stories* 88).

Publication History (October 1930; October 1938)

The sketch served first as an "Introduction by the Author" for Scribner's 1930 issue of *In Our Time,* perhaps to please Max Perkins. For the 1938 collection *First Forty-nine* Hemingway retained its place at the head of the *In Our Time* stories, but returned to one of his provisional titles, "On the Quai at Smyrna." Along this meandering path—first a late variety of the *In Our Time* chapters, then something of a thematic introduction to a reissue

of his first major volume of stories, and finally joining his last collection—
it achieved the status of a story.

Sources and Influences

Although Hemingway claimed in a letter to James Gamble on 12
December 1923 that he had been to Smyrna and Anatolia the year before
(*Letters* 107), he had arrived in Constantinople some three weeks after the
Turks had recaptured Anatolia and driven the Greeks to the quais at Smyrna
on 9 September 1922. He soon saw similar scenes of refugees in flight,
however, and reported them in his dispatches (*Dateline* 211–52), and the
details of the burning of Smyrna were at hand in recent newspapers, like
the *Chicago Tribune* (Paris edition) of 6 October:

> By last Saturday night, when the time limit for evacuation expired,
> 260,000 refugees had been taken from Smyrna. . . . From early
> morning until late at night, with searchlights from warships playing
> on the huddled crowd, American and British patrols shepherded the
> Greeks and Armenians aboard steamers. . . . Dr. Esther Lovejoy of
> the American Women's Hospital was present three days handling
> maternity cases in the streets and docks. More than 100 such cases
> occurred during the three days. Many women are going aboard ships
> expecting babies momentarily.

And if Hemingway did not recall the accents of Chink Dorman-Smith
from earlier days, he might have remembered the laconic dialect of the British
naval officers in Constantinople as they described their searchlights sweeping
over the dead and suffering refugees.

Critical Studies

Since the chaotic situation of the refugees and the brutality of both the
Turkish and Greek forces have their own grim and apparent eloquence, critics
have more often considered the implications of the story's narrative voice.
Once J. M. Harrison noted and explained the distinction between the speaker,
a British naval officer, and the voice of the author or narrator, which is
"heard only in the two puzzling introductory sentences"—the "he said" of
the first and fifth paragraphs—he went on to show how the device is related
to the other "dramatic monologues" in the *In Our Time* chapters (141–43).

Louis Leiter was the first to find a pattern in the officer's responses to
the seven scenes he recounts: they strike him serially as "strange," "uni-
maginable," "the worst," "extraordinary," "a hell of a mess," then "sur-

prising," and finally a "pleasant business . . . a most pleasant business" (*Stories* 87–88). This pattern "dramatizes the gradual numbing of human responses through repeated horrors"; yet the officer's "emotions are not entirely anesthetized," for, as he says, that "was the only time in my life I got so I dreamed about things" (Leiter 139; *Stories* 88). With this pattern in mind, the sketch becomes a story that "traces the curve of the storyteller's emotional cauterization—the tougher his emotions become, the more sensitive he grows in our eyes" (140).

Paul Witherington retraced this pattern to demonstrate how "sophisticated verbal solutions replace active solutions to pain and confusion, . . . as internalized events are controlled in art." Through repetition of words and phrases, distancing, and the dissolution of the narrative frame, the "conversation *becomes* a story in front of our eyes, showing the process by which the 'word' detaches itself from the event and takes on its own particular artistic 'flesh,' [and] the artist's version of giving birth" becomes an analogue of the story's only "answer to despair": the women giving birth in the dark holds of the ships (Item 18).

Works Cited

PRIMARY

Dateline: Toronto. Ed. William White. New York: Scribner's, 1985.

Death in the Afternoon. New York: Scribner's, 1932.

Ernest Hemingway: Selected Letters, 1917–1961. Ed. Carlos Baker. New York: Scribner's, 1981.

The Short Stories of Ernest Hemingway. New York: Scribner's, 1938, 87–88.

SECONDARY

Harrison, J. M. "Hemingway's *In Our Time.*" *Explicator* 18 (1960), Item 51; rpt. in *Critical Essays on Ernest Hemingway's "In Our Time."* Ed. Michael S. Reynolds. Boston: Hall, 1983, 141–43.

Leiter, Louis H. "Neural Projections in Hemingway's "On the Quai at Smyrna.' " *Studies in Short Fiction* 5 (Summer 1968): 384–86; rpt. in *Critical Essays on Ernest Hemingway's "In Our Time."* Ed. Michael S. Reynolds. Boston: Hall, 1983, 138–40.

Reynolds, Michael S. "Two Hemingway Sources for *in our time.*" *Studies in Short Fiction* 9 (Winter 1972): 81–86; rpt. in *Critical Essays on Ernest Hemingway's "In Our Time."* Ed. Michael S. Reynolds. Boston: Hall, 1983, 31–37.

Witherington, Paul. "Word and Flesh in Hemingway's 'On the Quai at Smyrna.' " *Notes on Modern American Literature* 2 (1978), Item 18.

28

Che Ti Dice la Patria?

Composition History (April–May 1927)

Hemingway returned from the Italian trip with Guy Hickok at the end of March 1927, and on 4 May he promised Max Perkins "two more stories—Italy 1927 and After the Fourth—these I am rewriting now" (Baker, *Ernest Hemingway: A Life Story* 184; *Letters* 250); the first was to be retitled "Che Ti Dice la Patria?" and the second "Ten Indians." The rewriting of "Italy 1927" must have come first, for it was published two weeks later in the *New Republic* on 18 May.

There are five manuscript items for the story (KL/EH 328A, 329, 330, 517, and 727). Probably the earliest is 727, a paragraph from a graph-lined notebook also containing the "Notebook" version of "Ten Indians"; it describes high winds and a scene similar to those in "Che Ti Dice." The first nearly complete version of the story rests in two manuscripts, again from graph-lined notebooks: 517 is three pages titled "Italy 1927" with a note to "go on in other book, page 3"; and 328 A is twenty-three pages of manuscript for the first section, titled "Italy 1927," the untitled third section, separated by a note, "A Meal in Spezia," the number "II," and the notation "1300 words." The only extant Hemingway typescript (330) is of the second section missing from manuscript 328 A. And the last version is a professional typescript (329) bearing the titles for sections 1 and 2 but not "After the Rain" for 3.

This confusion of manuscripts suggests that Hemingway followed his usual sequence of composition: first some notes (727), perhaps composed on the late-March trip; a manuscript (328 A), probably in mid-April; his own typescript (330) in late April; and the final typescript (329) sent off to the *New Republic* in early May. It also may indicate that in its earlier stages written in April, the three incidents of the story were not clearly fixed in his mind; and unless there were Hemingway typescripts of the first and third sections, it is possible that the "A Meal in Spezia" might have been intended as a story in itself, with its introduction and conclusion left out.

Publication History (18 May 1927; October 1927)

Although he had the working title "Italy 1927" in mind in April, at least for the first section, and used it for the *New Republic,* 18 May 1927, in late May he told Perkins he was considering others (*Letters* 252). There is a list of titles that includes four alternatives: "Thus to Revisit," "Italia Italia Beloved," "Dante's Country," and "Eviva Italia" (KL/EH 767 A). Each of them implies a revision of his original intention simply to report on Italy in 1927 in a piece of journalism to one that more clearly defines it as a story. In the letter to Perkins of 27 May he was worried about the length of the collection and suggested that the article might conclude the volume and offered a justification in that the "three sketches . . . were more on the story side than anything else" (*Letters* 252). Soon after that he settled on the last title "Che Ti Dice la Patria?"—"What do you hear from home?" or "What is the news from the fatherland?" (Baker, *Writer as Artist* 201)— a phrase that Jeffrey Meyers identifies as a "patriotic slogan of D'Annunzio" (84). And so it was titled in the October 1927 edition of *Men Without Women*.

Sources and Influences

Like "Now I Lay Me," "Che Ti Dice" seems to owe less to biography than biography owes to it, perhaps because it was first published in the *New Republic* and is so clearly antifascist in its depiction of Italy in 1927. Later biographers have drawn on it to describe the trip Hemingway and Guy Hickok took in March 1927, arriving at Genoa and Spezia on the 20th and racing for the French border at Ventimiglia ten days later. The report of the trip suggests that the journey was an unpleasant one; and, perhaps for the first time, what Hemingway left out was the middle of the story: it covers only some 20 kilometers before arriving at Spezia and some 180 from Genoa to the French border; missing is the distance from Pisa, through Florence, Rimini, Bologna, Parma, and back to Genoa. It was fascist Italy, the weather was bad; but Hemingway, with his approaching marriage to Pauline Pfeiffer, a Catholic, and his remorse at divorcing Hadley, had two reasons for contrite stops for prayer at roadside shrines (Baker, *Ernest Hemingway: A Life Story* 184, 595).

The rejected titles suggest other influences. "Thus to Revisit" recalls his experience of returning to Fossalta di Piave in the summer of 1922 to "recreate something for my wife [that] had failed" (*Dateline* 180). Two others, "Dante's Country" and "Eviva Italia" clearly indicate his contempt for Mussolini and his village puppets in an absurdist vision of hell and the irony of the translation of "long live Italy" to the "eye-bugging portraits of Mussolini, with hand-painted 'vivas' . . . with drippings of paint down the wall" (*Short Stories* 293). In another *Toronto Star* dispatch four years earlier, he had characterized Mussolini as a pretentious dictator with little real interest in his people; and he predicted that he would be deposed by an opposition "led by that old, bald-headed, perhaps a little insane but thoroughly sincere, divinely brave swashbuckler, Gabriele D'Annunzio" (*Dateline* 256). Recollecting that earlier experience with the fascist, Hemingway might well have decided on D'Annunzio's slogan "Che ti dice la patria?" for a title.

Critical Studies

The few critical remarks on "Che Ti Dice" either consign the story to journalism or attempt to distinguish it from that untidy realm of the discursive. Hemingway himself argued that it was "more on the story side"; but, as Carlos Baker noted, it was intended as a "true account of a motor-trip he made through Fascist Italy" and "left no doubt in the minds of *New Republic* readers . . . as to where Hemingway stood on Il Duce" (*Writer as Artist* 201).

J. F. Kobler noted that the story "has more thematic unity" than his other travel articles for the *Toronto Star,* and that the "episodes are linked by a vein of decay" in the images of the brown river and the mud and dust on the streets, making this "a highly unified and tightly constructed short story" (83). But Sheldon Grebstein is the only critic who has argued for a structure similar to those in other Hemingway stories, his concept of an "outside/inside antithesis." In this story there is not only the sequence of scenes from the road to the restaurant to the road again, but more important, the contrast between the "outside values . . . of the world outside Italy . . . suggested in the narrator's closing description of Mentone, just across the Italian border: 'It seemed very cheerful and clean and sane and lovely'" (Grebstein 11; *Stories* 299). Later Grebstein used this dramatic opposition to exemplify Hemingway's sensitivity to a "humor provoked by the differences between cultures and national identities," particularly in the second section in which the narrator and Guy assume the protective roles of South Germans from Potsdam (119).

Finally, Wirt Williams affirmed the story's dramatic structure but read it as a tragic pattern in which "Italy is the protagonist; she has sought meaning in fascism, and the corruption she has actually come to is the catastrophe" (96).

The question of whether one reads "Che Ti Dice" as an article for the liberal readers of the *New Republic* or as a short story has moment only, of course, if one's answer limits or enlarges the story's meaning. Criticism of the story so far has not significantly addressed that issue, as Hemingway might have suspected when he included among his fictions.

Works Cited

PRIMARY

Dateline: Toronto. Ed. William White. New York: Scribner's, 1985.

Ernest Hemingway: Selected Letters, 1917–1961. Ed. Carlos Baker. New York: Scribner's, 1981.

The Short Stories of Ernest Hemingway. New York: Scribner's, 1938, 290–99.

SECONDARY

Baker, Carlos. *Ernest Hemingway: A Life Story.* 1969. Scribner's, 1988.

———. *Hemingway: The Writer as Artist.* 1952. Princeton: Princeton UP, 1972.

Grebstein, Sheldon N. *Hemingway's Craft.* Carbondale: Southern Illinois UP, 1973.

Kobler, J. F. *Ernest Hemingway: Journalist and Artist.* Ann Arbor: UMI Research, 1985.

Meyers, Jeffrey. *Hemingway: A Biography.* New York: Harper, 1985.

Williams, Wirt. *The Tragic Art of Ernest Hemingway.* Baton Rouge: Louisiana State UP, 1981.

29
Ten Indians

Composition History (September 1925–May 1927)

The manuscripts of "Ten Indians" are unusual in several ways. The differences among them, especially their endings, argue that Hemingway found the story difficult to resolve. Each was written during a crucial period in the harrowing months between the dissolution of his first marriage in the fall of 1925 in Paris and the promise of his second in the spring of 1927 in Grau du Roi. Although each of the three versions of the story is an elegiac tale of the end of a childhood romance, the 1925 version turns the story away from Nick to the pathetic figure of Prudence, the 1926 version turns to the agony of Nick's father, and only the final version of 1927 ends with Nick's momentary solace "before he remembered that his heart was broken" (*Stories* 336).

The first, the "Chartres" version, is a sixteen-page manuscript in a notebook dated "Chartres/27 September 1925" (KL/EH 202 C). It approximates the final version up to Nick's first dialogue with his father, but there is no indication of Prudence's "betrayal" or his father's suspecting it. Nick goes happily to bed after a pleasant evening with his father, but is awakened later by Prudence at his window. Their final dialogue on the beach with the tearful Prudence's remark that she "won't ever kiss anybody again" and that her family "all came back drunk from town" bears a sinister implication, perhaps of abuse or incest, and suggests the beginning of another story.

The second, the "Madrid" version is comprised of two closely related Hemingway typescripts, the first of which is titled "Ten Indians" and marked "Madrid," and the second of which incorporates the revisions in the first and is titled "A Broken Heart" (KL/EH 728, 729). Again, this version written on or shortly after the marathon day of 16 May 1926, bears only a few revisions of the narrative up to the final dialogue between Nick and his father. But it was here that he not only worked in the complexity of that conversation that approaches a cross-examination but also dramatically directed the narrative into the consciousness of Nick's father after he has told his son of Prudence's betrayal:

> His father blew out the lamp and went into his own room. He undressed and knelt down beside the bed. "Dear God, for Christ's

sake keep me from ever telling things to a kid," he prayed. "For Christ's sake keep me from ever telling a kid how things are."

Then he got into bed. He lay crossways in the big double bed to take up as much room as he could. He was a very lonely man.

But he cannot sleep. He goes to Nick's door, finds he is asleep, and returns to his own room; "He would read for a while and perhaps it would put him to sleep" (KL/EH 729).

However unexpected this shift of narrative point of view, it is no more so than that in "A Canary for One" and is, in fact, prepared for in this version's last dialogue when the father intimates that Nick must come to terms with disillusionment as he has, lying alone and crossways on the big double bed. One could argue that this ending is neither better nor worse than the final version's—it is simply the ending of a different story.

The last, the "Notebook" version, is made up of six heavily revised pages in a notebook including a paragraph for "Che Ti Dice la Patria?" (KL/EH 727). In early May 1927 Hemingway wrote to Perkins that he was at work on both stories and that he would send them on in three weeks—the title in mind for this one was "After the Fourth" (*Letters* 250). For the last time he returned to the ending, revised some of the final dialogue and substituted the last paragraph on Nick's wakeful night and forgetful morning for the ending in the Madrid version. That ending brilliantly sets in contrast the story's two families, the Garners and the Adams, and the ways in which each would respond to Nick's first experience of the world of men without women.

The last typescript (KL/EH 730) is close to the published version; it was probably typed from KL/EH 729 and a lost typescript of the Notebook version (Smith).

Publication History (October 1927)

Of the last three stories to be included in *Men Without Women*, "Ten Indians" was either the latest to be completed or was held for further revision longer than the others: "Che Ti Dice la Patria?" was published in the *New Republic* on 18 May 1927, and "Hills Like White Elephants" appeared in the August issue of *transition*. Of the other stories that were first published in *Men Without Women*—"A Simple Enquiry," "A Pursuit Race," and "Now I Lay Me"—only the last might have been a candidate for earlier publication. That both "Ten Indians" and "Now I Lay Me" were not sent out to journals suggests that something common to the two stories restrained him. That shared feature, of course, is a depiction of Nick Adams's father in his silent conflict with, or separation from, his wife.

When Hemingway set the sequence of stories for *Men Without Women,* he placed "Ten Indians" immediately before "A Canary For One," his own version of the end of a marriage and, like "Now I Lay Me," which concluded the volume, a story of a brokenhearted man.

Sources and Influences

Nearly every detail of scene and character in "Ten Indians" has been traced to an original in Hemingway's Michigan summers in 1915–16. Constance Montgomery has walked the roads the Garners and Nick travel on the return to the farm from Petoskey and the trail Nick follows from the farm to the cottage on the lake; and she has interviewed Joseph Bacon, whose family were models for the Garners—Hemingway used their family name in the first manuscript (96–101). Prudence Mitchell appears as Trudy Gilby in two other stories, "Fathers and Sons" and "The Last Good Country"; her original was Prudence Boulton, the daughter of Dick Boulton of "The Doctor and the Doctor's Wife." She helped out in the Hemingway kitchen at the time Hemingway graduated to long pants. The only thing he ever forgot about her—and which he must have known—is that she committed suicide in 1918 when she was sixteen years old. (Smith 66–68.)

It was inevitable then that "Ten Indians" should be related to the other stories of Hemingway's Michigan boyhood. Philip Young drew the lines between it and the stories of fathers and Indians, "Indian Camp," "The Doctor and the Doctor's Wife," "Fathers and Sons," and "The Last Good Country" (7–8). Wirt Williams noted that the story "looks like a fugitive from *In Our Time,* fusing the actions of 'The End of Something' and 'The Three-Day Blow'" (93). And Joseph Flora suggested that the story is the last panel in a triptych with "Indian Camp" and "The Doctor and the Doctor's Wife" that records Nick's sexual maturation (51).

With this much evidence of the story's autobiographical origins and its intimate connections with others of its sort, one might not expect the usual citations of literary sources—especially for a story that seems a "fugitive from *In Our Time*." But in many ways "Ten Indians" is Hemingway's version of Joyce's "Araby." Both stories dramatize a young boy's awakening from romantic innocence: in "Araby" with the boy's witnessing the tawdry sexual encounter in the bazaar he has invested with almost sacred meaning, and in "Ten Indians" with Nick's hearing the witness of Prudence's profanation of their trysting place. Each story places the boy among other families, relatives, or neighbors, who seem to impede his unwitting and ironic quest for experience. Finally, each boy cries as he silently recognizes the end of an adolescent love and the emptiness of its sentimental nostrums for a "broken heart"; and each has gazed "into the darkness" and found both anguish and some solace:

the boy in "Araby" in imagining himself "as a creature driven and derided by vanity" and Nick in hearing the high wind and waves of his independence day.

Critical Studies

Both the manuscripts and the realized structure of "Ten Indians" seem to warrant the nearly unanimous critical interest in the character and behavior of Nick's father and only a passing interest in the resolution of the conflict between the scene with the Garner family and that with his father. Hemingway's rejection of the Madrid version with its dramatic and sympathetic portrayal of the father's lonely agony might justify a harsher view of his relationship with his son. Moreover, the story's symmetrical structure—two identical parts of three scenes of dialogue (each introduced by a narrative paragraph and with narrative transitions dividing the conversations) and a conclusion—"seems to establish the scene with the Garners as a standard for measuring what is diminished or missing from the scene at Nick's home" (Smith 54). But Robert Lewis identified the conflict as one "between what Nick really feels about his love affair with the Indian girl and what he is supposed to feel. . . . He thinks he cries for the broken heart he is supposed to have, but the greater hurt is probably to his pride" (9)—as it was to the vanity of the boy in "Araby."

If that is the story's true center, as it seems to be, then both the rejection of the Madrid version and the laborious revisions of the Notebook ending, with its distinction between the way Nick feels and his quick but trivial explanation that his heart must be broken, force a reconsideration of the roles of both the Garner family and Nick's father. That distinction "is a metaphor for the distance between the two families. . . . The image of a broken heart is a commonplace, and so offers the comfort of a shared and universal experience. It is . . . the sort of remark one might finally expect from Mrs. Garner. 'If I feel this way' rises out of the immediate experience of his father's telling him the way things are with Nick and, silently, with himself" (Smith 65).

Robert Fleming's recent article nicely reviewed the conceptions of the father as a "saint or sinner" that have occupied critics in the last two decades. He found three positions on the father's behavior: first, he "may be displaying a calculated cruelty toward his son"; second, "impelled by love for the boy, he may be acting for Nick's own good"; and third, "he is motivated on one level by altruistic principles and on another by an underlying hostility in his nature" (101).

Of those that find Nick's father deliberately cruel for his own reasons, Fleming cited Ann Edwards Boutelle's argument that in the last scene the father is wielding the knife against the huckleberry pie as he did in "another kind of brutal operation" against the woman in labor in "Indian Camp" (Boutelle 138). Fleming corrected this curious misreading of the two events later in his article and might have noted, less politely, that the operation in "Indian Camp" saves the woman's life while here he cuts the pie in the absence of the mother. (Boutelle twice used a revealing verb to identify the tenth Indian: in her account one Indian "blurs" into any other dead, male ("dead-snake") Indian, but never into the "customary" one, Prudence [137]). Gerry Brenner briefly extended this psychoanalytic vision to question the father's motives: "Had he gone off to the Indian camp to find Nick's girl for himself . . . ?" (18). Although literary biographers may have some trouble imagining an Oak Park doctor "threshing around" in the woods with a thirteen-year-old Indian girl, Brenner's question may hold us longer than Boutelle's article, for it draws on a closer reading of the story; but both notions, particularly Brenner's, might have found some support in the manuscripts (Smith 65–69).

Those who took a more benign view of Nick's father are exemplified in Fleming's review by Jarvis Thurston and Joseph Flora. Thurston recognized that Nick's questions "lead inevitably into an adult world of betrayal and infidelity—the kind of world Nick almost compulsively seeks to know and that the father wishes Nick did not have to know"; and his motive is a simple and "tender regard for his son's agony" (Thurston 175–76). Flora found the father's motives in "prudishness" in discussing Prudence's "threshing around" with a boy in the woods (49), and that is confirmed by his later reluctance to elaborate on "heinous" acts in "Fathers and Sons."

Then there are those who took the middle view that the father is "kindly in many ways, yet capable of cruelty" (Fleming 103). Understandably perhaps, most critics came to rest in this position. Joseph DeFalco saw the father as a guide figure: "He ministers to Nick's needs—feeds him—in a motherly fashion, but he also delivers the hurt" (52). Jackson Benson, like Flora later, found the father's prudishness a consequence not only of his wife's castrating acts but also of "the genteel environment that robbed him of his manhood" (12). Sheldon Grebstein could not decide whether the father's attitude was an act of "vengefulness" or an "an honest attempt to perform his paternal duty" (108). And Arthur Waldhorn, after describing the father's "mild but perceptible sadism" and "cunningly evasive" attitude, concluded that he "mingled burden with blessing." He, by the way, was the first to note the "vinegary innuendo" in the father's remark as he offers some cold pie, "You better have another piece" (56–57).

Robert Fleming concluded his article, which is informed with a reading of the story's manuscripts, by correcting those interpretations of the father's behavior as either sadistic or coddling. His analysis brought together the complex attitudes of both the father and son in their final dialogue, attitudes that are consequences of their personalities, their familial and social roles, and the parts each plays in the universal drama of father and son (108–10).

It is that very subtle drama of the relationship between father *and* son that is missed in those considerations of the story that exclude one or the other of its characters or ignore the buried questions beneath their end-of-day conversation. Nick may wonder for a moment why his father was walking "back of the Indian camp," but his question says more of his adolescent turmoil than of his father's improbable lust. On the father's side, there is the seemingly innocent moment when he asks his son what he did with his shoes. Nick says, "I left them in the wagon at Garner's," and the father senses that there is more there in his son's forgetfulness than easy summertime living, for he then invites him into the kitchen for a good cold supper and some good cold recognition of the way things are.

Much of the complexity of the story derives from Hemingway's recollections of his "adolescence and the lives and characters of those close to him: his boyhood friends, their parents and his own, and his first girl." Those memories must have been evoked in the difficult times between the fall of 1925 and the spring of 1927. His earliest experience of his disillusionment in love, his own remorse over the impending separation from Hadley, and his memory of his own father alone in the Windemere cottage must have had something to do with the title of his story. It comes from an old minstrel song, and it ends with fate of the tenth Indian:

> One little Injun livin' all alone,
> He got married and then there were none. (Smith 69)

Works Cited

PRIMARY

Ernest Hemingway: Selected Letters, 1917–1961. Ed. Carlos Baker. New York: Scribner's, 1981.

The Short Stories of Ernest Hemingway. New York: Scribner's, 1938, 331–36.

SECONDARY

Benson, Jackson J. *Hemingway: The Writer's Art of Self-Defense.* Minneapolis: U of Minnesota P, 1969.

Boutelle, Ann Edwards. "Hemingway and 'Papa': Killing of the Father in the Nick Adams Fiction." *Journal of Modern Literature* 9 (1981–82): 133–46.

Brenner, Gerry. *Concealments in Hemingway's Works.* Columbus: Ohio State UP, 1983.

DeFalco, Joseph. *The Hero in Hemingway's Short Stories.* Pittsburgh: U of Pittsburgh P, 1973.

Fleming, Robert E. "Hemingway's Dr. Adams—Saint or Sinner?" *Arizona Quarterly* 39 (Summer 1983): 101–10.

Flora, Joseph M. *Hemingway's Nick Adams*. Baton Rouge: Louisiana State UP, 1982.

Grebstein, Sheldon N. *Hemingway's Craft*. Carbondale: Southern Illinois UP, 1973.

Lewis, Robert W., Jr. *Hemingway on Love*. 1965. New York: Haskell House, 1973.

Montgomery, Constance. *Hemingway in Michigan*. Waitsfield: Vermont Crossroads, 1977.

Smith, Paul. "The Tenth Indian and the Thing Left Out." *Ernest Hemingway: The Writer in Context*. Ed. James Nagel. Madison: U of Wisconsin P, 1984.

Thurston, Jarvis A. *Reading Modern Short Stories*. Chicago: Scott, 1955.

Waldhorn, Arthur. *A Reader's Guide to Ernest Hemingway*. New York: Farrar, 1972.

Williams, Wirt. *The Tragic Art of Ernest Hemingway*. Baton Rouge: Louisiana State UP, 1981.

Young, Philip. " 'Big World Out There': The Nick Adams Stories." *Novel* 6 (Fall 1972): 5–19.

30

Hills Like White Elephants

Composition History (May 1927)

April and May of 1927 were crowded months for Hemingway; after his return from the grim trip to Italy with Guy Hickok, he saw his first wife and son off on the boat train on 16 April, turned to plans for his wedding to Pauline on 10 May and their new apartment, finished "Italy 1927" ("Che Ti Dice la Patria?") for publication in the *New Republic,* and, after two years, decided on the ending for "Ten Indians." Through May he listed the sequences of stories for *Men Without Women* and corresponded with Max Perkins over the last few stories to be included.

After promising Perkins "Che Ti Dice" and "Ten Indians," he told him he might have three others, "A Lack of Passion . . . and a couple more," for he wanted "the book to be full [$]2.00 size" (*Letters* 250–51, 4 May 1927). One of those two stories was probably "Hills Like White Elephants," for its title appears in a list of thirteen stories, on the verso of which are the four rejected titles for "Che Ti Dice."

Something of the story had been in Hemingway's mind for a long time. Carlos Baker suggested that he might have begun writing it as early as 31 March 1927, for in a letter on that date to Scott Fitzgerald there is the line "We sat at a table in the shade of the station" with Hemingway's note that "this is the start of something or other" (Baker 595; see *Letters* 248–50). If it was a brief start on the story, it is of interest, as Baker remarked, for its first-person point of view.

The first-person narration is also used in a related sketch from the early summer of 1925 (KL/EH 472). Kenneth Johnston erred in treating this sketch as if it revealed Hemingway's original intention for the story (234), and Robert Fleming provided the evidence that it does not (note 3). The unfinished sketch shares the story's setting and introduces the simile that became the story's title and most powerful image. But the events and the mood of the sketch could not differ more from those in the story: it opens on the train arriving at Caseta; Hemingway invents the simile, not Hadley; they order beer, and the rattan curtain, caught by the wind, sweeps the glasses to the floor; they race to get on the express train from Barcelona to Madrid and in happy conviviality join the other travelers. Some of the details of the trip are repeated in a letter to Gertrude Stein of 15 July 1925 that ends with the remark that it "was the best party almost I've ever been on. . . . It was very fine" (*Letters* 168). The mood of this letter and the sketch reflects the relief Ernest and Hadley felt at leaving Pamplona on their own after the ruined fishing at Burguete and the intrigues and arguments that troubled the Pamplona fiesta.

Aside from the setting and the comical incident of the curtain clearing the table, the earlier sketch is interesting for Hemingway's first try at the central simile. As is often the case, he first expands the comparison—sometimes to ungainly proportions—and later reduces it to a simple, nearly literal, statement (see Donaldson 207; Smith 40). In 1925 he wrote:

> beyond the river rose abruptly the |white|/mysterious/white/mountains.
>
> We had called them that as soon as we saw them. To be disgustingly accurate I had said, "*Look* at those god-dam/white/ mountains."
>
> Hadley said, "They are the most mysterious things I have ever seen."
>
> . . . On a cloudy day they might have been gray |but in| as a white elephant is gray in a circus |side show| tent; but in the |July sun|/ heat/they shone white as white elephants in the sun. (KL/EH 472)

The invention of the image, here almost a connubial venture, becomes solely and immediately Jig's creative act, which her companion neither participates in nor can understand.

The manuscript (KL/EH 473) that Hemingway must have had typed was sent off to Max Perkins on 27 May 1927 from Grau de Roi (*Letters* 251), and perhaps earlier to *transition,* for it was published in that journal in August of that year.

Its significant revisions or inserts are, for the most part, concerned with the story's images. Several describe Jig's perceptions of the beaded curtain (*Stories* 274, 275) and the shadow of the cloud (*Stories* 276); two suggest her companion's benighted vision of things. When he looks at their bags, Hemingway made two important changes, one of which he returned to its original: "There were |stickers| labels on them from all the hotels where they had |spent nights| stopped"—and he restored it to "spent nights." And at the end, he originally wrote, "There must be |an|/some/actual world. There must be some place where people were calm and reasonable./They were all waiting reasonably for the train./Once it had all been as simple as this bar," and he reduced the whole perception to the inserted sentence with its metaphoric adverb "reasonably."

Although Hemingway had sketched out the setting and the simile two years earlier, the narrative and dialogue he wrote in May 1927 were original.

And it seems to have come to him immediately, as its revisions were immediately apparent.

The only other earlier story for which there is one manuscript and which seems to have been written right off with a few significant revisions is "Out of Season," a story about another troubled couple in a foreign land where the landscape reflects their perceptions.

One last note on the manuscript: inscribed in pencil on the last page is this note, "Mss for Pauline—well, well, well." There is no telling what might be made of that note at the end of a story in which the conflict is over abortion, a story written by one who was about to marry a Catholic and had spent part of a recent trip to Italy to confirm that he had been baptized by a priest (Baker 183, 185). The only note to be made here is that the letter of 31 March 1927 to Fitzgerald, the one including an apparently introductory sentence for the story, which Hemingway noted as possibly the "start of something," also alludes to H. L. Mencken and adds, "Well well well pitcher that. That last is the Sinclair Lewis influence. That's the way his characters talk" (*Letters* 249).

Publication History (August 1927; October 1927)

One reason for suspecting that Hemingway finished "Hills Like White Elephants" earlier rather than later in May 1927 is that he sent it off to *transition* in time for it to be accepted and then published in August. In the latest list of stories he arranged, "Hills Like White Elephants" was placed third from last; in *Men Without Women* it came third after "The Undefeated" and "In Another Country," by which time his notion that the stories in this collection would demonstrate the absence of "the softening feminine influence" (*Letters* 245) had been forgotten. Perhaps he thought it would be best situated just after a story in which the central character still has hopes of marrying.

Sources and Influences

Although Lionel Trilling has noted an analogue between the story and "The Game of Chess" in Eliot's "The Waste Land," "Hills Like White Elephants," with its dependence on allusive dialogue and its suspended ending is almost universally considered a generic Hemingway story, a true original like "The Killers" or "A Clean, Well-Lighted Place," with no substantive literary indebtedness. In lieu of any literary source, speculation on the story's biographical origins is more than plentiful. Citing four sources, Robert Fleming argued that settling on any one source is "a disservice to readers as well as the reputation of the artist" (note 3). The earliest is an anecdote Robert

McAlmon reported to Hemingway at Rapallo in February 1923. He mentioned a rather blasé college girl who had an abortion and remarked, " 'Oh, it was nothing. The doctor just let the air in and a few hours later it was over.' . . . Later Hemingway informed me that my remark suggested the story" (159). The second source derives from reports of Hemingway's reaction to Hadley's pregnancy in 1923: Gertrude Stein recalled him saying he was "too young to be a father" (213); and Guy Hickok, through Lincoln Steffens, reported Hemingway's realization that "there is no sure preventative" (Steffens 835). The third source is the 1925 sketch (KL/EH 472); and the fourth is Hemingway's recollection in his 1958 interview with George Plimpton of meeting "a girl in Prunier. . . . I knew she'd had an abortion. I went over and we talked, not about that, but on the way home I thought of the story, skipped lunch, and spent that afternoon writing it" ("Interview" 35).

Together these four anecdotal remarks, remembered from four to forty years *after* the story was published, add little to it—especially McAlmon's memoir with the title *Being Geniuses Together,* published in 1938, a decade after Hemingway had become a bitter enemy and with good reason (Baker 206).

Although the couple in "Hills Like White Elephants" are not married, Jig, at least, has marriage on her mind; and the story may be read in the sequence of marriage tales: "Out of Season" (1923), "Cat in the Rain" and "Cross-Country Snow" (1924), and "A Canary for One" (1926). Written six months after the last of them, it predicts and in some ways explains the unhappy and inevitable end of that brilliant and tragic sequence of stories.

Critical Studies

In 1933 Hemingway complained to Max Perkins that of all his stories the one reviewers now call a " 'classic' Hills Like White Elephants not one damn critic thought *anything* of when it came out" (*Letters* 401). Not quite true, for Dorothy Parker praised the story as "delicate and tragic" even though Virginia Woolf's review was, as John Hollander has remarked, "most curious and suggests that she thinks the operation in question is a tonsillectomy" (Hollander 216).

Fifty years of criticism since then has included few dissenters to the judgment of the story as a classic. And almost all have turned first, as Hemingway directed them in the title, to the story's setting with its "line of hills . . . white in the sun" and Jig's sense that "They look like white elephants" (*Stories* 273). The simile is striking, but not so much as a visual image—it seems tentative, offhand, and approximate, as Jig admits later. It derives its power, of course, as an index to the girl's imaginative character, when during her dialogue she twice refers to her remark and twice looks to them as if for some respite from her terrible dilemma.

Even without the 1925 sketch, one could locate the setting in the town of Caseta, near the Ebro, at a small junction on the Barcelona-Madrid rail line. The two rail lines, with the station between them, divide the landscape between the brown, dry country and the white hills to the north and the fertile "fields of grain and trees along the banks of the Ebro" with mountains to the south (*Stories* 273, 276). Most commentators since Eusebio Rodrigues (1962) have noted the opposition between the two landscapes, one barren and the other fruitful, as an appropriate scene for a discussion of whether to abort or to bear a child.

There is some disagreement, however, over whether the image of the hills like white elephants itself implies both fertility and sterility. Sheldon Grebstein admitted only "the idiomatic sense of a thing now debased or devalued, the realization of a mistake" for the phrase "white elephant" (111). Mary Fletcher held that only on "the other side" is there any more promise than "the barrenness and sterility as represented by the dry hills" (17); and for Johnston even that vision of fertility is crossed by a cloud literally "foreshadowing the death of [the] unborn child" (235).

Joseph DeFalco was the first to argue that the term "white elephant" becomes "metaphorically an objectification of the inner conflict," for it "not only means an annoyingly useless gift; it may also be a possession of great value" (169). Lewis Weeks anatomized the image further by noting that, while for the man in the story the hills suggest the unborn child as a "white elephant that, in his selfishness, he wants to get rid of," when Jig mentions them a third time, "the image is of a fully pregnant woman . . . with her distended belly virtually bursting with life and with her breasts . . . making a trinity of white hills," an image closer to the meaning of the white elephant as a "rarity in nature, [to be] considered sacred and precious, . . . revered and protected" (76). John Hollander, in the most recent study, admitted both meanings and cites the origin of the proverbial meaning of a white elephant as an unwanted possession: it derives, "as *Brewer's Dictionary of Phrase and Fable* elegantly puts it, from the story of a Siamese king who 'used to make a present of a white elephant to courtiers he wished to ruin' " (214)—and that is somehow appropriate, too.

With the white elephants variously identified, the second most recurrent image in the story, the bamboo bead curtain has engaged some commentary. Gary Elliott argued that it "represents and functions as a rosary for [Jig], who must certainly be a Catholic," and therefore her resistance to an abortion derives from "religious sensibilities resurrected by the presence of the bead curtain" (23). Dennis Organ went further to suggest that Jig sees them as "familiar in infant's playthings" (11); and J. F. Kobler held that her "tactile responses" to the beads and her companion's walking through them indicate their opposed attitudes toward the abortion (7).

With the curtain drawn aside, only the drinks are left; and they too have been sampled for symbolism. Johnston, with some misinformation about the color and legality of absinthe, drew on popular beliefs that it causes sterility and is an aphrodisiac. When Jig drinks the Anis del Toro and recalls absinthe, her companion may be reminded that he introduced her to the aphrodisiac, but "it is doubtful that he has the wit to perceive the further irony of linking absinthe . . . to sterility and abortion" (237). Then Phillip Sipiora discovered the reason for the story's "peaceful ending": he miscounted the drinks and assumed the characters were of "average weight" to determine their blood alcohol level and to declare them "legally drunk in all fifty states" (50). No wonder Jig says "I feel fine," albeit in Spain.

If the critical conclusions in the last two paragraphs seem to range from the merely interesting to the wondrously bizarre, it may be that the story is simply, as Dorothy Parker said, "delicate and tragic." So delicate that its tenuous web of dialogue will not hold or respond to weighty associations with religion or the taste of licorice. Or, more likely, so simply tragic that the more perceptive interpretations of Joseph DeFalco (1963), Lionel Trilling (1967), Sheldon Grebstein (1973), and, now, John Hollander (1985) may have left little new to say.

Two earlier critics had assumed that the girl Jig "accepts her lover's demands," and simply reiterates that decision in a masochistic manner at the end of the tale (Wright 371–72); or that the essential drama of the story is a "struggle for speech which reveals the agonies beneath their composure" now that their "private language of love has become unbearable" (Lid 401–02). And each raised a crucial question: At the end of the story does the girl give in, masochistically or otherwise? And is the dialogue of the story inhibited by a private language they share or does it reveal *two* languages that reveal their irreconcilable differences?

The more recent interpretations responded to one or the other of these questions and are concerned with fundamental issues in the story's conflict: whether or not and in what way that conflict is resolved.

Joseph DeFalco saw the man as one of the "emotional and spiritual cripples of the 'marriage group,' " who refuses "to recognize and accept the natural processes of life." He "excuses moral sterility in the name of freedom"; while Jig, witnessing not only the brown hills but also the green "region of fecundity," realizes the "wider implications of the proposed abortion." The story ends with her "capitulation, . . . a pathetic resolution, for throughout the story she is the one who has had the insight" (168–72).

Lionel Trilling's commentary in his anthology was the first to find "a clue to where the point of the story lies" in the man's perception of the people in the bar, "They were all waiting reasonably for the train" (*Stories*

277–78). Trilling noted that *reasonably* "is a strange adverb for the man's mind to have lighted on," but that it pointedly expresses what little character the man has. His "line of detached reasonableness . . . achieves, of course, nothing better than plausibility" but is undercut by the fact that one "cannot say 'really' and 'just' (in the sense of *merely*) as often as he does without sounding insincere" (731). Although Trilling admitted that Jig's perception of the hills like white elephants may be a judgment on their lives as useless, "the chief effect of the simile is to focus our attention upon the landscape she observes" and its contrasting directions of sterility and fecundity. "She is aware of the symbolic meaning that the two scenes have for her, for after her second view she says, 'And we could have all this. . . . And we could have everything and every day we make it more impossible.' It is the sudden explicitness of her desire for peace and fullness of life that makes the man's reasonable voice ring false and hollow in her ears and that leads her to her climax of desperation" (731–32). Trilling did not venture an interpretation of the story's conclusion or any prediction of the couple's future—it was enough for him associate it with Eliot's poem and read it as a "comment—impassioned and by no means detached—on the human condition in the modern Western world" (732).

For Sheldon Grebstein the story approaches a drama of perception insofar as "the gesture or simple act of *looking* makes the most dramatic counterpart to what is said. . . . The girl looks at the distant hills, the bead curtain, the ground, the curtain again, the river, and the hills once more. Each of these looks corresponds with a phase in the conversation" (113). One should add to this analysis the three times the man looks at something: first "at her and at the table," a telling equation; second at their bags with "labels on them from all the hotels where they had spent nights," (the verb is a perfect choice); and finally at the people "waiting reasonably for the train" (*Stories* 277–78). Grebstein's sense of the ending is that it is "dynamically unresolved, not only open but with fuse lighted" (112).

John Hollander's essay on "Hemingway's Extraordinary Reality" is the latest, and may well be the last, commentary on the hills like white elephants. It is difficult to imagine a more perceptive reading, nor one so beautifully written. He, too, witnessed a drama of perception, but in finer detail.

> The girl's *looking* at the hills describes a totally different act from the disaffected sightseeing of the "look at things and try new drinks," of course, and the hills have been privileged by the narration to begin with. Even when she retracts her formulation about the white elephants, in the interests of maintaining the surface of the "fine time," she cannot abandon her observation entirely. What for the reader of novels constitutes her slip about the "skin" of the hills, operates in the poem of the sketch to reaffirm the truth and rightness and brightness of the

original and originating trope: The ridge of hills, low peaked and undulant, lined up in circus fashion, trunk to tail, parade across the middle-high horizon, calm, beneficent, reaffirming the health of distant vision. The narration, and the girl, both know this. But the image of possibility and delight is tragically and inevitably linked, by the ways of the world, to a darker, narrower emblem, and . . . the girl's pregnancy itself becomes part of the matter. (214)

Her second perception, the fields and the river, is, in Hollander's words, "a more pictorial landscape now, and less of a visionary one," and its "promise of plenitude [is] lost before the beyondness of the elephantine hills." The difference between the two acts of perception, first the visionary and then the pictorial, casts some doubt, like the shadow of the cloud at the moment, over the promise of the growing fields and the river. Hollander located the "riddling power of a figure like that of the hills . . . in the way Hemingway's narrative controls the mode of figuration. The hills are, at the outset, simply *there,* as given as given can be; then they are grasped by the girl, become more and more rhetorically problematic as the brief dialogue unrolls, and finally vanish behind a later, sadder kind of landscape. And yet their beauty is nobler than their narrowed emblematic meaning, and that beauty calls up a wider and stronger evocation" (215).

Hollander, like Trilling, made no predictions from the conclusion, but he lay an interesting claim for the story: with its "unfolding of the central tropes [it] has the kind of power of lyrical movement and tells the tale of the genesis of complex meaning . . . [that] may make even the Kilimanjaro and Macomber stories seem, some day, like anecdotes" (216).

The question raised at the end of the story, whether Jig's statement "I feel fine. . . . There's nothing wrong with me. I feel fine" (*Stories* 278) indicates a tacit agreement to the abortion (Wright, DeFalco, Johnston) or an unresolved issue that will erupt later (Grebstein), depends on her character and state of mind after the events of the narrative. No one has argued that she has decided to bear the child or even leave her companion, though many have wondered why she did not stalk off when he met her desperate appeal—"And we could have all this . . . and every day we make it more impossible"—with "What did you say?" (*Stories* 276).

If, however, these later interpretations of the story—each of which has affirmed her creative, even visionary, imagination more persuasively than the last—attest to the "truth and rightness and brightness" of her original perception, then how are we to interpret her enigmatic smile and the inflection of her last words. He has left her to drink yet another Anis del Toro among his "reasonable" kind waiting for the train. While he is gone, it seems at least possible that she might for the last time look at the hills like white elephants. And if so, could she not have smiled ironically at him and said,

"*I* feel fine. . . . There's *nothing* wrong with *me*," leaving him with the last remark of hers he has not the wit to understand?

Works Cited

PRIMARY

Ernest Hemingway: Selected Letters, 1917–1961. Ed. Carlos Baker. New York: Scribner's, 1981.

"An Interview with Ernest Hemingway." *Paris Review* 18 (1958): 60–89; rpt. in *Ernest Hemingway: Five Decades of Criticism.* Ed. Linda W. Wagner. East Lansing: Michigan State UP, 1974, 21–38.

The Short Stories of Ernest Hemingway. New York: Scribner's, 1938, 273–78.

SECONDARY

Baker, Carlos. *Ernest Hemingway: A Life Story.* 1969. New York: Scribner's, 1988.

DeFalco, Joseph. *The Hero in Hemingway's Short Stories.* Pittsburgh: U of Pittsburgh P, 1963.

Donaldson, Scott. "Preparing for the End: Hemingway's Revisions of 'A Canary for One.'" *Studies in American Fiction* 6 (Autumn 1978): 203–11.

Elliott, Gary D. "Hemingway's 'Hills Like White Elephants.'" *Explicator* 35 (1977): 22–23.

Fleming, Robert E. "An Early Manuscript of Hemingway's 'Hills like White Elephants.'" *Notes on Modern American Literature* 7 (1983), note 3.

Fletcher, Mary Dell. "Hemingway's 'Hills like White Elephants.'" *Explicator* 38 (1980): 16–18.

Grebstein, Sheldon N. *Hemingway's Craft.* Carbondale: Southern Illinois UP, 1973.

Hollander, John. "Hemingway's Extraordinary Reality." *Modern Critical Views: Ernest Hemingway.* Ed. Harold Bloom. New York: Chelsea, 1985.

Johnston, Kenneth G. "'Hills like White Elephants': Lean, Vintage Hemingway." *Studies in American Fiction* 10 (1982): 233–38.

Kobler, J. F. "Hemingway's 'Hills like White Elephants.'" *Explicator* 38 (1980): 6–7.

Lid, Richard W. "Hemingway and the Need for Speech." *Modern Fiction Studies* 8 (1962–63): 401–07.

McAlmon, Robert. *Being Geniuses Together.* London: Secker and Warburg, 1938.

Organ, Dennis. "Hemingway's 'Hills like White Elephants.'" *Explicator* 37 (1979): 11.

Parker, Dorothy. Review of *Men Without Women. New Yorker,* 29 Oct. 1927: 92–94; rpt. in *Hemingway: The Critical Heritage.* Ed. Jefferey Meyers. London: Routledge, 19, 107–10.

Rodrigues, Eusebio L. " 'Hills like White Elephants': An Analysis." *Literary Criterion* 5 (1962): 105–09.

Sipiora, Phillip. "Hemingway's 'Hills like White Elephants.' " *Explicator* 42 (1984): 50.

Smith, Paul. "Hemingway's Luck." *Hemingway Review* 7 (Fall 1987): 38–42.

Steffens, Lincoln. *The Autobiography of Lincoln Steffens.* New York: Harcourt, 1931.

Stein, Gertrude. *The Autobiography of Alice B. Toklas.* New York: Random, 1933.

Trilling, Lionel. *The Experience of Literature.* New York: Holt, 1967.

Weeks, Lewis E., Jr. "Hemingway's Hills: Symbolism in 'Hills like White Elephants.' " *Studies in Short Fiction* 17 (1980): 75–77.

Wright, Austin. *The American Short Story in the Twenties.* Chicago: U of Chicago P, 1961.

Winner Take Nothing
(October 1933)

31

Wine of Wyoming

Composition History (October 1928–May 1930)

The late summer and fall of 1928, from Pauline's long labor at Patrick's birth in June to Dr. Hemingway's suicide in early December, must have struck Hemingway as an epoch of endings, in both his life and his fiction, and a period that left little time for starting a story. In the late summer he finished the first draft of *A Farewell to Arms* and let it rest; most of the fall was spent traveling, from Wyoming to Arkansas to Chicago to Massachusetts, then back to Arkansas, down to Key West, up to New York, back to Chicago to settle his father's affairs, and finally returning to Key West and the manuscripts of his second novel.

But in the month between finishing the novel's first draft in late August and his return to Arkansas in September, he introduced Pauline to the Moncini family, their good new wine and chicken dinners, and discovered for himself the origins of his story "Wine of Wyoming" (Baker 195–97). Back in Piggott, Arkansas, Hemingway wrote to Max Perkins on 11 October that he had "a story about ¾ done. Will be leaving as soon as it is finished" (*Letters* 289). The first version of the story (KL/EH 837) is a typescript of the first three sections with the fourth and last in manuscript (*Stories* 462 ["The day before we had had good shooting . . ."]–67). And so it was left in late October when the travels and tragedy of the following months fell.

Three other features of this early draft are notable. In writing this version he used fictional names for the Moncinis, the Pichots; and in a false start (KL/EH 837, 14 verso) mentioned another couple, Larry (referred to in the story) and Martha, who drank with them—this fact and his sense of the story as three-fourths done on 11 October implies he had the whole fiction well in mind from the start.

But not the title: he considered several alternatives:

"Il Est Crazy Pour Le Vin"
"A Lover of Wine" (837, 1)
"Pichot Est Crazy Pour Le Vin" (837, 14 verso)

and

"September"
"A Lover of Wine"
"Wine of Wyoming"
"The New Country" (KL/EH 840 A)

The first set of three focuses attention on the character of Pichot/Fontan; in the second set, "September" turns to the autumnal and elegiac mood of the story's conclusion, and "The New Country," with its reference to the Fontans, their wine, and the social and political dimensions of the story, is gathered in the title he chose, "Wine of Wyoming."

The last aspect of this version to note is a deleted passage of dialogue between the narrator and his wife that both substantiates and qualifies Joseph Flora's interpretation of this story as one of the later "marriage tales" with "A Day's Wait" and "Fathers and Sons." Just after the couple agree that they should have had their last dinner with the Fontans, there is this passage, which was deleted from later typescripts:

> "They're the best people I we know in Wyoming I."
> "Yes, they're the best people," she said.
> I "How do you feel?"
> "I feel just like you do."
> "Elle est crazy pour lui." I (KL/EH 837, 23)

With *A Farewell to Arms* revised and out of the way, Hemingway wrote to Perkins in August 1929 that he was "cheerful again—have written three pieces—have some more in my head" (*Letters* 302), and one of the three must have been "Wine of Wyoming." But by then *Death in the Afternoon* was in the offing, and the potential story did not come to mind until April 1930 when Perkins asked for a submission to *Scribner's Magazine*. Hemingway sent him a typescript with the reassurance that it did not have too much French in it for *Scribner's* readers and that it was a "1st flight story" (*Letters* 323, 31 May 1930). Then to make certain the French in it was correct, he went to New York in early June, roused Lewis Galantière to check it, and submitted a setting copy (KL/EH 838–40: 838 bears inserts and corrections in the French; 839 is the setting copy with galley markings; 840 is a carbon of 838). And so to press, after a year and a half.

Publication History (August 1930; October 1933)

"Wine of Wyoming" was first published in the August 1930 issue of *Scribner's Magazine*. Two years later he began a list of "Stories for Book," all of which had been written before August 1932, and placed it first (KL/EH 221 A). Joseph Flora has commented on Hemingway's placing this, the first of the *Winner Take Nothing* stories to be written, nearer the end of that volume; his argument that Hemingway saw the story as related to "A Day's Wait" and "Fathers and Sons" is only slightly weakened by the fact that it is separated from the first by "A Natural History of the Dead" and from the second by "The Gambler, the Nun, and the Radio" (Flora 234). The story took that place between those grim tales in *Winner Take Nothing* in October 1933.

Sources and Influences

Carlos Baker's note that "Wine of Wyoming" follows "almost exactly the events of late August and early September, 1928, while EH and Pauline were in and around Sheridan" (597) may have chilled critical interest in the story's literary sources, as Joseph Flora claims (223). There was a Charles and Alice Moncini family who made their own wine and brewed beer and lived in a neat frame house that looked out toward the Bighorn Range (Baker 196). Whether that experience suggested the mode or the mode shaped the experience, Hemingway's first version of the story is elegiac and nostalgic: his rejected title "September" suggests an autumnal mood; and in his narrator's remarks on his country and its cuisine, "D'antan, oui. Mais maintenant, no," one hears the, perhaps ironic, echo of Villon's "Mais où sont les neiges d'antan?"

There is much in the story—as there must be in one that includes an immigrant French family and a writer who has lived in France—that contrasts European and American cultures, however simplistically. But a juxtaposition of the two cultures that is so sentimental, even trivial, makes Joseph Flora's suggestion that the story is Hemingway's "most Jamesian" a long reach (224).

Critical Studies

Only three critics have considered "Wine of Wyoming" with anything more than cursory notice. Sheldon Grebstein was the first with his analysis of the "I-witness-protagonist" narrator. He noted that the narrator is effaced through "three-fourths of the story's length"—precisely the moment at which Hemingway ended the first typescript and turned to manuscript (KL/EH 837)—but then his role changes and "his failure to keep an engagement with the Fontans . . . precipitates the story's crisis and provides the means by which characters are illuminated and values conveyed" (64). Those values, however, are not so much conveyed as they are undercut. Grebstein pointed out that the "narrator and the Fontans represent European values: the appreciation of good food and drink, friendship based on a shared ethos;

individual freedom and responsibility; self-respect as evidenced by cleanliness, order, and pride in one's work; and awareness of the greater worth of things because of their scarcity." Against these values we measure the behavior of the Fontans' unwelcome American visitors and their American daughter-in-law. Having established that European-American polarity, Grebstein then demonstrated that both M. Fontan and the narrator "behave like 'Americans'; that is, each betrays the relationship and its common values": the narrator fails to keep his appointment and Fontan, not one to waste new wine, finishes off three bottles (65).

Grebstein's analysis is a close one; perhaps too close, for the narrator has good reasons for failing to keep the dinner engagement; and Fontan, as the story and its rejected titles indicate, is "crazy for the wine"—his addiction and his final shame are a little less than cultural.

Not, however, for Kenneth Johnston. His essay on the story's social and political times placed the Fontans' predicament "between the dream and the reality of American life." Like them, the Indian girl, is a " 'foreigner' in America" when she is off the reservation, and her "Americanization . . . is often one of vulgarization, even corruption" (160). For the Fontans, "adapting to the new life is perhaps even more difficult," and the several "allusions to the [1928 presidential] candidacy of Al Smith" links his "political fate with the private fate of the Fontans" (161–62). Johnston documented that fate with contemporary political attacks on both Smith's Catholicism and his promised opposition to Prohibition. Johnston, like Grebstein, found Fontan's drinking an example of "one of life's simple pleasures when properly indulged," and the imminent defeat of Al Smith for his Catholicism a prediction of the frustration of their American dream. The "snow-capped mountains . . . finally emerge as symbols of illusion" (164–65).

Joseph Flora's study of "Wine of Wyoming" is the most recent, the most thorough, and the most original. He claimed the story for the Nick Adams series on the evidence of the narrator as "a writer who likes to hunt and fish . . ., has spent a great deal of time in Europe and has frequently compared the values of European culture and American culture" to the detriment of the latter (223–24). He further claimed it as a central story in a trilogy of late marriage tales with "A Day's Wait" and "Fathers and Sons," prophetic stories in which the wives are "cast in a curious, even alarming, nebulousness" (234).

That consideration of the trilogy illuminates this story and its depiction of three marriages—four, counting the poor fellow who sneaks out in his pajamas for a beer when his wife is at the movies: Sam and Maria Fontan's; their elder son's to an obese American Indian; and the narrator's to the other half of the plural "we" so unexpectedly referred to for the first time near the end of the second section (*Stories* 457). To Grebstein's analysis of the narrator's progression from "I" to "witness" to "protagonist," Flora added the gradual manifestation of the narrator's wife, emerging out of the pronoun to speak in the final section, but never with an identifying dialogue tag

(228–32). One may raise an eyebrow at the days and nights the narrator spends with the Fontans and his wife's anonymity; but Flora noted that although their marriage is unlike the French couple's, "there is a shared assumption between them about the significance of the Fontans" (232). More than that, they share some "good shooting" and at the end of the day, "We did not want a foreign language. All we wanted was to go early to bed" (*Stories* 462, 463). Finally, it is the wife who is most sensitive to their failure at keeping the dinner engagement: like Nicholas Adams's son at the end of "Fathers and Sons," it is she who recognizes the lost imperative: "We ought to have gone last night" (*Stories* 467, 499). How much more she recognized and might have envied in the Fontans' marriage might have been alluded to in the deleted dialogue in the first version. Just as Fontan is "crazy for the wine," she sees that Madame Fontan is "crazy pour lui" (KL/EH 837).

With all its contrasts—some broadly comic—between the older European culture and the American West, Catholicism and American protestantism, a tolerant marriage and versions of bondage, Flora recognized that although the story is "[p]otentially one of Hemingway's most topical, most political . . . stories, 'Wine of Wyoming' is more than that. It does, as Johnston says, have one eye on history—and in a very large sense." But finally, "Hemingway puts the emphasis not on America, or the Fontans, but on the narrator" and his "qualified" future (233–34).

Much of what seems to qualify the narrator's prospects for the future rests in his vision of the mountains so similar to the hills like white elephants in the earlier story. The "furrowed brown mountains" rising above yellow grain fields "looked like Spain, but it was Wyoming," and as they leave "they looked more like Spain than ever." Three times they are witnessed—at the outset of each of the three successive afternoons and once as the couple leave (*Stories* 450, 458, 462, 466). If we can find a persuasive meaning in the girl's vision of the hills in Spain, then it is hard to deny the narrator the meaning of his vision. What is different about the mountains of Wyoming is the snow-covered peaks. On the second afternoon the "snow looked very white and pure and unreal." And as they leave on the third day, the narrator knows that the "summer was ending, but the new snow had not yet come to stay on the high mountains; there was only the old sun-melted snow and the ice, and from a long way away it shone very brightly" (*Stories* 458, 462)—as the "snows of yesteryear" shone afar for Villon.

Works Cited

PRIMARY

Ernest Hemingway: Selected Letters, 1917–1961. Ed. Carlos Baker. New York: Scribner's, 1981.

The Short Stories of Ernest Hemingway. New York: Scribner's, 1938, 450–67.

SECONDARY

Baker, Carlos. *Ernest Hemingway: A Life Story.* 1969. Scribner's, 1988.

Flora, Joseph M. *Hemingway's Nick Adams.* Baton Rouge: Louisiana State UP, 1982.

Grebstein, Sheldon N. *Hemingway's Craft.* Carbondale: Southern Illinois UP, 1973.

Johnston, Kenneth G. "Hemingway's 'Wine of Wyoming': Disappointment in America." *Western American Literature* 9 (1974): 159–74.

32
The Sea Change

Composition History (January 1930–June 1931)

The manuscripts of "The Sea Change" are as difficult to date as those of "A Natural History of the Dead" completed two months later and similarly reflect a variety of occasions over a period of nearly two years. There are three complete versions of the story: a thirteen-page heavily revised pencil manuscript that is certainly the first version (KL/EH 679); a thirteen-page ink manuscript that appears to be a fair copy of a second version (KL/EH 680); and unrevised tear sheets from the story's first publication in *This Quarter* used as setting copy for *Winner Take Nothing* (KL/EH 222).

That fairly usual sequence of manuscripts is complicated by three sets of fragments that seem to be responses to a genial but peremptory letter on 28 June 1929 from Henry G. Leach, editor of *The Forum*, requesting a story (KL/EH). It was a form letter and it both infuriated Hemingway and inspired him to use it as an introduction or frame for stories he had in mind. On three occasions Hemingway copied *The Forum*'s prescriptions for a short story from the letter, for example this paragraph for KL/EH 681 A: "The editor writes that as the Forum reaches not only trained readers but the general public the story must contain narrative or at least plot. In other words it must not be merely a sketch. Two thousand words is the desired length. . . ."

In some forty words the editor managed to raise Hemingway's ire with misconceptions of the reading public, narrative or plot, and what is "merely" a sketch.

In a four-page manuscript fragment (KL/EH 681) Hemingway started a series called "Unsuited to Our Needs," quoted the letter, and added, "Let us see what we can do in twelve hundred and sixty-two words"—the word count on his fair copy of "The Sea Change" (680). This fragment includes a list of titles of "Three Love Stories," with "The Sea Change" first, and a brief rejected conclusion of that story. (The two other occasions on which he used *The Forum* letter as an introduction are: KL/EH 681 A, to introduce the death of the bullfighter Angel Carratala [see Chap. 16 above]; and KL/EH 734–35, from a notebook that includes a story about the death of Eldred Johnstone in World War I. Although that story has all the marks of the early 1920s, Hemingway met an Eldridge Johnson on his fishing trip to the Dry Tortugas in March 1930.)

Hemingway made two contradictory claims about the origins of this story: on 16 November 1933 in a letter to Max Perkins, he included it among those stories he "invent[ed] completely" (*Letters* 400); but in the late 1950s he remarked that he "had seen the couple in the Basque Bar in St.-Jean-de-Luz and I knew the story too too well" ("Art of the Short Story" 88). Although his first statement is more persuasive, his second does suggest that the story originated when he was in Spain and France, either in the fall of 1929 or 1931. 1930 was taken up largely with fishing in Key West, hunting in Wyoming, writing "Wine of Wyoming" and *Death in the Afternoon*, before his immobilizing accident in November.

In late September of 1929 Hemingway left Hendaye (near St.-Jean-de-Luz) for Paris, by which time he admitted to Perkins he had only "3 pieces" written and was signing his letters "E. Cantwork Hemingstein" (Baker 202; *Letters* 302). But in October and November he was again intimately involved with the Parisian literati. Edward Titus wrote a letter on 4 October to interest him in writing a preface to *Kiki's Memoirs* and another on 26 November to say that Ludwig Lewisohn had defended *A Farewell to Arms* against some of the early negative reviews (KL/EH). Then in early December he heard from Scott Fitzgerald some of the scurrilous tales Robert McAlmon was telling in New York to the effect that Pauline was a lesbian and Hemingway a homosexual (Baker 206). Earlier that fall he had resumed his friendship with Morley Callaghan after the disastrous boxing episode with Scott as the distracted timekeeper (Baker 202 ff.) In the interim Callaghan had been challenged by Edward Titus to a somewhat more literary contest with Robert McAlmon. Each was to write an au courant story about two well-known homosexuals. McAlmon lost by default, but Callaghan's "Now That April's Here" was published later in *This Quarter*. It describes one of the homosexuals deserting the other for a woman and being consoled by a character obviously based on McAlmon. A year later Callaghan modified the situation in a novella, *No Man's Meat*, to two lesbians, one of whom leaves her husband (Ford 154–57).

In December 1929 Hemingway wrote the preface to *Kiki's Memoirs*, published in a pamphlet the following month by Edward Titus. He then returned to Key West.

The intrigues gossiped about in the Parisian cafés in 1929 and Hemingway's close connection with Edward Titus, who had revived *This Quarter* and was soliciting manuscripts like Callaghan's, not only could have elicited the early manuscript of "The Sea Change" but also have suggested a congenial journal for immediate publication.

Although Hemingway might have submitted the story's second version (of which KL/EH 680 is a fair copy) in early 1930 when he was writing the *Kiki's Memoirs* preface for Titus, the curious coincidence of the unusual name Eldred Johnstone in the introductory fragment (KL/EH 681) and the name of the yachtsman he met in March 1930, Eldridge Johnson, argues for a later date.

Hemingway returned to Spain and France in May 1931, visited Hendaye again in June, and—if the later version of the story's occasion bears any weight—that visit could have revived interest in the story and led him to submit it to Titus for publication.

Two other considerations could have convinced Hemingway to wait a year. The thematic similarity between Callaghan's "Now That April's Here" and "The Sea Change" would have been rather noticeable in 1930, and if the vicious tales Robert McAlmon was telling about Pauline and Ernest were more widely known—and McAlmon was seldom given to reticence—the story might appear to confirm his gossip.

Publication History (December 1931; October 1933)

"The Sea Change" was first published in the December 1931 issue of *This Quarter*. Hemingway placed it second after "Wine of Wyoming" in the sequence of stories for *Winner Take Nothing* he jotted down sometime in the late summer of 1932 (KL/EH 221 A). But he apparently said little of it to Max Perkins in the eighteen months between its appearance in Paris and its publication with the more staid Scribner's. Given the subject of the story, he might well have felt that the less said of it the better until after its publication in *Winner Take Nothing* in October 1933.

Sources and Influences

Hemingway's two statements on the origins of "The Sea Change" seem to set the limits for considering its sources. In 1933 when he told Maxwell Perkins it was an invented story, he added "*nobody* can tell which ones I make up completely" (*Letters* 400); however, in the late 1950s he not only identified the origin of the story in a moment when he "had seen a couple in the Bar Basque in St.-Jean-de-Luz" but also added that he "knew the story too too well" ("Art of the Short Story" 88). His first remark suggests the story is a pure fiction, an invention, and in spite of that claim, perhaps because of it, literary biographers with a Freudian bent argue that the story is at least in part autobiographical. His second remark of some twenty-five years later appears to place the story's origin in the lives of another couple he had witnessed, perhaps had known, in St.-Jean-de-Luz. Yet when he adds that he knew the story "too too well, which is the squared root of well, and use any well you like except mine," he seems to admit that he knew the story more intimately than as a mere witness, and then immediately and rather brusquely demands that we readers keep his personal involvement out of our interpretations. With ambivalent statements such as these, it is little wonder that critics have read the story as a veiled account of either his conception or his experiences of bisexuality.

Michael Reynolds was the first to discover what was close enough to a lesbian relationship between Grace Hemingway and her young companion Ruth Arnold to stir Dr. Hemingway to banish the younger woman from their house—at least while he was there (78 ff.) Kenneth Lynn, in the most recent biography, reached further back into Hemingway's infancy when Grace dressed Ernest as a girl, somewhat unusually even for those times, and rather elaborately treated him and his older sister Marcelline as twins, unusual for any period (chap. 2 ff.) (On the verso of page 2 of the earliest manuscript of "The Sea Change," two sentences read: "They were a brother and sister who lived together and loved each other very much. This was considered admirable in the old days" [KL/EH 679].)

With the recent search for sources or earlier intimations of *The Garden of Eden* (1986), critics will inevitably consider this story as an early version of David Bourne's discovery of his wife's bisexuality and their later transsexual exercises (chap. 11 ff.) At the end of that chapter David ostensibly leaves for Paris when Catherine leaves his bed for Marita's; although he returns in the following chapter from Cannes, one can imagine the story's conversation in the Paris bar forming an epilogue to Catherine's confession of bisexuality. The similarity between the story and this part of the novel lends support to Robert Fleming's claim that Phil, in the story, is a writer like David Bourne—and, one would add, like Hubert Elliot who, somewhat more passively, suffers the same revelation in "Mr. and Mrs. Elliot" of April 1924 (215).

Hemingway's remark that he "knew the story too too well" might have been made by anyone who had frequented the literary cafés of Paris, that tolerant city so unconcerned over its own and expatriate homosexuals and, in Jeffrey Meyers's phrase, the "leading literary lesbians" of the 1920s (78). Hemingway knew most of them well—Sylvia Beach, Janet Flanner, Nathalie Barney, Margaret Anderson, and Hilda Doolittle—and knew, too, that H.D.'s lover Bryher had left her husband, Robert McAlmon and their businesslike merger (Ford 78–79, Lynn 320–22).

It was McAlmon, a homosexual married to a lesbian, who had hissed the stories about Hemingway and Pauline in 1929. And in the same year it was he who did not rise to Edward Titus's challenge to him and Callaghan to write competing stories about those two literary homosexuals—"clever little devils," according to McAlmon, who turned their "snickering wit" against him in his absence, according to Callaghan (131–36).

All this café gossip and literary tattle, at the very least, offered Hemingway more than enough material for his story, some of which he may have returned to in *The Garden of Eden*. And if, as it seems, the story was begun in late

1929, then it might have served to pay back McAlmon—not in kind, but with a remarkably subdued and perceptive study of a man's reactions to losing his lover to another woman.

Critical Studies

It may be that there is little criticism of "The Sea Change" because the story has been subsumed as a fact of biography, or because our attention is distracted by the narrator's intrusions (Grebstein 114), or simply because there is little to say—or *was* until *The Garden of Eden* recalled it to consideration. Those few who have commented on it began with the two literary allusions Philip Young cited in notes to his study of 1952. The title is from Ariel's song in Shakespeare's *The Tempest*:

> Full fathom five thy father lies;
> Of his bones are coral made;
> Those are pearls that were his eyes:
> Nothing of him that doth fade
> But doth suffer a sea-change
> Into something rich and strange. (1. 2. 396–401)

And the lines Phil tries to remember are from Alexander Pope's "An Essay on Man":

> Vice is a monster of so frightful mien,
> As, to be hated, needs but to be seen;
> Yet seen too oft, familiar with her face,
> We first endure, then pity, then embrace.
> (2. 11. 217–20)

Young's brief comment was that both quotations allude to the change Phil experiences and that the lines from Pope trace the stages of that change (178–79 n.)

Joseph DeFalco followed Young's suggestion to claim that Phil's progression from repulsion to "acceptance of vice" occurs not through his own "magnanimity, or some spiritual impulse as much as the [woman's] appeal to the abnormal within him. In fine, he has embraced vice, not the woman" (178). Sheldon Grebstein agreed that the woman's rather cryptic remark "You've used it well enough," and Phil's acquiescing to the fact that she probably will come back (*Stories* 400), imply that the "couple's relationship has been in some ways as 'corrupt' as the homosexual affair" (114).

The thread of implication running through all these commentaries was finally picked up in J. F. Kobler's analysis of Phil's progression from hating his wife's bisexuality, to enduring it with the admission that he understands (*Stories* 398), to pitying both of them with the recognition that she probably will come back to him (*Stories* 400). Others, like Grebstein, had suggested that the last stage in the progression, at which one embraces vice, lies in the conclusion's "hints at the man's degradation" (114); but Kobler sees the final scene, in which the two men at the bar "make room" for Phil and then move "down a little more, so that he would be quite comfortable" (*Stories* 401), as evidence of his "moving toward a homosexual affair" (322). Phil sees himself as "quite a different man," one for whom vice is no longer a "monster of frightful mien" but a "very strange thing"—perhaps "something rich and strange" as Ariel sang to Ferdinand.

Robert Fleming reviewed the arguments from DeFalco to Kobler that first suggested and then stated that the progression of Phil's attitude from hating to embracing vice or perversion ends with his identification with the two, probably homosexual, men at the bar, and offers another interpretation. His is a complex, at times tenuous, argument that Phil is "a writer and that his perversion is more degrading than the lesbian tendencies of his former lover"; indeed, he finds it analogous to Nathaniel Hawthorne's concept of the "Unpardonable Sin" (215). His textual evidence rests in the climactic dialogue in which others, like DeFalco, inferred from the woman's most telling remark that their own relationship has been one of "unrecognized vice" (DeFalco 177). The passage follows Phil's use of the word "perversion":

> "I'd like it better if you didn't use words like that," the girl said. "There's no necessity to use a word like that."
> "What do you want me to call it?"
> "You don't have to call it. You don't have to put any name to it."
> "That's the name for it."
> "No," she said. "We're made up of all sorts of things. You've known that. You've used it well enough." (*Stories* 400)

The crucial issue in the passage depends on the antecedents of "it": In all but her last lines, the antecedent is what he calls "perversion"; but in the last line the antecedent of "it" is "that" in the previous sentence, and its antecedent is the fact that "We're made up of all sorts of things." Beyond that, of course, the pronoun "we" could refer to women, or lesbians, or men and women, or the two of them themselves. Over against those critics who claim that she is charging him with sexual perversion, if that is the term he insists on, Fleming argued that Phil has used his intimate knowledge of " 'all sorts of things' in human nature to enrich his writing," again, like the probing artists or scientists in Hawthorne's fiction. Thus, he concluded, "homosexuality should not be viewed as Phil's own vice but as a metaphor for a writer's perverse willingness to use others for the sake of art" (216).

There may be a way to mediate between these two readings, if only by noting that one can be both a homosexual and a writer. Fleming's position that Phil is not, as Kobler said, "moving toward a homosexual affair," is hardly proven by the misconception that Hemingway's "attitude toward homosexuality is, from first to last, anything but understanding." In fact, there is a good deal of understanding in the two stories cited as evidence (217).

Nor did Fleming make his point with a reference to a discarded fragment of the story's ending (KL/EH 681). In that fragment Phil moves to the bar to order a drink and in two deleted sentences asks James, "What do the punks drink, James?" and "What can you recommend to a recent convert?" The first is clearly an insult, the second close to an invitation. Then, before rejecting this ending, Hemingway wrote, "Whatever |the punks| they drink, James," apparently referring to the other two men at the bar. Fleming argued that Hemingway's rejection of this ending reveals his intention to dissociate Phil from the two men; but Kobler might argue that it just as legitimately supports his interpretation of that last scene.

Fleming's original insight that Phil is a writer is persuasive and is supported by Joseph Flora's similar interpretations of other stories—like "An Alpine Idyll"—but the analogy with Hawthorne's idea of the Unpardonable Sin, and that concept's confusion of art and morality, does not capture the complexity of this story. What is taken as a charge against Phil's morality—"We're made up of all sorts of things. You've known that. You've used it well enough."—may be read simply as the woman's affirmation of his understanding *as an artist* of the complexity of human nature. (Hemingway, after all, was closer to Henry James, who claimed his right as an artist to use any experience in his fiction with the remark "Where emotion is, there am I.") If we can modify both Kobler's and Fleming's persuasive interpretations, one with the other, then "poor old Phil's" conflict lies in that what he has known and used well in his life as an artist he cannot, at least until the end of the story, accept in his life as a man. His lost lover comes close to it when she tells him that it is not necessary to use a word like perversion.

Works Cited

PRIMARY

"The Art of the Short Story." *Paris Review* 23 (Spring 1981): 85–102.

Ernest Hemingway: Selected Letters, 1917–1961. Ed. Carlos Baker. New York: Scribner's, 1981.

The Garden of Eden. New York: Scribner's, 1986.

The Short Stories of Ernest Hemingway. New York: Scribner's, 1938, 397–401.

SECONDARY

Baker, Carlos. *Ernest Hemingway: A Life Story.* 1969. New York: Scribner's, 1988.

Callaghan, Morley. *That Summer in Paris.* New York: Penguin, 1963.

DeFalco, Joseph. *The Hero in Hemingway's Short Stories.* Pittsburgh: U of Pittsburgh P, 1963.

Fleming, Robert E. "Perversion and the Writer in 'The Sea Change.'" *Studies in American Fiction* 14 (1986): 215–20.

Flora, Joseph M. *Hemingway's Nick Adams.* Baton Rouge: Louisiana State UP, 1982.

Ford, Hugh. *Published in Paris.* New York: Pushcart, 1980.

Grebstein, Sheldon N. *Hemingway's Craft.* Carbondale: Southern Illinois UP, 1973.

Kobler, J. F. "Hemingway's 'The Sea Change': A Sympathetic View of Homosexuality." *Arizona Quarterly* 26 (1970): 318–24.

Lynn, Kenneth S. *Hemingway.* New York: Simon, 1987.

Meyers, Jeffrey. *Hemingway: A Biography.* New York: Harper, 1985.

Reynolds, Michael S. *The Young Hemingway.* Oxford: Blackwell, 1986.

Young, Philip. *Ernest Hemingway: A Reconsideration.* 1952. New York: Harcourt, 1966.

33

A Natural History of the Dead

Composition History (January 1929–August 1931)

The writing of "A Natural History of the Dead" reflects so many of the events and experiences of Hemingway's life—from his boyhood reading of nineteenth-century naturalists through his war service in Italy to his mature reading of the reviews of *A Farewell to Arms*—it is curious that it had little to do with the writing of *Death in the Afternoon* in which the "story" was first published.

There are seven items from an early sketch to galleys that suggest the history of the story's composition and then indicate the later revisions for inclusion in *Death in the Afternoon*. Hemingway was singularly reticent about the story until 1931, but twenty years later he wrote to Charles Poore that he was certain he wrote the story in Key West (*Letters* 799). Between January 1929 (a likely date for the early fragments) and March 1931 (when he mentions the story in a letter to Archibald MacLeish [*Letters* 338]), he was in Key West from January or February to April or June of those three years.

The two early fragments bear traces of the winter of 1928–29. The first (KL/EH 508 A) is a brief but nearly complete four-page sketch (numbered 1–4) of the dramatic conclusion of "A Natural History of the Dead" (close to the text in *Stories* 446 ["In the mountains . . ."] to 447 ["They went out."]) The sketch ends with a line that realizes an incipient allusion in the story: "He [the wounded soldier] was alive all the next day. By that time there was a report around that he was Christ." When Hemingway began the composition of "A Natural History," he expanded the argument between the doctor and the officer and reinstated the ironic allusion to Christ to conclude his satire on the morality of Christian and latter-day humanists.

The second fragment (KL/EH 812) is a three-page manuscript (numbered 10–12) that is apparently all that remains of the story's earliest version. It is written in the story's parodic style, proclaims itself part of a "monograph," and might well have followed the passage in the text on the death of animals (*Stories* 444). It begins: "The way fish die is most instructive or easily instructive as the death of one's parents or friends," particularly since "if either of the parents . . . end their lives themselves by violent means, the naturalist is again deprived of the moment of observation since he may be in another part of the country. . . . This is unfortunate." Near the conclusion it considers someone dying in bed and so is linked with the "natural death" from Spanish influenza that follows in the text. This fragment reveals Hemingway's first attempt to contain his grief and anger at his father's suicide and to bear witness to the sight of the shattered head of the first "natural historian" in his life.

But, as he wrote in "Fathers and Sons," it was still too early to write of his father's death, and this passage, like another allusion in a rejected conclusion of the first extant manuscript of the story, had to be deleted. Nevertheless, it and the early version of the story's conclusion mark the beginning of "A Natural History," perhaps as early as January 1929 when he returned from settling his father's affairs in Oak Park and turned in a fury of revision to the manuscripts of *A Farewell to Arms,* with its weary surgeon and often self-righteous officers.

The summer of 1929 began badly; he wrote to Owen Wister in late July, "I have been trying to write stories or a story rather and can't a damn bit" (*Letters* 301). And although a month later he told Perkins he was "cheerful again—have written 3 pieces" (*Letters* 302), the term "pieces" is not promising. That summer, while he was cleaning up the language in the galleys of his novel, he was worrying about the competition it would face from Erich Remarque's *All Quiet on the Western Front.*

His worst fears were realized when Robert Herrick, without having finished *A Farewell to Arms,* attacked it in a comparison with Remarque's novel in the November issue of *The Bookman.* Susan Beegel has demonstrated the informing influence of this review on the story's first complete version (KL/EH 31; Beegel 35–36). Herrick's review "What is Dirt?" answered the question with a comparative analysis of the scenes of sex, defecation, and drunken vomiting in the two works, and Hemingway fared badly. Herrick followed the antique line of *The Bookman,* edited by Seward Collins, in affirming the moral idealism of Paul Elmer More and Irving Babbitt. For *The Bookman,* dirt was unidealized dirt, unmarried dirt, dirt with no redeeming social virtue, dirty dirt. Letters followed and finally Henry S. Canby resolved the issue by slapping Herrick on the wrist for not reading the book he reviewed and chastising Hemingway for using "the most striking talent in recent American writing" to offer us a "dehumanized love story" (Stephens 86, 99).

Hemingway's response, written sometime in the early months of 1930, again at Key West, was a typescript with a manuscript version of its rejected ending, and it identified the literary humanists with the sentence "A persevering traveler like Mungo Park or me lives on and yet will see the death of Irving Babbitt or Paul Elmer More or watch the noble exit Seward Collins makes" (KL/EH 31). That manuscript, with its rejected conclusion, which returns from the conflict between the doctor and the officer to a reprise of the attack on the humanists, is the subject of Susan Beegel's study.

But the story had another year to wait. By this time Hemingway was well along with the first manuscript of *Death in the Afternoon,* worked on it through the summer of 1930, and then broke his writing arm in November in an automobile accident (Lewis 32–35; the earliest or "Texas Manuscript" does not include the story).

When he returned to Key West in February 1931, the arm was still bothering him, as he wrote to MacLeish: "I'd be glad to let Caresse [Crosby] have the Natural History [of the Dead] for the [$]1500. You can read it when you come. I didn't answer because I couldn't write nor go over the story—will write her soon" (*Letters* 338, 14 March 1931). MacLeish, then, had seen or heard of the unrevised version of the story (KL/EH 31). Caresse Crosby had been writing Hemingway for a story—any story—since February 1930 with little success; and in early May of 1931 asked specifically for "A Natural History of Death [*sic*]." By mid-July she wrote to chide him that he had been in Paris and neglected to see her; but sometime in the next two months she received a typescript of the story, read it, and on 15 October wrote, "I am returning your mss. very reluctantly" (KL/EH, Crosby to Hemingway, 5 May, 6 May, 17 July, 15 October 1931; see also Ford 221).

Sometime in August or early September, then, Hemingway managed two typescripts of "A Natural History" for publication as a story: KL/EH 32, signed with a word count; and KL/EH 40, with his name and word count typed. He used the first (32) as a setting copy for *Winner Take Nothing* and the second (40), with manuscript additions for the version that appeared in *Death in the Afternoon.*

With a rejected story on his hands, he added in manuscript the first versions of the dialogues between the Old Lady and the Author to KL/EH 40, and from that the setting copy for the end of chapter 12 of *Death in the Afternoon* was typed (KL/EH 34) to appear in the galleys he corrected in the spring of 1932.

A long history, indeed, but worth following if only to demonstrate that "A Natural History of the Dead," gathering a host of earlier sketches and drawing on earlier publications, was meant in its original form but later publication as a story, even though it appeared in an earlier publication and later form as a part of his book on bullfighting.

Publication History (September 1932; October 1933)

Textual critics may argue over which of the two published versions represents the better text: the first published in *Death in the Afternoon* in September 1932 or that published a year later in *Winner Take Nothing* but derived from the 1931 typescript sent to Caresse Crosby.

The differences between the two texts are slight except for the dialogues between the Old Lady and the Author that were omitted from the 1933 story collection. Hemingway added the detailed description of a death from Spanish influenza sometime after the abbreviated version in 1932 (see *Stories* 445 and *Death* 139). In the first edition of *Winner Take Nothing* he added a petulant footnote on the story's first publication in a "rather technical book" and its poor sales (*Winner Take Nothing* 137; see Carlos Baker 302); the note was omitted beginning with the *First Forty-nine* edition (1938). The footnote on the humanists was added to the 1933 edition, when he could refer to that literary movement as "an extinct phenomenon" (*Stories* 445).

The Old Lady/Author dialogues (*Death* 131, 135, 137, 138, 139, 140, 144) functioned in part to meld the story into the bullfight book with a device he had begun in chapter 7. But in November and December of 1931, as he wrote the first versions of those dialogues, his anger at the humanists from the year before was waning. He deleted the references to Babbitt, More, and Collins; and after summoning the Old Lady to testify that Collins was no humanist because he knew neither Latin nor Greek but "used to edit Vanity Fair," he cancelled the passage and added in galleys her familiarity with T. S. Eliot (KL/EH 40, p. 110 H; *Death* 139).

Sources and Influences

Both the structure and the style of "A Natural History of the Dead" depend upon the ironic contrast Hemingway draws between his reading of earlier natural historians and his own writing drawn from observations of the dead. His introductory allusions to naturalists and explorers from the eighteenth-century Mungo Park and Gilbert White to the nineteenth-century Bishop of Norwich, Edward Stanley, and to W. H. Hudson of the generation before Hemingway's, are meant, in various ways, to establish a style for parody and, more important, a Christian humanist attitude to satirize. John Portz first identified these allusions and their contribution to the story's structure; and Susan Beegel has pointed out that all but Park's work (which is quoted) are listed in Michael Reynolds's survey of Hemingway's reading (103, n. 9).

With Mungo Park's and Bishop Stanley's happy inferences of a divine and beneficent hand in all things great and small, Hemingway tests the hypothesis on the battlefield dead. The gender of the dead leads to a digression on mules and the opportunity to cite the "Introduction by the Author" to the 1930 edition of *In Our Time* (later published as "On the Quai at Smyrna," which the Old Lady of *Death in the Afternoon* has read). The parodic tone diminishes as he recalls his experiences at the Milan munitions factory in June 1918, and later that month after the Austrian offensive, in passages that are close to others in "A Way You'll Never Be."

With these passages he returns to "that persevering traveler, Mungo Park," again considering the ways in which men die like animals, and then to the only natural death he had seen, the death of a "patient" dying of Spanish influenza. This memory, recalled from an earlier manuscript (KL/EH 260), which immediately precedes his attack on the second and literary generation of humanists, Paul Elmer More and Irving Babbitt, could well have been occasioned by their spokesman Robert Herrick and his review of *A Farewell to Arms*. "What is Dirt?" would have galled Hemingway for its contrast between Remarque's novel, told by a "professional," and Hemingway's, by an "amateur," and in particular the fact that Herrick found some "eternal significance" in a "scene over the sanitary buckets" in *All Quiet on the Western Front,* which told him "far more of war than all the vivid pictures of mangled flesh" in Hemingway (Stephens 87–88). So Hemingway expanded the image of the patient who "shits the bed full" (*Death* 139) to "one vast, final, yellow cataract that flows and dribbles on after he's gone," and savagely added, "So now I want to see the death of any self-called Humanist" (*Stories* 445).

That attack on the literary humanists and its footnote—an odd one in a passage that ends with a sneer at footnotes—derived from more than Herrick's review. The evidence of "Banal Story" indicates that Hemingway kept abreast of intellectual matters by reading *The Forum*. In the February 1928 issue he read Irving Babbitt's essay "The Critic and American Life," for in the rejected conclusion of the 1930 manuscript (KL/EH 31) he mentions that "Someone has observed that our bodies are made from dust and return to dust." The general reference, as Beegel has noted, is to Ecclesiastes 3:20; but the more immediate reference is to Babbitt's essay, which quotes "a recent poet" claiming that dust is our "common source," and—*pace* the Preacher—proceeds to consider the "substantial sacrifices" such a position entails: "depth and subtlety, . . . beauty in almost any sense of that elusive term, . . . delicacy, elevation, and distinction," to say nothing of being driven to an "inordinate interest in sex for its own sake" (139). Hemingway's ironic strategy is to agree, for the moment, since "my own observations [have] led me to the conclusion that our bodies are originally made from the elements contained in semen, a pleasantly viscous liquid with an odor rather like that of a freshly caught barracuda" (KL/EH 31, quoted in Beegel 42).

One ironic consequence of that passage and its footnote is that it provoked twice as much commentary as all the rest of the story. In the *New Yorker* of July 1939, Russell Maloney, "purely by way of amplification," recalled Babbitt's devoted teaching and his death from "ulcerative colitis" as, according to Maloney's doctor, "definitely heroic" (26). Only sixteen years later in the *National Review,* John A. Clark sniffed in Maloney's piece the source of the "strong whiffs of humanism" he had noticed in the intellectual atmosphere of the 1950s (20). In 1963 and finally, one hopes, John A. Yunck found the issues of the humanists and the naturalists, the deaths of Babbitt and Hemingway, fading indistinguishably into recent history in which the conception of *nada* is more real than either of them imagined. And from this distance, as Yunck said, both men are closer in their shared sense of decorum than they seemed separated by the brief issue of their times (41–42). To which one should add that Hemingway's footnote, like the humanists', is, as he implied, of only "mild historical interest" (*Stories* 445).

From there on the story turns to an objective narration of the conflict between the doctor and the artillery officer (with one first-person intrusion mentioning Goya), which may well have been the earliest segment of the story (KL/EH 508 A). The mood and narrative point of view of this section is enough to deny Lewis Weeks's claim for some relevant similarity between the story and Mark Twain's chapter 20 in *Life on the Mississippi* (15–17), for it is precisely the sentimental piety to which Twain retreats that Hemingway condemns.

Critical Studies

If one discounts the commentary on "A Natural History of the Dead" that is largely concerned with its allusions or writes the story off as less than a story, there is little criticism to consider. John Portz's identification of the allusions to earlier naturalists and John Yunck's moving essay on how a burning issue of the early 1930s has been lost in the ashes of Hiroshima offer interesting insights of literary history but say little about the story. Nor is there much light cast in the comments of Sheridan Baker or Richard Hovey or Sheldon Grebstein. The latter dismissed the story as "a personal essay, with a tacked on fictional episode," exemplifying Hemingway with his "craft unbuttoned" (77).

Most of these critics ignore the story because it appeared first in *Death in the Afternoon*—Sheridan Baker called it a "tricked piece of journalism" (87)—or because it violates, as Gerry Brenner noted, "the Jamesian requirement of maintaining a single narrative perspective" (74).

Those critics who are less concerned with distinctions between discursive and literary prose or, like Brenner, understand Hemingway's "studied disregard of narrative conventions," not only display more tolerance for literary invention but also avoid association with those literary humanists and the implications of their distinctions between reality, which may not be edifying, and their notions of the moral purpose of literature.

Arthur Waldhorn was the first to consider the story seriously, albeit as a part of *Death in the Afternoon,* when he argued that the doctor in the final section "knows what the officer must learn, that holding tight is almost all a man can salvage." And although Waldhorn related "holding tight" to the Spanish term *"pundonor,* meaning . . . pride, honor, and courage"—and this seems a large claim for a simple necessary act—he did direct attention to the implications of the story's concluding drama (134).

Wirt Williams nicely demonstrated that the final section is a "dramatization of what the 'lecture' has suggested by its heavy irony," but for the fact that the discrepancy between statement and meaning in the essayistic section is complicated by the fact that at the end "the two disputants are on the same side," although the doctor has a greater understanding of the real issues embodied, as it were, in the dying man that so troubles the living. When he throws iodine in the artillery officer's eyes, he is "trying to make him see though he temporarily blinds him," to make him "like himself, red-eyed as from weeping at the plight and the impotence of men against their adversary," a plight that is no less than *nada* (103). And Joseph Flora followed both Waldhorn and Williams in deciding that "the doctor has acted very ably in the most difficult of circumstances," which "have caused the lieutenant to act as he has" (127).

One might leave the story at that were it not for Gerry Brenner's skeptical interpretation of the concluding section. He argued that its "omniscient perspective detaches Hemingway, for it objectively takes sides with neither the doctor's cynical humanism nor the officer's humanistic heroics." For Brenner, Hemingway's point is, simply or not, that "it is stupid, when confronted with dying or dead human beings, to expect only one perspective, one feeling, one solution of how to respond humanely." The story offers a variety of perspectives if we take it as a whole: the romantic idealism of the humanists, the parodist's excessive and immature contempt, the doctor's cynical humanism, the officer's empty heroics, even the stretcher bearers' natural and selfish interests. From all these perspectives, Brenner concluded, Hemingway "dares us to choose only one as the correct one." And he does so by refusing to "give his story a traditional form or conventional structure . . . to prod his readers tolerant of experiment to acknowledge the complicated feelings they have toward death. And the object upon whom the sketch focuses so much concern? He is the man whose head, broken like a flower-pot, . . . better transmits its message than the clichéd image of the bone-white skull: memento mori" (74–75).

That is a complex and challenging reading of the story, and it returns us not only to the image of the dying man in the cave but also to the image of the general who shot himself in the head so that there was a "hole in front you couldn't put your little finger in and a hole in back you could put your fist in" (*Stories* 446). If the image of such a broken head is central to the story, and if the story was begun shortly after Hemingway returned from witnessing "the handsome job the undertaker had done on his father's face" (*Stories* 491, "Fathers and Sons"), and if two of the related manuscripts allude to his father's suicide (KL/EH 31, 812), it is difficult to escape the conclusion that the story began when Hemingway saw his father's embalmed body and turned almost desperately to revise his war novel. It was Dr. Clarence Hemingway, after all, who was the first natural historian to instruct his son in the observation of nature, inform it with the idealism of the nineteenth century, and then blow it all away with a bullet in his head.

Works Cited

PRIMARY

Death in the Afternoon. New York: Scribner's, 1932.

Ernest Hemingway: Selected Letters, 1917-1961. Ed. Carlos Baker. New York: Scribner's, 1981.

The Short Stories of Ernest Hemingway. New York: Scribner's, 1938, 440-49.

Winner Take Nothing. New York: Scribner's, 1933.

SECONDARY

Babbitt, Irving. "The Critic and American Life." *Forum,* 79 (Feb. 1928): 161-76; rpt. in *On Being Creative.* Boston: Houghton Mifflin, 1932, and *Literary Opinion in America.* Ed. Morton Dauwen Zabel. New York: Harper, 1937, 133-45.

Baker, Carlos. *Ernest Hemingway: A Life Story.* 1969. Scribner's, 1988.

Baker, Sheridan. *Ernest Hemingway.* New York: Holt, 1967.

Beegel, Susan F. *Hemingway's Craft of Omission.* Ann Arbor: UMI Research, 1988.

Brenner, Gerry. *Concealments in Hemingway's Works.* Columbus: Ohio State UP, 1983.

Clark, John A. "A Footnote to a Footnote to a Footnote." *National Review* 28 Dec. 1955: 19-21.

Flora, Joseph M. *Hemingway's Nick Adams.* Baton Rouge: Louisiana State UP, 1982.

Ford, Hugh. *Published in Paris.* Yonkers, NY: Pushcart, 1980.

Grebstein, Sheldon N. *Hemingway's Craft.* Carbondale: Southern Illinois UP, 1973.

Hovey, Richard B. *Hemingway: The Inward Terrain.* Seattle: U of Washington P, 1968.

Lewis, Robert W. Jr. "The Making of *Death in the Afternoon.*" *Ernest Hemingway: The Writer in Context.* Ed. James Nagel. Madison: U of Wisconsin P, 1984.

Maloney, Russell. "A Footnote to a Footnote." *New Yorker* 15 July 1939: 26.

Portz, John. "Allusion and Structure in Hemingway's 'A Natural History of the Dead.'" *Tennessee Studies in Literature* 10 (1965): 27–41.

Reynolds, Michael S. *Hemingway's Reading, 1910–1940.* Princeton: Princeton UP, 1981.

Stephens, Robert O. *Ernest Hemingway: The Critical Reception.* N.p.: Burt Franklin, 1977.

Waldhorn, Arthur. *A Reader's Guide to Ernest Hemingway.* New York: Farrar, 1972.

Weeks, Lewis E., Jr. "Mark Twain and Hemingway: 'A Catastrophe' and 'A Natural History of the Dead.'" *Mark Twain Journal* 14 (1968): 15–17.

Williams, Wirt. *The Tragic Art of Ernest Hemingway.* Baton Rouge: Louisiana State UP, 1981.

Yunck, John A. "The Natural History of the Dead Quarrel: Hemingway and the Humanists." *South Atlantic Quarterly* 62 (1963): 29–43.

34

After the Storm

Composition History (April 1928–June 1932)

The manuscripts of "After the Storm" suggest that, like other stories conceived during a period in which he was engaged in longer works—here *A Farewell to Arms* and *Death in the Afternoon*—it was sketched out soon after its initiating experience, set aside, and then revised when a propitious opportunity to publish it arose. On a fishing trip to the Dry Tortugas in April 1928, Captain Eddie "Bra" Saunders told Hemingway and his guests Waldo Peirce, John Dos Passos, and Bill Smith "a yarn, direct from life, piratical in flavor, with its own intrinsic form" about his discovery of the wreck of the *Valbanera* (Baker 193–94; *Letters* 358).

Susan Beegel's chapter on the composition of the story—to which this summary is indebted—confirms that the first manuscript (KL/EH 226) was written soon after Hemingway's hearing the tale. Like many of his immediate versions of a story close to his life, this one includes the names of others who figure in the tale, in this case "Waldo" and "Dos," as well as a note to add the scene in which "Bra" is to "dive down and see the woman."

A second manuscript, fourteen pages numbered 14–27 and beginning with "I drifted over her with the boat" (*Stories* 373), adds the diving episode in response to that earlier note (KL/EH 226 A). There is no evidence to suggest when that fragment was written.

A third manuscript of twenty-eight pages is close to the published version and radically changes the first. This version deletes the identified narrator and his quizzical Conradian audience of shipmates; substitutes the diving episode, nearly a third of the story, for the first version's long account of even more piratical battles between the Key West "conchs" and Greek sponge fisherman; and excises Bra's dating the events at Christmas six years earlier and his curious scruples over a fisherman's place in the food chain following "jewfish" who have fed on the drowned passengers of the *Valbanera* (Beegel 80–88; see "Sources and Influences" below). This manuscript, too, is difficult to date. It might be one of those Hemingway referred to in a letter as early as 29 January 1931 to "Bud" (a fishing companion) in which he remarked that the "editor of Cosmopolitan came down [to Key West] and offered me 5000 apiece for stories. Have two and if they take either one I can finance the trip" (KL/EH).

The fact that there is no intermediary Hemingway typescript of the story but there is one by someone else that was used as a setting copy for publication in *Cosmopolitan* supports the conjecture that the story was "finished" and accepted for publication before a final typescript was submitted. (The typescript KL/EH 222 is an unrevised copy of the setting copy submitted to *Cosmopolitan* now in the Morris Library, Southern Illinois University; see Howell.) That Morris Library typescript incorporates some significant revisions in Hemingway's hand, which John Howell has noted. It was mailed to William Lengel, editor of *Cosmopolitan,* on 11 February 1932; and on 1 March Hemingway returned the proofs the day he received them (Howell 42; KL/EH, Hemingway to William Lengel). If this conjecture stands, then the final version of "After the Storm" was typed and revised sometime in late 1931 or January 1932.

Publication History (May 1932; October 1933)

Whenever William C. Lengel, editor of *Cosmopolitan,* solicited a story from Hemingway—in January 1931 or in the following months (see KL/EH, Hemingway to "Bud," 29 January 1931)—Hemingway wrote him on 19 February 1932 suggesting a fee of five thousand dollars, and on 1 March that he had "sent back the proofs the day I received them" (KL/EH). The story was first published in the May 1932 issue of *Cosmopolitan,* without any editorial emendations (Howell 42), but at their dollar-a-word rate; Hemingway agreed, for in a letter to Guy Hickok that fall he remarked, "Well well well this depression is hell" (*Letters* 373).

The story seems to have held a primary place in Hemingway's sense of his forthcoming volume, for until June 1933 his working title was *After the Storm, and Other Stories* (Baker 241). In October of that year the story introduced *Winner Take Nothing*.

Sources and Influences

Two critics have commented on sources for "After the Storm," one briefly on a classical myth, and another at length on contemporary accounts of the wreck of the *Valbanera*. Robert Walker found an allusion in the story to Plato's use of the myth of Gyges in *The Republic:* in each a man, after a storm, descends (into the earth or the sea), discovers (a bronze horse with little doors or a ship with portholes), sees a corpse with a ring on its finger, and retrieves the ring. In the myth the ring enables the man to become invisible and commit evil deeds, thus demonstrating that "no one is just of his own will"; in the story the man fails to retrieve the ring, which demonstrates—something else (Walker 375).

Although Walker's perception of the story's irony needs little from Plato to prove it, his note reminds us in a roundabout way that precisely *because* Hemingway later claimed that the story was recalled "word for word as it happened to Bra" (*Letters* 400), one should expect more than a little of the storyteller's shaping art, particularly in a tale told by a conch fisherman to Key West visitors about an event worn smooth by a decade and, in the first version, merged with an event from nearly a decade before that.

Susan Beegel's exhaustive reconstruction from newspaper and Coast Guard reports of the sinking of the *Valbanera* in the hurricane of September 1919 confirms the details of the location and condition of the wreck and the story's concluding account of how it probably occurred. Those same sources, however, show that the wreck was neither looted nor dynamited, and that the first version's account of a war between the conch and Greek sponge fishermen that ended with the burning of two Greek vessels is drawn from events of 1911 (69–75).

There are elements in the story's first draft that suggest a literary influence from Joseph Conrad. (That these marks of influence are erased in the final version would offer evidence, at least to Harold Bloom, of a more interesting version of influence.) Beegel recognizes the difference in the first draft between Bra's relationship with his audience and Marlow's in *Heart of Darkness,* but the similarities between the two narrations are more interesting. Both are narratives within narratives, with an "I" who recounts another's narration— a device Hemingway had used several times in his Chicago fiction. Both inner narratives are told on a boat swinging at anchor at night to a group of listeners with varying experiences of the sea but all less than the storyteller's. As in Conrad's novel, Bra's friends interrupt his narration, at times with naive questions, at others with restive remarks on his digressions (Beegel 78). Marlow is no barroom brawler like Bra, but both leave their societies and, in a sense, bear their immoralities like burdens. Both descend to witness some ultimate horror, in which greed overcomes humanity. And Hemingway implies what Marlow says of Kurtz and Conrad's narrator implies of Marlow: He "was a remarkable man. He had something to say. He said it" (151).

When Hemingway disembodied his narrator and dismissed his audience— Waldo and Dos—he may well have been covering his tracks back to Conrad. And when he did so he did not necessarily write a better story but a different one, one that was, one suspects, somewhat easier to write and probably more suitable for *Cosmopolitan.*

Critical Studies

Whatever the story's origins and influences, once published it seldom held critical attention for more than a note. Earl Rovit saw in the narrator a prototype of Harry Morgan in *To Have and Have Not* (71). Joseph DeFalco linked the story to the earlier "Fifty Grand," to demonstrate a similarity between two characters who refuse to yield "to the rule of conventional morality" and "illustrate man's victory over himself and adjustment to the world in which he lives" (212).

Others were less forgiving, either toward the narrator or the universe. John Howell, once he had commented on stylistic aspects implied in the revisions of the setting copy, turned to evidence of Hemingway's "metaphysics" in the "confrontation between two beings, one physically dead [the drowned woman], one spiritually dead [the narrator] . . ., himself a shark, . . . a moral scavenger" (45). Wirt Williams invoked the "caprice of the universe": from the absurd fight in the bar to the vessel run aground in quicksand to save her, "random violence and absurdity have created a stream of causation that has taken [the narrator] close to a gratification of his greed. . . . [T]he teasing universe has promised him everything, then left him with nothing" (98).

The latest of the brief notes on the story is Gerry Brenner's psychoanalytic reading of the analogy between the story's narrator and Harry Morgan in *To Have and Have Not*. Underlying this "brilliant dramatic monologue" by an "amoral opportunist, . . . who sees only loot, not human suffering" and the later novel, is a drama of conflicting attitudes toward the father figure: parricidal in Harry but, in both Harry and this narrator, mingled with a desire for "paternal understanding and approval" (140). For Brenner this accounts for the last third of the story in which the narrator tries to "reconstruct for his listener precisely what must have occurred and how the captain of the sunken liner must have felt, . . . an act of imagination, compassion, and empathy . . . for a father figure (255, n. 3).

The two most extensive analyses of the story appeared some twenty years apart, Anselm Atkins's in 1967–68 and Susan Beegel's in 1988. In his close and perceptive reading, Atkins demonstrated that two ironic contrasts are focused in the narrator: on the stylistic level, the contrast between the "flat, feelingless narration" and the profound "emotion which the story generates"; and on the structural level, the contrast between narrator's story of his attempts to loot the wreck and the "secondary action of the ship's misfortune." At each level—and they are sometimes indistinguishable—these ironic contrasts are suppressed. The narrator's first reaction to the ship's size is to wonder "how much she must have in her"—not *what* but how much (*Stories* 374); his cold and methodical attempts to break the porthole glass beneath which the drowned woman floats, almost as if she's watching him—"I could see her floating plain and I hit the glass twice with the wrench" (*Stories* 374); and his remark on "the pieces of things" that "you couldn't tell what they were," which, as Atkins noted, means they were *anatomically* unidentifiable, but may also suggest that he, the narrator, could not, for other reasons, tell us—all these and other instances dissolve "the staggering contrast between the petty loot [the goal of the narrator's story] and the human remains on which the birds were feasting [the tragic outcome of the story of the wreck]" (Atkins 227–28).

Atkins noted at the end that the narrator's diction unites the two stories: "I wonder how *fast* [the ship] made it" in the quicksands; and the Greeks "must have come *fast* all right"; the crew and passengers "must have took *it* [death] inside"; and "Well, the Greeks got *it* all [the loot]" (*Stories* 377–78; Atkins 228–29). The "maimed, sub-human viewpoint of the narrator-hero precludes the reader's experiencing the impact of the story" until the end, when it suddenly explodes—"a time bomb without a tick" (230).

Susan Beegel's study of the manuscripts confirmed and applauded Atkins's earlier essay, even though she found a similarity between the narrator and the captain that Atkins did not. Both, she argued, are winners who take nothing, but still winners "because they confront death bravely," with a courage that "is the proud but futile defiance of death's inevitability" (81). That conclusion, however, seems to equate the motives and behavior of the captain who tried to save his passengers, among them the drowned woman, and those of the narrator who wants to strip her of her rings. There is a difference between a captain who dies at the wheel and a sponger who suffers a nosebleed, and the narrator recognizes that difference at the end. The implicit identification of the fisherman with the wheeling birds does not suggest the struggle between "unaccomodated man and natural law" (81) so much as it implies his ruthless complicity in its fundamental amorality.

With that matter of interpretation aside, Beegel's chapter is an exemplary and original study of the creative process through which Hemingway achieved this apparently so simple but finally profound story. Her strategy was to identify all the disparate "factual" elements that Hemingway might have heard from Bra Saunders and others at Key West or from contemporary newspaper accounts, then to trace the ways in which these are included and then deleted through the progression of the three major manuscript versions, and finally to isolate the three elements of the final version that were clearly invented: the diving episode, the vision of the drowned woman, and the understated conclusion that replaces the first version's burning of the Greek sponging vessels. Each of these elements contributes to the "creation of a fictional mainplot that provides an ironic counterpoint to the factual subplot" (84). Beyond that she traced the development of the character of the narrator from something of a rummy and old salt, a near parody of Conrad's Marlow, into someone as "brave and amoral as a predatory animal" whose narration "chills because it is a tragedy narrated by a hollow man" (87).

Indeed, a hollow man. And the allusion returns us to Conrad's *Heart of Darkness,* which provided T. S. Eliot with an epigraph for "The Hollow

Men" and which Hemingway had read and alluded to in the manuscripts of *A Farewell to Arms*. A hollow man is neither brave nor courageous any more than a seabird or a shark is in their instinctual scavenging. What distinguishes the narrator of "After the Storm" and Kurtz of Conrad's novel from the world of predatory nature, is that they both speak. Hemingway's narrator does not identify "The horror! The horror!" but his story does reveal "the appalling face of a glimpsed truth—the strange commingling of desire and hate" (151) that moved Kurtz to speak those words.

Works Cited

PRIMARY

Ernest Hemingway: Selected Letters, 1917–1961. Ed. Carlos Baker. New York: Scribner's, 1981.

The Short Stories of Ernest Hemingway. New York: Scribner's, 1938, 372–78.

SECONDARY

Atkins, Anselm. "Ironic Action in 'After the Storm.' " *Studies in Short Fiction* 5 (1967–68): 372–78; rpt. in *The Short Stories of Ernest Hemingway: Critical Essays.* Ed. Jackson J. Benson. Durham: Duke UP, 1975, 227–30.

Baker, Carlos. *Ernest Hemingway: A Life Story.* 1969. New York: Scribner's, 1988.

Beegel, Susan F. *Hemingway's Craft of Omission.* Ann Arbor: UMI, 1988.

Bloom, Harold. *The Anxiety of Influence.* Oxford: Oxford UP, 1975.

Brenner, Gerry. *Concealments in Hemingway's Works.* Columbus: Ohio State UP, 1983.

Conrad, Joseph. "Heart of Darkness." *Youth and Two Other Stories.* Garden City: Doubleday, 1929.

DeFalco, Joseph. *The Hero in Hemingway's Short Stories.* Pittsburgh: U of Pittsburgh P, 1963.

Howell, John M. "Hemingway's 'Metaphysics' in Four Stories of the Thirties: A Look at the Manuscripts." *ICarbS* 1 (1973): 41–51.

Rovit, Earl. *Ernest Hemingway.* Boston: Twayne, 1963.

Walker, Robert G. "Irony and Allusion in Hemingway's 'After the Storm.' " *Studies in Short Fiction* 13 (1976): 74–76.

Williams, Wirt. *The Tragic Art of Ernest Hemingway.* Baton Rouge: Louisiana State UP, 1981.

35

God Rest You Merry, Gentlemen

Composition History (February–December 1932)

When Carlos Baker was writing his biography of Hemingway, he received from Waring Jones six letters left in Hemingway's files that were originally sent to Dr. Logan Clendening of Kansas City from persons seeking help in his "column of medical advice, 'Diet and Health,' . . . syndicated in hundreds of newspapers" (604). Baker's account suggests that Hemingway received the letters by early 1932, and that by 24 February he could include among "After the Storm" and "six others for a new collection" two that derived from these letters—"One Reader Writes" and "God Rest You Merry, Gentlemen" (227).

Although they were inspired by those letters, other evidence suggests that both stories were written later than February 1932: "One Reader Writes" probably a year later, and "God Rest You" probably between the late spring and fall of 1932 (for "One Reader Writes" see Chap. 42 below).

Although the speculation is at best tenuous, it seems likely that the three "fine" or "swell" stories he mentioned to Max Perkins and Henry Strater on 7 and 9 February would not have included those already published, "Wine of Wyoming" and "The Sea Change," or "A Natural History of the Dead," which he had just included in the galleys of *Death in the Afternoon* (Baker 604; *Letters* 353). When he wrote to Waldo Peirce, however, on 15 April that he had "*about* six done for a book," he might well have been referring to the two published stories, "After the Storm" (to be published in May), two others, and "Homage to Switzerland," which he was about to finish.

Two candidates for those unidentified stories are "God Rest You Merry, Gentlemen" and "The Mother of a Queen." In a list of "Stories for Book" he cited those two stories, three he had published by then ("Wine of Wyoming," "The Sea Change," and "After the Storm"), "A Natural History of the Dead"—at that time a candidate for a collection—and two he was working on through the summer of 1932 ("Homage to Switzerland" and "The Light of the World"). Two stories usually dated in the first half of 1932, "One Reader Writes" and "A Way You'll Never Be," do not appear on that list for reasons to be considered later (KL/EH 221 A).

If the letter sent to Dr. Clendening and then to Hemingway from a troubled "youth in West Englewood, New Jersey, who had spent many years worrying about the problem of sexual desire" (Baker 227) initiated "God Rest You," Hemingway had little time to do more than sketch the first false start (KL/EH 426) before he embarked on a fishing marathon that lasted through June 1932.

In July, "seething with 'damned good stories' " and recuperating from bronchial pneumonia, he set off for Piggott and Wyoming, passing through Kansas City (Baker 229). It is likely that the second false start describing that city and the first eleven-page pencil manuscript (KL/EH 428) were written sometime early in that summer.

On the first manuscript he made a note to change the doctors' names from Fisher to Fischer and Cox to Wilcox—to put off both Jungians and Freudians?—and probably in late fall incorporated those changes in a typescript he signed, addressed at Key West, Florida, adding "1st Serial Rights only (all names are fictitious)" (KL/EH 429, an ink-corrected carbon of the original 430). This typescript must have been the one given to Louis H. Cohen in January 1933 for the limited edition of the story published by House of Books in April.

But Hemingway was not finished with the story. Although George Monteiro has taken Scribner's to task for their "principles of censorship" and so chosen the House of Books edition as his text (213, n. 2), in both the pencil manuscript and the typescript for Louis Cohen, Hemingway left a dash for the offensive "Oh go and [jack off]" (*Stories* 395). He tried to return those words in the House of Books tear sheets he submitted for setting copy to Scribner's, to no avail, but more important, he added several lines to the concluding dialogue between the two doctors, all but one of which are Doc Fischer's: "It was an amputation the young man performed, Horace"; "undoubtedly *your* Saviour"; "I have even had a very small look into it [hell]. No More than a peek, really. I looked away almost at once." Finally, in those tear sheets, Hemingway added the concluding interchange between the two doctors, which appears in neither the first manuscript nor the last typescript: " 'You hear him, Horace?' Doc Fischer said. 'You hear him? Having discovered my vulnerable point, my achilles tendon so to speak, the doctor pursues his advantage.' 'You're too damned smart,' Doctor Wilcox said' " (*Stories* 395–96).

Publication History (April 1933; October 1933)

Louis H. Cohen had published an early bibliography of Hemingway's works in August 1931, corresponded with him in early 1932 (KL/EH, Louis H. Cohen to Hemingway, 29 February 1932), and asked for a story for a limited edition to offset the recent negative reviews of *Death in the Afternoon* in January 1933. Although Baker noted that Hemingway wanted to "fight his own battles," he must have agreed and handed him the typescript he had signed, addressed, and noted for publication rights with a disclaimer as fiction (KL/EH 429). Cohen published it in a House of Books edition of three hundred copies; and with revised tear sheets from that limited edition it was included in *Winner Take Nothing*.

Sources and Influences

For this odd and, as some would argue, curiously reticent story there are a variety of sources, and two are biographical. Charles Fenton was the first to claim that "God Rest You" was from a "memorable harvest of his [Kansas City] *Star* assignments" and suggested that it was one of those stolen from Hadley in 1922 (49). That it was not so early a story is established by both the manuscripts and the compelling letter passed on from Logan Clendening of 1932, the second biographical source for the story.

Whatever its modern origins, any story set at Christmas about a young man who may be dying after mutilating himself for Christian principles, however misconceived, and told through the dialogue of two doctors, one a Jew named Fischer, simply cannot be denied its timeless archetypal sources. Peter Hays first associated the story with Jessie L. Weston's study of the fisher king legend and its central figure of the "medicine man" in *From Ritual to Romance*. So profound a shaping influence on T. S. Eliot's "The Waste Land", it seems likely that Hemingway knew the book either from his reading or Ezra Pound's passionate interest in Eliot's poem in its early version (225–27). Then George Monteiro followed the implications of the Christmas carol quoted in the title to allusions to Corinthians, Matthew, and Luke in the New Testament (208–11).

Julian Smith, in a rather daring critical leap, confronted the difficult question of the identity of the story's narrator, and concluded that he is very like a young Jake Barnes, a newspaperman from Kansas City, who hears and tells a story prophetic of his own emasculation in the novel he narrates, *The Sun Also Rises* (135–47).

Critical Studies

Other than the three articles by Peter Hays, Julian Smith, and George Monteiro, there are few more than passing mentions of "God Rest You" and those are summarized in Monteiro's introduction. He noted that the criticism of the story has developed from Carlos Baker's naturalistic reading ("a sardonic Christmas tale . . . of mistaken piety"), to Joseph DeFalco's psychological analysis ("The refusal to accept the stage of puberty . . . is the extreme of the *via negativa*"), to Peter Hays's archetypal interpretation ("Fischer is a Christ figure . . . a 'fisher of men' ") (207).

Peter Hays drew on some complex aspects of the fisher-king legend to demonstrate its analogies with the story. He noted that in Jessie Weston's study of the myth there is often a "doubling, dividing the ritual tasks of a hero between two characters who are usually related." Thus in the story "the roles in the tale of a fisher king wounded in the genitals, and healed by a young, pure knight, have been divided and reassigned: it is the young innocent who is wounded, and it is the fis(c)her who is the healer" (225–26). Other contrasts between the legend and the story abound. In the legend the king is wounded, and the wound is both a cause and symbol of the land's sterility; in the story the boy wounds himself, or was his wound not the cause but the result of the land's sterile religiosity? (Doc Fischer's suggestion that the cross-indexing from symptoms to treatments in *The Young Doctor's Friend and Guide* might also be cross-indexed in reverse from treatments to symptoms, as "an aid to memory," is not an offhand remark [*Stories* 392].) Such memory is desperately needed in an ironic world where the once "vital and honored role of the healer, the medicine man" of legend, is now held by "bungling doctors" (Hays 226).

Finally, Hays argued that Fischer and the mutilated boy not only exchange the roles of legend but also are united in their separation from others. Fischer's "intelligence, self-confidence, and compassion" make him "too damned smart" for Wilcox and this world; and he shares a "spiritual kinship" with the boy, who is "set apart from a normal life by abnormal sensitivity and religiosity" (224, 227).

The role and motives of the narrator, Horace, have troubled some critics. Hays found him impassive and equated him, unfairly, with Doctor Wilcox for their "harsh treatment" of Fischer and the boy (227). For Julian Smith it is just that impassive aspect that lead him to conclude that "the thing left out" of the story is the narrator's reason for telling it, a reason we may infer from the similarity between the boy's wound and Jacob Barnes's. Smith argued that Hays "underrates the narrator," who has "acquired true sophistication, so much so that he can now speak objectively of his youthful naiveté." Admiring the story for its "incompleteness," he still wondered why the story ends with a "pointless argument between the two doctors" (146).

But the pointlessness of the doctors' argument may be its point: each of them is shocked at the boy's self-mutilation and even more at their own helplessness, for different reasons. Even Wilcox may understand the truth of Fischer's penultimate remark, "The significance of the particular day is not important." Yet they argue as if to unburden their horror at what they have witnessed in their anger at each other and themselves. If this is the case, it seems clear that the story must have a third person to tell it, and a third person who is a witness, especially if Hemingway meant to embed the boy's story within the doctors', and their story in turn within the narrator's drama of perception.

George Monteiro began with the fact of the story's "nested narrative structure" and, with a sensitive and persuasive reading of the "perspectives" of the two inner narratives, discovered deeper ironies. Out of a rich pattern of biblical echoes and allusions he brings us to troubling questions at the heart of the boy's story: "Is the boy's fate an exemplum for those who would follow Pauline dictates on purity of the self by obeying the strictures against lust and sin? Or is he an example to those who would apply Christian teachings literally in the secular world?" (211) Similarly, he demonstrates how the doctors' story "complicates the neat conflict of emotional involvement versus professional neutrality. The doctor who bodies forth, unprofessionally, excessive emotional involvement is also, in skills, the better practitioner of medicine. . . . The doctor who is objective and unfeeling, on the other hand, is not at all well-versed in medicine. The objectivity he manifests is a direct function of his personal callousness" (211). But when he arrived at the outer narrative, Monteiro found "no solid connections" between the two inner narratives and Horace's narration, and concluded it is useless "to try to fathom out his reason for telling us about what he has heard in the ambulance waiting room" (212).

His criteria for "solid connections" seem more strict than they need be, for there are at least two that deserve consideration. First, however impassive, Horace is intimately aware of the two doctors' backgrounds: he knows of Wilcox's dismal performance in medical school, and he watches Fischer's gambler's "hands that had, with his willingness to oblige and his lack of respect for Federal statutes, made him his trouble" (*Stories* 393, 395). If he is sophisticated enough to recognize his own former naiveté, he might recognize as well that his knowledge of the doctors' histories implicates him in their narrative. And second, the boy's story and the doctors' part in it is not simply what he "heard in the ambulance waiting room," but what he saw. He was a witness—"I had been there when he came in"—and it is he who tells the story of the boy's appearance the day before. He recalled the way the boy looked and dressed, that he "was very excited and frightened but *determined*," and that he responded to Doctor Wilcox's profanities "with dignity" (*Stories* 394, 395).

The story has a variety of affinities with others: as in "The Killers," three—not two—characters respond in radically different ways to a horrible and ineluctable event; and, as with "In Another Country," a retrospective narrative begins with a long recollection of a setting, unfolds in a hospital, and ends with a once naive narrator's implicit revelation. If those two stories can stand alone, then "God Rest You Merry, Gentlemen" neither needs nor deserves the return of Jacob Barnes. After all, his presence trivializes the story: one need not be emasculated to witness and suffer the agony of another who is; it is enough to have said, "I had been there when he came in," and so to imply some complicity with the doctors in the boy's tragedy.

Works Cited

PRIMARY

Ernest Hemingway: Selected Letters, 1917–1961. Ed. Carlos Baker. New York: Scribner's, 1981.

The Short Stories of Ernest Hemingway. New York: Scribner's, 1938, 392–96.

SECONDARY

Baker, Carlos. *Ernest Hemingway: A Life Story.* 1969. Scribner's, 1988.

DeFalco, Joseph. *The Hero in Hemingway's Short Stories.* Pittsburgh: U of Pittsburgh P, 1963.

Fenton, Charles A. *The Apprenticeship of Ernest Hemingway.* New York: Farrar, 1954.

Hays, Peter L. "Hemingway and the Fisher King." *University Review* 32 (1965–66): 225–28; rpt. in *The Short Stories of Ernest Hemingway: Critical Essays.* Ed. Jackson J. Benson. Durham: Duke UP, 1975, 222–27.

Monteiro, George. "Hemingway's Christmas Carol." *Fitzgerald/Hemingway Annual* (1972): 207–13.

Smith, Julian. "Hemingway and the Thing Left Out." *Journal of Modern Literature* 1 (1970–71): 169–72; rpt. in *The Short Stories of Ernest Hemingway: Critical Essays.* Ed. Jackson J. Benson. Durham: Duke UP, 1975, 135–47.

36

Homage to Switzerland

Composition History (March–June 1932)

Biographical references within "Homage to Switzerland" would set its composition in 1929—Mr. Harris's father committed suicide "last year," and the story shares its locale with the end of *A Farewell to Arms*—and one false start in which the protagonist is named Higgins may have been written early (KL/EH 476 A). But all the evidence in letters and lists of titles points to a period in the late spring of 1932.

In early February he had only three, albeit "swell," stories written (*Letters* 353). The first pencil manuscript (KL/EH 476, 476 B) could have been completed between fishing trips to the Dry Tortugas in February and March to become one of "about six done for a book" he mentioned in mid-April (*Letters* 358). If not then, it was ready for typing in May, probably during the two week-long visits Pauline made that month to join her husband on his "Cuban holiday," for she had it "copied in Key West" before they left for Wyoming in early July (Baker, *Ernest Hemingway: A Life Story* 229; *Letters* 367).

That typescript (KL/EH 477) was sent to William C. Lengel, editor of *Cosmopolitan,* in mid-August after several telephone calls. Hemingway signed and addressed it from the L-Bar-T Ranch, noted first serial rights only, and requested the manuscript's return—probably suspecting they would reject it, as they did. That typescript became the setting copy for the *Scribner's Magazine* publication in April 1933.

The major revisions of the story are deletions from the pencil manuscript at the conclusions of parts 1 and 2, and—perhaps more significant—the late decision to divide the experiences in the three parts among three different characters: in the manuscript and typescript all three characters are named Mr. Wheeler; in the typescript Hemingway changed the part title and name to Mr. Johnson in part 2, and to Mr. Harris in part 3 (KL/EH 476, 476 B, 477).

Before the concluding sentence of part 1 Hemingway deleted a passage that confirms Mr. Wheeler's homosexuality: "He was very careful about money and did not care for women | except to talk to and of course his own dear mother and sisters. He had stopped off on the way from Rome to see a friend at Territet but the friend had left Territet and Mr. Wheeler would meet him in Paris. From Paris it was only a step to London and from London really only a step to New York if that was the way you felt about it. |" This is followed by another deletion: "| and to tease. Mr. Wheeler was a great tease. He had tormented a good many people in his day |" (KL/EH 476).

This deletion not only italicizes Wheeler's homosexuality and adds a titillating note on his mother and sisters, it adds a whisper of implication that Hemingway might have, at this point in the narrative, been thinking of more than a "metaphysical" meeting of the various "Wheelers," later named Johnson in Vevey (ten minutes from Montreux by train) or Harris in Territet (a ten-minute walk from Montreux, and incidentally not a stop of the Simplon-Orient Express).

The second deletion is a rejected conclusion of part 2 of the pencil manuscript (KL/EH 476 B). Here Mr. Wheeler/Johnson is a writer embittered over his wife's divorcing him for another man. He neither wants to meet anyone nor to be alone; a woman, his wife (?), had said he lacked "courage to face life" and "ought to go out more with people"—which he had just done, but "they were Swiss of course." Now "his heart was gone. She had his heart and it was lost now. She couldn't help it. She never could help anything. He knew it and did not blame her and his heart was gone. . . . He could live without his heart because he had to and everything went on and he did not care. He could not write without his heart. It was all hollow like this story." An interesting passage that deserved deletion, it may have been a recollection of Hemingway's dark days before his divorce from Hadley in the fall and winter of 1926–27; but it was written in May of 1932 in Cuba when, as Carlos Baker so decorously notes, "Pauline was there, [and] they saw a good deal of Jane Mason" (*Ernest Hemingway: A Life Story* 228).

Publication History (April 1933; October 1933)

The rejected typescript sent to *Cosmopolitan* served as setting copy sent to *Scribner's Magazine* that fall, and Hemingway returned proofs on 26 January 1933 (Baker, *Ernest Hemingway: A Life Story* 606); it was published without revision in April 1933. Tear sheets from that publication, again without revision, served as setting copy for the October 1933 publication in *Winner Take Nothing*.

Sources and Influences

For a story so reminiscent of Hemingway's dark season before his divorce from Hadley, his father's suicide and the nearly therapeutic revision of *A Farewell to Arms* a month later, but written in a later season when he was embarking on a fishing trip to Cuba and an affair that would predict the dissolution of his second marriage, the biographical sources are unsurprisingly legion.

Hemingway had known the Vevey-Montreux/Territet stations along the shore of Lac Leman from his vacations and *Toronto Star* assignments in 1922; he had been near there in Gstaad in early 1927 and stopped in Montreux in December for the night; and finally he had passed through on his way to visit Gerald and Sara Murphy at Montana/Vermala in December of 1929. Each stop must have recalled the first bright, cold days at Chamby with Hadley, then their long separation and divorce, and the last chapters of the novel that coalesced those years with his father's suicide.

It might have been chance that he drew on those memories in early 1932, but the fishing trip to Cuba that stretched from two weeks to two months, the alluring presence of Jane Mason, for whom Pauline was no match, might have recalled the end of his first marriage—not that hindsight or foresight then, or ever, did him any good.

The story is Hemingway's second "Canary for One," which ends on a cement station-platform as do the first two parts of this one. So it is linked with the first group of marriage tales—"Out of Season," "Cat in the Rain," "Cross-Country Snow"—and even "Hills Like White Elephants," which begins and ends on a station-platform with a contrast between a troubled American and those foreigners who are "reasonably" waiting for a train.

However much Hemingway paid for this story in his troubled past, he still owed something for it to his literary contemporaries. When he began to explain it to William Lengel (and also justify its length), he said "it's a new form for a story. The fact that the three parts all open the same way or practically the same is intentional." But then, perhaps realizing that Lengel would not be listening or that the experiment was not all that new, he drifted off, claiming that it represented "Switzerland metaphysically where it all opens in the same way always" and where young men will not marry until the bride's father buys his daughter false teeth, and so on. He dismissed the thought with, "But, possibly, Mr. Lengel, you have been in Switzerland yourself" (*Letters* 367, ca. 15 August 1932; see also John Howell's remarks on the letter).

A curious comment, with a wit similar to the story's, it probably should not be taken as a serious literary statement. Fictional collations of simultaneous narratives gathered about a shared thematic center had been around at least since Browning's *The Ring and the Book*, and then there was Joyce's *Ulysses*, and most recently Faulkner's *As I Lay Dying*, which Hemingway praised in January 1932 (Hemingway to Owen Wister, cited in Baker, *Ernest Hemingway: A Life Story* 227, 603). Hemingway's claim for literary originality is justified as far as it goes, if that is no further than the opening scenes of the three narratives. The significance of that experiment is a matter for literary criticism.

Critical Studies

"Homage to Switzerland" may be an oddity among Hemingway's short fiction; but a larger oddity is that a story so obviously dependent upon its form for its meaning has failed to catch the lasting attention of any critic in thirty years dominated by formalist criticism. Carlos Baker's interest in it was only biographical (*Writer as Artist* 138); and Sheridan Baker declared it a "trivial experiment with form that nevertheless condemns American society with a final note of suicide" (85). His judgment of the experiment as trivial probably followed from the curious idea that the suicide condemns American society.

Joseph DeFalco, in the most extensive comment on the story—some four pages—worked through the three parts of the story to discover that: in the first, there is "something abnormal in [Mr. Wheeler's] sexual tendencies; in the second, Mr. Johnson's divorce is, to the three porters, implicitly not normal; and in the third, Mr. Harris reports that his father shot himself, "oddly enough" (181–82). From this he legitimately concluded that these characters are "illustrative of a cross section of society on the journey of life"; but like others before him he misconstrued Mr. Johnson's divorce as the "metaphorical basis for the examination of the process of adjustment to emotional hurt" (183, 179).

Two critical assumptions, then, have delayed any serious consideration of the story: first, that the formal experiment is trivial; second, that the problems of a homosexual (Mr. Wheeler) and the son of a suicide (Mr. Harris) may be subsumed in those of a divorced man (Mr. Johnson).

But critical interest in "Homage to Switzerland" may be reviving, for Michael Reynolds recently presented a delightful and challenging paper with the subtitle "Einstein's Train Stops at Hemingway's Station." He took seriously the simultaneity of the story's three parts and the nearly exact repetition of their opening scenes to suggest that had this story been written by, say, James Joyce, not a few critical careers might have been launched with serious studies of its ironic treatment of the relativity of time and space. If Hemingway did not attend or read of Albert Einstein's lectures in Paris in March 1922, he could hardly have missed the newspaper accounts of his work—from 1922 to 1928 "the *New York Times* carried 172 stories about Einstein . . . and almost 100 articles appeared in English and American general periodicals" (Reynolds 4). And, of course, the classic example of the relativity principle involves two men, one on a train and the other on a platform, each simultaneously measuring a window and recording the time, with different results, as the train passes by at the speed of light—which perhaps it would have had to do to arrive on time in the story's three parts, particularly if Hemingway had left the three gentlemen with the same name as he did in his early draft.

However that may be, Reynolds was the first critic to appreciate the story's wit, particularly in the meeting between E. D. Harris and Dr. Sigismund Wyer, Ph.D. in part 3, and their discussion of some of the memorable issues of the *National Geographic*. Finally, he suggested that for those of us who are concerned with when the story was set or written, it has its own inner relativity in its biographical and historical references. Clarence Hemingway's suicide "oddly enough" places the story in 1929; the *Geographic*'s foldout picture of the Sahara, in 1926; and the reference to T. E. Lawrence, in 1931–32—"perfectly appropriate in a universe where time is relative" (Reynolds 8–9). The moral, he concludes—let us not take ourselves *too* seriously.

Works Cited

PRIMARY

Ernest Hemingway: Selected Letters, 1917–1961. Ed. Carlos Baker. New York: Scribner's, 1981.

The Short Stories of Ernest Hemingway. New York: Scribner's, 1938, 422–35.

SECONDARY

Baker, Carlos. *Ernest Hemingway: A Life Story.* 1969. New York: Scribner's, 1988.

———. *Hemingway: The Writer as Artist.* 1952. Princeton: Princeton UP, 1972.

DeFalco, Joseph. *The Hero in Hemingway's Short Stories.* Pittsburgh: U of Pittsburgh P, 1963.

Howell, John M. "Hemingway's 'Metaphysics' in Four Stories of the Thirties: A Look at the Manuscripts." *ICarbS* 1 (Fall–Winter 1973): 41–51.

Reynolds, Michael S. " 'Homage to Switzerland': Einstein's Train Stops at Hemingway's Station." Unpublished paper.

37

The Light of the World

Composition History (May–July 1932)

The only evidence for the date of composition for "The Light of World" is Hemingway's vague recollection some twenty years later of writing it in "either Key West or Havana. It probably was Havana" (*Letters* 799, 23 January 1953). The first draft, of which only a fragment remains (KL/EH 548), was probably completed sometime in May or June 1932, and either typed while Ernest was in Cuba or, more likely, brought along for revision at the Nordquists' L-Bar-T ranch that summer. The manuscript fragment reveals some indecision over the story's ending, a matter Hemingway would have reasonably postponed until the relative calm of a Wyoming vacation in July. The signed typescript is addressed from Cooke, Montana.

In the manuscript's rejected conclusion, Alice invites the narrator (Nick) "to stay for nothing"—that is to say, something for nothing—and he declines. The cook, who had offered to accompany the boys earlier, is rebuffed in the lines that conclude the final version of the story; and Alice remarks, "That's right." The boys leave and walk up the tracks a little way past the three Indians and stop. They discuss Alice's offer; Tom says that Nick refused because he was "afraid of her"; he takes the challenge and they "went back a little way, and I stopped."

"I don't want to go," I said. "I like her but I'm spooked."
"I know you are." (KL/EH 548)

All this is deleted and a final page close to the published conclusion is added.

Publication History (October 1933)

The carbon of the typescript later used as a setting copy for *Winner Take Nothing* (KL/EH 222) makes evident Hemingway's original intention to submit the story to a more tolerant journal than *Scribner's Magazine* as well as their reasons for rejecting it sometime in the fall: "You know where" was originally "Up your ass" and "interfere" is the polite locution for "bugger" (*Stories* 384–86). With that rejection, Hemingway sent them "The Gambler, The Nun, and the Radio" and then cleaned up the language for publication in *Winner Take Nothing* (Baker, *Ernest Hemingway: A Life Story* 238, 606).

Sources and Influences

Joseph Flora remarked that "The Light of the World" is "perhaps the most 'literary' " of the Nick Adams stories, and in his discussion of sources and analogues he comes close to proving it the most literary of all Hemingway's stories.

Although every reader has recognized the source for the story's title (John 8:12), Peter Thomas's exhaustive study of the tale "within a mode . . . of biblical parody and analogy" adds other allusions from John (8:13–14); suggests that, in Peroxide's memories at least, Ketchel has become William Blake's Tyger; and concludes that the narrator's attraction to Alice ("as big as three women") is a "parody of religious adoration (trinitarian Alice)" that is interrupted by his companion, a Doubting Thomas (14, 17–18). Later, Gary Elliott argued that Christ's calling his disciples "the light of the world" (Matt. 5:14–16), turns the story's meaning away from Ketchel as an ironic Christ to Nick as an ineffectual disciple who fails to let his "light so shine before men, that they may see your good works."

Hemingway certainly knew his Bible, but for him its words were made visible and exact in a copy of Holman Hunt's painting "The Light of the World" his mother gave to her church to memorialize her father, Ernest Hall. Michael Reynolds is persuasive in arguing that Hemingway, who from the age of six would have found blessed relief from dull sermons in that painting, must have wondered what was behind the cottage door at which Christ knocks. Reynolds argued that when Hemingway finally opened it in 1932 "to discover five whores and a homosexual cook—not exactly what middle-class Christians expected," given "his mother's associations with the painting, this brutal little story became a private memorial to Grace's preoccupation with the Hall family" (105).

From 1933 on Hemingway thought that "The Light of the World" was "as good or better a story about whores than [La] Maison Tellier" of Guy de Maupassant (*Letters* 393). Constance Montgomery considered the parallels, but concluded the two "stories have little in common" (95). James Martine, and later Joseph Flora, disagreed: Martine cited the "same number of 'girls' (five) taking a trip by rail, . . . the central scene . . . awash with the tears of maudlin sentimentality, . . . [and] the description of Mme. Tellier, very like that of big Alice." More important, however, is that the two writers share a "sacrilegiously comic" authorial intention: Martine cites

Maupassant's description of the Tellier house where "all night long a little lamp burned . . . such as one still sees in some towns, at the foot of the shrine of some saint." So the lantern borne in Holman Hunt's painting becomes "the archetypal light on the archetypal houses of the oldest profession in the world" (465–66).

Barbara Maloy found some six unpersuasive parallels between the story and Lewis Carroll's *Alice in Wonderland* and *Alice through the Looking Glass*: extremes of argument, crying, and laughter; "fallen" characters, including Tweedledum (Nick) and Tweedledee (Tom), and, of course, the two Alices (83). Flora agreed with Carlos Baker's suggestion that Hemingway's Alice shares much more with Chaucer's Alice, the Wife of Bath (*Writer as Artist* 140). The two ladies are women of the world, and their haystack proportions accommodate their expansive visions of the world and their largess—each knows well "the olde daunce" of the art of love.

Flora cited two other works that might have shaped the story. Almost as an aside he mentioned Nathaniel Hawthorne's "My Kinsman, Major Molineaux" (75 n. 13). Although there is no evidence that Hemingway ever read the story, the shared elements are impressive: a night journey of initiation in a strange town, belligerent encounters with the townfolk, a meeting with a prostitute interrupted by another person, a threateningly ambiguous world, often misconstrued, and a young boy who considers himself a "shrewd youth" at the center of it all. The other work is James Joyce's "An Encounter." Flora notes that it is a "first-person account of an unnamed boy" who instructs his companion to use pseudonyms when they meet a homosexual at the end of an adventure inspired by their reading of wild-west fiction (77).

Constance Montgomery's early study identified the original Michigan setting for the story, Kalkaska, just north of Cadillac and south of Mancelona on the Grand Rapids & Indiana Railroad, and the fastidious cook from a lumber camp on Walloon Lake (92–93). But the more important history behind the story is "Steve" Ketchel's, for the controversy the cook began and Alice and Peroxide joined over his sainted memory has been carried on in critical journals, in rather more polite language. Sheridan Baker and Matthew Bruccoli drew on several boxing records to establish the facts of Ketchel's career: born Stanislaus Kiecal in 1886, he was middleweight champion from 1908 to 1910, and his most famous fight was as the White Hope against Jack Johnson, the heavyweight champion, in 1909 in California; in that fight, which some say was fixed, Ketchel floored Johnson and then was knocked out in the twelfth round. A notorious free-spender, he had, as Bruccoli noted, a "heroic appetite for women," and was murdered in 1910 ("Light of the World" 125–27).

Everything else claimed in the story by the two whores or even the "shy man" is either false or unsubstantiated. There is some irony, then, in the fact that the cook's quiet suggestion that Steve's name was Stanley represents the one recollection that is true, however brief and tentative. Bruccoli held that Stanley "seems to have preferred being addressed as Steve"; James Martine, in 1970, noted that there was a "Steve Ketchell who, on July 31, 1915, fought Ad Wolgast (the Ad Francis of 'The Battler')" five years after Stanley's murder (466); and five years after that Bruccoli reaffirmed his original point ("Stan Ketchel" 325-26).

All this interest in the fighter's brief fame is meant, of course, to answer the question of which, if either, of the two whores could have known him, in any sense of the word—a question of critical significance.

Critical Studies

On the relative veracity of the two whores' memories, most critics would rather believe Alice than Peroxide; like Nick, they may have been moved for a moment by the blonde's "high stagey way" and her epiphanic vision (*Stories* 388-89), but Alice's "simple concrete memory, . . . the kind of memory that adheres within the spirit," as Arthur Waldhorn had it, is finally more convincing (60). James Barbour ("Comedy of Errors"), Matthew Bruccoli, and Joseph Flora were in general agreement, and Scott Donaldson put it most simply: "Nick correctly perceives that the massive whore Alice, despite her profession, is capable of love, the true 'light of the world' " (*By Force of Will* 238).

Others might argue that those critics have been deceived by the stereotype of the "whore with the heart of gold," particularly one who, like Hemingway, understands the persuasive power of the simple phrase "You're a lovely piece, Alice" (*Stories* 390). Not that they found Peroxide a true bride of Christ, but William Stein, Joseph DeFalco, and James Martine doubted Alice's motives, as does Nick's companion Tom. Stein argued that any narrator who witnesses such a travesty of Christian love and is still tempted must be damned; DeFalco agreed that Nick is "taken in by the seductive voice and appearance of the 'Queen,' who emerges victorious in this Walpurgis Night congregation" (87); and Martine believed that the cook's identification of the real Stanley Ketchel "establishes that both Peroxide and big Alice are lying" (466).

There is, however, a good deal of agreement on other issues. Nearly every commentator shared Carlos Baker's appreciation of the story's Chaucerian comedy, with its "raucous play of human emotion" in contrast to the "furtive yearnings of the homosexual cook" (*Writer as Artist,* 140), although some, like DeFalco, found the comedy darker, more ironic. Few argued with Philip Young's consideration of this as a Nick Adams story (56); indeed, Flora's extended analysis of the story as part of a trilogy with "The Battler" and

"The Killers" is persuasive. And, of course, none can ignore Peroxide's enraptured and innocent parody of the three Christian motifs DeFalco noted: Christ's death ("His own father . . . killed him. Yes, by Christ, his own father"); his struggle with Satan (Jack Johnson, "that black son of a bitch from hell"); and the Bride of Christ ("We were married in the eyes of God") (*Stories* 388-89; DeFalco 84-86; see also Thomas, cited above).

As with other Hemingway fictions, the first allusion to some Christian or classical myth is often the first warning to be wary and wait for the end, especially if the story's light is dim. Alice is the first one to mention Christ, and then as a profanity in the midst of her laughter at the cook (*Stories* 386). Her laughter continues through Peroxide's ecstatic vision of the "White Hope" as Christ the tiger in language she might have heard working some revivalist's tent. And if the story's title is meant to recall Christ's challenge to the Pharisees who would condemn the adulteress, "He that is without sin among you, let him first cast a stone at her" (John 8:7), then the only honest characters in the story are the three Indians who know when to leave. Love may be the light of the world, but a "lovely piece" is less than that; and Nick, with the bravado of a teenager, wonders what it would be "like getting on top of a hay mow" (*Stories* 386). This much would suggest that the story is less an orthodox or even liberal Christian parable and more a chapter in the education of Nick Adams in the language of the world.

In that light, Joseph Flora's analysis is most relevant: for him the story dramatizes Nick's "learning to read voices, to distinguish where the true may be found" (82). One must read voices to understand and measure character; and, with a cue from Joyce's "An Encounter," Flora suggested that the characters' names—true or false or verging on the allegorical—are "crucial for the story's theme" (77). Tom and (we assume) Nick never reveal their names. None of the nine other men is named but only identified by occupation (the cook, the lumberjacks), by origin (the two Swedes, the three Indians), or by their propensity to talk ("the one who talked," "the shy man," the one "ready to say something," the silent Swedes and Indians). But all five whores have names, assumed or acquired: the fat ones, Alice, Hazel, and Ethel; one of the blondes, Frances Wilson, and the other whom the narrator names Peroxide, a sobriquet that unites her with the false "White Hope" and matches her against the cook with his white face and hands.

Flora's detailed analysis of the general conversation singled out the cook's subtle and insistent destruction of Peroxide's deification of Ketchel: it is he who mentions Cadillac and leads the shy man to recall the fighter, remembers his given name, suggests that Peroxide should have married him, and brings up the fight with Johnson—"nothing if not persistent," he leads "Peroxide on to trap herself," and leaves Alice to finish her off (*Stories* 388-89; Flora 78-80).

The crux of the argument between Alice and Peroxide is again a matter of voice and character. Peroxide insists that "it would have been impossible for Steve to have said" that Alice was "a lovely piece." But Alice remembers "when he said it and I *was* a lovely piece exactly as he said" (*Stories* 390). The ambiguity of the story, and the source of the critical controversy over its meaning, resides in Nick's perception of Alice's "sweet *lovely* voice" which, however truthful it may seem, is finally vicious.

One last note on the fourth Indian. Nearly every reader has remarked that one of the four Indians on page 385 disappears on page 386, and most have agreed that the subtraction adds to the story's bewildering atmosphere. But only William Schafer has attempted to explain the deeper meaning of the Indian's silent departure. The obvious resolution of the mystery, he argued, lies in the fact that the four are obviously not American Indians. His source is "the twenty-second book of the *Rhama Gondagetsha,* the Book of Instructions of India." Unfortunately, Schafer could only consult a fragment of "this curious document . . . pasted on the bottom of a large urn (now shamefully filled with sand and used as an ashtray) in the British Museum" (103, 104, n. 4). A delightful article that is dutifully listed in the Hemingway bibliographies, it was taken seriously by at least one later critic.

But not Scott Donaldson. He read the story's manuscripts to discover that Hemingway's typescript bears a handwritten correction of four to three Indians (KL/EH 549; *Stories* 385), dispelling what James Barbour calls the story's "funny math" ("Comedy of Errors" 6). The correction, however, was not incorporated in the setting copy (KL/EH 222), and the error was overlooked by both Hemingway and his editors (Donaldson 18). A nice example for the theoreticians of authorial intention.

Works Cited

PRIMARY

Ernest Hemingway: Selected Letters, 1917–1961. Ed. Carlos Baker. New York: Scribner's, 1981.

The Short Stories of Ernest Hemingway. New York: Scribner's, 1938, 384–91.

SECONDARY

Baker, Carlos. *Ernest Hemingway: A Life Story.* 1969. New York: Scribner's, 1988.

———. *Hemingway: The Writer as Artist.* 1952. Princeton: Princeton UP, 1972.

Baker, Sheridan. *Ernest Hemingway.* New York: Holt, 1967.

Barbour, James J. " 'The Light of the World': Hemingway's Comedy of Errors." *Notes on Contemporary Literature* 7 (1977): 5–8.

———. "'The Light of the World': The Real Ketchel and the Real Light." *Studies in Short Fiction* 13 (1976): 17–23.

Bruccoli, Matthew J. "'The Light of the World': Stan Ketchel as 'My Sweet Christ.'" *Fitzgerald/Hemingway Annual* (1969): 125–30.

———. "Stan Ketchel and Steve Ketchel: A Further Note on 'The Light of the World.'" *Fitzgerald/Hemingway Annual* (1975): 325–26.

DeFalco, Joseph. *The Hero in Hemingway's Short Stories*. Pittsburgh: U of Pittsburgh P, 1963.

Donaldson, Scott. *By Force of Will: The Life and Art of Ernest Hemingway*. New York: Viking, 1977.

———. "The Case of the Vanishing American and Other Puzzlements in Hemingway's Fiction." *Hemingway Notes* 7 (Spring 1981): 16–19.

Elliott, Gary D. "Hemingway's 'The Light of the World.'" *Explicator* 40 (Fall 1981): 48–50.

Flora, Joseph M. *Hemingway's Nick Adams*. Baton Rouge: Louisiana State UP, 1982.

Maloy, Barbara. "The Light of Alice's World." *Linguistics in Literature* 1 (1976): 69–86.

Martine, James J. "A Little Light on Hemingway's 'The Light of the World.'" *Studies in Short Fiction* 7 (Summer 1970): 465–67.

Montgomery, Constance. *Hemingway in Michigan*. Waitsfield: Vermont Crossroads, 1977.

Reynolds, Michael S. *The Young Hemingway*. Oxford: Blackwell, 1986.

Schafer, William J. "Ernest Hemingway: Arbiter of Common Numerality." *Carleton Miscellany* 3 (Winter 1962): 100–04.

Stein, William Bysshe. "Love and Lust in Hemingway's Short Stories." *Texas Studies in Literature and Language* 3 (Summer 1961): 234–42.

Thomas, Peter. "A Lost Leader: Hemingway's 'The Light of the World.'" *Humanities Association Bulletin* 21 (Fall 1970): 14–19.

Waldhorn, Arthur. *A Reader's Guide to Ernest Hemingway*. New York: Farrar, 1972.

Young, Philip. *Ernest Hemingway: A Reconsideration*. 1952. New York: Harcourt, 1966.

38

The Mother of a Queen

Composition History (Fall 1931–August 1932)

There is little evidence for a precise dating of the composition of "The Mother of a Queen"—nothing in the surviving manuscripts or the available letters—but there are some hints elsewhere that warrant a speculation. Hemingway told Arnold Gingrich in June 1933 that the story was about a matador named Ortiz (*Letters* 393), and Carlos Baker surmised that he had "learned the story from Sidney Franklin," the bullfighter from Brooklyn whose career he had followed since the summer of 1929 (606). By the summer of 1931, they were fast friends, and in Hemingway's "Short Estimate" of him appended to *Death in the Afternoon* he wrote that he was "one of the best story tellers I have ever heard" (475).

If Franklin did tell him the story of Ortiz—and Franklin would have known it—a likely time would have been in mid-summer of 1931. In the last chapter of *Death in the Afternoon* he recalls a day with Franklin and "the unsuccessful matadors swimming with the cheap whores out on the Manzanares along the Pardo road; . . . playing ball on the grass where the fairy marquis came out in his car with the boxer; where we made paellas, and walked home in the dark" (271). An unpublished sketch titled "Portrait of Three or The Paella" describes that swimming party with Sidney, the bullfighters preparing a paella, and the appearance of a homosexual marquis and his lover (KL/EH 660). The late summer of 1931, then, seems the earliest date for the writing of "The Mother of a Queen."

The latest date would have been in late August of the following year when he listed the "Stories for a Book," including only those written by that date, "The Mother of a Queen" (fourth on the list) and "|Portrait of Three| The Paella" (KL/EH 221 A). To include the last two would have been a bit much, so Hemingway never completed the story of the bullfighters' picnic that could well have been the occasion on which he heard the tale of Ortiz from Sidney Franklin.

All through the fall of 1931 Hemingway was occupied with the last few chapters of his bullfighting book; but when he came to the recollection of the Manzanares picnic or the brief biography of Franklin, he might have sketched out the story—KL/EH 583 seems to be a fair copy of an earlier draft. During the winter and spring of 1932 he was at work on the galleys, and again he might have recalled Franklin's story and decided to write it down. Like "God Rest You Merry, Gentlemen," it might have been one of the three fine stories he referred to in early February, or one of the six "done for a book" in mid-April (*Letters* 353, 388; see Chap. 35 above). A probable date for the story's first typescript would be April 1932; that typescript (KL/EH 584) was taken from the fair copy manuscript and was used as the setting copy for *Winner Take Nothing* (KL/EH 222)—neither bears any startling revisions or emendations.

Publication History (October 1933)

When Hemingway referred to a set of stories as "done for a book," he meant that rubric to include those he knew could not gain entry to the more conservative magazines but, in the company of his more reserved stories, would be allowed into a collection. "The Mother of a Queen" was one of those, and it found its way in to *Winner Take Nothing* in October 1933.

Sources and Influences

Biographers and critics have claimed two sources for the story from its title. One, as noted, was Sidney Franklin; the other Grace Hall Hemingway or, at least, what is taken to be Hemingway's feelings towards her, particularly after his father's suicide in 1928. The virulence of Roger's monologue is exceeded only by that of two recent biographers. Jeffrey Meyers's contempt is directed at "Sidney Franklin (né Frumpkin)" as an overrated matador and political naif who, according to letters and interviews, was "a secret 'homosexual despite his rugged appearance and bravura' " (230–31, 598 n. 14). Add to this Hemingway's own estimate that Franklin's "business judgement . . . is terrible" (*Death* 476) and we have not only a source for the story but also for two aspects of Paco. Kenneth Lynn read the story as an updating of Hemingway's "quarrel with Grace . . . dealing symbolically with their current financial relationship; unfortunately . . . nothing but a revolting expression of a famous man's resentment at having to send a woman he hated a monthly allowance" (408).

Both these biographical notes may touch on subsidiary motives for the story, but they miss the formal intent it shares with other dramatic monologues, and not only Hemingway's "My Old Man," "Fifty Grand," and "After the Storm." This one in particular seems closely modeled on those of Robert Browning that Hemingway read aloud over a jug of wine to Ted Brumback until four in the morning back in 1918 (Baker 37). To consider it only, or even principally, Paco's story is tantamount to ignoring the Duke of Ferrara who speaks of "My Last Duchess" and failing to see this as Hemingway's

"Soliloquy in a Spanish Cloister," Browning's delightful portrait of jealousy and hatred.

Critical Studies

Most of the earlier critics cited the story as evidence of Hemingway's intolerance of "those whose sexual inclinations are aberrant" (Waldhorn 228, n. 6) or, more politely perhaps, his "savage concern with homosexuality" (Rovit 70). Sheldon Grebstein also noted "Hemingway's scorn for homosexuals," but his interest in the "unreliable I-witness" led him to consider the story "much more interesting and substantial than anyone had thought." Roger's litany of Paco's "breaches of conduct: miserliness, dishonesty, treachery to friends, incompetence, disregard of obligations to filial duty and family honor, total absence of pride as a man and as a Spaniard . . . arouse our suspicions about *his* reliability" (57). Moreover, "in almost every episode the narrator himself is the hero." So Grebstein asked some questions about Paco's sexuality that have rather easy answers; but he also wondered why Roger calls "the matador a bitch?—a strange epithet for a man to use, even to a homosexual. It seems more typically what one homosexual would call another" (58).

Gerry Brenner took Grebstein's tentative conclusion as an obvious fact: "Roger is not only an unreliable narrator but also a jealous and thus vindictive 'closet' homosexual. His peremptory dismissal of Paco's defensible values richly earns Hemingway's implied scorn," which, he later notes, is *not* scorn for his homosexuality (11-12, 239, n. 16).

Charles Stetler and Gerald Locklin attempted to answer Grebstein's questions by arguing that Roger is "possibly but not likely" a homosexual, but has "allowed himself to slip into the essentially feminine role of a mother"—the second mother of a queen (68). Here, a good deal rests on that verb "allowed" and the assumption that a man may not be both homosexual and motherly. They admitted Roger's calling Paco a "bitch" is troublesome, but they countered with a question about his calling him a "queen": "Would the pot call the kettle black?" (To which the answer is, yes, hence the phrase.) So even if, as they maintained, "it is unlikely that [Paco and Roger] are lovers," it does not follow that Roger is heterosexual (69). There is a way, then, to draw their evidence together with Grebstein's and Brenner's to discover the ambivalent referents in the title "The Mother of a Queen."

At least two questions remain about Paco's attitudes toward his mother and her death. Stetler and Locklin asked the first: Is Paco's patent lie that his mother died when he was young "a conscious or subconscious vengeance against the source of his homosexuality?" (69) Brenner, and certainly Lynn, would say it was. Then, again, even though by default he consigns her remains to the "common boneheap" in violation of his native traditions, he is hardly a conventional Spaniard, much less a bullfighter, and may truly believe that now "she will always be with me" (*Stories* 416).

Paco, like Sidney Franklin, was a phenomenon that must have piqued Hemingway's curiosity. He might have wondered over what we assume must be the conflicting roles a homosexual must play as a matador. What drew him first to bullfighting, that most masculine profession? Roger cannot understand why he "had only fought twice in Spain . . . , and he had seven new fighting suits made and . . . had them packed so badly that four of them were ruined by sea water on the trip back and he couldn't even wear them" (*Stories* 417). His insistent question—"What kind of blood is it that makes a man like that?"—is Hemingway's; and Roger's blind rage is Hemingway's dramatic demonstration of one way in which the question will never be answered.

Works Cited

PRIMARY

Death in the Afternoon. New York: Scribner's, 1932.

Ernest Hemingway: Selected Letters, 1917–1961. Ed. Carlos Baker. New York: Scribner's, 1981.

The Short Stories of Ernest Hemingway. New York: Scribner's, 1938, 415–19.

SECONDARY

Baker, Carlos. *Ernest Hemingway: A Life Story.* 1969. Scribner's, 1988.

Brenner, Gerry. *Concealments in Hemingway's Works.* Columbus: Ohio State UP, 1983.

Grebstein, Sheldon N. *Hemingway's Craft.* Carbondale: Southern Illinois UP, 1973.

Lynn, Kenneth S. *Hemingway.* New York: Simon, 1987.

Meyers, Jeffrey. *Hemingway: A Biography.* New York: Harper, 1985.

Rovit, Earl. *Ernest Hemingway.* Boston: Twayne, 1963.

Stetler, Charles, and Gerald Locklin. "Beneath the Tip of the Iceberg in Hemingway's 'The Mother of a Queen.'" *Hemingway Review* 2 (Fall 1982): 68–69.

Waldhorn, Arthur. *A Reader's Guide to Ernest Hemingway.* New York: Farrar, 1972.

39

A Way You'll Never Be

Composition History (May–November 1932)

In July 1955 Hemingway returned to Key West to arrange for the sale of the Whitehead Street house. A. E. Hotchner was with him when he went through his writing room in the "Pool House" and recalled "A Way You'll Never Be": "I had tried to write it in the Twenties, but had failed several times. I had given up on it but one day here, fifteen years after those things happened to me in a trench dugout outside Fornaci, it suddenly came out focused and complete. Here in Key West, of all places. Old as I am, I continue to be amazed at the sudden emergence of daffodils and stories" (Hotchner 162–63). Although one might doubt the remark on daffodils, Hemingway had told Charles Poore in January 1953, "I know I wrote A Way You'll Never Be [in Key West] and A Natural History of the Dead" (*Letters* 799). In another letter to Clifton Fadiman on 26 November 1933, just after the publication of *Winner Take Nothing,* he explained the story's "enigmatic title." Carlos Baker paraphrased that explanation: "[T]he heat of Havana had reminded him of the way it was on the lower Piave in the summer of 1918. At the same time, said he, he was watching a hell of a nice girl going crazy from day to day. He gave the story its title in order to cheer her up on the grounds that the 'citizen' in the story, Nick Adams, had been 'much nuttier' than this girl was ever going to be" (228, 608). From this letter and some of the details of Hemingway's affair with Jane Mason, Carlos Baker dates the completion of the story during Hemingway's "Cuban holiday" from late April to late June 1932, and Jeffrey Meyers and Kenneth Lynn have followed suit (Baker 228, Meyers 245, Lynn 405).

These three accounts of the story's occasion, coming a year-and-a-half to twenty-two years after the event, offer a nice array of contradictions. To both Hotchner and Poore Hemingway was certain he had written the story in Key West, there in the "Pool House"; but to Fadiman it was the heat in a Havana hotel in May or June that reminded him of Italy—on his return home he was in bed with pneumonia before leaving for Piggott on 2 July (Baker 229). The letter to Fadiman reveals the instincts of a squid: although it explains the title (and marks it as his worst), it implies that Nick Adams's condition is exaggerated to assist in Mrs. Mason's psychotherapy. But when she left Cuba for a New York hospital from 10 May to 11 June 1932, it was for minor surgery, and Hemingway knew it. It was not until a year later that she attempted suicide, was hospitalized for five months in New York, and began psychotherapy (Lynn 405–07). It was just as she was starting that therapy that Hemingway wrote to Clifton Fadiman in November 1933; and if Hemingway's recollection and arithmetic are to be trusted, his remark to Hotchner would have the story "focused and complete" earlier in that summer of 1933.

To date the completion of the story in the spring of 1932 on anything other than the suspect letter to Fadiman raises the question of Hemingway's conspicuous silence on the story until the following year. The "Stories for Book" list includes the eight from "Wine of Wyoming" to "The Light of the World," all completed by late summer 1932. Two other titles are crossed out: one is "Portrait of Three" or "The Paella" (see Chap. 38, "The Mother of a Queen"), the second is "Nothing Better to Suggest" and is marked "Provisional" (KL/EH 221 A). The latter title could have been intended for "A Way You'll Never Be"—it is certainly no worse. There are several moments in the story when Paravicini or Nick is reduced to some final and desperate suggestion for lack of anything better to say—Nick's closing exhortation in his "lecture" to the Italian soldiers, "Gentlemen, either you must govern—or you must be governed," is one of those moments for which the title is appropriate.

Hemingway returned to Key West in late October 1932; Pauline returned to Piggott within a week to attend the two younger children with whooping cough, and he was left with Bumby for a full month of "working like hell writing." By mid-November he could count "four stories ready to be typed [and] ten ready for a book"; and three weeks later he told Max Perkins that "Pauline had 3 of the last stories copied" before she left (*Letters* 376, 380). So he had at least ten and at most fourteen stories typed or about to be and ready for the book. One of those could well have been "A Way You'll Never Be"; the only complete version of the story is a typescript (not by Hemingway), but its title was added later in pencil (KL/EH 815).

Two other remarks in his letters of November and December 1932 may confirm his completion of the story then. In November he wrote Perkins that the "odd thing is that my head is in better shape than it has ever been and I am certain of doing better work than I have ever done. The one thing I will not do is repeat myself, . . . people always want a story like the last one" (*Letters* 377). And in December he asked Perkins to "spread this statement around": "Mr. H., who is a writer of fiction, states that if he was in Italy during a small part of the late war it was only because a man was less liable to be killed there than in France. He drove, or attempted to drive, an ambulance and engaged in minor camp following activities and was never involved in heroic actions of any sort" (*Letters* 379). With his head in good shape and determined not to repeat "In Another Country" or "Now I Lay

Me," that ironic disclaimer as a minor camp follower suggests he was preparing his editor and his audience for his new story of Nick Adams in the war.

The last discrepancy among the three accounts is the most interesting. Baker's summary of the Fadiman letter suggests the story was inspired by the heat of Havana and Jane Mason; but Hotchner's memoir recalls Hemingway saying he had "tried to write it back in the Twenties, but had failed several times." Both recollections are partly true and partly false: to Fadiman, Hemingway was recollecting only the *completion* of the story; and to Hotchner he told a little less than he knew, for there is a complete thirty-five-page, first-person manuscript version of the story, probably written in the late 1920s (KL/EH 746 A). Perhaps the most provocative of his unpublished manuscripts, it echoes and even repeats lines and images from "A Natural History of the Dead" and *A Farewell to Arms*. So when Hemingway wrote to Charles Poore in 1953 that "I *know* I wrote A Way You'll Never Be [in Key West] and A Natural History of the Dead," he might have been associating the writing of the story's first version with "A Natural History" as well as his revision of his novel in the winter and spring of 1929 when he was living there on South Street.

As in *A Farewell to Arms* and the earlier war fiction there are discussions here of drinking *grappa,* not the "Americanos" (Campari and soda) of the Milan cafés, and of D'Annunzio and his slogans; there is the image of the "dark sausage balloons" in the sunset, an image he cut from the novel (KL/EH 64–110; *Farewell* 46); and like Frederic Henry, Paravicini is an architect and at times affects a British dialect. The similarities with "A Natural History of the Dead" are more substantive. The opening section of this version (746 A) is similar in its concentration on the surprising amount of postcards and papers around the dead with an early fragment of "A Natural History" (KL/EH 33); in both this version and the early version of the argument between the doctor and the artillery lieutenant of "A Natural History," there is an officious officer and a sensible doctor; and finally the parodic style of the lecturer on natural history is in this version assigned to Paravicini who speaks in the "tone of a lecturer in a popular course at a university," the tone, of course, that Nick adopts in his lecture on locusts in the finished story.

What is most striking, however, about this early manuscript is that its general structure of seven scenes is almost exactly that of "A Way You'll Never Be," but the action within three of the most crucial scenes is so radically different that one might better think of them as two different stories, rather like the "Madrid" and "Notebook" versions of "Ten Indians" (see Chap. 29). The published story's seven sections follow this scheme:

1. Return to the battlefield and meeting the officer (*Stories* 402–05)
2. First conversation with Paravicini (405–07)

3. First "dream" (407–09)
4. Nick's "lecture" (409–12)
5. Second conversation with Paravicini (412–14)
6. Second "dream" (414)
7. Departure (414).

This pattern, slightly revised from E. R. Hagemann's analysis (25), is the familiar "embedded" scheme Hemingway discovered early in his career, with the seven sections related in this way: (A [B&C] D [B&C] A). Although the two versions share this pattern, they differ most radically in sections 3, 4, and 6 (the two "dreams," hallucinations or whatever, and the "lecture"). In the early manuscript those three sections are linked in the narrative. In 3, the "red-eyed" lieutenant brings in two soldiers he has caught in a homosexual act; in 4, Paravicini delivers a lecture on the difference between this "childishness" and true vice and the extenuating circumstances of the two soldiers' recent bravery in battle; and in 6, after another shelling, the lieutenant is revealed as having shot himself in the hand and is charged and sent away.

As Hemingway told Hotchner in 1955, he "failed several times" to complete the story, and there are several one- or two-page false starts that confirm that memory (KL/EH 813, 814). When the story finally did emerge, like a daffodil but not so suddenly, between the spring and fall of 1932, it came from what some would argue are rather dark roots. Whatever critics call that transformation between the manuscript and typescript—simple revision or complex sublimation—the two texts tease us into speculation. What did the "red-eyed" lieutenant's officious charge against the two brave but homosexual soldiers have to do with his own cowardice and self-mutilation, and why did Hemingway turn those two scenes into Nick Adams's hallucinations centering on his own wound in the head? And why did he replace Paravicini on the podium and his tolerant lecture on homosexuality with Nick and his ironic lecture, which mocks his own role but insists that one must govern oneself or be governed?

The simplest answer is that he remembered a better story, but somehow the parallel structures in the two versions insist on some buried analogies between those divergent scenes.

Publication History (October 1933)

If the story was completed sometime in the latter half of 1932, Hemingway had little time and probably less inclination to submit it for journal publication; and by the end of the year *Scribner's Magazine* was already planning to publish three other stories ("A Clean Well-Lighted Place," "Homage to Switzerland," and—under an earlier title—"The Gambler, The

Nun, and The Radio.") By early 1933 it was among those he counted in the fourteen he had done for the book, and it was published in October in *Winner Take Nothing* (*Letters* 384).

Sources and Influences

Although a literary allusion or two has been dug out of the story, no critic has suggested any informing literary influence on "A Way You'll Never Be." On the other hand, no one has neglected its relationship with the other war and postwar fictions ("Big Two-Hearted River," "In Another Country," and "Now I Lay Me"), *A Farewell to Arms,* and, finally, Colonel Cantwell's ritual burial of "merde, money" and his memories at Fossalta in *Across the River and into the Trees* (18–19).

The story stands at the end of a twenty-five-year period in which Hemingway recalled or imagined his wounding on 18 July 1918 at Fossalta di Piave and his return to that front three months later on 19 October. By the time he returned to Oak Park in January 1919, he had citations, a tailored uniform (with cape), souvenirs, a strong taste for wine, and an elaborate story of heroism for the home folks. And he elaborated its details in lectures and his "Chicago" stories, like "The Woppian Way," and "The Visiting Team." In the spring of 1922 he returned to Fossalta a second time, now with Hadley, and found the place so changed that he wrote a *Toronto Star* article advising veterans not to revisit their old fronts lest it make them "believe that the places and happenings that had been the really great events to you were only fever dreams or lies you had told to yourself" (*Dateline* 176). In the spring of 1924 that partial and implicit confession was dramatized in the mind of Krebs in "Soldier's Home" who pretended to have been "badly, sickeningly frightened all the time" (*Stories* 146).

In the two stories of the fall of 1926, Nick Adams is candid about his leg wound ("an accident"), afraid of dying, and sleepless ("In Another Country," *Stories* 270); that latter condition verges on a battlefield trauma in "Now I Lay Me," in which he has been wounded "a couple of times" (*Stories* 370). Frederic Henry also deprecates his behavior in battle—it is Gordini and Rinaldi who would make him a hero—and he is bored with Ettore, the "legitimate hero," and his medals (*Farewell* 63, 121). His head wound is not severe—lacerations and a possible skull fracture—but his dreams are frightening (59, 88).

Without these stories and the novel—perhaps only without "Now I Lay Me"—it would be difficult to make the connections that many have made between "A Way You'll Never Be" and "Big Two-Hearted River." Philip Young, of course, was the first to suggest that Nick's experiences on that river are to be explained by the traumatic head wound, imperfectly treated, and the hallucinations in this story. Kenneth Lynn, after a long controversy with Young and Malcolm Cowley, has argued that the connection is an invention of the critics that Hemingway tacitly approved until he himself came to believe it—Lynn reviews that argument in his recent biography (102–08).

The story of Hemingway's wounding was first rather credulously told by Carlos Baker (44–45), and in recent years has been questioned in part by Jeffrey Meyers (30–36) and more seriously by Kenneth Lynn (79–86). Lynn's account is convincing, and the discrepancy between what probably happened at Fossalta that night in July 1918 and the dramatic versions Hemingway and others invented over twenty-five years would explain that later sequence of stories in which he played down his heroism. But while those heroic accounts were being revised toward reality, the portrayals of Nick as a shell-shocked victim, who could only find courage in a bottle, were repeated and elaborated toward their final version in "A Way You'll Never Be," almost as if the trauma might pardon the lie.

Critical Studies

Since Philip Young's influential study in 1952, critical commentary on the story has often begun—and sometimes ended—with Nick's two hallucinations. Both occur, ironically, when Paravacini convinces him to lie down; the apparent effect is to increase pressure on his head wound, which, as his friend believes, should have been trepanned. His mind follows a logic of association: as he drifts off, the sight of the dugout recalls his driving frightened young recruits to attack when he, having no time to drink away his fear, is terrified. The attack is "up that slope," and that recalls Gaby Deslys, a Parisian feather dancer, to whose show Nick and his girl had often gone "up the hill" in Montmartre with its dome of Sacré Coeur "blown white, like a soap bubble." (For an intriguing account of the historical Gaby Deslys see Hagemann.) On those nights when his girl is with someone else, he dreams of the river that "ran so much wider and stiller than it should and outside of Fossalta there was a low house painted yellow with willows all around it and a low stable and there was a canal."

Philip Young argued that it is the "change in the width of the river" that terrifies Nick here, and in "Big Two-Hearted River" makes "the swamp horrible" (52). But this is a selective reading. To Nick the "house meant more than anything," because he "had been there a thousand times and never seen it" and even now "there was no house."

Joseph DeFalco's analysis is more precise, and his conclusions startling. For him, the importance of the recurrent image of the house and stable and canal lies in its psychological function, since when it recurs the second time it comes *in place of* the vision of "the man with the beard" who shot him and the experience of his wound. This traumatic event, given us in a curious aside by the narrator, is what "Nick has sublimated into the triadic image" of the yellow house (119). If this is an act of sublimation, as it seems to be, then DeFalco was justified in maintaining that the images of the still, wide river and the yellow house are "comforting and alluring manifestations of the death state conjured up by Nick's unconscious," especially when they include the boat among the willows and "the classical association with the river Styx" (118-19). DeFalco's point, then, is that Nick's journey of return to Fossalta is paralleled by a dream journey back to the image that lies behind the vision of the yellow house, and that once he can "make the association demanded by the dreams" he is, at the least, "equipped to leave this symbolic realm of death" (119).

DeFalco's analysis of Nick's two dreams is part of a larger conception of the story of an archetypal descent and return. Nick does wander through a land of the dead; and, as Joseph Yokelson pointed out later, the bearded and red-eyed lieutenant seems an analogue to Dante's Charon, "who has 'shaggy cheeks' and 'around whose eyes flames in a circle wheeled' " as he "tries to turn away the living Dante from the realm of the dead" (280). DeFalco's sense that Nick not only returns from the land of the dead but is returned to sanity rests in his reading of Nick's "emphatic rejection of the romantic in war" when he dismisses the question of where he saw the "cavalry regiment riding in the snow with their lances" and looks for his "damned bicycle" (120). (Hemingway himself rejected exactly that image when he revised the manuscripts of the passage on abstract words in *A Farewell to Arms* [184-85; KL/EH 64-355-56].)

For nearly twenty years after DeFalco's study, critics generally dismissed the story: Earl Rovit felt its "obvious hysteria . . . fails to create a meaningful tension" (80); Sheridan Baker thought "Hemingway was beginning to tire of his hero" (34); and Arthur Waldhorn agreed that "[h]ysteria is clearly the mode, but the modality . . . stains the narrative method" (64). Only Sheldon Grebstein connected the two elements of the journey motif, as DeFalco had done, by noting the "outside/inside" pattern into the dugout and into Nick's mind (18)—and he did add a nice phrase, "the rhetoric of hysteria," but failed to notice that that rhetoric is not hysterical (118).

Beginning with Joseph Flora's book in 1982 some interest in the story has been revived. His study is largely devoted to demonstrating the story's place in the Nick Adams canon—although that fit is not always neat. A detailed reading, it drew on DeFalco's interpretation of the image of the yellow house as a "dream prefigurement of his death" (132), and closely analysed Paravicini's role as a "something of a father figure, . . . aware of the limitations and injustices of life," but acting with honor and dignity in the face of them (128). But Flora, for once in his book, seemed at odds with the story: the chapter is replete with the details of allusion—Gaby's song recalls both Eliot's "The Waste Land" and dadaism ("tadada!"), and she is both the Gaby on board ship in "Night Before Landing" (*Nick Adams Stories* 137) and the famed Gaby Deslys, while the recollection of her as "the great Gaby" alludes to Fitzgerald's title as does the phrase "the far side of the taxis" (131-32). If these literary echoes and puns are relevant, as for example are the allusions to Dante, then one wonders why Flora did not pursue them to dissociate Nick as actor and Nick as writer.

The critical history of "A Way You'll Never Be," with next to nothing between 1963 and 1982 and little since then, is something of an embarrassment. When perceptive critics in that period dismissed the story as hysterical, they mistook a carefully ordered sequence of symbolic associations for incoherent rambling and then attributed that incoherence to one of Hemingway's most intricate and patterned narrative structures. There is, indeed, a hidden "rhetoric of hysteria" in the two dream scenes just as there is a kind of "rhetoric of sanity" in Nick's mocking military lecture on locusts. His audience, like some of Hemingway's, are so alarmed by his seeming incoherence that they miss the ironic analogy between the "medium-brown" locusts and the color of the uniform upon which he tells them to fix their eyes. Earlier he had fixed his eyes on the details of the dead; and if, however distraught, he can "govern" himself enough to utter the analogy that is so exact and prophetic of the slaughter to come, he has come some way toward realizing that the vision of the yellow house *is* a sublimation by which he had been governed and from which he must free himself.

"A Way You'll Never Be" deserves a place among Hemingway's major stories. One of his most original, even daring fictions, its challenge has yet to be met.

Works Cited

PRIMARY

Across the River and into the Trees. New York: Scribner's, 1950.

Dateline: Toronto. Ed. William White. New York: Scribner's, 1985.

Ernest Hemingway: Selected Letters, 1917-1961. Ed. Carlos Baker. New York: Scribner's, 1981.

A Farewell to Arms. New York: Scribner's, 1929.

The Nick Adams Stories. New York: Scribner's, 1972.

The Short Stories of Ernest Hemingway. New York: Scribner's, 1938, 402-14.

SECONDARY

Baker, Carlos. *Ernest Hemingway: A Life Story.* 1969. New York: Scribner's, 1988.

Baker, Sheridan. *Ernest Hemingway.* New York: Holt, 1967.

DeFalco, Joseph. *The Hero in Hemingway's Short Stories* Pittsburgh: U of Pittsburgh P, 1963.

Flora, Joseph M. *Hemingway's Nick Adams.* Baton Rouge: Louisiana State UP, 1982.

Grebstein, Sheldon N. *Hemingway's Craft.* Carbondale: Southern Illinois UP, 1973.

Hagemann, E. R. "The Feather Dancer in 'A Way You'll Never Be.' " *Hemingway Notes* 6 (Spring 1981): 25–27.

Hotchner, A. E. *Papa Hemingway.* New York: Random, 1966.

Lynn, Kenneth S. *Hemingway.* New York: Simon, 1987.

Meyers, Jeffrey. *Hemingway: A Biography.* New York: Harper, 1985.

Rovit, Earl. *Ernest Hemingway,* New York: Twayne, 1963.

Waldhorn, Arthur. *A Reader's Guide to Ernest Hemingway.* New York: Farrar, 1972.

Yokelson, Joseph B. "A Dante-Parallel in Hemingway's 'A Way You'll Never Be.' " *American Literature* 41 (May 1969): 279–80.

Young, Philip. *Ernest Hemingway: A Reconsideration.* 1952. New York: Harcourt, 1966.

40

A Clean, Well-Lighted Place

Composition History (Fall 1932)

The manuscript of "A Clean, Well-Lighted Place"—or at least its fourth page—is by far the most celebrated of any Hemingway ever wrote. That single page, reproduced in two articles, has generated more criticism of the story, raised more theoretical questions on issues of textual evidence, authorial intention, and even editorial ethics than all the commentary on any four of the other stories in *Winner Take Nothing*.

Some part of the controversy over the significance of the manuscript evidence might be resolved if there were any extant typescript version between the twelve-page pencil manuscript (KL/EH 337) and the unrevised tear sheets from the *Scribner's Magazine* version (KL/EH 222), which was used as setting copy for publication later in 1933, although one may infer that the differences between the manuscript and the tear sheets were incorporated in that lost typescript.

In 1977 Hans-Joachim Kann was the first to turn to the manuscript to resolve some of the confusion about the waiters' dialogue; he reproduced the crucial page and reviewed the major revisions in the manuscript. Two years later, Warren Bennett studied the revisions in precise detail to discover its composition history. He concluded that the story was "by all appearances, written at one sitting," with pencil revisions and insertions "evidently made at three different stages": two during the composition of the story and one "much later, perhaps another day" ("Manuscript and Dialogue" 616).

Bennett's elaboration of Kann's brief note isolated three crucial passages of dialogue revised in the manuscript:

The first occurs when the younger waiter rejoins "|the other waiter|/ his colleague/again."

> "He's drunk now, he said."
> "He's |stewed|/drunk/every night." (See *Stories* 380.)

Hemingway drew a run-on line between the end of the paragraph and the first remark, marking it as the younger waiter's line, a revision that has not been incorporated to this day.

The second, and most controversial, passage occurs near the end of that dialogue, with the following sequence of revisions in the younger waiter's remark and the older waiter's response. First, two alternating lines of dialogue are spoken by the young waiter:

"His niece looks after him." |They treat|
"I wouldn't want to be that old. . . ."

Then Hemingway separated the two lines with the older waiter's response:

"His niece looks after him." |They treat|
/"I know."/
"I wouldn't want to be that old. . . ."

Finally, Hemingway added a line slightly above "I know" (here in boldface):

"His niece looks after him. |They treat|
        /You said she cut him down."/
"I know."
"I wouldn't want to be that old. . . ." (See *Stories* 381.)

From the *Scribner's Magazine* version until the 1965 edition of the stories, the last insert was reprinted as part of the older waiter's line, "I know," indicating that it was the younger waiter who knew the details of the old man's attempted suicide (Bennett, "Manuscript and Dialogue" 619-22).

The third passage again involves confusion over who speaks the two lines of dialogue after a soldier and his girl pass by:

"The guard will pick him up," one waiter said.
"What does it matter if he gets |his tail|/what he's after/?"

The revision of this indelicacy, Bennett argued, is consonant with two other revisions of the older waiter's dialogue, and he therefore assigns the line to him ("Manuscript and Dialogue" 622-23).

Although the significance of these revisions has been argued, sometimes in raised voices, the evidence that the manuscript was written at one sitting and revised soon after lends some support to dating it in the fall of 1932. Carlos Baker noted that it was one of the three stories Hemingway submitted in December 1932 to *Scribner's Magazine* and one of "the last stories copied when [Pauline] had to go to St. Louis" late in the previous October (*Letters* 380). (A typescript of the story recently acquired by the University of Delaware does not settle the issue of the confusing dialogue, except to exonerate *Scribner's Magazine*'s typesetters, for if this or a carbon was their setting copy, they did their work with accuracy. It might have been typed by Pauline from Hemingway's manuscript, or from a Hemingway typescript by someone else; in either case, the ambiguity in the manuscript is repeated in this Delaware typescript. See Smith.)

Publication History (March 1933; October 1933)

Scribner's Magazine published the story in March 1933 and set in print the seeming confusion in the dialogue that was to last for twenty-two years, for the unrevised tear sheets of that version were used as setting copy for *Winner Take Nothing* in October.

By 1964 several critics had expressed their perplexity over the dialogue, and John V. Hagopian stated that the "obvious typographical error" should be corrected by moving the line "You said she cut him down" one line up to the younger waiter's comment. In the 1965 edition of the *The Short Stories* Scribner's followed that advice and subsequent editions continue that editorial change.

One ironic footnote to this controversy was published in 1974 when George Monteiro discovered that "Hemingway himself was once asked to comment on the confusion arising from the 'messy' dialogue." Judson Jerome had brought the issue to his attention in 1956, and Hemingway scrawled a brief reply to the effect that "the story as originally published continued to make perfect sense to him" (Monteiro 243).

Sources and Influences

The mere mention of "A Clean, Well-Lighted Place" among scholars evokes allusions to modern philosophical and religious thought, and at least a footnote to existentialism seems obligatory in scholarly articles on its meaning. They all draw upon or conclude with the story's famous *"nada* prayer." Steven Hoffmann, for example, took the clean, well-lighted place as the dark haven of "the existential hero, both in the Kierkegaardian and Heideggerian senses of the term. In the former, he is content to live with his *angst,* and because there is no other choice, content to be in doubt about ultimate causes. . . . In the latter, he can face the unpleasant realities of his own being . . . and can accept with composure the reality of his own death" (95).

The issue the *nada* prayer raises in most critics' minds rests in the degree to which it suggests a nihilistic blasphemy or, as Daniel Barnes argued, "attributes of a *positive* force which affects those who live in fear of" *nada*. Although critics from Robert Penn Warren in 1947 on through Carlos Baker in 1952 and others later far outnumber those seeking a little more positive light in the prayer, Barnes suggested that the parody of the "Our Father" and "Hail Mary" prayers is initiated by the older waiter's contemplation of light, reminiscent of "the light shines in the darkness; and the darkness grasped it not" in John 1:5; and, moreover, that it has a "rhythmic correspondence" with the opening of that gospel: "In the beginning was the Word" (Barnes 17). And Ely Stock offered a later source that would make the prayer an affirmation of a mystical experience. He discovered a quotation in William James's *The Varieties of Religious Experience* from the American theosophist H. P. Blavatsky: "He who would hear the voice of Nada, the 'Sound-less Sound,' and comprehend it, [will] become the Light, . . . become the Sound, . . . that resounds throughout eternities," and so on in a transcendental vein (Stock 54).

No one yet, however, has traced the story to any persuasive literary source. Philip Young, without much conviction, mentioned Stephen Crane's "An Episode of War" (195–96); and Earl Rovit found some similarity with T. S. Eliot's "The Hollow Men" (111–12)—a somewhat more convincing notion, for Hemingway found the poem important enough to consider quoting it in the manuscript of *A Farewell to Arms.*

In their two studies Earl Rovit and Steven Hoffman drew intricate lines of relationship between this story and nearly twenty of Hemingway's other fictions. For Rovit the story reads like "a metaphor of the code" (114), and so is central to his outline of that concept. The older waiter shares qualities with Mr. Frazer in "The Gambler," the major in "In Another Country," Santiago in *The Old Man and the Sea,* and others; its setting serves metaphorically as do those in "The Killers," "The Battler," "Fifty Grand," "The Undefeated," and "Big Two-Hearted River" (115–16). Hoffman's longer list is meant to isolate a central unity in the short stories: the threat of nothingness is often close, as in "Now I Lay Me" and "A Way You'll Never Be"; naifs, like the younger waiter, ignore it or explain it away as in "Indian Camp" and "The Killers"; and "the central crisis" of the story achieves its "resolution" in "The Short Happy Life" and "The Snows of Kilimanjaro" (91 ff.) If all this is so, then there is warrant for Arthur Waldhorn's remark that the story is Hemingway's "somber paradigm of the world" (28).

Critical Studies

The critical controversy over the confusion, ambiguity, inconsistency— various critics use a variety of terms—in the dialogue of "A Clean, Well-Lighted Place" has lasted as long as any other issue in Hemingway scholarship: it began in 1959 and is still, in some part, unresolved. Something of its endurance, fortunately, derives from the fact that it has confronted critics with fundamental issues of literary evidence and interpretation.

The question was raised in independent articles by F. P. Kroeger and William Colburn in 1959: both felt that the line indicating the younger waiter knew first of the old man's suicide and the apparent assignment of two indented speeches to the same character ("antimetronomic" dialogue, it was later called) were the result of someone's carelessness, but ultimately Hemingway's responsibility when he read proof or even reread the published story (Kroeger 241). To counter that argument was to assume that the "mistakes" were deliberate, which Otto Reinert did with the claim that the antimetronomic dialogue was meant to imply a "reflective pause" between one speaker's two lines (417–18).

For the next twenty years the two sides in the debate were evenly divided, and each was at some loss without the evidence of the manuscripts. But in one way, at least, that loss was a gain: for each side was obliged to place the text under microscopic analysis and to invoke some rather general principles of interpretation.

Following Reinert, Joseph Gabriel (1961) admitted the inconsistency in the dialogue but argued that it was deliberate. In the first two conversations the lines were "attributable to either waiter and to both," and that ambiguity was part of Hemingway's original "experiment in multiple meaning" through the "semantic possibilities inherent in the words *nada* and *nothing* . . . in the manner of Henry James." The "logical inconsistency" in the third and crucial dialogue was a "necessary means toward a higher consistency" between the story and the world it reflects (542–44).

From the other side, John Hagopian (1964) cited three principles to deny the argument of deliberate intent: it was neither "the simplest solution," nor was it supported by either Hemingway's practice in his other fiction or the story's context (141). With a reading of the dialogue from his colleague Martin Dolch that does not depend on the "absurd aesthetics of Tristan Tzara," he suggested that it was "far kinder to Hemingway to label a single line of dialogue as the obvious typographical error that it is than it is to torture his prose into ambiguous chaos" (142, 144). In 1965 Charles Scribner, Jr., and his editor made that change with Carlos Baker's advice and Mary Hemingway's permission—and the predictable hue and cry called for Hagopian's head.

Some critics came to his defense. Warren Bennett (1970) discovered a four-part pattern in the dialogue that moves through 1) a serious question, 2) a verbal irony, 3) a turn to another subject, to 4) a final serious reply; and that pattern consistently identifies the older waiter with the ironic response and the knowledge of the suicide ("Character, Irony" 263 ff.). The following year, Nathaniel Ewell risked reducing the debate to the absurd by suggesting *two* slugs of type had been not misplaced but omitted (306).

The decade of the seventies began with two more interpretive articles and ended with another two. In 1971, Charles May took Hagopian to task for his three critical principles. Although objecting to his criterion that the simplest explanation is the best on the now manifestly inaccurate assumption that Hemingway invariably read his manuscripts and proofs with "consummate care" (327), Hagopian's principle does confuse a simpler editorial solution with a simpler interpretation. May also challenged the notion that Hemingway rarely used antimetronomic dialogue. (That issue was to be settled later in Scott MacDonald's article [1973] and David Kerner's two articles [1979, 1985], with a veritable anthology of examples from Hemingway's "The Three-Day Blow" to *Across the River* and others from Turgenev to Forster.) Turning to the evidence of the context, May argued that the "functional violation" of the dialogue convention allows for a "simpler, yet more pertinent reading of the story." If it is the younger waiter who tells the older waiter of the suicide, then "forced to confront his affinity with the old man's despair, he arrives at his nada prayer at the end as a *result* of the story." Whether this is in fact a simpler reading, it derives from a theoretical distinction "between seeing the story as a static or a dynamic action" and a value judgment for the latter; and, closer to the text, it assumes that the older waiter needs to be told by his colleague in order to confront the act of suicide and the sense of nothingness (328).

In the same year David Lodge considered the textual revision suggested by Hagopian and reviewed the critical debate. For him the revision was the right solution, and he singled out Joseph Gabriel's objections for critical analysis. Lodge made the perceptive distinction between the ambiguities in the first two dialogues and the logical inconsistencies in the third:

> The *ambiguities* which Gabriel rightly observes in the text, are all, in the end, capable of resolution or, if left open, do not affect the authority of the story. This cannot be said of the *inconsistency* [at ll. 4–5, Stories 381]. . . . A logical inconsistency of this kind, if deliberate, can only have the effect in narrative of radically undermining the authority of either the narrator or the characters or both. . . . That the facts about the old man are "true," and that the older waiter is a reliable character, are essential preconditions if the latter's interior monologue is to be at all moving or persuasive. The story works by packing meanings under its realistic surface, not by undermining that surface so that it collapses. (191–92)

Like others, Lodge is beguiled by the notion of Hemingway's care with his manuscripts, but he finds it "odd" that he would have missed the inconsistent third conversation as long as his readers did. Beyond its scrupulous concern for interpretive implications and its judicious examination of competing analyses, this essay is notable for the evenhanded distinction between the early ambiguities that enhance the story and the later inconsistencies that do not and so deserve, as does Hemingway, a sensible revision.

Before the end of the decade, Scott MacDonald had challenged Hagopian and called for other scholars to petition Charles Scribner, Jr., to restore the lines to their original confusion. Warren Bennett (1973), too, had second thoughts and felt that the editorial change only complicated matters. In 1976 C. Harold Hurley offered a reading of the second dialogue based on a question-answer pattern in the story that assigns the first speech to the older waiter. (When he returned to the passage with the evidence of the manuscripts in 1982, he supported his argument with the evidence of the deleted diction more appropriate to the younger waiter.)

When the evidence of the manuscript was revealed in 1977, it raised again the crucial issue of the inconsistency in the third dialogue and, ultimately, the question whether Hemingway's revisions of that passage initiated an unintentional or deliberate confusion of the two waiters' roles. Although Warren Bennett's detailed description of the revisions of the lines on the manuscript's fourth page and its sequence of penciled insertions went unchallenged, David Kerner objected strongly to his speculative reconstruction of Hemingway's intention—and momentary misconceptions—when he made those insertions. The language each critic used to describe this moment of composition is revealing: Bennett suggested that Hemingway "probably forgot" and "probably thought," and mentioned a "first confusion," a *"lapsus memoriae,"* and the story's "bad luck" ("Manuscript and Dialogue" 620, 622); Kerner stated that Hemingway "could not have thought" and "was perfectly aware," and if he "made the alleged error, we can be sure he would have caught it" ("The Foundation" 288). The issue between these two seems to rest on the one insertion, "You said she cut him down." Bennett suggested that Hemingway "added [this] second revision," perhaps "to replace 'They treat [him well enough],'" and then considered more likely motives (620). Kerner stated that Hemingway "added 'You said she cut him down' *to the earlier insertion,* 'I know'" (287).

In 1983, with the critical argument as confused as the story's dialogue, George H. Thomson surveyed what seemed a minor discipline of literary scholarship, sorted out the essential questions, and offered a variety of answers. He first established the nature of the textual problem and summarized three explanations: the text is confused and should be emended; the text violates normal dialogue conventions; and the text is correct but incorrectly interpreted (32–38). His final section assumes that the text is not corrupt, that the dialogue may violate convention, and, more interesting, that a new reading of the text as it was first printed could "justify the interpretation that it is the older waiter who is aware of the old man's history" (39). His gloss of the crucial line has the younger waiter presumptuously stating that the old man's "'niece looks after him'—something he cannot know" and the older waiter chastising him with " 'I know [which is more than you do]. *You said* she cut him down [but you don't know at all what happened]' " (38). Thomson's conclusion admits that either his or the alternative interpretation "requires some ingenuity of reading," but his preference is founded on his sense of the older waiter's character and of his line "as an ironic jibe at his presumptuous colleague" (42).

This attempt to moderate the debate, however, did not impress David Kerner. In the following year he challenged Thomson's assumptions about the waiters' characters and argued that he had missed what Kerner had claimed in 1979 was evident in the two lines of dialogue on the manuscript's fourth page.

It now seems as if the critics have set their camps, each on one of the two original lines of dialogue, martialed their critical compatriots, and are struggling to win over to their side the contested sentence lying in the little field between them.

There were others, however, whose purview was so panoramic that the inconsistency in two lines of dialogue must have seemed, if they noticed it at all, insignificant. Their criticism followed Robert Penn Warren's essay of 1947 in which he claimed that, in the phase reflected in this story, Hemingway was a "religious writer," writing of "the despair felt by a man who hungers for the certainties and meaningfulness of a religious faith but who cannot find in his world a ground for that faith" (83–84). Nearly all of the later commentaries, some with allusions ranging from the Paternoster to Jean-Paul Sartre, divide along the two lines of Penn Warren's phrases: some read the story largely for the moral landscape of a world with no ground for faith, *nada,* to which the only possible response is despair. Others—and there are more of them—are more concerned with whatever meager fare there may be for those who hunger for certainties.

The first of these two critical views found support in some of the early comments on the story—from Ray B. West, Joseph DeFalco, and Sheridan Baker—which located the subject in nothingness and "the pessimism and despair of the human response to it" (Benert 186; see also Hoffman). William Bache assumed that both the old waiter and old man express a "nihilistic . . . way of life," and the clean, well-lighted place is a "symbolic substitute for the spiritual life," at best a "known and tangible and dignified nothingness" (62). Sam Bluefarb portrayed that place as an "Absolute—a perfect but negative, vacuum" in which all the characters are caught in the "private purgatories" of Martin Buber's "I-It" relationship, except for the old waiter who manages only a "slight sign" of achieving the "I-Thou" in his compassion for the old man (5, 9). Those critics, like Daniel Barnes, who attempted to read the "nada-prayer" as critical only of "orthodox Christianity" and "carrying on in the true Christian tradition" (22–23), were contradicted by Jackson Benson's argument that "Christianity, in Hemingway's design, must be considered to be aligned with sentimentality," for its "ego-centered" and "anthropomorphic" assumptions. "There is no help for man except in the 'clean, well-lighted places' that he carves out of the darkness for himself" (116).

This is not to say that those with a darker vision of the story did not see some hopeful, if only faint, light; but others stated or implied that more affirmative view with more conviction. Carlos Baker began this trend with his sense of the paradoxical transformation of the younger waiter's "mere *nothing* into the old waiter's Something—a Something called Nothing which is so huge, terrible, overbearing, inevitable and omnipresent that, once experienced, it can never be forgotten" (*Writer as Artist* 124). Never forgotten, but not beyond challenge. John Killinger held that the "only entity truly capable of defying the encroachments of Nothingness is the individual" (14); and Cleanth Brooks defined that defiance: the clean, well-lighted place does "*not* reflect an inherent, though concealed, order in the universe. What little meaning there is in the world is imposed upon that world by man" (6). Earl Rovit noted that Hemingway's resolution of this metaphysical crisis is, unlike Eliot's, "not a presage . . . of theological existence," but remains a "structure that man imposes on the chaos to wrest order and a temporal regularity out of the meaningless flux of sensations" (115).

Two articles, Annette Benert's and Steven Hoffman's, concluded the affirmative argument on this issue. Both took careful notice of earlier criticism, and both kept a keen eye on the text. Benert began with the story's central paradox, that the older waiter's affirmation of the clean, well-lighted, and quiet place are *negations,* functioning as the absence of the dirt, darkness, and sound of *nada,* and yet "all three are posited as barriers against the ultimate negation, against Nothingness itself" (183). Her sense of the older waiter as smart enough to have "gone one step beyond Beckett's tramps" and ironic enough to call his condition insomnia, an "act of humility eliminating the last possibility of error," led her to conclude that he "actively demonstrates that life against *nada* is achieved by awareness, sensitivity, human solidarity, ritual, . . . humor, and courage. Together these qualities make dignity, or to use Jamesian terms, style or form." For her, "A Clean, Well-Lighted Place" is "without cheating, a totally affirmative story." The older waiter is "neither a hero nor a saint, but, to borrow from Camus, that more ambitious being, a man" (184–85, 187).

Steven Hoffman advanced Benert's argument in several directions: back to the Nick Adams and forward to the late African stories, and out to contemporary existentialist philosophy. Although some may question his notion that the older waiter's crisis is resolved by Macomber in his short, happy life or Harry in his vision of Kilimanjaro, he persuades us that the older waiter "willingly embraces the impact of universal nothingness on his own person" when he responds to the barman's question, "What's yours?" and answers, "Nada." At that instant he is "the 'winner' who truly takes 'nothing' as his only possible reward" and in so doing reaches the "highest level of heroism in Hemingway's fictional world" (101).

With this long and sometimes bitter controversy over the story's true text, its author's intention, and its range of meaning, a final note may seem unnecessary, perhaps unmerciful. But when Cleanth Brooks wrote that any meaning "there is in the world is imposed on that world by man," and Wayne Booth added that the struggle between darkness and light may be fought finally only in "the clean, well-lighted place of art itself" (299), they made explicit the buried questions in both the criticism that arose from the confusion over the story's dialogue and the continuing discussions of the story's meaning in whatever philosophical context: Who tells this story; and what is, after all, the clean well-lighted place of his art?

Works Cited

PRIMARY

Ernest Hemingway: Selected Letters, 1917–1961. Ed. Carlos Baker. New York: Scribner's, 1981.

The Short Stories of Ernest Hemingway. New York: Scribner's, 1938, 379–83.

SECONDARY

Bache, William B. "Craftsmanship in 'A Clean, Well-Lighted Place.'" *Personalist* 37 (Winter 1956): 60–64.

Baker, Carlos. *Hemingway: The Writer as Artist.* 1952. Princeton: Princeton UP, 1972.

Baker, Sheridan. *Ernest Hemingway.* New York: Holt, 1967.

Barnes, Daniel R. "Ritual and Parody in 'A Clean, Well-Lighted Place.'" *Cithara: Essays in the Judaeo-Christian Tradition* 5 (May 1966): 15–25.

Benert, Annette. "Survival through Irony: Hemingway's 'A Clean, Well-Lighted Place.'" *Studies in Short Fiction* 11 (1974): 181–87.

Bennett, Warren. "Character, Irony, and Resolution in 'A Clean, Well-Lighted Place.'" *American Literature* 42 (Mar. 1970): 70–79; rpt. in *The Short Stories of Ernest Hemingway: Critical Essays.* Ed. Jackson J. Benson. Durham: Duke UP, 1975, 261–69.

―――. "The Manuscript and the Dialogue of 'A Clean, Well-Lighted Place.'" *American Literature* 50 (1979): 613–24.

―――. "The New Text of 'A Clean, Well-Lighted Place.'" *Literary Half-Yearly* 14 (1973): 115–25.

Benson, Jackson J. *Hemingway: The Writer's Art as Self-Defense.* Minneapolis: U of Minnesota P, 1969.

Bluefarb, Sam. "The Search for the Absolute in Hemingway's 'A Clean, Well-Lighted Place,' and 'The Snows of Kilimanjaro.'" *Bulletin of the Rocky Mountain MLA* 25 (1971): 3–9.

Booth, Wayne. C. *The Rhetoric of Fiction*. Chicago: U of Chicago P, 1961.

Brooks, Cleanth. *The Hidden God*. New Haven: Yale UP, 1963.

Colburn, William E. "Confusion in 'A Clean Well-Lighted Place.'" *College English* 20 (Feb. 1959): 241–42.

DeFalco, Joseph. *The Hero in Hemingway's Short Stories*. Pittsburgh: U of Pittsburgh P, 1963.

Ewell, Nathaniel M., III. "Dialogue in Hemingway's 'A Clean, Well-Lighted Place.'" *Fitzgerald/Hemingway Annual* (1971): 305–06.

Gabriel, Joseph F. "The Logic of Confusion in Hemingway's 'A Clean, Well-Lighted Place.'" *College English* 22 (May 1961): 539–46.

Hagopian, John V. "Tidying Up Hemingway's 'A Clean, Well-Lighted Place.'" *Studies in Short Fiction* 1 (1964): 140–46.

Hoffman, Steven K. "*Nada* and 'A Clean, Well-Lighted Place.'" *Essays in Literature* 6 (1979): 91–110.

Hurley, C. Harold. "The Attribution of the Waiters' Second Speech in Hemingway's 'A Clean, Well-Lighted Place.'" *Studies in Short Fiction* 13 (1976): 81–85.

―――. "The Manuscript and the Dialogue of 'A Clean, Well-Lighted Place': A Response to Warren Bennett." *Hemingway Review* 2 (Fall 1982): 17–20.

Kann, Hans-Joachim. "Perpetual Confusion in 'A Clean, Well-Lighted Place': The Manuscript Evidence." *Fitzgerald/Hemingway Annual* (1977): 115–18.

Kerner, David. "Counterfeit Hemingway: A Small Scandal in Quotation Marks." *Journal of Modern Literature* 12 (Nov. 1985): 91–108.

―――. "The Foundation of the True Text of 'A Clean, Well-Lighted Place.'" *Fitzgerald/Hemingway Annual* (1979): 279–300.

―――. "The Thomson Alternative." *Hemingway Review* 4 (Fall 1984): 37–39.

Killinger, John. *Hemingway and the Dead Gods: A Study in Existentialism*. Lexington: U of Kentucky P, 1960.

Kroeger, F. P. "The Dialogue in 'A Clean, Well-Lighted Place.'" *College English* 20 (Feb. 1959): 240–41.

Lodge, David. *The Novelist at the Crossroads and Other Essays on Fiction and Criticism*. Ithaca: Cornell UP, 1971.

MacDonald, Scott. "The Confusing Dialogue in 'A Clean, Well-Lighted Place': A Final Word?" *Studies in American Fiction* 1 (Spring 1973): 93–101.

May, Charles E. "Is Hemingway's 'Well-Lighted Place' Really Clean Now?" *Studies in Short Fiction* 8 (Spring 1971): 326–30.

Monteiro, George. "Hemingway on Dialogue in 'A Clean, Well-Lighted Place.' " *Fitzgerald/Hemingway Annual* (1974): 243.

Reinert, Otto. "Hemingway's Waiters Once More." *College English* 20 (May 1959): 417–18.

Rovit, Earl. *Ernest Hemingway*. Boston: Twayne, 1963.

Smith, Paul. "A Note on a New Manuscript of 'A Clean, Well-Lighted Place.' " *Hemingway Review,* forthcoming, 1989.

Stock, Ely. "*Nada* in Hemingway's 'A Clean, Well-Lighted Place.' " *Midcontinent American Studies Journal* 3 (Spring 1962): 53–57.

Thomson, George H. " 'A Clean Well-Lighted Place': Interpreting the Original Text." *Hemingway Review* 2 (Spring 1983): 32–43.

Waldhorn, Arthur. *A Reader's Guide to Ernest Hemingway*. New York: Farrar, 1972.

Warren, Robert Penn. "Ernest Hemingway." *Kenyon Review* 9 (Winter 1947): 1–28; rpt. in *Ernest Hemingway: Five Decades of Criticism*. Ed. Linda Welshimer Wagner. East Lansing: Michigan State UP, 1974, 75–102.

West, Ray B. Jr. *The Short Story in America: 1900–1950*. Chicago: Gateway, 1952.

Young, Philip. *Ernest Hemingway: A Reconsideration*. 1952. New York: Harcourt, 1966.

41

The Gambler, the Nun, and the Radio

Composition History (Summer 1931–Fall 1932)

Although Hemingway's automobile accident on 1 November 1930 introduced him to the characters of "The Gambler, the Nun, and the Radio," in an ironic stroke he must have contemplated, it broke his writing arm so badly he could not write for six months. In a letter to Ivan Kashkin in August 1935, he recalled writing it after he regained the use of his arm and during a period when "one is discouraged," before *Death in the Afternoon* and the "other stories" in *Winner Take Nothing* (*Letters* 418). However improbable that sequence, he was accustomed in the early 1930s to sketching stories he had heard or lived through soon after they occurred. So the first version (KL/EH 417, 420) might have been written in the summer of 1931.

But *Death in the Afternoon*, interrupted by the accident and long recovery, was first on his agenda; and it is more likely that "The Gambler" had to wait a year, for it does not appear on his list of stories in August of 1932. At about that time, however, the story might have been called to mind. Letters from Paul Romaine in July and August questioned his political stance, and this "presumptuous poppycock" led him to claim that he did not follow "the fashions in politics, letters, and religion," to imply that he was familiar with revolutions, and that others could not understand "the heat of rage, hatred, indignation, and disillusion that formed or forged what they call indifference" (*Letters* 363, 365). In October he told John Dos Passos, "I suppose I am an anarchist"—perhaps the best position for someone who on the same day could write that the "country is all busted," two hundred thousand homeless "are on the road like the wild kids of Russia," and in the next sentence say that with the extraordinary sales of his novel he would spend next summer in Europe "along with the other tourists" (*Letters* 372, 375). During his stay in the hospital in 1930, he had a private room; and after talking with the impoverished Chicanos in the wards, he would dictate letters to Pauline with the news that "63 banks a day failed in Arkansas" and he had sold the movie rights to *A Farewell to Arms* for "80,000 dollars" (*Letters* 333).

When Hemingway began the first version of the story (KL/EH 417), he rejected its working title "Three Ambitions," and chose a first-person narration. Whether or not that point of view served his memory, the story came easily until the ending, but then the manuscripts show *four* tentative conclusions.

The first seventeen pages of the nineteen-page Hemingway typescript bring the story to the moment when the narrator and Cayetano wish each other luck in the passing of their pain (*Stories* 484); the narrator remarks that he does not know whether Sister Cecilia or Cayetano realized their ambitions, but he at least has "left the hospital and the radio," implying, that is, the third ambition of his tentative title. He concludes, "I have never returned to Billings, Denver, Salt Lake City, Los Angeles, or Minneapolis. Sometime I would like to go to Portland, Oregon" (Seattle in the published version)—the first tentative ending for the story.

Then he continued the narrative in pencil through the next long paragraph, describing the other broken patients in the ward (*Stories* 484–85), and paused again after deleting this passage (similar to the related fragment, KL/EH 230): "All are damned twice, some more, but it is not so simple because many never realize it, others will not admit it, others forget it, many listen to the radio, and some do not care. It is more than a question of health or environment or training or heredity or the state of the liver. It is perhaps a question of maintaining an interest. Assuredly, it is not entirely to be explained by economics." A second and more cryptic ending—All are damned twice?—but one in which his act of listening to the radio gathers the significance that will suggest his final title.

A related manuscript, still in the first person, takes up the story again and brings it to the third tentative ending with his remark "Play the Cucaracha another time. It is better than the radio" (KL/EH 421; *Stories* 486). (See below for Paul Rodgers's explanation of the song's ironic significance.)

If Hemingway did begin "The Gambler" in 1931, it is possible that, with everything else he had to write, this recalcitrant story's refusal to end could have kept him occupied until the late summer of 1932. In any case, he then had it typed, gave it its final title, and changed to the third-person narration, Mr. Frazer's (KL/EH 418, 419). This typescript incorporates the third ending of KL/EH 421.

The last tentative ending came later with the *Scribner's Magazine* version, "Give Us a Prescription, Doctor," which concludes three lines later with Mr. Frazer's rejection of revolution (*Stories* 486–87 [". . . opiums are for before and after."]) The typescript for that version is titled, signed, noted for serial rights, and addressed at Key West (KL/EH 420). It, too, must have been one of the "four stories ready to be typed . . . [or] ten ready for a book" he mentioned to Perkins on 15 November in the midst of that month of "working like hell writing" (*Letters* 376).

The fifth and final ending came in the following summer when he added it to the tear sheets from the *Scribner's Magazine* version used as setting copy for *Winner Take Nothing*.

Publication History (May 1933; October 1933)

"The Gambler, the Nun, and the Radio" first appeared in the May 1933 issue of *Scribner's Magazine*. In that version the last radio station to sign off was Portland, Oregon. That town was changed to Seattle, probably when Hemingway checked a map; as Edward Stone explains the change, with an assist from Maurice Beebe, Hemingway may have heard a Portland announcer refer to Vancouver, Oregon, just across the Columbia River, and thought it was the Canadian Vancouver, 300 miles to the north, but only a mere (for westerners) 150 from Seattle (378).

The last three sentences of the story were added to the version published in October in *Winner Take Nothing*.

Sources and Influences

To avoid seeming repetitious or less than literary, it is tempting to suggest that "The Gambler, the Nun, and the Radio" is Hemingway's American version of James Joyce's "Grace," but reason prevails—once again, there seem to be no obvious literary sources for the story. Granting that all fictions are in some sense autobiographical, some incorporate more details of their original occasions and so seem closer to discursive prose or, as Hemingway said, "straight reporting." Theoreticians may argue this, but Hemingway saw some distinction between six stories, nearly half of those in *Winner Take Nothing* ("Wine of Wyoming," "After the Storm," "The Mother of a Queen," "The Gambler," "One Reader Writes," and "A Day's Wait"), written "absolutely as they happen," and those he "invent[ed] completely" (*Letters* 400). With the exception of "Che Ti Dice" perhaps, it would be difficult to demonstrate that distinction among any of the stories of the two earlier collections.

Carlos Baker's account in his biography confirmed the story of the accident and the details of Hemingway's hospitalization with some six contemporary letters and as many later recollections (216–18, 602). Hemingway's letters to Archibald MacLeish and Guy Hickok in November and December 1930 identify the characters' originals, mention the "raddio" (his spelling), and express the ordinary convalescent's obsession with the details of his operation and abiding restlessness (*Letters* 329–34).

Sister Cecilia in the story was identified as Sister Florence (Baker 602); and perhaps the proof positive of her abiding and cheerful faith is that when she was interviewed in the late 1930s she happily repeated the details of the short story with an inspired unconcern for fact. (The interview is quoted in George Monteiro's delightful article [51–52].) The good sister's powers of prayer, or Hemingway's memory, lapsed, however, with the bases loaded in the third game of the 1930 World Series, for "Bing Miller struck out despite the nun's pleas"; still, as Frederick Murolo admitted, "a nun that goes three for four" has a respectable average (52–53).

Finally, Hemingway moved the hospital from Billings, Montana, confusing Mr. Frazer, who says to Cayetano, "Listen, amigo, . . . The policeman says that we are not in Chicago but in Hailey, *Montana*" (*Stories* 470), and leading Carlos Baker to assume that mythical town was Hailey, Idaho, "Ezra Pound's birthplace" (602). Hemingway's broken arm becomes Frazer's broken leg, and Edward Stone recalls the line "Mr. Frazer had been through this all before" (*Stories* 480) to suggest an association with Frederic Henry's and Hemingway's earlier wound (379). One changed detail such as this may weigh more in meaning than all those unchanged between the experience and the fiction, but the story still has the surrounding details of Billings, Montana, rather than Hailey, in whatever state.

Critical Studies

In 1952 Philip Young set the terms for the critical consideration of "The Gambler" for nearly two decades. He placed the story in Hemingway's experience with the passage from *Green Hills of Africa* in which Hemingway recalls the worst horror of his life as the "time in a hospital with my right arm broken. . . . Alone with the pain in the night of the fifth week of not sleeping" (148). Although the passage demotes to second place the traumatic war wound, Young finds in Frazer "our old friend Nick" with his insomnia and bad nerves, avoiding "thinking" with alcohol and the radio in "another rite with which to keep off the 'evil spirits' " (67). Sister Cecilia offers a faith that Frazer rejects as naive, while Cayetano exemplifies the code he may admire but being "too tortured, too thoughtful, too perplexed" cannot attain (68).

The criticism of the story in the 1960s presented variations on this central trio of characters and their positions. Joseph DeFalco gathered all three attitudes under the rubric of "adjustments people make to the exigencies of life." Frazer begins as "the unadjusted one, the victim of total unfaith," but ends making a "tentative truce. . . . in much the same way as the gambler" (214–15). Marion Montgomery was more affirmative: Frazer "warms from detachment to humanness," adopting both the "human concerns" of the nun and the "quiet determination" of the gambler. The evidence for Montgomery rests in the final section where Frazer questions the Marxist and seems to affirm the values of a "tolerant knowledge" over the "imposed knowledge" of education—another "opium of the people"—a confirmation of Hemingway's romantic antiintellectualism. With that, Montgomery concluded that Frazer has undergone "a spiritual rehabilitation"; but he still found a void at the center of the story, for we "do not understand what pain the opium of the radio helps him to bear" (204, 209–10).

Earl Rovit agreed with Young's perception of Frazer as a tyro who failed, but also condemned Cayetano as an "inadequate father image" and the story in general as a "text for a moralizing sermon" (70, 98). Sheridan Baker, however, found Cayetano one of "the undefeated" and then offered an answer for Montgomery's question: Frazer, with his social awareness of "the Marxist thirties," discovers in " 'that well-lighted part of his mind' " that bread is " 'the real, the actual opium of the people.' Life itself, the daily bread, in other words, is a narcotic that keeps one from the awful truth" (85–86). If that equation of bread and life is justified, the story is far more nihilistic than its predecessor from another "well-lighted" part of Hemingway's imagination.

Most of the critics, while nodding to the story's humor, viewed it as one that approaches tragedy (see Williams 100–01). But Sheldon Grebstein found the story exemplary of Hemingway's humor, interweaving "both light and dark comedy" and employing "incompatible perspectives and the contrast of tongues to achieve his comic effects" (194). More than a comic device, the "linguistic contrast signifies a deeper contrast not only of mental alertness and acuity but also of value and attitude" (196). That important point was made in Delmore Schwartz's article of 1938 exploring Hemingway's "extension of the rhetorical possibilities of speech, . . . his most valuable contribution to writing." Schwartz noted that in the "heightening of the kinds of speech of our time, . . . *the foreigner* is necessary for this rhetoric. The foreigner carries over into English the idiom of his native tongue, and in that modified English he makes clear the fact that he is living by the values which constitute the code." When Frazer serves as translator in this "conversational system," even though Cayetano knows English well, Schwartz implied that Frazer is more than fluent in Spanish, he understands the code (121–22).

With Grebstein's study of the story's "dark comedy," two other articles appeared in the early 1970s to give "The Gambler" its due. After considering some of the textual problems of the story, Edward Stone turned to the differences between its magazine and final endings, to answer Montgomery's question about the source of Frazer's despair—his broken leg, his failure as a writer, or his political disillusionment. "None and all" is his answer: all three force us to read the story as "fictionalized autobiography," and the third, moreover, requires us to read the "disillusionment of American intellectuals" with Marxism in 1937 and 1939 back into a story of 1932. Yet "Frazer is all three, figuratively: the patient in a state of nerves, . . . the writer who has lost his audience, and the thoroughly conscious citizen of the years following the collapse of the American economy" (379–80). Stone argued that if the story's weakness is its "topicality, its strength is that it authentically re-creates the American temper in what even then seemed a kind of premature twilight of our civilization" (382). Then, in a vivid and compelling re-creation of his own, Stone drew on contemporary sources and later histories to recall the dangerous despair of "the Great Doldrums." He cited the article Hemingway must have read in which Bernarr MacFadden called for "dictatorial powers" for the president and the abrogation of the Constitution in a periodical called *Liberty,* and another in which the leftist Louis F. Budenz said "potatoes became the opium of the people" (383; *Stories* 486).

Whether in spite or because of the economic collapse, the "lines were long in front of the movie houses as well as the banks and soup kitchens," for the years just after 1929 were marked by a passion for entertainment; and among the most popular forms, as Stone pointed out, were gambling (Cayetano), sports events (Sister Cecilia), and radio musical programs (Frazer) (384).

Finally, Stone considered the two endings. The *Scribner's Magazine* version ends with a condemnation of revolution (one with at least the partial appeal of its epigrammatic form). When Hemingway reviewed the story for the collection, he "would appear to have realized that resignation, not defiance—radio, not revolution—was its theme" (387). Although earlier Frazer had thought the revolutionary song of the past, "La Cucaracha," was "better than the radio," in this ending he turns to his newfound opiate, which, in Stone's words, is "guaranteed to be effective all through the night. Especially recommended, 'Little White Lies.' The more faintly heard, the better" (388). Edward Stone's reading is dark with our own history.

Paul Rodgers's analysis of the story's ironic levels was the first to consider the function of the story's narrator. He began with a detailed reading of the story's closing scene, identified Frazer's problem not in his physical pain but in what "the narrator repeatedly and somewhat mysteriously refers to as 'thinking.' " The consequence of that thinking is the "meditation" on opiums that ends with the conclusion that the fundamental opium is bread. "Whatever one's level of awareness, life means privation, frustration, pain. The very staff of life is a crutch. This is the bleak conclusion to which thinking leads Mr. Frazer" (440–41).

The narrator points to no "flaw in Frazer's thinking"; indeed, his "expository comments echo Frazer's tone and vocabulary so faithfully that we can scarcely distinguish one man from the other ('She went right down and prayed for him'), and at least once the two voices appear actually to merge: 'This does not sound so funny now but it was funny then.' " The consequence is that "the narrator is usually regarded as an uncritical sharer of Frazer's pessimism" (442). (The manuscripts with the wholesale shift from first- to third-person narration account for this impression.)

But Rodgers claimed that the "narrator's understanding and consequent pessimism very probably exceeds Frazer's; for in reporting Frazer's meditation, he suggests an irony that Frazer does not recognize": if any opiate is good in that it "serves to make *life* tolerable," that is one thing; but "if *bread* [presumably life itself] is an opiate, then one may wonder whether the whole complicated involvement with pain and opiates makes sense. . . . In short Frazer's philosophizing may affirm nothing . . . except the absurdity of all affirmation; and although he does not perceive this possibility, we must infer that the narrator does" (442–43).

There are two ways out of this quandary, and for each "Cayetano is the key." Others have argued that Cayetano is the code-hero and that Frazer fails to meet that code. Rodgers countered that he "makes not the least attempt to emulate Cayetano." It is more likely then that Frazer "does not *and cannot* recognize" what Cayetano stands for. The change in the title, "with its odd arrangement of non-coordinates in parallel structure, directs attention away from Frazer's philosophizing and focuses on the man himself, apparently in order to judge him" (444–45).

All this, however, "collides with another of the narrator's calculated ironies." If Frazer is denied the faith of Sister Cecilia, whose namesake was the patron saint of the blind and of music, and "the fortitude and dignity of Cayetano, that ironically admirable 'victim of illusions,' " he is, in his final conversation with the Marxist, revealed to have one last devotion, knowledge (446–47). And here Rodgers came close to destroying his argument. He entertained the possibility that that knowledge is not simply another opiate; but if it is not, then how does it differ from the narrator's knowledge that allows him to see the irony of Frazer's meditations?

But Rodgers did not let the story go, "for there is one last irony to recognize." As the story ends, Frazer hears the strains of "La Cucaracha" the Chicanos will take with them when they leave, and he will play the radio. Were Frazer to listen to the words as well as the "sinister lightness and deftness" of the tune, he would hear: "The cockroach, the cockroach,/ It cannot walk,/Because it lacks, because it no longer has/Marijuana to smoke." To Rodgers, it "does not matter whether Frazer knows these words or recalls them, for he is blind to their significance for him. But the narrator is not blind, and the inference we draw is surely his implication. Frazer . . . is just as nerveless and immobile and insignificant as the revolutionary cockroach that lacks its marijuana. His knowledge is a paralyzing opiate" (448–49).

These two articles, different in their critical assumptions, are both exemplary in that they challenge received opinions. Edward Stone's, with its ranging social history, refuses to accept the notion of Hemingway as uninterested in the politics of his time; and Paul Rodgers's, with its sensitivity to subtle and ironic narrative inflections, dismisses the concept of the code, which has been so restrictive of late.

Works Cited

PRIMARY

Ernest Hemingway: Selected Letters, 1917–1961. Ed. Carlos Baker. New York: Scribner's, 1981.

Green Hills of Africa. New York: Scribner's, 1935.

The Short Stories of Ernest Hemingway. New York: Scribner's, 1938, 468–87.

SECONDARY

Baker, Carlos. *Ernest Hemingway: A Life Story.* 1969. Scribner's, 1988.

Baker, Sheridan. *Ernest Hemingway.* New York: Holt, 1967.

DeFalco, Joseph. *The Hero in Hemingway's Short Stories.* Pittsburgh: U of Pittsburgh P, 1963.

Grebstein, Sheldon N. *Hemingway's Craft.* Carbondale: Southern Illinois UP, 1973.

Monteiro, George. "Hemingway's Nun's Tale." *Research Studies* 46 (Mar. 1978): 50–53.

Montgomery, Marion. "Hemingway's 'The Gambler, the Nun, and the Radio': A Reading and a Problem." *Forum* 7 (Winter 1962): 36–40; rpt. in *The Short Stories of Ernest Hemingway: Critical Essays.* Ed. Jackson J. Benson. Durham: Duke UP, 1975, 203–10.

Murolo, Frederick L. "Another Look at the Nun and Her Prayers." *Hemingway Review* 4 (Fall 1984): 52–53.

Rodgers, Paul C., Jr. "Levels of Irony in Hemingway's 'The Gambler, the Nun, and the Radio.'" *Studies in Short Fiction* 7 (Summer 1970): 439–49.

Rovit, Earl. *Ernest Hemingway.* Boston: Twayne, 1963.

Schwartz, Delmore. "Ernest Hemingway's Literary Situation." *Southern Review* 3 (Spring, 1938): 769–82; rpt. in *Ernest Hemingway: The Man and His Work.* Ed. John K. M. McCaffery. Cleveland: World, 1950, 114–29.

Stone, Edward. "Hemingway's Mr. Frazer: From Revolution to Radio." *Journal of Modern Literature* 1 (Mar. 1971): 375–88.

Williams, Wirt. *The Tragic Art of Ernest Hemingway.* Baton Rouge: Louisiana State UP, 1981.

Young, Philip. *Ernest Hemingway: A Reconsideration.* 1952. New York: Harcourt, 1966.

42

One Reader Writes

Composition History (February 1932-February 1933)

Whenever "One Reader Writes" was written between February 1932 and February 1933, it could not have taken up more than an hour of Hemingway's morning composition. In Carlos Baker's account, the story was one of seven he "had assembled . . . for a new collection" in February of 1932. It was "composed"—if that is the word for it—from one of six letters Dr. Logan Clendening of Kansas City had received from readers of his nationally "syndicated medical column" and sent to Hemingway.

The letter, now in Baker's files, was from "a woman in Harrisburg, Pennsylvania, whose husband had contracted syphilis while serving with the United States Marines in Shanghai. . . . Hemingway edited the letter slightly, changing the date and the place-name and adding a short introduction and conclusion" (Baker 227, 604). Indeed, when Hemingway described the woman writing the letter "steadily with no necessity to cross out or rewrite anything" he was also very nearly describing his own transcription of the letter (*Stories* 420).

Baker's date of February 1932 may indicate when Hemingway received the six letters from Clendening, but in both the surviving manuscripts he changed the place from Harrisburg to Roanoke, Virginia, and the date to 6 February 1933. Hemingway might have figured in 1932 that the collection would not come out until 1933 and simply advanced the date a year, but what made him "post" the letter from Roanoke? Both the place and the date might have been snatched from the air, but on 6 February 1933 Hemingway had just returned to Key West after driving from Piggott, Arkansas, to Roanoke to leave the car, entrain to New York for two weeks, and return to Roanoke to finish the drive home (Baker 236-37). It seems probable, then, that the story was written closer to the later date of February 1933.

In the first pencil manuscript (KL/EH 635) Hemingway made only one revision in the body of the letter to obscure the husband's service in the marines. The only revisions in the introductory and concluding paragraphs are three immediate inserts establishing the woman reading the newspaper, looking at the doctor's picture, and thinking that he looks smart. Hemingway paused, however, over the ending after the line "It's such a long time though."

Then, in darker ink, he ended the story with the woman's moving appeal to Christ (*Stories* 420–21). The only minor difficulty Hemingway had with the story was finding a title: twice he considered "The Syndicated Column," and once, significantly, "Light from the East."

The typescript used as setting copy for *Winner Take Nothing* (KL/EH 222) incorporates all the revisions in the first manuscript. It was typed by Jane, the wife of Hemingway's journalist friend Richard Armstrong, from whom there is correspondence on her work beginning on 31 July 1933 (KL/EH).

Publishing History (October 1933)

As with other stories about which Hemingway, for whatever reasons, had some doubts, he was reticent with "One Reader Writes." When he mentioned it to Max Perkins a month after its publication in *Winner Take Nothing,* he referred to it as "the letter one" among those he wrote "absolutely as they happen" (*Letters* 400).

Sources and Influences

Hemingway met Dr. Logan Clendening in November 1931 when Gregory was born in Kansas City, and—like the correspondent in "One Reader Writes"—thought "he was a hell of a fine guy." Clendening was nationally known for his "column of medical advice, 'Diet and Health,' . . . syndicated in hundreds of newspapers"; and early in 1932 he sent Hemingway six letters he had received from persons seeking his advice (Baker 227, 604).

The doctor was a "fine guy" in more than professional ways. He was a brilliant writer whose ironic style originated in his deep compassion for human suffering and his vehement scorn for those beliefs and institutions that ignore it to preserve their cruel moralities. Like Hemingway, he would have been struck by the correspondent's turning to him because she "often heard my Father say one could well wish themselves dead if once they became a victim of that malady" (*Stories* 420). In Clendening's bestselling book *The Human Body,* published in 1928 and selling a half-million copies, he writes on the prevention of syphilis, the question raised by the benighted woman in this story: "Prevention is possible. Public prevention can never be accomplished until prostitution, irregular prostitution, is abolished, which I suppose everyone admits is an unattainable ideal. The public regulation and supervision of prostitutes has always been prevented by the false sanctimony of public opinion. Christian ministers would always prefer to have boys diseased, women ruined and made barren, and babies blinded than admit the seventh commandment was ever broken by any of their flock" (315).

This wise and humane book is not noted in catalogs of Hemingway's reading, but he owned Clendening's second book, *The Care and Feeding of Adults, With Doubts about Children* (1931) (Reynolds 111), and there are interesting analogies between Clendening's concluding thoughts on death in *The Human Body* and rejected versions of the ending of *A Farewell to Arms*.

"One Reader Writes" is not the first instance of Hemingway's lifting an actual letter, adding an ironic frame, and considering it a story. Sometime in 1921 he did it with another letter, now published as "Portrait of an Idealist in Love" (Griffin 162–64; see Smith 579, n. 13). Later still, he originally intended to publish a letter from the boxer Larry Gains, for which he left a space in the manuscript of *The Sun Also Rises* (Svoboda 28).

Critical Studies

"One Reader Writes" has the distinction of being the most neglected of Hemingway's short stories—and most would say the distinction is deserved. Only one critic writing before the publication of Carlos Baker's biography in 1969 took it seriously, and he, Joseph DeFalco, gave it no more than a paragraph. Once Baker revealed the story's origins, few to this day have afforded it more than a brief allusion or a footnote.

It is an oddity in a variety of ways, not the least of which lies in the evidence of its origin, and for that reason alone one can imagine critics shying away from a story of which only one-third is fiction. Moreover, it is likely that some critics have been offended by Hemingway's opportunism in writing, as Baker called it, "the easiest short story he ever devised" (227). Yet in this latter day of "found" poetry, collages, and the theoretical shadings on the spectrum of fiction and nonfiction, such critical strictures seem a trifle too nice, particularly with a writer whose style has been praised on the evidence of his revisions of a 1922 cable for chapter 3 of *In Our Time* (Fenton 229–36).

The only extended analysis of the story is Mark Edelson's, and it seems strained here and there. He first noted that the irony of title calls attention to the writing of the semiliterate "reader" and the writing of the story. By virtue of her class and predicament, this portrait of the woman is in "ironic contrast" with those of "James, Eliot and all the others" who have written a "Portrait of a Lady" (329). Unable to find advice from her husband, her father, or even a local doctor, she turns to "a kind of mail-order medicine"; and her isolation is formally reflected in the frame that encloses her "public thoughts" in the introduction of the scene and the conclusion, "a cadenza of distress and doubt" (330–31).

The most recent mention of the story is Wirt Williams's; and it is curious that his study of Hemingway's tragic art from the perspectives of the major theories of tragedy should simply praise Hemingway for avoiding "sentimentality and . . . ludicrous failure" with an "enlightening demonstration" of a narrative point of view that "sets up a distance between reader and character sufficient to maintain detachment and coolness" (100).

The story cannot, must not, leave us so temperate and distant. It would not if we were to read the letter in our morning paper, any more than it did Dr. Clendening or Ernest Hemingway. Those who have read the story with a modicum of sympathy have remarked its irony and pathos, but it was Joseph DeFalco in 1963 who left an unnoticed clue to the source of that irony: "In her absolute ignorance and remorse, the girl resorts to faith in an anonymous 'god-doctor' figure who appears in a newspaper. The irony of her pathos is revealed in the last lines of the sketch: 'I wish to Christ he hadn't got any kind of malady. I don't know why he had to get a malady'" (159–60).

Her questions are finally as troubling as Job's, perhaps more so in that she invokes a merciful Christ. One of Hemingway's rejected titles was "Light from the East," and in obedience to that allusion he added the last few lines of the woman's appeal, not to her husband, nor her father, nor even the doctor, but to the Light of the World.

Works Cited

PRIMARY

Ernest Hemingway: Selected Letters, 1917–1961. Ed. Carlos Baker. New York: Scribner's, 1981.

The Short Stories of Ernest Hemingway. New York: Scribner's, 1938, 420–21.

SECONDARY

Baker, Carlos. *Ernest Hemingway: A Life Story.* 1969. New York: Scribner's, 1988.

Clendening, Logan. *The Human Body.* New York: Knopf, 1928.

DeFalco, Joseph. *The Hero in Hemingway's Short Stories.* Pittsburgh: U of Pittsburgh P, 1963.

Edelson, Mark. "A Note on 'One Reader Writes.'" *Fitzgerald/Hemingway Annual* (1972): 329–31.

Fenton, Charles A. *The Apprenticeship of Ernest Hemingway.* New York: Farrar, 1954.

Griffin, Peter. *Along with Youth: Hemingway, The Early Years.* New York: Oxford UP, 1985.

Reynolds, Michael S. *Hemingway's Reading: 1910–1940.* Princeton: Princeton UP, 1981.

Smith, Paul. "Hemingway's Apprentice Fiction: 1919–1921." *American Literature* 58 (Dec. 1986): 574–88.

Svoboda, Frederic J. *Hemingway and "The Sun Also Rises."* Lawrence: UP of Kansas, 1983.

Williams, Wirt. *The Tragic Art of Ernest Hemingway.* Baton Rouge: Louisiana State UP, 1981.

43

A Day's Wait

Composition History (March-July 1933)

There is little evidence for dating the composition of "A Day's Wait," for the last note on the "original manuscript" is Richard Armstrong's to Hemingway assuring him that it was "safely in the cover which I described to you" (KL/EH, 31 July 1933). The typescript, used as a setting copy for *Winner Take Nothing,* was one of those done by Jane Armstrong on a typewriter with large block letters (KL/EH 222).

The earliest date of composition could not have been before late January 1933; the incident Carlos Baker recounts as the story's source happened in the previous month, and Hemingway spent most of January on the road. But by mid-March 1933 Hemingway wrote to Arnold Gingrich that he had "written three stories" since one he had sent him in December, and that for "the book of short stories I have 14 done. Will write one more" (*Letters* 383–84). Whatever stories he was counting as those fourteen, or even the fifteenth he had in mind, it is likely that "A Day's Wait" was among them.

So it seems the story was written sometime between late March of 1933, sent to Jane Armstrong for typing, and returned that summer. If the manuscript is still "safely in the cover" Richard Armstrong mentioned, his wife's typing might have been or still may be richly rewarded.

Publication History (October 1933)

By July of 1933 Hemingway had no reason to send "A Day's Wait" to a magazine; by then he was thinking of the concluding set of stories for *Winner Take Nothing,* and the story took its place introducing the later triad of "marriage tales" in October 1933.

Sources and Influences

Carlos Baker related the incident of December 1932 that Hemingway drew on for the story, and it was confirmed by John Hemingway (Bumby in life and Schatz in the story):

Shortly before the Hemingways were due to leave Piggott, Bumby came down with influenza. On learning that his temperature was 102, he turned pale, and could not seem to concentrate even when Ernest read aloud to him from Howard Pyle's *Book of Pirates*. Ernest went out quail shooting with a young Irish setter belonging to the Pfieffers. When he came back, Bumby was still behaving strangely. His schoolmates in France had told him that no one could possibly survive with a temperature of 44. Since his own was more than twice that high, he was sure he was going to die. He relaxed visibly when Ernest explained the difference between Fahrenheit and Centigrade. (*Ernest Hemingway: A Life Story* 236).

It made a good story—almost too good, for apparently Baker had to remind Jack Hemingway of the incident to confirm it—and, as in so much of Hemingway's life and fiction, it seems almost as if he prepared the event. On 15 November 1932, when he was about to bring Bumby to Piggott where Gregory and Patrick had come down with "whoop cough," he asked Max Perkins to send him Howard Pyle's "book on pirates" since he had "promised it to Bumby" (*Letters* 376-77).

How much of Bumby's recollection of the event when he was nine was refreshed by Baker's inquiry when he was forty and the story thirty years old, is a matter for conjecture. Hemingway told Perkins the story was one of those written "absolutely as they happen" (*Letters* 400)—and if that is so, Hemingway was once again remarkably lucky to discover such an artful story ready at hand.

Critical Studies

The story has had its share of adverse criticism and reluctant apologies. Sheridan Baker dismissed it as "almost straight journalism" (88)—an odd perception—and Allen Shepherd labored to demonstrate how much the story differed from the biographical account only to conclude that it was, "as a work of art, . . . unimpressive" (39). Finally, Peter Hays argued that this "charming, sentimental story" of a "prototypical code hero" and his "juvenile heroics" is meant with self-relexive irony to direct "some gentle laughter at the inappropriateness of the code . . . in the present circumstances" (25)—a comment that seems singularly insensitive to those circumstances.

Most critics follow Carlos Baker (*Writer as Artist* 134) in considering "A Day's Wait" a Nick Adams story (Waldhorn, Grebstein, and Flora). Some do not, and among them—curiously—is Philip Young, who excluded it from the 1972 edition of *The Nick Adams Stories* (see also DeFalco and Williams). Some might argue that the narrator is not named, or that even if he were, it is not his story but Schatz's. (That nickname—German for treasure, darling, or love—appears in the manuscripts of "Fathers and Sons" for Nicholas Adams's son.)

But if the father is unnamed and away hunting during the boy's crisis, his son's behavior in the ordeal marks his lineage with both the tyros, like Nick Adams, and the heroes to whose code they aspire (Waldhorn 71). Like Nick Adams before him, Schatz endures an initiation, but a far more terrifying one than his predecessor/father faced, for here it is the certainty of his immediate death, however misconceived. Joseph DeFalco argued that Schatz, confronted with the "trauma of reality, . . . undergoes a complete transformation from child to adult." Before he hears the doctor's offhand sentence of death, "One hundred and two," he is a typical child refusing to go to bed. Then, in an "ironic reversal, . . . he assumes the authoritarian role," excusing his father from witnessing his death, if it bothers him (53–54). At the end, of course, he becomes a child again.

That sequence of roles from child to adult to child is reflected, as Sheldon Grebstein noted, in the alternation between inside and outside scenes and between dramatic scenes of dialogue and the central narration of the hunt (9–10). And those structural elements relate in turn the father's release of tension and expression of emotion in hunting with his son's unburdening himself with confession (10).

Patrick Mahony, in a detailed explication, described the hunting scene as a "focus of ironic counterpoint" between the father's "successful self-entertainment" and his "futile attempts in reading" to his son, his pleasure in finding birds "for another day" on his son's last day, his role as a hunter/killer and his son's as the hunted/victim of his fear. Even the imagery of the wintry scene is repeated in Schatz's white face; and when the father returns from "flushing" birds, he finds his son's face "flushed" with fever (Item 18).

These studies all support Joseph Flora's argument that the story is not simply the boy's story but is a drama of the father-son relationship. He suggested that Hemingway deliberately chose a first person narration to emphasize that relationship, for if the story had been only "about the lad's brave wait for death, third person would have done just as well." That emphasis might also account for the fact that after the opening sentence, the wife in bed is never mentioned—indeed, when the father returns it is "they" who tell him his son "refused to let anyone come into the room" (*Stories* 436, 438). Whatever the reason—and feminist critics will have others—the narrator "does the proper things" and shows "his gentleness as a father" (218–19).

Although the father "misses some important signals" and assumes "that his son will accept his own confidence" (Flora 219), he is hardly unfeeling or negligent. In fact, at the story's climactic revelation of Schatz's mistake, the dramatic release of tension occurs not only in Schatz's mind but in his father's as he shares both his son's profound relief and the lingering memory of his agony. As Wirt Williams notes, "The drama of his psyche is seen in the perspective of his father's; the tension between the two is the tension of the finished work" (104).

Joseph Flora is convincing in his study of the story as one of the last concerned with Nick Adams, now mature, married, and a writer; and he argued that "the use of the first person narrative for a story about a writer suggests that the writer knows what is significant in it—for the boy and for himself" (222–23). And with that concluding remark, Flora opened up a new dimension of the story. Earlier he had identified dramatic and verbal similarities with other Nick Adams stories to place "A Day's Wait" in that canon, but he had left their implications adrift. He noted, for example: Schatz "seemed very detached from what was going on," as the Arditi lieutenant of "In Another Country" who "had lived a long time with death . . . was a little detached" (*Stories* 437, 269); he insists on staying awake, as does Nick in "Now I Lay Me" (*Stories* 437, 362); he "can't keep from thinking," as does Nick in "Big Two-Hearted River" and others elsewhere (*Stories* 438, 218). Finally, the "courageous little boy takes us all the way back to the haunting question of 'Indian Camp': 'Is dying hard, Daddy?' " (Flora 219–22). Time and again, Nick, as the attendant "father, hears but does not hear" the echoes from the stories he has written (Flora 220, 222).

If this much is given, then there may be more. Nearly every critic has remarked on the "ironic counterpoint" in the wintry hunting scene and taken without question Nick's pleasure in the event. But the scene "along a frozen creek . . . [with its] high clay bank and overhanging brush" makes for difficult, even dangerous hunting—he falls twice and once drops his gun. He returns with two quail, and his pleasure is less in the hunting than in knowing he can return to hunt the threatening place "on another day" (*Stories* 437–38). The scene is a little winter metaphor of the summer day that ended "Big Two-Hearted River."

What finally unites and identifies the father and the son is that both misconceive experience for a brief but ominous day: the boy, innocently, measures his fate with a scale from another country of his youth; the father fails to measure his son's terror with that scale of behavior he had so finely calibrated in his fiction. For both, however, there is at least another day. On this day's wait, the father discovered his true treasure and the son earned the name Schatz.

Works Cited

PRIMARY

Ernest Hemingway: Selected Letters, 1917–1961. Ed. Carlos Baker. New York: Scribner's, 1981.

The Nick Adams Stories. Ed. Philip Young. New York: Scribner's, 1972.

The Short Stories of Ernest Hemingway. New York: Scribner's 1938, 436–39.

SECONDARY

Baker, Carlos. *Ernest Hemingway: A Life Story.* 1969. New York: Scribner's, 1988.

———. *Hemingway: The Writer as Artist.* 1952. Princeton: Princeton UP, 1972.

Baker, Sheridan. *Ernest Hemingway.* New York: Holt, 1967.

DeFalco, Joseph. *The Hero in Hemingway's Short Stories.* Pittsburgh: U of Pittsburgh P, 1963.

Flora, Joseph M. *Hemingway's Nick Adams.* Baton Rouge: Louisiana State UP, 1982.

Grebstein, Sheldon N. *Hemingway's Craft.* Carbondale: Southern Illinois UP, 1973.

Hays, Peter L. "Self-Reflexive Laughter in 'A Day's Wait.'" *Hemingway Notes* 7 (Fall 1980): 25.

Mahony, Patrick J. "Hemingway's 'A Day's Wait.'" *Explicator* 17 (Nov. 1968), Item 18.

Shepherd, Allen. "Hemingway's 'A Day's Wait': Biography and Fiction." *Indiana English Journal* 4 (Spring 1970): 37–39.

Waldhorn, Arthur. *A Reader's Guide to Ernest Hemingway.* New York: Farrar, 1972.

Williams, Wirt. *The Tragic Art of Ernest Hemingway.* Baton Rouge: Louisiana State UP, 1981.

44

Fathers and Sons

Composition History (November 1932-August 1933)

Sometime late in the summer of 1933, Hemingway added a line in pencil to the typescript of "Fathers and Sons" he would soon send to Max Perkins for setting copy. After Nick recalls the "handsome job the undertaker had done on his father's face," he wrote: "But there was no use going over it/again/until he needed it" (KL/EH 222). The line was rejected, but it offers a reason for his reticence in writing the "good story" of his father's suicide other than that "there were still too many people alive for him to write it" (*Stories* 491).

He had alluded to the suicide in a rejected fragment of "A Natural History of the Dead" in early 1929 (KL/EH 812), and it is possible that he sketched the story out in that year. In the next few years, the anniversary of his father's death seemed to conspire with events in the first week of December. Harry Crosby shot himself in December 1929, and Hemingway spent December 1930 in the hospital in Billings, Montana; these events are reflected in the dark mood of "The Gambler, the Nun, and the Radio." In December 1931 he was revising "A Natural History", and in late November 1932, with the recent word of the death of Uncle Willoughby, he made the trip west with Bumby through the landscape that recalled hunting with his father as a boy (Baker 234-35).

There is a one-sentence fragment written on Hotel Ambos Mundos stationery, but it is too brief to date the first manuscript in the early summer of 1932 or of 1933 (KL/EH 385). The two other fragments suggest longer attempts at an early version of the story: one leads into the narrative after the introductory scene (KL/EH 384; *Stories* 491 ["His father had summed up"]); and the other leads into the narrative just before the reverie is ended with the boy's question about the Indians (KL/EH 382; *Stories* 497 ["What was it like"]). Thus, either might indicate a version of the story without the midwestern setting and might have been written before November 1932. KL/EH 382 is clearly the earliest fragment, but both were written either out of an anger so deep and a perplexity so unsettling that they argue for a date closer to Dr. Hemingway's suicide in 1928 and give good reasons for his decision not to finish the story.

That is, "until he needed it," as he wrote in the final typescript, and he *did* need it in the summer of 1933. In April he wrote that the book was "nearly done"; in June he settled on a title for the collection, composed its epigraph, and said he had "13 stories" for the book; and on 26 July he wrote Perkins that he would "start re-writing The Tomb of My Grandfather today" (*Letters* 386, 393, 395). The story took on two other tentative titles, "Indian Summer" and "Long Time Ago Good," before its final title, and each of the two fragments associates Indians and late summers with the narrator's memories of his tortured father.

The earliest (KL/EH 382) begins with the contrast between his father's keen eyesight and myopic advice on sex. When the boy interrupts his reverie with his question about the Indians, his father replies:

"There was an Indian girl named Prudy Gilby that I was very fond of. We were very good friends.
"What happened to her?"
"She |had a baby| went away to be a hooker."
"What's a hooker?"
"I'll tell you sometime."

But he cannot tell him then of what it was like, any more than Nick can reveal his thoughts later (*Stories* 497). He says simply, "I always liked them. We had good times then and later on we played a lot of baseball. Her brother Dick was a very good ballplayer." Then suddenly he begins to "wonder what my father knew beside the nonsense that he told me and how things were with him because when I asked him what the Indians were like when he was a boy he said that |they| he had very good friends among them, that he was very fond of them and that they called him Me-teh-ta-la [unclear in text] which means Eagle Eye."

The second fragment (KL/EH 384) approaches uncontrollable rage as the narrator recalls his parents' marriage: the things "a man suffers in his own home are only proof of his own weakness," and the only thing to do with a selfish and hysterical wife is to "get rid of her"; for whoever

in a marriage of that sort wins the first encounter is in command and, having lost, to continue to appeal to reason, to write letters at night, hysterically logical letters explaining your position, to have it out/again/before the children—then the inevitable making up, . . . everything that had been told the children cancelled, the home full of love, and mother carried you, darling, over her heart all those months and her heart beat in your heart. Oh yes and what about his |poor bloody| heart and where did it beat and who |beats it now and what a hollow sound it makes.|

Then abruptly the passage evokes the enigmatic ending of "Indian Camp":

> I've seen him when we used to row in the boat in the evening, trolling, the lake quiet, the sun down behind the hills, widening circles where the bass rose, ask me to take the oars because it was too uncomfortable.
> "It's the hot weather," he said. "And the exercise."
> I would row, not knowing what it was about, watching him sitting in the stern [,] the |big| bulk of him, the blackness of him, he was very big and his hair and beard were black, his skin was dark and he had an indian nose and those wonderful eyes, and I didn't know what it was that made him so uncomfortable. I had not started to be uncomfortable that way yet and when I was young all he ever told me about sex was that masturbation produced blindness, insanity and death. . . .

Remembering the bitter sympathy of these passages—and one wonders, for once, why Hemingway saved them—one might almost feel that when Nick, later, has his father in his sights, to have pulled the trigger would have been close to an act of mercy.

The first complete manuscript was titled "The Tomb of My Grandfather" from the boy Schatz's remark near the end of what is still a first-person narrative. Hemingway must have been thinking of its revisions before his 26 July letter to Perkins, in order to have typed his second version (KL/EH 385 A), revised it, have it typed again, and finally revised for the setting copy published in October 1933 (KL/EH 222).

He had several passages to correct and more to add to the first manuscript. One of the most startling is that the narrator is not only driving with his son but, for a moment, with his sister who figures so significantly in his reverie. Prudy (later Trudy) is with her brother Dick (later Billy)—recall "The Doctor and the Doctor's Wife." Long passages like the first hunting scene are heavily and tentatively revised; others have yet to be added, and when they are in the first typescript, they are still incomplete: two examples are the long paragraph about his inability to write of his father's death (*Stories* 491) and the later evocation of his father, the whipping for "losing" the hand-me-down underwear, and the terrifying scene when he imagines shooting him from the woodshed (*Stories* 496–97).

All these passages took on other additions and revisions in his own typescript, again in the typescript he sent to Scribner's, and although there are no galleys available, from the differences between that setting copy and the published text, they too must have been revised.

Two other more distantly related manuscript fragments deserve notice. The earliest (KL/EH 816) begins "We are the generation whose fathers shot themselves" and blames their suicides on financial loss "although their wives are almost invariably a contributing cause." A reference to humanists and *The Bookman* in this fragment associates it with "A Natural History." In another set of notebook fragments (KL/EH 513), the second describes Nick sitting in a woodshed looking out at his *new* father on the porch; the fourth describes Robert Thompson's hatred of his mother, his shame over his father's suicide, which the family has explained away as a hunting accident.

No other manuscripts show more extensive and detailed revisions and additions through so many versions than do those for "Fathers and Sons." With his first typescript he cast it into the third person, but still he worked at revisions—and not only because its subject was difficult for Hemingway to contemplate and still maintain the distance it required.

Publication History (October 1933)

Late in the summer of 1933, Hemingway knew he was writing the concluding story for his third major collection, and he must have sensed something of the challenge he had set himself earlier with "Big Two-Hearted River" at the end of *In Our Time* as well as something of the conflicts calling for resolution in the characters of both Nick Adams and his father, the last two "men without women" in "Now I Lay Me." Even if the story had had nothing to do with Hemingway's own experience, it would have been no mean accomplishment to bring it to completion before the publication of *Winner Take Nothing* in October 1933.

Sources and Influences

As with *Torrents of Spring* earlier, Hemingway took his title from a Turgenev novel, *Fathers and Sons;* but those who suggest a literary influence do so only in general and tentative terms. Joseph Flora, for example, finds it neither "difficult to imagine Hemingway's being deeply moved by Turgenev's study of the conflict between generations" nor, apropos of a son's interest in his father's youth, may it "be amiss to recall the embarrassment . . . between Nikolai Kirsanov and his liberal son Arcady when the father explains that he has taken a mistress . . . and has a child by her" (245, 247). Myler Wilkinson's recent volume on Hemingway and Turgenev is more concerned with contemporary concepts of what may count as an influence than proving any constitutive influence from the Russian.

Hemingway read Russian fiction avidly in the winter of 1925; at times, it seems, in order to make olympian pronouncements in his letters: he did judge Turgenev to be an "artist"—not a "professional writer" like Balzac or an "amateur" like Chekhov—but his admiration was more for *A Sportsman's*

Sketches than the novel, which he felt "can never be as exciting again as it was when it was written" (*Letters* 179, 176).

His cultural sources were closer to home. Conveniently close for Leslie Fiedler's dramatic account of the "failure of the American fictionist to deal with adult heterosexual love and his consequent obsession with death, incest, and innocent homosexuality." "Fathers and Sons" served Fiedler as an example of Hemingway's characteristically American "sense of how simple it all was once" and how "the rejection of a sentimental happy ending in marriage involves the acceptance of the sentimental happy beginning of innocent and inconsequential sex, camouflag[ing] the rejection of maturity and of fatherhood itself" (xi, 305). Fiedler's headlong analysis, often relieved of the weight of the texts, can too easily be ignored. For if the story is read less as a personal than as a cultural confession, then only some synoptic view like Fiedler's can account for the story's dramatic juxtaposition of the hunter-father who died in a domestic trap, his son's education as a hunter and sexual initiation troubled with fears of miscegenation and incest, and the resignation of guilt and grief as the son recognizes that he can do little more for his own son than his father did for him. Taken out of Hemingway's biography, this story is one of those "dangerous and disturbing" works Fiedler insisted on, as disturbing in its cultural implications for us reading as it was to Hemingway remembering.

What he remembered has been told and retold in biographies and memoirs. First, in the story, he recalled the trip by car from Key West to Piggott with young Bumby, stopping the last night in late November 1932 in northern Mississippi ("not his country" but Faulkner's as he would recall years later [*Stories* 488; Baker 234–35, 605]). The good hunting country reminded him, with pride, of his father's farsighted skills as a marksman and, with affectionate humor, his nearsighted notions of sex.

Then the suicide four years before: he was with Bumby then, too, in Trenton on the train to Key West when the telegram came from his sister Carol on 6 December 1928. He sent his son on, took the all-night train to Chicago, learned the details the next day, and might well have seen the body before the "handsome job the undertaker" did on the face (*Stories* 491). (Two years later as a senior, Carol Hemingway wrote a story, "The Eleven o'Clock Mail Plane," for the Oak Park High School literary magazine, *Tabula;* a fine story that must have astonished her teachers, it tells of hearing the shot, the confusion in the house, the inquest, and the gathering of the relatives to view the body, all through the memory of the young son Miles [Leicester]. It, too, recalls "the undertaker's work of art"; and it may add another inflection to Hemingway's sentence "It was a good story but there were still too many people alive for *him* to write it" [*Stories* 491].)

From the memory of his father's advice on sex, he then turned to his "own education in those earlier matters" (*Stories* 491). Most biographers follow Carlos Baker in discounting this scene as more "wishful thinking than . . . fact" (26). But the actors in this fantasy were all there in the summers of 1914–16 at Walloon Lake. Donald St. John found in the township school records that in 1914 Prudence Boulton (Trudy) was twelve, her brothers Richard (Billy), nine, and Edward (Eddie), seventeen—probably more than a match for Ernest at fifteen (83). Prudence was remembered by the older Indian residents of Charlevoix as a strikingly attractive girl, precocious and apparently generous. (In a passage from the manuscript of "The Last Good Country," deleted by its editors for its "dubious" taste [Young 6], Nick's sister Littless dissuades him from seeking out Trudy with the warning "You wouldn't go and make her another baby would you?" Nick replies, "I don't know" [KL/EH 542].) Her life ended in tragedy when she committed suicide in February 1918 with her lover, a paroled convict; and it may be that the deepest association between the first two parts of the story and between Trudy and Nick's father is that their originals were the first and the latest persons he knew, much less loved, who took their own lives.

With the son's abrupt and unsuspecting questions in the concluding return to the present scene, the story opens to embrace three generations. And as it does, the conflicts among them recede before the recognition of what they shared or might have shared. After his father's death, Hemingway passed through Chicago from time to time but never returned in 1933 or later to "pray at the tomb" in Oak Park, although "Fathers and Sons" is something of a prayer in itself, an invocation of the past and an appeal for the future.

Biographers and critics have looked ahead to later works in which Dr. Hemingway's suicide figures: Carlos Baker cited a deleted passage in the manuscripts of *Green Hills of Africa* (609); Robert Fleming has compared the deaths of the fathers in the story and *For Whom the Bell Tolls*. Finally, Joseph Flora's chapter, "Father and Son," places the story in the Nick Adams canon, reaching back to "Indian Camp" and "The Three-Day Blow" and ahead to "The Last Good Country" (213–50). His most original insight, however, is the placement of this story with "Wine of Wyoming" and "A Day's Wait" to form a little trilogy of late marriage tales, now with children.

Critical Studies

The issue that has divided most critics of the story rests in its resolution, or rather in the question of its nature and permanence, for few disagree that Nick Adams has achieved some sort of accomodation with his past. Those who find the ending more affirmative and lasting are most often those who consider the story integral to the Nick Adams canon; while those who find it more transitory and negative place the story within the psychic history of American culture or Hemingway himself.

Joseph DeFalco concluded his study of the hero in Hemingway's stories with the presentation of the "theme of reconcilement" in "Fathers and Sons." The presence of Nick's son moves Nick toward his "acceptance of the father figure" and the "forces of authority"; with a "return from isolation and dissociation," he recognizes that "he too will pass away and that the only hope for personal immortality rests in the continuity from his father to his own son" (217–18). So, too, Sheldon Grebstein found that the story's inward journey to "the sources of the protagonist's psyche" approaches an inner resolution and, finally, "predicts still another journey soon to be made . . . to the father's grave, perhaps the final reconciliation" (19–20). And lately, Wirt Williams found three "keys" to unlock the story: the father (a key to the past), the Indians (Nick's engagement with a "life force" in his own present), and the son (a key to the future), together "establish a cycle and continuity." The story does not achieve a tragic transcendence but achieves a reconciliation with the "dramaturgy of 'happy ending' " (104–05).

Joseph Flora, in one of the most recent and detailed commentaries, began with the important distinctions between Nick's thinking here, which is almost "a solace," and his compulsion to avoid "thinking" in "Big Two-Hearted River" or his chaotic memories in "A Way You'll Never Be" (237). That Nick is like his father in his nervousness in other stories and like him as a hunter, whose sense of smell is as good as his father's sense of sight, implies that Nick's "sleeping son will one day judge" him as he has judged his father (238).

Flora's reading of the scenes of Nick's childhood was notable for his perception of their subtle counterpoint of the elegiac and the comic. Without denying their burden of oedipal hatred, incest, and miscegenation, Flora noted the deliberate distancing of those events. Nick's recollection is, perhaps curiously, dispassionate and ordered. Much as he violates his father's conventional advice, in the midst of his sexual encounter with Trudy he "becomes comically traditional" when she tells him that *her* brother has designs on *his* sister: with "outraged honor . . . Nick, the writer to be, . . . sees a good story" and acts out his father's Victorianism in a bravura performance (240). Nor did Flora deny the significance of the argument over the underwear or Nick's anger as, with an armed shotgun in the woodshed, he watches his father on the porch. But even that scene is faintly comical, with his father sniffing "indignantly" to test his own underwear and Nick realizing now that a sharp sense of smell "was good for a bird dog but it did not help a man" (*Stories* 496–97). As Flora notes, such "murderous instincts" are "not unnatural," and if the "buried wish is now fulfilled," it is "ironically and sadly" so (241–43).

Although several critics have noted Hemingway's gift for comedy and satire—even called for a book on it—seldom have they considered the effects of the comic stance in their separate studies of this story. For all its somber themes, "Fathers and Sons" is filled with comic scenes: Nick's imagining Caruso "doing something strange, bizarre, and heinous with a potato masher"; Trudy's natural insouciance over Billy, "I no mind Billy. He my brother"; and Billy, oblivious of Leslie Fiedler, saying, "What we come? Hunt or what?" (*Stories* 491, 493, 495).

But Flora, for one, perceived the story's lighter tones, and that perception directs his reading of the last scene. The story, for him, returns to the tolerant mode of comedy with its traditional union of the societies of the fathers and the sons. Now, with his "greater understanding of his youth and his parents" and with his quiet and amused responses to his own son's questions, "his love reaches forward and backwards" through his life (250).

Other critics have been less sanguine. Like Jackson Benson, they found little evidence of surcease in the "turmoil of love and hate, guilt and gratitude that tortures Nick in his relationship with his father" (16). Nick's "loss" of the underwear and his brooding anger in the woodshed suggest his frustration at "assuming manhood . . . within the pattern held up for him by his father." That frustration is a consequence of the larger cultural conflict Benson adopts from Leslie Fiedler between "male/female, Victorianism/realism, and repression/emotional freedom" (17).

The central moment of that conflict usually occurs during the rite of passage and sexual initiation. Benson alluded to Fiedler when he noted that Nick's early sexual experiences are associated with hunting, indeed the two acts "go on simultaneously" (10). One would expect, then, a reenactment similar to Fiedler's American revision of the European sexual initiation fable: "In the forest, rather than brothel or bedroom, through murder rather than sex, the child enters manhood, trembles with nausea over the broken bird or lifeless rabbit rather than the spread-eagled whore" (355). By this definition, however, Nick's encounter with Trudy is, if not continental, perhaps mid-oceanic. In fact, there is good evidence that this is not a moment of *initiation* but one of several regular occasions that Nick takes in a matter-of-fact rather than trembling manner.

Psychoanalytic strategies are used with a vengeance in Ann Boutelle's study of patricide in the Nick Adams stories. She continued the curious reading of "Ten Indians" that identifies Dr. Adams as the tenth victim. Here she drew on Leicester Hemingway's distant memories of Ernest's behavior after the suicide. When Hemingway insisted, according to Leicester, on having the suicide gun, "he knew, either consciously or unconsciously, [he] had a right to that gun. In his fiction he had *already* killed his father, . . . especially because of his conviction of the power of writing. When he claimed that the imagined part of a story was 'what made everything come true,' he meant it literally and superstitiously. It didn't just give the story authenticity; it altered future reality." Thus the story becomes a "public confession of Hemingway's complicity in his father's suicide" (140–41).

Larry Grimes's study of the religious dimensions of Hemingway's fiction cast the conflict between generations into "ethico-religious" terms to argue that Nick's rebellion against the "fantasies of potency he attributed to his father" is half-hearted and ineffective and that, finally, he "cannot face the fact that his father has died," thus the "hint of procrastination in Nick's response to his son's plea" to visit the tomb of his grandfather (70). Grimes, like Benson and Flora before him, entertained the facts that Nick is a writer, this is a story, and—with some uncertainty—that "perhaps we are reading that account now" (69).

The implications of Nick's role as a writer in and of this story had to wait until Richard McCann's essay in 1985, a sensitive and convincing essay that is a delight to read. He gathered all the relevant passages in a scrupulous reading particularly attentive to nuances of style and the rhetorical structure of Nick's recollections (12). He caught the illuminating pun in Nick's hunting "the country in his mind" (*Stories* 488), which conjoins the evocations of hunting quail and hunting the memory of his father who is repeatedly likened to a bird (13).

McCann might have left it at that but went on to demonstrate that "the hunt for the father also becomes the hunt for the father within the self—the father internalized in Nick." Although Nick turns away from the story of his father, we are given "Nick's *rehearsal* of the story he will one day write. . . . Thus 'Fathers and Sons' becomes the search for the means of writing a story." Nick becomes two characters: "One is the writer, Nicholas Adams, who seeks to order an experience which resists resolution; he plays it over and over in his mind. The other is his child-self, the self 'Nicholas' looks back upon." Add, then, to the relationships between the three "generations" in the story a fourth and parallel relationship of another sort of "generation," which the "autobiographer has to the protagonist he creates" (13–14).

In his interpretation of the scene with Trudy, McCann invoked the universal story of the Edenic fall without denying or affirming the local American version others insisted upon. With Trudy Nick deliberately enjoys a prelapsarian "sexuality without inhibition or shame," embracing the "world his father warned against." But then in the romantic outrage of his fantasy, he betrays the idyllic scene and reveals the power of his father's sentimentalized law, and falls. Earlier, McCann had stated that in one sense Nick "admits" the past, but in another "he falls into it, falling into himself" (12). This Edenic scene, then, becomes the story in little, in that the fall was a fall into history, into time.

When Nick returns to the present, McCann insisted that, even with Nick's son, there will be a "cycle without release." To deny as much would be dishonest and to violate the meaning of the myth that informs the story. But if in Adam's fall we sinnèd all, it was a necessary and "fortunate fall." Thus McCann returned to his conception of Nick as a writer, one who "has begun, by rehearsal, to write the story we have read." Still noncommittal, still, as it were, with his first draft, Nick "agrees to 'visit' the tomb of the father, but not to 'pray'" (16–17).

This essay on the last of the *Winner Take Nothing* stories clearly calls for a reconsideration not only of "Fathers and Sons" but also of the other late stories in the last of Hemingway's original collections.

Works Cited

PRIMARY

Ernest Hemingway: Selected Letters, 1917–1961. Ed. Carlos Baker. New York: Scribner's, 1981.

The Short Stories of Ernest Hemingway. New York: Scribner's, 1938, 488–99.

SECONDARY

Baker, Carlos. *Ernest Hemingway: A Life Story.* 1969. New York: Scribner's, 1988.

Benson, Jackson J. *Hemingway: The Writer's Art of Self-Defense.* Minneapolis: U of Minnesota P, 1969.

Boutelle, Ann Edwards. "Hemingway and 'Papa': Killing of the Father in the Nick Adams Fiction." *Journal of Modern Literature* 9 (1981–82): 133–46.

DeFalco, Joseph. *The Hero in Hemingway's Short Stories.* Pittsburgh: U of Pittsburgh P, 1963.

Fiedler, Leslie. *Love and Death in the American Novel.* Cleveland: World, 1962.

Fleming, Robert E. "Hemingway's Treatment of Suicide: 'Fathers and Sons' and *For Whom the Bell Tolls.*" *Arizona Quarterly* 33 (Summer 1977): 121–32.

Flora, Joseph M. *Hemingway's Nick Adams.* Baton Rouge: Louisiana State UP, 1982.

Grebstein, Sheldon N. *Hemingway's Craft.* Carbondale: Southern Illinois UP, 1973.

Grimes, Larry. *The Religious Design of Hemingway's Early Fiction.* Ann Arbor: UMI Research, 1985.

Hemingway, Carol. "The Eleven O'Clock Mail Plane." *Tabula* (Apr. 1930): 17.

McCann, Richard. "To Embrace or Kill: 'Fathers and Sons.'" *Iowa Journal of Literary Studies* 3 (1985): 11–18.

Smith, Paul. "The Tenth Indian and the Thing Left Out." *Ernest Hemingway: The Writer in Context.* Ed. James Nagel. Madison: U of Wisconsin P, 1984.

St. John, Donald. "Hemingway and Prudence." *Connecticut Review* 5 (Apr. 1972): 78–84.

Wilkinson, Myler. *Hemingway and Turgenev: The Nature of Literary Influence*. Ann Arbor: UMI Research, 1986.

Williams, Wirt. *The Tragic Art of Ernest Hemingway*. Baton Rouge: Louisiana State UP, 1981.

Young, Philip. " 'Big World Out There': The Nick Adams Stories.' *Novel* 6 (Fall 1972): 5–19.

The Fifth Column and the First Forty-nine Stories
(October 1938)

45

The Capital of the World

Composition History (November 1935-February 1936)

Between the publication of *Winner Take Nothing* in the fall of 1933 and the winter of 1935, Hemingway either turned to longer fiction than the short story or what he began as a short story became, in spite of himself, a novel. From the first safari in November 1933 came *Green Hills of Africa*, which even a year later he was considering as a long story to open his next collection, "The First Fifty-Four Stories" (Baker 268). And when "One Trip Across" (*Cosmopolitan*, April 1934) was followed by "The Tradesman's Return" (*Esquire*, February 1936), it was clear that the Harry Morgan stories were becoming early chapters in a novel—the latter was probably the story he said he would begin the next day in a letter of 16 November 1934 (*Letters* 410).

Whether Hemingway was tiring of doing "pieces," as he called them, for *Esquire*—he had written twenty-three in two years and would write only two more or found in his African and Gulf Stream experiences new reasons to return to the story form, it was the writing of "The Capital of the World" that signaled his return to short fiction. In December 1935 he wrote to Dos Passos that he had "written two stories, had just finished one ['The Tradesman's Return'] and saw my next three months clear" (*Letters* 426–27). The letter indicates that he was reluctant to send it to *Esquire* as part of his agreement to write twelve pieces a year, for *Cosmopolitan* was paying more, but it would at least hold them off.

The second "story" was the manuscript of "The Capital of the World" (KL/EH 311). When the editor of *Cosmopolitan* came to Key West in late March 1936, Hemingway offered him the story and he turned it down; whereupon Hemingway wrote to Arnold Gingrich promising the story he had finished two months before, in early February, and which "Pauline is typing while I write this" (*Letters* 441, 5 April 1936). Hemingway may have sent the original of that typescript; two other carbons exist, one of which was used as setting copy for *The First Forty-nine* (KL/EH 312, 313).

The differences between the first manuscript (311) and the setting-copy typescript show significant revisions. The manuscript was begun as a typescript but continued in pencil after page 4, suggesting an earlier draft copied out for review in late March. Between then and Pauline's typed version, several passages were added and the ending revised. Hemingway added the last two sentences of the description of the banderillero (*Stories* 41 ["His legs were . . . out of it"]); all but the first sentence on the three waiters (*Stories* 41 ["It was the rule . . . table for him"]); the long paragraph describing the cowardly matador's recollection of the times when he fought without fear (*Stories* 43–44 ["He could remember . . . that laughed at him"]); and several lines adding details to the two priests' pastoral complaints (*Stories* 44–45).

Finally, as is often the case, Hemingway's ending was first sketched and later revised. In the manuscript the last two paragraphs began: "The boy Paco had never known about any of this I which raises the question of when is death a misfortune I nor about what all these people would be doing on the next day and on other days to come. He had not even had time to be disappointed in the Garbo picture which disappointed all Madrid for a week." Then two sentences were written below this passage and arrowed up to precede the final sentence: "He died, as the Spanish phrase has it, full of illusions. He had not had time to lose any of them, nor even, at the end, to complete the act of contrition" (KL/EH 311). An interesting sequence of revisions: the sense that Paco had died "full of illusions" was an afterthought, and although it found its way into the ending, it was placed in a penultimate position to his original ironic note that Paco had missed a disappointing movie.

Publication History (June 1936; October 1938)

When Hemingway finally sent the story off to Arnold Gingrich in early April 1936, he gave him permission to clean up the text and suggested a variety of titles: "Outside the Ring; The Start of the Season; The Capitol [*sic*] of Illusion; A Boy named Paco—too easy; To Empty Stands; The Judgment of Difference?; The Sub-Novice Class" (*Letters* 441).

The story was published in the June 1936 issue of *Esquire* as "The Horns of the Bull"—a title not much better than some of the others. The final one was entered in pencil on the typescript used for setting copy for *The First Forty-nine,* published in October 1938.

Sources and Influences

In the winter of 1935–36, when Hemingway returned to writing stories that would *stay* short, he was clearly attempting something new, at least for him. Each of the three stories finished by the spring of 1936 is structured about shifting points of view, as in "The Short Happy Life," or radical shifts from the present to the past in the central character's mind, as in "The

Snows." "The Capital of the World" similarly shifts the narrative away from the central story of Paco's tragedy to the bullfighters, priests, and waiters.

Joseph DeFalco qualified the analogy with Nick in "The Killers" and "The Battler" by noting that in this story the innocent central figure facing a threshold experience "operates on the periphery and is exposed to contingent forces" (92). That, of course, was Hemingway's intention, and he had any number of literary models by 1936, including some of his own. The two stories he had completed that became the early chapters of *To Have and Have Not* would juxtapose "contingent forces" even more deliberately. And, as Bernard Oldsey has noted, that juxtaposition was familiar in Joyce's *Ulysses* and in the *U. S. A.* trilogy John Dos Passos was completing at the time (104).

In spite of that literary tradition, Oldsey contends that Hemingway's structural technique owes something to cinematic "cross-cutting" and, more importantly, to Greta Garbo's "second talking film" of 1932, *Grand Hotel* (105). That may be so, but since Hemingway had been so indebted to Joyce before this and was so much in competition with Dos Passos in the mid-1930s, and, not incidentally, was contemptuous of the movies, it seems more sensible to locate his sources in literature.

Which is not to say that events in his own life may not have suggested the subject of his story. The question he raised and deleted in his manuscript, "When is death a misfortune?" is one he was deeply moved by in March 1935 when he wrote to comfort Gerald and Sara Murphy over the loss of their son Baoth: "I know that anyone who dies young after a happy childhood . . . has won a great victory . . . with his world all intact and the death only an accident" (*Letters* 412). With this story of an accidental death of an innocent, and with "The Short Happy Life" and "The Snows of Kilimanjaro" soon to come, the idea of a fortunate death was much on his mind.

Critical Studies

The earliest critical study of "The Capital of the World" found the story's scene thick with allusions to Christ and attendant figures or events—from the bullfighting pass named for Saint Veronica, as Hemingway noted in *Death in the Afternoon,* to Eugene O'Neill's Anna Christie, who "derives her name from a medieval prayer, *Anima Christi*," and the various bullfighters who imitate or fail to follow aspects of Christ's Passion—all finding a center in Paco. Named with the diminutive of Francisco, he "dies a Christ-figure," and just as the people of Madrid "fail to recognize Christ in Anna," so they fail to "see Him in Paco" (McAleer 2–4). So thoroughly explained with one fixed idea, the story seems simple—and hardly worth reading.

There were two studies in 1963—Joseph DeFalco's chapter and Stephen Reid's article—each of which considered the story from a complex theoretical position, which to this day has been ignored or simply dismissed. DeFalco's interpretation followed the archetypal pattern of a "threshold experience," in which Paco is the typical pastoral hero. Fatherless, he arrives from the humble and pure provinces in pursuit of his "great fantasy," to become a bullfighter. The exemplar of the natural man, filled with nearly universal love for his sisters, his work, his ideal, and Madrid (his Jerusalem), he goes without fear or disillusion to his "accidental" crucifixion and, "in a sense, . . . dies for all mankind" (91–96). Enrique, the dishwasher, takes the role of the "knowing one," both warning the innocent Paco and participating in his fatal, albeit partial, recognition. And when life empties from Paco like "dirty water . . . from a bathtub" (*Stories* 50), Paco is cleansed of the "chthonic aspects of mortality" (97).

DeFalco drew on the Christian allusions McAleer noted, but he attempted to give them some order and meaning within this narrative which, as he remarks, is "in a sense an *imitatio Christi*" (93). But it is that qualifying phrase that begs the large question: In what sense? Paco is not Christ or even Christ-like, even with his innocence and obscure paternity; his death is "accidental," and only in his "great fantasy" to become a bullfighter could he be imagined to have died "for all mankind," represented by Madrid.

In the same year Stephen Reid found psychological referents in many of those aspects of the story that DeFalco had read as an archetypal conflict. Hemingway wrote that Paco died, "as the Spanish phrase has it, full of illusions" (*Stories* 51). Reid, unlike other critics, tried to identify those illusions and argued that he died "*because* of his illusions" (37). Those illusions, he stated, are centered in bullfighting. The characters who are *dis*illusioned are those, like the three matadors, who are either ambivalent, cowardly, or physically inadequate, or, like the anarchic waiter, misconstrue an analogy between bullfighting and the church (38). Reid held that Paco's illusion, his utter fearlessness in the face of an imagined bull, derives from his fatherlessness. Hemingway's statement that Paco is distinct from all the other Pacos of Madrid in that he "had no father to forgive him, nor anything for the father to forgive" (*Stories* 38), is inverted to read that "This Paco had nothing for the father to forgive *because* he had no father" (Reid 41–42). This much depends on the psychological analogy between, as Reid has it, "an acting-out, in a rigidly controlled, highly stylized form, of Oedipal conflicts," in which the son is identified with the matador, the father with the bull, and the mother's love with the prize for the conflict (37).

Reid's interpretation includes the female figures of the story as variants of the mother: the owner of the pension Luarca, older, chaste (pace the bolster), and maternal; the sister, a "mother tempted"; and Anna Christie, enacted by Greta Garbo, the whore, or "mother fallen" (41).

Finally, the dishwasher Enrique, in acting out the role of the bull and presumably of the father, "kills Paco" in an "accident" that, Reid believed, "we are to take . . . as a meaningful happening." Enrique's motive to disillusion Paco—"all I wanted was to show the danger" (*Stories* 49)— associates him with all the other disillusioned of Madrid who, if they do not teach him a fatal lesson, stand as exemplars of what he must learn.

Reid concluded that the story "is a fable," and with its number and variety of characters, all more or less emblematic and its title universalizing the story's irony, it has some fabulous qualities. But what is its "moral": Reid's rather timid conclusion that "the Oedipal conflicts are at the center of all our lives" (43), or something more local, more Spanish, something arising from the priest's remark before Paco's mock battle, "Madrid kills Spain" (*Stories* 45)? If Madrid, with its almost allegorical procession of characters displaying disillusionment in listless irony or passionate cynicism, has killed the pastoral innocence of provincial Spain, is Paco's death not a peripheral accident but central to a cultural tragedy as profoundly Spanish as the informing ritual of the bullfight? Put another way, if the story may be moralized, does the tragedy rest in the fact that Paco died "full of illusions," or that all the others gathered about but unaware of his death will die empty of illusions? Hemingway raised this question earlier in *The Sun Also Rises* with Jake Barnes's conversation with the waiter after the death of Vicente Girones—"All for morning fun. Es muy flamenco," the waiter says (198). Although Reid's article did not quite resolve the issue, it is valuable for presenting it once again.

Through the next two decades comments on the story were brief and often introduced as transitions to the two African stories. Earl Rovit suggested that Paco "sacrifices himself with the same kind of naive idealism" that motivates Emilio, the young revolutionary in *To Have and Have Not,* and this sacrifice marks a movement in Hemingway's fiction away from the disengaged stance of Frederic Henry's "separate peace" (72). Richard Peterson, in questioning the legitimacy of Hemingway's "objective" and "disciplined" tone in this story and others, found the mood of "outrage and bitterness" unjustified: Paco's death is pathetic and foolish, and so "why should others not be interested in their own affairs" (75)? Sheldon Grebstein was more sympathetic in his brief consideration of the story's alternation of sparse dialogue and narrative passages encircling the central event. The effect "verges on the blackest of dark comedy" (103) and reaches its height in Paco's partial absolution of Enrique, "Don't worry. . . . But bring the doctor" (*Stories* 49).

The most recent, and only extensive, commentary since the early 1960s is Bernard Oldsey's essay at "analysis . . . along the interconnected lines of theme, technique, and social commentary" (103). His consideration of the cinematographic technique of "cross-cutting" and its literary antecedents is noted above. A sense of Spanish society led him to reduce Reid's classification of the women in the story, close to Robert Graves's "triple goddess," to two derived from "the emphasis placed on the concepts of virginity and whoredom in a country like Spain, a center of Mariolatry . . .: the good mother, sister, wife; and then all the rest." He dismissed Reid's interpretation as "presumptive," presumably on the evidence that Paco is "one of the most scorned objects in Spain, 'un hio de puta,' or whoreson" (106), although that fact is not inconsistent with Reid's model. Finally he noted that Hemingway's final title was added after the outbreak of the Spanish Civil War in 1936, by which time Madrid had "become something of a capital of the world" and the "center of conflict between fascist and anti-fascist forces" (107). With that note one might reconsider the details of the story as prophetic of the civil tragedy Spain was ineluctably approaching when Hemingway first wrote it.

The theme of this "fictive anatomy of illusion-disillusion" seemed for Oldsey to lie between the two extremes and is figured in the characters who "find a good balance between the two"—the bolstered woman who owns the pension Luarca and, perhaps, the more tolerant middle-aged waiter (108). That accomodation through the resignation of the one and the tolerance of the other may well bear the meaning of this story, but it offers only a momentary surcease and does not finally speak to the story's urgent question.

Works Cited

PRIMARY

Ernest Hemingway: Selected Letters, 1917–1961. Ed. Carlos Baker. New York: Scribner's, 1981.

The Short Stories of Ernest Hemingway. New York: Scribner's, 1938, 38–51.

SECONDARY

Baker, Carlos. *Ernest Hemingway: A Life Story.* 1969. New York: Scribner's, 1988.

DeFalco, Joseph. *The Hero in Hemingway's Short Stories.* Pittsburgh: U of Pittsburgh P, 1963.

Grebstein, Sheldon N. *Hemingway's Craft.* Carbondale: Southern Illinois UP, 1973.

McAleer, John. "Christ Symbolism in Hemingway's 'The Capital of the World.' " *English Record* 12 (Spring 1961): 2–4.

Oldsey, Bernard. "*El Pueblo Español:* 'The Capital of the World.' " *Studies in American Fiction* 13 (1985): 103–10.

Peterson, Richard K. *Hemingway: Direct and Oblique.* The Hague: Mouton, 1969.

Reid, Stephen. "The Oedipal Pattern in Hemingway's 'The Capital of the World.' " *Literature and Psychology* 13 (Spring 1963): 37–43.

Rovit, Earl. *Ernest Hemingway.* Boston: Twayne, 1963.

46
The Short Happy Life of Francis Macomber

Composition History (November 1934–April 1936)

The four extant manuscripts of "The Short Happy Life of Francis Macomber" include only Hemingway's first fragmentary attempts to begin the story and the typescripts he submitted as setting copy for publication in *Cosmopolitan* in September 1936 and again two years later to Scribner's for *The Fifth Column and the First Forty-Nine Stories*. With evidence missing for the usual two intermediate stages in the story's composition—the holograph manuscript and a Hemingway typescript—nothing final may be said of the composition of this story. And, for a story as unusual in its narrative strategy, that missing record is particularly unfortunate.

The critical controversy over Mrs. Macomber's motives at the end of the story has, however, occasioned some close and intelligent analysis of the remaining manuscripts. Bernard Oldsey, in a sensitive study, related the two early fragments (KL/EH 689, 690, untitled four- and five-page manuscripts) to the published story (224–34). Each fragment is a first-person narrative in the voice of an admiring assistant introducing the white hunter, "O.M.," or old man, who is "gone about" Dorothy, the wife of his client, Denny Macomber. The hunter, a more paunchy and raunchy original for Robert Wilson, is of less concern than the Macombers: Dorothy has the predatory qualities of the later Margot, and when her target is game she "could hit them fine and miss them just as well and didn't know why she did either"; Denny, however, is a fine marksman; but after demonstrating his skill, is curiously thoughtful as they sit around the campfire in the evening (Oldsey 225–28). Something of the realized story is planted in these fragments; but as Oldsey suggests, so are several other possible denouements.

These fragments are undated, but the arguments of those critics who find the immediate source for the story in the period from the Hemingways' safari in the early months of 1934 and the writing of *Green Hills of Africa* through the fall of that year suggest a possible early date. The acronym "O.M." echoes those in *Green Hills* as a descriptive passage on the flight of flamingoes in the first fragment recalls others in the African book. Hemingway wrote to Arnold Gingrich on 16 November 1934 that he had "finished the long book. . . . Going to start a story tomorrow" (*Letters* 410); and within a week his safari trophies arrived from the New York taxidermist. So in November 1934 he might have used some of the impulse to write fiction he claimed he suppressed in the writing of *Green Hills,* at least, to begin a story with a similar setting and cast.

But almost immediately his attention was turned away: a trip to Piggott, a recurrence of African dysentery, fishing at Key West and Bimini, the stories that became *To Have and Have Not,* and then the furious hurricane in the fall of 1935 (Carlos Baker 268–84). In the last three months of 1935, the reviewers almost unanimously answered Hemingway's question whether it was possible to write "an absolutely true book to . . . compete with a work of the imagination" with a resounding negative (Meyers, *Hemingway: Critical Heritage* 210–22). That rejection of the experiment Hemingway intended in *Green Hills* may have returned Hemingway to a more obviously fictional version of his African experiences and led to the writing of the lost holograph and typescript versions of the story. In any case, by 9 April 1936, he wrote to Max Perkins that he had finished "day before yest. . . . a very exciting story about Africa which I think I can publish in Cosmopolitan"(*Letters* 442).

The two typescripts used as setting copies are, in fact, one: the first is the original typescript and the second, KL/EH 691, is a carbon. John Howell and Charles Lawler, in a detailed study of the original used as setting copy for the *Cosmopolitan* version (in the Morris Library of Southern Illinois University), noted that "eight passages, three which alluded to sex and five which contained questionable language," caught the eye of the editors as they tried to shape "the masculine story into something fit for a special female magazine"; they allowed "hell," "four-letter man," "five-letter woman," "cuckoldry," and "loss of virginity" but drew the line at "bitch," "bitchery," and "bastard" (229–33).

Howell and Lawler note that the title was apparently added in a type different from the story's just before it was submitted to *Cosmopolitan* (217); the typescript's carbon (to which they did not have access) was titled in pencil when it was submitted to Scribners and used as setting copy for the *First Forty-nine* publication. It bears a variety of pencil revisions and what Leger Brosnahan has demonstrated is an accidental deletion of some 100 words. Mishandling the carbon and carbon copy, Hemingway apparently left some scratched lines on the carbon copy that the Scribner's editor took for cancelations and so red-penciled the passage (Brosnahan 329–30). The passage occurs just before the hunters enter the bush after the wounded lion (*Stories* 16–17; the italicized passages were retained):

> *There was dark blood on the short grass that the gun bearers pointed out with grass stems,* and as they followed this toward the swale of

high grass/*that ran away behind the river bank trees,*/the gun bearers on each side of the trail pointing each shot[?] with their grass stems, they found a trail of splatters of light red frothy blood that led into the high grass.

"It's as I said," said Wilson, looking over the high grass. "You gut shot him and you hit him forward./There's the dark and light blood./He may be dead in there now, or he may be lying doggo waiting for us." He took out his tobacco pouch and filled a pipe. (KL/EH 691)

This apparently accidental deletion leaves a rather ragged cut, with an awkward sentence and a curious situation in which the lion has taken cover in the *short grass*.

When Hemingway settled on his title in April 1936, he selected it from two lists: one of sixteen (reprinted in Oldsey 232–33 from KL/EH 692) and another of ten in a "List for Francis Macomber" (reprinted in Howell and Lawler 217–18). The KL/EH 692 list includes:

> A Marriage Has Been Arranged
> The Coming Man
> The New Man
> The Short Life of Francis Macomber
> The End of a Marriage
> Marriage is a Dangerous Game
> The More Dangerous Game
> A Marriage Has Been Terminated
> The Ruling Classes
> The Fear of Courage
> Brief Mastery
> The Master Passion
> The Cult of Violence
> The Struggle for Power
> Marriage is a Bond
> Through Darkest Marriage

Oldsey considers these titles in the context of Hemingway's usual practice and applauded his rejection of the allusions to "a cheap thriller of his day" with "The More Dangerous Game" and to the common phrase "through darkest Africa" with the last on the list (233). One would add that six of the titles directly, and several others indirectly, refer to an unstable marriage, while at least two ("The Ruling Classes" and "The Struggle for Power") suggest that Hemingway had somewhere in mind the notion of class distinctions that later critics have noticed.

The "List for Francis Macomber" in Howell and Lawler adds the final title and nine others:

Than a Dead Lion
The Manner of the Accident
Fear's End
The Short Happy Life of Francis Macomber
The Tragic Safari
The Lion's Portion
Mr. and Mrs. Macomber
The Macombers
The Macomber Safari
The Safari of Francis Macomber

As Howell and Lawler suggested, the first contradicts the sense of Macomber's "heroic growth" with the allusion to Ecclesiastes 9:4 "a living dog is better than a dead lion," and the second, taken from Wilson's directive at the end of the story, indicates Hemingway's initial sense of the "accident" as the crux of the story (218, 221).

"The Short Happy Life," like "A Clean, Well-Lighted Place," has drawn critical attention to its manuscripts largely because of some critical disagreement over a crucial matter of interpretation. But like Francis Macomber, those manuscripts will have only this brief a life until the intermediate manuscripts come to light.

Publication History (September 1936; October 1938)

In the first week of April 1936, Hemingway had begun negotiations with Harry Burton, *Cosmopolitan*'s editor, for the publication of "The Short Happy Life" and referred to it in a letter to Perkins with the twenty-seventh possible title, "A Budding Friendship"—one he hoped to God he could beat and did (*Letters* 442, 444). In the letter of 9 April he raised the question with Perkins of the possibility of a collection including his three previous volumes and five new stories ("One Trip Across," "The Tradesman's Return," "The Capital of the World," and the two African stories) or a fourth "separate book" of those five and some others. By 11 July, however, he had decided on a "Key West-Havana novel [*To Have and Have Not*] of which One Trip Across and The Tradesman's Return were a part," and he had sent Perkins typescripts of both African stories (*Letters* 442–43, 447–48).

Thomas Jackson's summary review of the editorial changes in the *Cosmopolitan* typescript has been superseded by Howell and Lawler's definitive study of its first publication. By the time Hemingway submitted the carbon of the typescript to Scribner's, Perkins had become inured to Hemingway's inflammatory language that so disturbed *Cosmopolitan*'s editors, and he published the story without editorial question in *The First Forty-nine* of 1938.

Sources and Influences

It is a commonplace that by the mid-1930s Hemingway's public image had begun to dominate studies of his fiction, so it is little wonder that autobiographical sources for his fiction outweigh literary antecedents in the criticism of his stories in that period. This, in spite of R. S. Crane's passing comment on "a long literary tradition of characters like Macomber, cuckolds in subjection to their wives who are also . . . cowards." Comic figures in the nineteenth century, these characters "have often been given the status of protagonists in serious plots" in the twentieth and allowed a "certain impression of nobility . . . by making them unexpectedly act or speak like heroes" (321–22).

Philip Young was the first to suggest that "The Short Happy Life" was a reworking of Stephen Crane's "study of cowardice and heroism" in *The Red Badge of Courage* (198). William Bache followed this suggestion somewhat further to notice that both Henry Fleming and Macomber are transformed "without much apparent motivation . . . from being a frightened rabbit to . . . a fighting wildcat," both receive head wounds, red badges of courage; and that both stories end on a "false high note": "Henry's assurance will not last" and Macomber's "previous life is a categoric denial" of the possibility of his redemption (83–84).

Robert Stephens's consideration of the Somali proverb, "A brave man is always frightened three times by a lion" (*Stories* 11) as a part of the "male-cult world of Somali gunbearers and British professional hunters," led him to review the earlier accounts of hunting in Africa by Stewart Edward White, which Hemingway had read. In White's *The Land of Footprints* (1912) Stephens finds close analogues with the hunter's "code of honor" in confronting a wounded lion, its mystical aura, and other matters like the question of the ethics of whipping rather than fining the natives, and those analogues are persuasive ("Macomber" 139).

Harbour Winn argued that Hemingway's reading in his early Paris years suggests a similarity between both African stories and Leo Tolstoy's "The Death of Ivan Illich." For Macomber the similarities with Illich lie in their loveless marriages to selfish and materialistic wives and in the moments before their deaths when "both men live more intensely than ever before and experience a sense of birth or rebirth in the moment of death" (452).

Most recently, Mark Spilka's articles on Victorian sources for Hemingway's fiction have found intriguing parallels in the fiction of Captain Frederick Marryat with "The Short Happy Life." It is likely that Hemingway read

Marryat in his impressionable school years, and it is certain that he was slow to outgrow it. Spilka noted that Robert Wilson's embarrassed quotation of the talismanic line from Shakespeare, "By my troth, I care not; a man can die but once; we owe God a death" (*Stories* 32), is cited or paraphrased no less than three times in Marryat's *Percival Keene,* setting it in Hemingway's memory several years before he heard the phrase from Chink Dorman-Smith. Beyond that, he found in that novel incidents of a deliberately "accidental" gunshot to the head, comic parallels in a cowardly response to a charging cow, as well as long disquisitions on the kinds of courage in Marryat's *King's Own* ("Source for Macomber" 30–35).

When Edmund Wilson first reviewed *Green Hills of Africa* in December 1935, he deplored the fact that "something frightful seems to happen to Hemingway as soon as he begins to write in the first person. In his fiction, the conflicting elements of his personality, the emotional situations which obsess him, are externalized and objectified; and the result is an art which is severe, intense, and deeply serious." Three years later when he remarked on "The Short Happy Life," he found it "as good as 'Green Hills of Africa' was bad," for it concerns a theme implicit in the earlier book but "disengages and fully develops this theme" (Meyers, *Critical Heritage,* 218, 268)

Wilson never identified that theme, but in the late 1960s four critics, Robert Lewis, John Howell, Sheridan Baker, and Robert Stephens drew the numerous connections between the account of the safari and the short story, and Stephens went further with similarities between the story and the *Esquire* articles of 1935 (*Hemingway's Nonfiction* 268–73). The other three all drew on the implicit congruency between the triangles in *Green Hills* (Hemingway, "Pop" the hunter or Philip Percival, P.O.M. or Pauline Hemingway) and the story (Francis, Wilson, and Margot). And Sheridan Baker noted the similarity between Hemingway's transcribed name "Bwana M'Kumba" and Macomber (101). Howell and Baker both cited the event in *Green Hills* when Hemingway "wounds a buffalo that escapes into high grass, thus forcing him and Phillip to move in after it," while the tracker (with "P.O.M.'s Mannlicher") and Pauline were told to remain behind. When Pauline and the tracker inadvertently follow, and Hemingway and the hunter hear a noise, Percival was furious and Hemingway was "spooked" (Howell, "Macomber Case" 171–72; *Green Hills* 113–16).

Robert Lewis, however, was the first and most thorough in exploring the relationship between the triangles implicit in *Green Hills* and explicit in the story. If Hemingway transmuted his own dysentery into Harry's gangrenous leg in "The Snows of Kilimanjaro," so may he have turned Poor Old Mama's deep affection for Pop into the adultery of "The Short Happy Life" (80). Lewis's argument, sensibly qualified, seems most persuasive: thinking back on the safari, Pauline noted sadly that her memory of Pop was fading; Hemingway said, "I can remember him, . . . I'll write you a piece some time and put him in." And, as Lewis remarked, "Hemingway fulfilled his promise in the 'Macomber' story" (79–81; *Green Hills* 295).

Critics like Robert Lewis, interested in the literary biography of the story, were soon overwhelmed by those interested only in biographical sources who took their cue from Hemingway's bristling preface for a proposed "school" collection of his stories, "The Art of the Short Story." In this essay, now maudlin and self-pitying, now combative and reacting to an adrenalin rush of the true "gen," he tells us that he knew the woman of the story, and although she was not "my dish, not my pigeon, not my cup of tea, . . . I was her all of the above" (93). He then characterizes her husband as a "nice jerk"—a better "four-letter" word than shit—the White Hunter as "his best friend," and Margot as clearly *not* one of those "bitches" who shot their husbands accidentally (93–95).

Hemingway's two latest biographers, Jeffrey Meyers and Kenneth Lynn, have searched for the story's origin. Meyers found his in British Colonial Office Papers and a "scandalous case of adultery and suicide" involving John Henry Patterson and Mr. and Mrs. Audley James Blyth. For Meyers the buried account is "significant not only for the way it influenced Hemingway but for the way he changed it." Those changes—the hunter from a villain to a hero, the negative consequences of cuckoldry to positive, the husband from a suicide to a victim of murder—raise questions about what counted for Meyers as "significant" (267–73).

Kenneth Lynn, on the other hand, was as much convinced that Margot, except for her hair and age, is the "spitting image of Jane Mason," and that Hemingway affirmed in "The Art of the Short Story"—"without mentioning her name"—that "Jane had indeed been the model for Margot" (432).

Each biographer, with the authority of some psychoanalytic displacement, depended on what Hemingway does *not* mention and what he *significantly* changes in the two sources of the story. And each cited the Jackson Burke interview of 1953 in which Hemingway affirmed that Margot deliberately murdered Francis for his cowardice (7). Meyers used it to prove the charge of murder, and Lynn to suggest that Hemingway, once again, wrote better and differently than he knew (Meyers 273, Lynn 432). With these summations, the crucial question of the story is returned to the critical jury to consider the persuasiveness, even the legitimacy, of autobiographical and biographical evidence.

Critical Studies

On New Year's Day 1980, William White, the master bibliographer of Hemingway studies, counted 101 entries on "The Short Happy Life," 37 since Jackson Benson's *Critical Essays* only five years earlier; and to that number even a cursory review would add some 20 through 1985, to maintain the story's record as "the most written about of Hemingway's short fiction"—not to say the most formidable for one reviewing that record (35–38).

The very range of that criticism suggests that no stone, animal, gun, gimlet, or word—whether in Swahili or English—has been left unturned, often twice.

Theodore Gaillard has classified the story's "animal menagerie" into those that suggest Macomber's background as a society hunter, those that imply some negative view of his character, and, most important, those that serve as "personified foils with which the main characters are identified and compared" (32). Macomber's moral achievement is marked by the associations in the "transition from 'rabbit' and 'laddybuck' to lion, to bull (with its implications of size and virile strength), and to manhood" (35).

Two critics have remarked on the guns: Jerry Herndon challenged G. B. Harrison's earlier claim that the 6.5 Mannlicher, with a kick "like a peevish camel," was inappropriate for a woman, and with it Margot could not have *intentionally* hit either the buffalo or her husband. Herndon stated that the Mannlicher has a light recoil, but considering Margot's position relative to the others and the buffalo, "her foreshortened view [of] the distance between buffalo and man . . . makes an accidental shooting much more plausible" (291). Robert Fleming, in turn, corrected Hemingway twice on the .505 Gibbs with a "muzzle velocity of two tons" (*Stories* 21): it has "a muzzle *energy* of . . . more than three tons"—this to mark Hemingway "as an amateur among professional guides and hunters" and to add to the recent resistance to "the view of Hemingway as a realist or naturalist" (Item 17).

Then there are the notes on specific aspects of language. Joseph Harkey, with assistance from the linguist Elsa Liner, opened up some ironies in the story. " 'Macomber' is a *near* phonetic equivalent of the Swahili word *mkubwa* [and] *very close* phonetically to Hemingway's spelling of the word *(M'Kumba)*" in *Green Hills*. The Swahili word means "leader, manager, superior, or employer; when combined with *bwana,* it means 'sir' with a high degree of respect." Furthermore, "Africans use the compound *bwana mkubwa* humorously at times, to suggest the absence of masterly qualities" (346–47). Although the compound does not appear in the story, Hemingway used it at least once in *Green Hills* to deflate his "long-winded and rather pompous discourse on American fiction," and it may be of some note that the term is used ironically by his wife (*Green Hills* 29; Harkey 347). Harkey's interpretive point is that Macomber's transformation is from one who deserves the ironic associations of the title to one who finally deserves its original and honorable implications.

Other notes have filled in the sexual or scatalogical blanks: C. Harold Hurley pointed to Robert Wilson's description of his night's sleep as "topping" (*Stories* 23), implying copulation, which Macomber recognizes (9). All agree that a five-letter woman is a "bitch"; but J. F. Kobler, citing the OED and dictionaries of slang, decided on "shit" for the four-letter man ("Francis Macomber" 296); while John McKenna, drawing on Carlos Baker's sources, argued for "jerk" ("Macomber" 73). Perhaps, but j-e-r-k hardly needs so coy a counting, whereas. . . .

These articles have been summarized partly because their specific concerns are in most cases tangential to the one issue that has so dominated critical commentaries on the story: whether Margot Macomber deliberately murdered her husband or shot him accidentally while aiming "at the buffalo" (*Stories* 36). Some critics find a "double-barrelled" resolution in that she *consciously* shot at the buffalo and *unconsciously* at her husband, and there are even a few who hold that since the question is unanswerable she did both. However the issue may be resolved in the future, it is clear that Hemingway's ambivalent ending—like the contradictory dialogues in "A Clean, Well-Lighted Place"— have engendered all but a few of the many commentaries on this story.

Until the mid-1950s, nearly every critic followed Edmund Wilson's assumption in 1939 that Margot shot her husband when and because he was about to save his soul (Meyers, *Critical Heritage* 312). Robert Holland has conveniently summarized the various charges of murder through the witness of Ray B. West, Philip Young, Carlos Baker, John Killinger, Leslie Fiedler, Joseph DeFalco, Theodore Bardacke, and André Maurois—an impressive jury rendering unanimous verdicts between 1939 and 1963 (171–73). One tentative exception in these early years was R. S. Crane's (published first in 1949, then more widely in 1957). With little love for Hemingway, he said that if he "meant to leave us in doubt whether the killing was accident or murder . . ., then Hemingway has bungled his job" (316). And that remark raised the question that has fueled the controversy for some thirty years since 1955—what evidence does one allow for determining what Hemingway meant?

The critical issue might be isolated in the relatively minor question of the significance of Robert Wilson's rather embarrassed quotation of a passage from Shakespeare: " 'By my troth, I care not; a man can die but once; we owe God a death and let it go which way it will, he that dies this year is quit for the next.' Damned fine, eh?" (*Stories* 32). Indeed, it is damned fine from one perspective: the one that cites Hemingway's high school reading of Marryat (Spilka) or his hearing it from Chink Dorman-Smith in 1919 (Carlos Baker 54) and taking it as a maxim irrespective of its context. But it is somewhat less fine if it is situated in the context of Shakespeare's *Henry IV, Part 2* (3. 2). Virgil Hutton first noticed that context in 1964 and that the lines are spoken by Francis Feeble (note the name), a lady's tailor of undetermined sexual preference, and a fool (253–63). He was challenged by John McKenna and Marvin Peterson, arguing that the force of that context is overcome by Hemingway's longtime sense of it, like Wilson's, as "damned fine" (82–85).

The issue of the larger meaning of "The Short Happy Life" is represented in little in the opposed associations with poor Francis Feeble's words: those derived from Hemingway's own sense of them as talismanic, affirmed on several occasions, or those that resonate with the irony of their literary source, one that Hemingway may well have forgotten, or never understood.

The sides of that controversy found their champions in Warren Beck, arguing in 1955 that Mrs. Macomber shot her husband accidentally, and Mark Spilka accusing her with, at least, the dominating motive of murder. Both critics returned to the issue on the occasion of the twenty-first year of publication of *Modern Fiction Studies* in 1975, and Spilka added his latest argument in 1984. Over the thirty years of this debate there have been as many critics joining the two camps, more who believe Margot's aim was accurate, but several who argue as persuasively that she missed her target.

Warren Beck's 1955 article opened the debate with three central assertions that are essentially revisionist in that they contradict earlier and more traditional interpretations:

The first reconsiders Mrs. Macomber's character: she is a more complex figure than a "bitch for the full course," as Hemingway later claimed ("Art of the Short Story" 93), one who had her own "happy moment of a kind, in which she wished and tried to save her husband, with that access of recognition and penitence and hope in which love can renew itself" (Beck 37).

The second challenges Robert Wilson's character and role: rather than being a percipient witness, he "has been seen plain as an uncertain spectator, given to oversimplification, a man of one admirable talent and no other" (35).

The third follows from these two interpretations of the characters to reread the story's ending: Mrs. Macomber did indeed shoot "at the buffalo" and not at her husband, for had "she wanted him dead, she could have left it to the buffalo"; and Wilson, imperceptient to the end, misconstrues her motive and her agony. With this reading, Beck found "The Short Happy Life" a "more profound story, more humane in substance, and a larger and more subtly executed story than Hemingway has been credited with by those who have taken Wilson's word for it" (37).

For all of this essay's complexities and its high praise for the story's potential subtleties, it clearly challenged two traditional assumptions of Hemingway criticism: the canonical views of the irredeemable bitch-wife and the infallible white hunter.

When Mark Spilka first responded in 1960, then again in 1976 and finally in 1984, he did so not only to rebut Beck's interpretation but also to set it in the perspective of the waning years of New Criticism and the growing critical reaction to its methods and assumptions. Beck's misreading of the story, in Spilka's view, was a consequence of a larger failure of the New Critics to attend to that "necessary" style, not only "a characteristic way of arranging experience for aesthetic ends," but also a style that "adapts itself to theme, or to an author's working vision of existence," one that "persists, even in changing aspects, throughout their whole production." Spilka's concept of style is close to Leslie Fiedler's definition of an author's "signature," and it found support in the then recent work of E. D. Hirsch and others. Given a "characteristic way of arranging experience" in Hemingway's "working vision of existence," which "persists . . . throughout [his] whole production" ("Necessary Stylist" 287), there is little chance for a fallible white hunter or bitch with a brief moment of sensitivity and love.

The complexity of the two critics' arguments, the fine points of fictional details upon which they rest, and even the critical fervor—just this side of animosity—in which they are expressed make this sequence of stated positions, rejoinders, and rebuttals too long and intricate for summary here but mark them as essential for an informed reading of the issues of this important story.

Beyond that, the exchange between Warren Beck and Mark Spilka is one of the few in Hemingway criticism that, largely through Spilka's urging, makes explicit the critical assumptions that underlie opposed readings of Hemingway's fiction. At one point in Spilka's 1976 rejoinder he recalled an editor's remark that his disagreement with Beck was "only an honest difference of opinion" (247), a remark that dismissed as trivial most of what scholars and teachers do when they read Hemingway. No, the issue was crucial, then as now, not simply for a resolution of the crux of the story, but more importantly for how we read and interpret any fiction and connect it with our lives.

However much it may seem to oversimplify a complex matter, it may be useful for others to begin with the radical assumptions over which these two critics disagree. Beck, rather ingenuously identifying himself as an impressionist and as slyly suggesting that Hemingway was a more complex writer than he knew, mined the text for contradictions in Robert Wilson's character and vision and Mrs. Macomber's perception of her husband and triggering motive. Although he cited other Hemingway works, he rested his case largely on the evidence of the story as a discrete text. Spilka's contrary reading of the white hunter as both a more accurate witness of the events and a credentialed spokesman for the author and Margot as an irremediable bitch, even for a moment, rests on the evidence for his concept of Hemingway's "necessary style."

It is indeed true that any writer worth reading is valued for some persistent "vision of experience" made manifest in a style, although in this essay Spilka did not reveal the necessary connection between Hemingway's vision and any conventional description of his prose style. But insofar as that construct of a writer's vision, stylistic or otherwise, limits the possibility of our finding complexities in character and narrative, or even, in a sense, restrains the writer from exploring subtleties of personality and experience beyond the purview of that vision, it would seem to limit the value for which it was originally praised.

Beck's interpretation of "The Short Happy Life" is attractive for its suggestion that Hemingway could write a story that transcended the restrictions of a necessary style, while it risks the charge that such a reading is too ingenious, too involuted, too much what we would like Hemingway to have meant in spite of what we suspect that he, in his own impercipience, probably meant.

When Spilka responded to Beck's rebuttal twenty years later, he insisted that the issue was "a question of validation, of how we proceed when honest comprehensive readings cancel each other out" ("Warren Beck" 247). And through the 1960s critics attempted two validations of Spilka's position with evidence drawn from the Macombers' response to the "primitive world" of Africa or from psychoanalytic interpretations.

Arthur Waterman argued that, confronted with that world, Macomber is transformed into a man while Margot "degenerates into an hysterical savage who murders her mate in blind, primitive hate" (Item 2). William Bysshe Stein corrected this ethnocentric notion by condemning "Wilson's principles with the ruthless and selfish philosophy of British imperialism, in particular with the affectation of humanitarian interest in the fate of the regimented natives." Wilson's cuckolding Macomber marks the insulation of his "emotions from man as man," and in disgusting Francis "enables him to conquer his fear," but only for a delusory moment; thus there is a compounded irony: Francis did not attain manhood, and Margot need not have murdered him *or* shot at the buffalo (Item 47).

Joseph DeFalco drew again on the "construct of the nursery drama" in which Wilson assumes the role of an "authority-father figure," Margot that of the "dangerous mother-temptress," and Francis the young hero who must undergo a "trial of learning." His dream of the "the bloody-headed lion" transforms the beast into a "totemistic symbol of both the father-authority" associated with the red-faced Wilson and "the symbol of the [new] self he must become" (203–05). DeFalco suggested that Macomber's near triumph must inevitably fail in an "ideal-less world" inhabited by men like Wilson who have "adjusted" to that world and women like Margot who fear the consequences of that brief victory (206–07).

Beginning with Earl Rovit, whose study appeared with DeFalco's in 1963, critics returned the story's psychological implications to the context of Hemingway's character and career. Rovit found the story marking the moment when Hemingway revoked the identification of disengagement or flight with "heroic nobility," as in *A Farewell to Arms,* and transferred blame from the "impersonal 'world'" to the self-conscious tyro, signalling the first stage in the return to health and creativity," if only to die, as in *To Have and Have Not* and *For Whom the Bell Tolls.* In Hemingway's "fantasy life," such a transition marks a dismissal of the mother and an identification with the father (73–74). A decade later Arthur Waldhorn elaborated on Rovit's suggestion in arguing that the two African stories, both experimental for Hemingway, signal the return of the "adventurer" in *Green Hills* to "his early commitment to art," and to maintaining a "distance from characters whose obsessions reflect his own. . . . [T]heir fears—Macomber's of death and Harry's of unfulfilled promise—are Hemingway's fears." Following the "inexorable logic of his story, compelling each of his heroes to die at the moment of insight," Hemingway paid his debt to art and "may have benefited from the psychological relief of having survived his 'double'" (150–51). A year later H. H. Bell suggested that in obedience both to the hunter's code on wounded animals and Hemingway's code in the story, Wilson perceives Margot as a "wounded lioness in the brush," and he moves in after the death of Macomber to "kill her by killing her spirit" (Item 78). And a decade after that, Gerry Brenner went further to suggest that when mother-Margot is subjected at the end to father-Wilson's withering irony, Hemingway might even have experienced a "paroxysm of pleasure" in restoring his own father's "masculine domination" (147). Validations of a sort, but perhaps not altogether the sort Mark Spilka had in mind.

Since the early 1970s some critics have moderated the murder charge against Margot by disallowing Spilka's delineation of her character and Robert Wilson's. James Gray Watson argued that after the Macombers' "sound basis of union," founded on a "security derived from mutual dependence" and complementary weaknesses, is destroyed at the story's midpoint, Margot's motive is to meet the "higher imperative of the hunt. When she shoots with the 'manly' Mannlicher 'at the buffalo,' she is quite literally bidding to rejoin the society of her hunter-lovers by shooting well, and her primary motive is neither to murder her husband nor to save him but to save herself." Her attempt fails "not because she is a bitch, or even a woman, but because she violates the first principle of the society which she is trying to join" (217–19). Watson's argument rests on a detailed analysis of the role reversal that has as its fulcrum the central passage in which the narrator describes the history of the Macombers' relationship—Francis's early cowardice is reenacted later in Margot's infidelity, for example.

Robert Hellenga admitted the force of Warren Beck's charge against Wilson but turned to consider the ways in which Macomber's "generosity and openness" ennoble him and make Wilson's hunterly maxims irrelevant. However much Hemingway "admired (and preferred) men like Wilson, men who, in a dark and meaningless universe will hold to a heroic code," Macomber is the "more attractive figure than the hard-bitten white hunter. . . . This is not to invalidate Wilson's code; it is to transcend it" (Item 10).

Two articles in 1980–81 will serve as examples of recent modifications and reaffirmations of Spilka's original position. The first was Barbara Lounsberry's precise and pointed listing of instances in which Robert Wilson is not only an uncertain and ambivalent witness, as Warren Beck argued, but also that he is at crucial moments dead wrong "in his first assessments of Macomber's courage, of the significance of the moment of cowardice, and of the nature of [Macomber's] relationship with his wife" (30). So the story becomes a complex weaving of three narratives of education: Francis learns to face death with courage; Margot learns of her husband's transformation; and Wilson learns, as do we, of the "ways of American life and death" (32). Lounsberry's argument depends on her sense of the function of the last scene, to depict the "mutually tainted 'survivors' " continuing in the "pretense of Macomber's accidental death" (32). But the question still abides, for Wilson's willingness to pretend that Macomber's death was an accident is not equivalent in any moral sense to Macomber's suggestion that they ignore the wounded lion earlier, except in one rather interesting way. Macomber does not mean to pretend that the lion has not been hit, he is simply unaware of the consequences, which, when he understands them, make him immediately agree with Wilson; it is *Wilson*'s assumption that Macomber means "to pretend to ourselves that [the lion] hasn't been hit" (*Stories* 18). So it may be that Wilson's pretense at the end of the story is similar only in that it derives from an ignorance of Margot's true motives, in which case one might wonder whether he *has* learned anything equivalent to the short happy education of the Macombers.

If Barbara Lounsberry's article seems about to defect to Warren Beck's side, Bert Bender's in the following year might well be the sort of support that Mark Spilka could do without. Bender began with the sexual allusions in the story's opening dialogue over the drinks—a phallic "gimlet" or a "lemon squash" (*Stories* 3)—to set the conflict in sexual terms: "Margot needs something—to be dominated sexually, physically, psychically; and the quashed Francis is incapable of setting things right." He demonstrated that this "opening volley of off-color puns penetrates the story's heart, where the arts of hunting, story-telling, and love lie grotesquely intertwined" (14–15). It is this texture of "Hemingway's violent sexual allusions" that Macomber must come to learn to complete his education; he must come to recognize the "primitive regenerative power in Hemingway's male world of blood, violence, and sex" (14–18). Bender agreed with Spilka that Margot "might well have unconsciously shot at Francis, . . . but it seems of little consequence"—something with which Spilka might well disagree (18). Citing "what we know of [Hemingway's] style and vision, in general," Bender seems to have been led by Spilka's sense of that vision; but with some reluctance, for his "purpose is not to defend Hemingway's primitive sexist values, but to show how they are embodied in the story from beginning to end" (19). Bender raised at least two questions in his analysis: First, if the "arts of hunting, story-telling, and love are grotesquely intertwined," may we not take that very grotesqueness as proof that Wilson's notion of the art of hunting is irrelevant and the art of love, other than in its "double-cot" sense, is tragically absent? And second, might we not admit that Hemingway, if only in a flash of insight as brief as Macomber's, could have recognized the possibility of a regeneration that transcends primitive, sexist, even puerile attitudes?

Such questions, inadmissable within the boundaries of the convention of Hemingway's vision, serve as initial assumptions for most of those critics who challenge Mark Spilka and agree, by and large, with Warren Beck. There are fewer of them, but their responses are longer, for they seem to assume the burden of proof. All but a few were written in the decade between 1965 to 1975, and they share certain necessary critical strategies. With Beck these critics found Robert Wilson an unreliable witness and Margot Macomber deserving of sympathy, and some seriously questioned Macomber's brief victory over cowardice—most recently John Seydow with a devastating attack on what he cites as Macomber's "spurious masculinity" (39–41). And often these critics sought to answer Spilka's "question of validation" within the contexts of cultural, psychological, or archetypal criticism. But the most interesting difference between them and the "traditionalists"—as they have dubbed them—is their reliance on the detailed analysis of the story's narrative structure, its shifting points of view, and their thematic implications—precisely the strategies of the New Critics Spilka found wanting if not moribund.

Virgil Hutton was first in 1964 to defend Warren Beck's position. For him, Hemingway's portrait of Robert Wilson was an "unrelenting satire of . . . an unwitting hypocrite who harshly judges others on the basis of various false and strict codes that he himself does not follow" (239). To take one example: for a man who carries a double-cot "to accomodate any windfalls" to be repelled by Macomber's innocent but ignorant suggestion they leave the wounded lion in the bush is one thing, but to conceive of his repulsion with the metaphor of having "opened the wrong door in a hotel and seen something shameful" is quite another: either Wilson is a hypocrite or Hemingway has lost his way in the search for an appropriate image. With his rather inflated sense of decorum, Wilson misses the complexities of experience to the very end. "When he says what he does not think—'Of course it's an accident'—he speaks the truth; and his comical British reverence for good form slips out when he asks Margaret, 'Why didn't you poison him? That's what they do in England' " (242–44). Finally, Hutton returned to the crucial question raised by R. S. Crane before the Beck and Spilka confrontation. He argued that Crane's interpretation depends on his (and Spilka's) evaluation of Wilson as Hemingway's moral arbiter as well as his expectation of Macomber's "change from boyish cowardice to heroic manhood" (248). But without these two assumptions, Hutton argued, Crane's criticism of Hemingway's failure to control our estimation of the characters and the tragic valuation of Macomber's short happy life are beside the point.

Robert W. Lewis's interpretation of the story in 1965 should be read with Joseph DeFalco's of 1963. Both draw on psychological and archetypal constructs to arrive at opposing interpretations of the story. Lewis's reading derives from the organizing principle of his study, the persistent juxtaposition in Hemingway's fiction of three informing conceptions of love: the romantic, figured in the story of Tristan and Iseult, demanding an unattainable love; the erotic, realized in sexual desire; and that of agape, found in some sublimated and idealized love, as in Plato (chaps. 1–2). That these three conceptions of love sometimes merge—one diminished or ennobled with another, as the romantic is with the concepts of eros or agape—is obvious and essential in Lewis's interpretation. And with that sense of complexity, he demonstrated how each of the three major characters in the story enacts the conflicts among those conceptions of love: Wilson, the latter-day Tristan who must have a competitive husband to fulfill his drama; Macomber, who discovers the erotic in his final confrontation with the buffalo and, paradoxically, confirms the identification Wilson himself recognizes between them, something close to agape; and Margot, who toys with with erotic infidelity, and both fears and respects, and finally may affirm some conception of a higher love, agape (89–93). A subtle and persuasive reading.

In 1968 Robert Holland wondered at what for him had become an "astounding misreading" among the majority of commentators—he counts ten—with only a "few sensible critiques"—two, to be exact (173). Not wholly unwilling to assume that the majority "scanned the words and heard the Edmund Wilsons and the Bakers," Holland offered three other possible explanations for ignoring the fact that Margot "shot at the buffalo": first, that "the stereotype of the Hemingway Bitch has become a critical commonplace"; second, that under the sway of "new criticism devoted to ambiguities as a virtue in art, the blunt directness of Hemingway may be old-fashioned"; and third, that "critics of the present generation are likely to fall prey to *a priori* judgments based on the Freudian psychology, existentialism, myth, or some other frame of reference" (174–75). Of the three possibilities, it seems that only the first is likely, for those who find complexity in Margot's character arrive at as much ambiguity and irony in the story and often through Freudian or mythic frames of reference—Robert Lewis is but one of them. In fact in the same year John Hill neither exonerated Margot nor denied Wilson's veracity as a witness, but argued that Wilson, believing Macomber's death was accidental, "will not allow an accident to deprive Francis of his rightful victory" (132).

Anne Greco offered the best defense of Margot after Warren Beck's. She rather adroitly answered Wilson's charge against dominating American wives by suggesting that "[p]erhaps it's not the women who pick men they can handle, but the men who pick women that can handle them" (274). She found that Margot speaks at times in support of Francis, and that her "verbal attacks are an attempt to force her husband into recognizing her disgrace so that he might work out some means of atonement. Ironically, by committing adultery, Margot causes Francis to submerge his fear in a hatred that enables him to perform an act of great courage," and at the end "she was consciously trying to save him from a very real danger" (278–79).

To argue against the conventional notion of Hemingway's vision of experience with its domineering women and sharp-eyed hunters demanded a return to the narrative and narration of the story. Jackson Benson held that "Wilson *thinks or chooses to think*" that Margot consciously murdered her husband, and that "masterful stroke" placed the emphasis of the story's ending precisely where it must be, on "the anger of the white hunter who had 'begun to like' Macomber." To have focused on Macomber's "tragic death" or to have unambiguously characterized Margot's grief as genuine would have ended the story in sentiment. With her response "completely overshadowed by the clear power of Wilson's rage," Hemingway places the "theme of the story squarely on Macomber's life, rather than on his death" (147–48).

Not until James Nagel's essay of 1973—rather late in the day—was there a systematic analysis of the story's structure and various points of view. Nagel demonstrated that each of the story's three parts is narrated from a variety of points of view, but in two there is a dominant dramatized narrator. In the first (the afternoon and early evening of the day of the lion hunt), "most of the narration of this section comes from the mind of Robert Wilson." The second (from the night before to the return from the lion hunt) is "told largely from Macomber's point of view." And the third (from the second night through the final day) is "essentially three dimensional and views the action from the viewpoint of each of the three major characters" (21–23). In the first part, then, Macomber's failure is "measured against Wilson's ethic"; while in the second the emphasis is on "the workings of [Macomber's] mind, on his fears, his lack of knowledge and poise," and are measured "against the superior knowledge of the omniscient narrator" (21). At two places in the story a moment of time is "reduplicated" from two points of view: in the second part, from the wounded lion's and Macomber's; and in the third, with its medley of perspectives, at Macomber's death, from his own and the omniscient narrator's. This complex construct of narrative and narration isolates the account of "the role of each major character at the critical moment" with an "objective, omniscient viewpoint [in] one of the few 'reliable' passages in the story" (25–26). Thus, Macomber's death was an accident.

In 1982 Paul Jackson reviewed the revisionists' argument, drawing largely on James Gray Watson and James Nagel's analyses of the story's structure and multiple points of view. With that evidence Jackson considered in detail how the "point of view and distancing of reader from character and character from event . . . provide access to the story" (2). The effect of the entry into the lion's perception is to both distance Macomber from the lion and the reader from Macomber; the effect of the placement of the flashback to Macomber's act of cowardice is to make it seem that, "while it is not a formal interior monologue, [it] functions as the narrative equivalent of one" (6). Although we may judge Wilson by his behavior, "it is the heavy exposure of [his] thoughts that both creates interest in him as a developed character"—more so than either of the Macombers—and also allows us to judge well or ill of him (8). Finally, Margot's "thoughts are mostly denied the reader except by indirection"; most often we are cast in the "spectator's role of watching Margot watching" (11–12). At the end, then, "all the strategies seem designed to increase Margot's isolation, to distance her from her husband and the reader from her. It is the lion hunt all over again. . . . Margot's shooting in every way parallels that of her husband earlier. She shoots, as he did, not so much out of the demands of the situation as she does out of the demands of her own isolation" (14–15).

There is one sign that the controversy between the traditionalists led by Mark Spilka and the revisionists by Warren Beck has ended or, possibly, that all the antagonists lie exhausted on the field. With the exception of Spilka's epilogue to his recent article on the story's sources, no critic other than the biographers has joined either side. A harbinger of this armed truce was evident in the early 1970s in two articles suggesting the issue was irreconcilable. Arnold Davidson rather finely calibrated the distinction between Margot's having "shot" at the buffalo and having "aimed" at it, and then concluded that she shot at "both the buffalo and her husband" in obedience to a "perfect objective correlative for her own mixed feelings" (14–15). Then J. F. Kobler relieved us all with the judgment that with "equal care and artistic skill Hemingway makes 'absolute truth' about the death of Macomber undiscoverable" and dismissed the case ("Short Happy Illusion" 65).

Whether one sides with the traditionalists or the revisionists on this issue, the controversy has been not only the most arousing and the longest but also among the most consequential. Early in the history of Hemingway criticism, R. S. Crane, first and rather distantly, and then Warren Beck and Mark Spilka, with more commitment, raised perhaps the primary issue in Hemingway criticism: whether we can or should consider the evidence of an authorial intention embedded in the general vision of experience we find in his other works, or deny that evidence to allow the possibility of other, perhaps momentary, glances at that experience that are as compelling and as demonstrative of his complex art. One cannot say for sure, but it seems likely that the burgeoning variety and sharpening acuity in the last quarter century of critical studies of not only this story but all of Hemingway might well have been delayed without these critics who took a stand. We are all in their debt.

Works Cited

PRIMARY

"The Art of the Short Story." *Paris Review* 23 (Spring 1981): 85–102.

Ernest Hemingway: Selected Letters, 1917–1961. Ed. Carlos Baker. New York: Scribner's, 1981.

Green Hills of Africa. New York: Scribner's, 1935.

The Short Stories of Ernest Hemingway. New York: Scribner's, 1938, 3–37.

SECONDARY

Bache, William B. "*The Red Badge of Courage* and 'The Short Happy Life of Francis Macomber.'" *Western Humanities Review* 15 (Winter 1961): 83–84.

Baker, Carlos. *Ernest Hemingway: A Life Story*. 1969. New York: Scribner's, 1988.

Baker, Sheridan. *Ernest Hemingway*. New York: Holt, 1967.

Beck, Warren. "The Shorter Happy Life of Mrs. Macomber." *Modern Fiction Studies* 1 (Nov. 1955): 28–37.

―――. "Then and Now—Hemingway." *Modern Fiction Studies* 21 (Autumn 1975): 377–85.

Bell, H. H., Jr. "Hemingway's 'The Short Happy Life of Francis Macomber.'" *Explicator* 32 (May 1974), Item 78.

Bender, Bert. "Margot Macomber's Gimlet." *College Literature* 8 (1981): 12–20.

Benson, Jackson J. *Hemingway: The Writer's Art of Self-Defense*, Minneapolis: U of Minnesota P, 1969.

―――, ed. *The Short Stories of Ernest Hemingway: Critical Essays*. Durham: Duke UP, 1975.

Brenner, Gerry. *Concealments in Hemingway's Fiction*. Columbus: Ohio State UP, 1983.

Brosnahan, Leger. "A Lost Passage from Hemingway's 'Macomber.'" *Studies in Bibliography* 39 (1986): 328–30.

Burke, Jackson. "Ernest Hemingway—Muy Hombre." *Bluebook* (1 July 1953): 7.

Crane, R. S. "Ernest Hemingway—'The Short Happy Life of Macomber.'" *The Idea of the Humanities and Other Essays Critical and Historical*. 2 vols. Chicago: U of Chicago P, 1967. 2:315-26.

Davidson, Arnold E. "The Ambivalent End of Francis Macomber's Short, Happy Life." *Hemingway Notes* 2 (Spring 1972): 14-16.

DeFalco, Joseph. *The Hero in Hemingway's Short Stories*. Pittsburgh: U of Pittsburgh P, 1963.

Fleming, Robert E. "When Hemingway Nodded: A Note on Firearms in 'The Short Happy Life.'" *Notes on Modern American Literature* 5 (1981), Item 17.

Gaillard, Theodore L., Jr. "The Critical Menagerie in 'The Short Happy Life of Francis Macomber.'" *English Journal* 60 (January 1971): 31-35.

Greco, Anne. "Margot Macomber: 'Bitch Goddess' Exonerated." *Fitzgerald/Hemingway Annual* (1972): 273-80.

Harkey, Joseph H. "The Africans and Francis Macomber." *Studies in Short Fiction* 17 (Summer 1980): 345-48.

Hellenga, Robert R. "Macomber *Redivivus*." *Notes on Modern American Literature* 3 (Spring 1979), Item 10.

Herndon, Jerry A. "No 'Maggie's Drawers' for Margot Macomber." *Fitzgerald/Hemingway Annual* (1975): 289-91.

Hill, John S. "Robert Wilson: Hemingway's Judge in 'Macomber.'" *University Review* [Kansas City] 35 (Winter 1968): 129-32.

Holland, Robert B. "Macomber and the Critics." *Studies in Short Fiction* 5 (Winter 1968): 171-78.

Howell, John M. "The Macomber Case." *Studies in Short Fiction* 4 (Winter 1967): 171-72.

Howell, John M., and Charles A. Lawler. "From Abercrombie & Fitch to *The First Forty-nine Stories:* The Text of Ernest Hemingway's 'Francis Macomber.'" *Proof: The Yearbook of American Bibliographical and Textual Studies*. Ed. Joseph Katz. Columbia: U of South Carolina P, 1972. 2: 213-81.

Hurley, C. Harold. "Hemingway's 'The Short Happy Life of Francis Macomber.'" *Explicator* 38 (Spring 1980): 9.

Hutton, Virgil, "The Short Happy Life of Macomber." *University Review* [Kansas City] 30 (Summer 1964): 253-63; rpt. in *The Short Stories of Ernest Hemingway: Critical Essays*. Ed. Jackson J. Benson. Durham: Duke UP, 1975, 239-50.

Jackson, Paul R. "Point of View, Distancing, and Hemingway's 'Short Happy Life.'" *Hemingway Notes* 2 (Spring 1980): 2-16.

Jackson, Thomas J. "The 'Macomber' Typescript." *Fitzgerald/Hemingway Annual* (1970): 219-22.

Kobler, J. F. "Francis Macomber as Four-Letter Man." *Fitzgerald/Hemingway Annual* (1972): 295–96.

———. "The Short Happy Illusion of Francis Macomber." *Quartet: A Magazine of the Arts* [College Station, TX] 6 (Winter-Spring 1974): 62–67.

Lewis, Robert W., Jr. *Hemingway on Love.* 1965. New York: Haskell, 1973.

Lounsberry, Barbara. "The Education of Robert Wilson." *Hemingway Notes* 2 (Spring 1980): 29–32.

Lynn, Kenneth S. *Hemingway.* New York: Simon, 1987.

McKenna, John J. "Macomber: The 'Nice Jerk.'" *American Notes & Queries* 17 (Jan. 1971): 73–74.

McKenna, John J., and Marvin V. Peterson. "More Muddy Water: Wilson's Shakespeare in 'The Short Happy Life of Francis Macomber.'" *Studies in Short Fiction* 18 (Winter 1981): 82–85.

Meyers, Jeffrey. *Hemingway: A Biography.* New York: Harper, 1985.

———, ed. *Hemingway: The Critical Heritage.* London: Routledge, 1982.

Nagel, James. "The Narrative Method of 'The Short Happy Life of Francis Macomber.'" *Research Studies* [Washington State U] 41 (Mar. 1973): 18–27.

Oldsey, Bernard. "Hemingway's Beginnings and Endings." *College Literature* 7 (1980): 213–38.

Rovit, Earl. *Ernest Hemingway.* Boston: Twayne, 1963.

Seydow, John J. "Francis Macomber's Spurious Masculinity." *Hemingway Review* 1 (Fall 1981): 33–41.

Spilka, Mark. "The Necessary Stylist: A New Critical Revision." *Modern Fiction Studies* 6 (Winter 1960–61): 289–96.

———. "A Source for the Macomber 'Accident': Marryat's *Percival Keene.*" *Hemingway Review* 3 (Spring 1984): 29–37.

———. "Warren Beck Revisited." *Modern Fiction Studies* 22 (Summer 1976): 245–69.

Stein, William Bysshe. "Hemingway's 'The Short Happy Life of Francis Macomber.'" *Explicator* 19 (Apr. 1971), Item 47.

Stephens, Robert O. *Hemingway's Nonfiction: The Public Voice.* Chapel Hill: U of North Carolina P, 1968.

———. "Macomber and that Somali Proverb: The Matrix of Knowledge." *Fitzgerald/Hemingway Annual* (1977): 137–47.

Waldhorn, Arthur. *A Reader's Guide to Ernest Hemingway.* New York: Farrar, 1972.

Waterman, Arthur E. "Hemingway's 'The Short Happy Life of Francis Macomber.'" *Explicator* 20 (Sept. 1961), Item 2.

Watson, James Gray. " 'A Sound Basis of Union': Structural and Thematic Balance in 'The Short Happy Life of Francis Macomber.' " *Fitzgerald/Hemingway Annual* (1974): 215–28.

White, William. " 'Macomber' Bibliography." *Hemingway Notes* 5 (Spring 1980): 35–38.

Winn, Harbour. "Hemingway's African Stories and Tolstoy's 'Illich.' " *Studies in Short Fiction* 18 (Fall 1981): 451–53.

Young, Philip. *Ernest Hemingway: A Reconsideration*. 1952. New York: Harcourt, 1966.

47

The Snows of Kilimanjaro

Composition History (February–April 1936)

Hemingway's letter to Max Perkins on 9 April 1936 reviewing his recent writing argues that he had been at work on "The Snows of Kilimanjaro" for one and perhaps two months. The writing of "The Short Happy Life" had gone so well he refused to "interrupt [it] to write an article" for *Esquire* and had sent them, reluctantly, "The Capital of the World." Now, with that story to be published in June and "The Short Happy Life" finished at eleven thousand words, he told Perkins of "The Happy Ending, which is between 7200 and 7500 words long and a major story" (*Letters* 442). However easily the two African stories might have come to him, some nineteen thousand words would have meant at least a month or six week's work.

The weak and provisional title and the estimated word count he gave the story suggest, too, that he was referring either to his earliest typescript (KL/EH 702) or to that probably typed by Pauline (in the University of Delaware Collection). His typescript bears "The Happy Ending" title in pencil and many revisions; those revisions and the title are incorporated in the Delaware typescript. Both of these typescripts identify Harry as "Henry Walden," the American poet as Malcolm Cowley, and the later Julian as Scott Fitzgerald; but in all the many revisions neither includes the story's epigraph.

Two of the four manuscript fragments may say something about that marathon of Hemingway's writing and Pauline's typing. One (KL/EH 703) includes pages 2 and 6 (the latter missing from Item 702); both pages are revised in pencil and both are passages of bitter dialogue between Harry and Helen (*Stories* 53, 57). The other (KL/EH 705) is in another hand, is numbered page 26 (Item 702 ends at page 25), but describes the last approach of the hyena before Harry's dream-flight (*Stories* 74–75). Whether there was some discussion between the author and his typist over "the way it was" is a matter for conjecture. It seems likely, however, that in the rush to complete the typescript, Hemingway dictated the later scene.

The remaining two fragments are in Hemingway's hand. The first is a three-page description of the mountains surrounding Schruns in the fall and is marked "Use in The Happy Ending" (KL/EH 706). In both the Kennedy and Delaware typescripts, the Schruns recollection (*Stories* 56–57) is one of

349

the most heavily revised; that this autumnal memory of the place before the snows fell was not used marks a decision to concentrate those recollections on scenes of deep winter and the recurrent imagery of snow.

The last manuscript fragment (KL/EH 704) is a set of drafts of the story's epigraph and its rejected epigraph quotation from Vivienne de Watteville's *Speak to the Earth* (See Lewis and Westbrook). The second page is clearly Hemingway's first draft, for the first page begins as a fair copy titled "The Snows of Kilimanjaro" and then is heavily revised. Both drafts, however, include the unrevised quotation from Watteville:

> "The difficulties, he said, were not in the actual climbing. It was a long grind, and success depended not on skill but on one's ability to withstand the high altitude. His parting words were that I must make the attempt soon, before there was any risk of the rains setting in."

Hemingway could have had these two epigraphs in mind on 9 April when he estimated the story's length between 7200 and 7500 words; more likely they came, as did the final title, as afterthoughts sometime between then and his departure for Cuba on April 24th. It is difficult to imagine that he would have left for a month of fishing without his third and final typescript in hand (the University of Texas typescript on which Robert Lewis and Max Westbrook's studies are based.)

Even if Hemingway had considered the strategic use of one or two epigraphs earlier, when he came to write them he was clearly undecided about the emphasis and relationship he would give to their three elements: Kilimanjaro as the Masai's conception of the House of God; the Watteville quotation on the difficulty of the ascent to that altitude; and the story of the leopard. In his first draft he seems first to have associated the mountain as the House of God with man's ascent, more a matter of altitude than skill, and then added the story of the leopard's ascent. In the second draft, he mentioned the mountain, then the story of the leopard, and then the Masai conception of the House of God, leading to the Watteville passage. His last revision was to arrow the sentence on the House of God to its position as the second sentence in the epigraph.

Both epigraphs introduce the University of Texas typescript, although next to the Watteville quotation Hemingway wrote "Maybe better out. E.H." Arnold Gingrich felt it added "an awkward amount of 'business' " and it was finally deleted for the *Esquire* publication (Lewis and Westbrook 75–76).

Robert Lewis and Max Westbrook's 1966 study of the Texas version and its critical implications was the first endeavor to introduce manuscript evidence into Hemingway scholarship—a landmark then, it still serves twenty years later to orient that discipline. Lewis's introductory essay on the "Text and the Critic" draws in part on the typescript to establish both the potential values of manuscript and textual studies and also some of its critical pitfalls. Lewis noted the manuscript changes from those that are editorial—matters of style or decorum—to those that are substantive, additions and deletions that add to our understanding of the final text (70–74).

In 1966, however, Lewis and Westbrook did not have access to either the Kennedy or Delaware typescripts, which would have revised two of their conclusions and might have qualified, if only slightly, their interpretations of the two epigraphs. Although the Texas version was apparently submitted as "the author's final copy" (70), it was clearly not the earliest working draft. Finally, Lewis noted that the Texas version does not indicate a spacing break introducing Harry's dream-flight, while the last page of the typescript (reprinted on page 73) indicates a break after it. The Delaware typescript does show two lines (=====) both before and after that section. Lewis knew that "a textual critic . . . can never be certain that he has all the information" (74).

In 1970 Lewis and Westbrook completed their work on the Texas typescript with detailed annotations and a collation of it and three relevant editions (*Esquire* 1936 and 1949, and the Jonathan Cape edition of 1939) with that in *The First Forty-nine*. Now with the manuscripts in the Kennedy Library, there is more than enough material to warrant a revised version of their original work including the story's three typescripts.

Publication History (August 1936; October 1938)

Robert Lewis suggested that the preparation of "The Snows of Kilimanjaro," and perhaps the later stages of its revision, were hurried under the pressure of a deadline from *Esquire*. On a copy of the September 1949 *Esquire* in which the story was reprinted, Hemingway wrote: "A story I was forced to sell to Esquire due to haveing [*sic*] my name on the cover and haveing to produce something on time and being unwilling to interrupt work on the story to write an article. EH" (Lewis and Westbrook 70). Lewis was sceptical of the accuracy of Hemingway's memory some thirteen years after the story's first publication, and probably with good reason. He may have been confusing the submission of this story with that of "The Capital of the World." In April 1936 he used a similar explanation in a letter to Perkins: "I was going so well on this long one I've just finished ["The Short Happy Life"] that I would not interrupt to write an article so sent them that story ["The Capital of the World"] at considerable loss." He added that he thought he could publish "The Short Happy Life" in *Cosmopolitan* (*Letters* 442). In fact he was under contract with that magazine, and according to an editorial recollection in the September 1949 *Esquire,* Hemingway "cabled them that he owed *Cosmopolitan* a story and since their deadline came first, he was sending them ["The Short Happy Life"] and would write them another ["The Snows"]" (Cited in Hanneman 164).

An apologetic note seems to run through all of this, especially in the letters to Perkins; it is as if his contracts for *Esquire* articles and *Cosmopolitan*'s munificent fees at a time when he was writing at a rate close to that of the spring of 1924 compelled him to submit his two African stories to fashionable journals that were a far cry from the literary magazines of his earlier years. (Both stories, by the way, direct derogatory remarks at the advertising and the readers of such slick and trendy publications [*Stories* 4, 67].)

In any case "The Snows of Kilimanjaro" appeared in the August 1936 issue of *Esquire* and was based on the heavily revised and far from clean copy of the University of Texas typescript. It attributed the remark about the rich to "poor Scott Fitzgerald and his romantic awe of them"; Fitzgerald reasonably objected to Hemingway's "praying aloud over my corpse" simply because he had written "de profundis" in *The Crack-Up;* Hemingway responded with singular obtuseness, and later changed the name to "Julian" (*Stories* 72; Baker, *Ernest Hemingway: A Life Story* 290–91). The change, as Kenneth Lynn noted, "left Fitzgerald still visible, for Julian was the name of the autobiographical hero of Fitzgerald's story, 'The New Leaf' " (438).

Through the spring and early summer of 1936, Hemingway toyed with the prospect of publishing the two African stories and others with the first two chapters of *To Have and Have Not* in a separate story collection, then a story collection and the "Key West-Havana novel"; but by the end of the summer he returned to the plan of 1934 to publish a collection of all his stories (*Letters* 442–49; KL/EH, Max Perkins to Hemingway, 6 October, 10 November 1934, 21 July 1936). Two years later it was published with its revisions in the 1938 collection, *The Fifth Column and the First Forty-nine Stories*.

Sources and Influences

"The Snows of Kilimanjaro" is an exception to the rule that pervasive biographical sources for a story seem to chill critical interest in its literary analogues, for there are as many articles finding sources in the life as those finding them in literature. Philip Young was the first to cite the story as a "fictionalized purge" and to remark that there were few writers like Hemingway "who stuck so rigorously to writing of themselves, and—in a way—*for* themselves" (74–75). Carlos Baker found the story's outline in "Hemingway's own grave illness, the flight out of the plains country, and the distant view . . . of Kilimanjaro" in January 1934 (*Writer as Artist* 192; *Ernest Hemingway: A Life Story* 251). More recently Kenneth Johnston and the later biographers, Jeffrey Meyers and Kenneth Lynn, have accepted the notion that the story served Hemingway as a "dying writer's attempt to explain, to rationalize, to evade full responsibility for his failure to fulfill his early promise as a writer" (Johnston 224). Robert Stephens had demonstrated early on that the story had "perhaps a greater number of nonfictional analogues, sources, and echoes" than any other Hemingway story, listing those analogues in articles from the *Toronto Star* of 1922 through those in *Esquire* of 1934 and 1936 and then the later versions of his memoirs of Paris in *A Moveable Feast* (273–82).

Then there are the literary analogues. The "dream-flight" to the approaches of Kilimanjaro—imagined in such detail that for the moment we may read it as if it were one of the italicized passages—has been attributed several times to Ambrose Bierce's "An Occurrence at Owl Creek Bridge" (Young 197; Montgomery 281; Crane 362–65). But the differences between Bierce's "trick" ending and Hemingway's, so much more a part of the rest of the story, make the similarity seem almost trivial. William Bache suggested similarities with the setting, circumstances, and ironic death in Joseph Conrad's *Nostromo,* and concluded somewhat broadly that the novel "seems to have functioned for Hemingway as a thematic inspiration, as a critical model, as a source" (34).

In the 1960s both Carlos Baker and Marvin Fisher found sources for Harry's failings as an artist in Henry James's fiction. Baker cited the remarks of Henry St. George in "The Lesson of the Master": " 'Don't become in your old age what I have in mine,' he tells his young admirer, '—the depressing, the deplorable illustration of the worship of false gods . . . the idols of the market, money and luxury' " (*Writer as Artist* 192); and Fisher noted that Hemingway's "introspective writer-hero, possessing intelligence, wit, and a high degree of self-knowledge" and the story's "central problem . . . growing out of the interrelatedness of aesthetic and moral issues" is a hallmark of James, as in his "The Real Thing" (346, 352).

Since then three other more distant or tenuous sources have been suggested. Led on by the name in the manuscripts, Henry Walden, Charles Bassett found analogies between Harry's perception of Kilimanjaro and Henry Thoreau's of Mount Katahdin and Wachusett Mountain in a 1906 edition of his works—which it is unlikely Hemingway read. Harbour Winn made a somewhat better case for Tolstoy's "The Death of Ivan Illich" with similarities between the two characters' minor but fatal "wounds," the manner of their dying in a dream with the "decomposing body . . . counterpointed to the awakening soul" (453). And finally, Alice Petry discovered interesting parallels between the story and Beryl Markham's account of the last hours of a man dying of blackwater in *West with the Night*—but as she noted, the story could have influenced Hemingway only if he had heard it when he and Markham met during his 1933–34 safari (10).

Both of the story's epigraphs—the one Hemingway composed from his reading and the deleted quotation from Vivienne de Watteville—have been taken as sources for the story itself. In 1960 Robert Stephens was the first to find a source for the "leopard" epigraph in the account of the "first European to climb the peak of Kilimanjaro," Hans Meyer. Meyer's account of 1891, in the usual breathless prose of climbing chronicles, mentions finding an antelope, wondering for a moment over its motive, and settling for "adventurous curiosity." Stephens drew on the division of animals between the noble and the obscene, to account for the substitution of the leopard (85–86). Three years later, Barney Childs found the source in Meyer "completely untenable," since H. W. Tilman had climbed Kilimanjaro twice in 1930 and 1933, to report—in print, at least—in 1938, an outcropping known as Leopard's Point, "on top of which lies the dessicated remains of a leopard," and "that I have never heard any explanation of how it came to be there, but presumably it went up of its own volition" (3). In 1968 R. W. Bevis, M. A. J. Smith, and G. Brose, pointed out that although according to Carlos Baker Hemingway got the legend from Philip Percival in 1933, published accounts of three ascents of the mountain by Richard Reusch had mentioned Leopard's Point and appeared in 1928 and 1932. John Howell gathered the evidence with a letter to Reusch in 1968, and published a convenient collection of source materials and essays on the two African stories in 1969.

John Howell's collection of sources deserves to be read with some care, for they clarify what Hemingway knew of the phenomenon of the frozen leopard and what he chose to omit from his first epigraph. Richard Reusch knew, as anyone familiar with animal behavior would, that "what the leopard was seeking at that altitude" (*Stories* 52), was food, specifically a mountain goat found some three hundred feet from its pursuer (quoted in Howell, *Hemingway's African Stories*, 99; see also Thomaneck, 326–27). To assume that "[n]o one has explained what the leopard was seeking at that altitude," or to imply by juxtaposition that the animal might have absorbed the Masai's myth of the mountain as the "House of God," is an obvious and long leap of anthropomorphism reminiscent of Walt Disney. With that in mind, it is obvious that the leopard's natural instincts were motivated by precisely those that Harry believes corrupted him, the instinctual desire to feed well. The omitted seven-eighths of this epigraph is perhaps best left underwater, even though it has governed much of the interpretation of the story.

The implications of the Vivienne de Watteville quotation have been more carefully considered in two essays. Although Hemingway was willing to delete the quotation, Robert Lewis pursued the similarities between Watteville's *Out in the Blue* (1927) and *Speak to the Earth* (1935), from which he took the deleted quotation. In Watteville's later book and in Hemingway's story there is an abiding concern "with the nature of death," with the almost desperate need "to climb Kilimanjaro," and the perception of Africa as a place that offered both a resolution of the problems of the past and a realization of future possibilities, to suggest a close thematic parallel between the two works that contemplate Kilimanjaro as the "divine mountain" (Lewis and Westbrook 78, 80, 87). Adeline Tintner questioned the influence of *Out of the Blue* on the weak evidence that Hemingway's own copy was published in 1937, but more convincingly suggested that Hemingway came by *Speak to the Earth* through Edith Wharton, who had written its preface.

Critical Studies

It is idle, of course, to speculate on how the story would have been received and read with its original title, "The Happy Ending," or without the late addition of the remaining epigraph. Yet it seems another instance of Hemingway's remarkably good luck at the eleventh hour, for the late title and epigraph have served critics variously as touchstones in in the long controversy over the meaning of Harry's dream-flight to the mountain.

Gloria Dussinger's article of 1967 serves as a review of the three major positions critics had taken:

> *First:* "to grant the leopard and the mountain their full idealistic value but to deny Harry a place among them"—O'Connor, Stallman, Maloney;
>
> *Second:* to accept "the metaphysical meaning of the symbols and . . . the apotheosis of Harry," but refuse "to reconcile the two"—Gordon and Tate, West; and
>
> *Third:* to subscribe "to both the transcendental import of the symbols and the transfiguration of the protagonist"—Tedlock, Evans, DeFalco. (Dussinger, " 'Snows of Kilimanjaro' " 55 and notes)

As Dussinger framed the question of the story, its two major symbolic elements and their meanings—the leopard of the epigraph and the mountain in the protagonist's dream—can only be related and evaluated through the story's narrative, particularly the italicized passages of reminiscence.

Although most commentaries do that, some do not. In 1949 Charles Walcutt read the leopard as a symbol of Harry's "fundamental moral idealism" triumphing over the "aimless materialism" of the generation of the 1920s; although as "naturalistically illogical" as the leopard's ascent, his idealism, marked by his sense of "failure to record perceptions of human dignity and integrity," may be a mystery "but there it is" (Item 43; see also Tedlock, Item 7). Even the two longer essays of 1961 were trained on symbolic elements abstracted from the text. Marion Montgomery, fixed on the symbolic contrast between the leopard and hyena, found a similar polarity between

Harry's "present ignoble situation and the memory of a more heroic past" (277). Dussinger's objection that this transformation of the animals' hunting habits into an "aesthetic code" ignores the "extraordinary behavior of the leopard" (" 'Snows of Kilimanjaro' " 54–55, n. 2), is unnecessary since there is no evidence that Harry's past is any more heroic than his present. Later in 1961 Oliver Evans reviewed some of the brief and negative responses to the story between 1945 and 1956—Ray B. West, Jr., Caroline Gordon and Allen Tate, and William Van O'Connor—and challenged most of the identifications of the leopard with the beasts from Revelation and the *Inferno*. Evans drew on Carlos Baker's more general mountain-plain opposition in Hemingway to establish the major contrast here with the mountain representing "life-in-death" and the plain representing "death-in-life," each with its emblematic animal, the leopard and the hyena. Nearly everything on the plain, from the vultures to Harry's gangrene and his inability to love, is associated with death-in-life; even Helen "thrives, as would the hyena, on *what is dead* in him." Given this symbolic polarity, the story must end "on a note of triumph. Harry does gain the mountain top, not merely *in his delirium* . . . but *in death*" (Evans 603–05, 607).

Other variations have been worked on the symbolic leopard and hyena. Alfred Kolb linked that pair with another, the mimosa tree and the airplane, drawing on evidence in as disparate works as James George Frazer's *The Golden Bough* and Shelley's "The Sensitive Plant." In both sets of symbols the opposition is complicated with each element embodying either life or death, movement or stasis, the natural or mechanical, so that no univalent interpretation of the ending is possible (Item 4). And the hyena, in particular, has enjoyed a couple of literary roles. Earl Rovit, for whom Harry "is, not at all, a nice man," saw the beast joining Helen in "weeping for the dead artist, because the hyena becomes the distended identification of the audience the artist must serve. . . . [I]t is quick to lament the loss of the artist, even as it is quick to harry [*sic*] him down when he is alive" (37–38). Like Rovit, Kenneth Johnston drew upon the description of the wounded hyena tearing out its intestines in *Green Hills of Africa,* but here the animal represents Harry in his "frantic circling back to feed upon his dead past and his dying self. Thus, the sound of hyenic 'laughter' is a most fitting note on which to end the story" (227). To which one might add a final lugubrious question: Did Harry in his dream stick his leg "out straight to one side of the seat where Compton sat," or was Helen unable to look at the leg with the dressings "all come down" because she recognized why the "hyena made the same strange noise that had awakened her" (*Stories* 75)?

If a reasonable answer to that question is, yes, then certainly a multivalent meaning is probable in the symbol of the snows of Kilimanjaro and elsewhere. Again, the epigraph with its implication of a frozen immortality for extraordinary achievement skewed most readings of the story until Bernard Oldsey's essay of 1963. Following Hemingway's suggestion, Oldsey read the weather through all his fiction. In an expansive and detailed study, he discovered that in Hemingway's first forty-nine stories, over one-third begin or "make important internal use of snow, ice, cold, white, and light imagery" (64). Of the eleven that begin with a snow image, this one is first among equals. But, following other critics' early warnings against polarized readings of such symbols, Oldsey demonstrated that the snows of the story are preeminently plural in their meanings, as they are throughout Hemingway's fiction. Hemingway might have titled his story, as Oldsey says, "The *Snow* of Kilimanjaro" but did not, for his title "can represent both the dreamed-of snow in Harry's mind as well as the actual snow of the mountain; it can represent the destroying quality of a snow like a cloud of locusts as well as the preserving quality of Kilimanjaro's snow" (70). And finally, Oldsey recognized the *ubi sunt* note that sounds throughout this story. And that makes sense, for a story that is so reminiscent of his early days in Paris, when Hemingway liked to think he wrote in Villon's apartment, what better tacit epigraph than Villon's refrain "Mais où sont les neiges d'antan"?

Whatever meaning one gives to the symbolic snows, the leopard's ascent, or the hyena's laughter, it must be supported, as Dussinger suggested, by the story's intricate narrative of reminiscence and present dialogue. R. W. Stallman was the first to argue that the italicized passages are "not irresponsible reminiscences," but "progress toward the final and climactic image of Williamson," emboweled on barbed wire and pleading for death and so projecting Harry's own "death-wish" (193-95). Although Stallman misconstrued the epigraph as the first of Harry's memories, his sense of their progression through a thematic pattern of "flight, retreat, and betrayal" (197) argues for the organic unity earlier critics had missed. Joseph DeFalco, following an archetypal pattern, had found a similar achievement within the "logic of [Harry's] own inner drama, to a kind of redemptive Avalon" (208). Max Westbrook, in the article shared with Robert Lewis, argued persuasively that the italicized reflections are "exercises in attaining [an] 'impersonal state,'" free from the "sickness of the temporal," in which one can create the "pure and concrete and permanent" (100).

But Robert Lewis had demurred a year earlier, with the note that Harry's role as a writer is "not of great consequence" (*Hemingway on Love* 97). What is more important for Lewis is the fact that each of the five reminiscences returns to "scenes of death or love" and the "combination is significant" (100). In a complex reading of the italicized passages, Lewis relates the triad of love relationships governed by eros, agape, or romantic love with the recurrent images of death. Helen is viewed more sympathetically here than elsewhere, even though Lewis seriously considered that the two are not married, as Alfred Engstrom was the first to suggest. Harry remains to the end a "Tristan reacting against his sick vision which ends in memories of death and violence" (107). One might for a moment expect that Lewis would find something transcendent in Harry's dream-flight, something approaching a redemptive vision of agape; but Harry's vision is too strongly fixed in the erotic and its association with death. So, although Harry may be "flying to the House of God," the sceptical analyst notes that "the 'old cock' Harry is put in the Puss Moth, where there is, naturally, only room for one," and the "Pilot says, 'I'll be back for the Mem,' as indeed he may" (110).

Between Gloria Dussinger's summary of the critical meaning of the reminiscences in 1967 and Scott MacDonald's review in 1974, two critics seem to have reluctantly taken the middle ground. Jackson Benson found the story exemplary of typical rituals of avoidance in Hemingway but the dream-flight a "slick magazine exit" (133); and Arthur Waldhorn concluded that the only redemption in the story for its "simplistic life message: a corrupt life breeds a corrupt death," lay in Hemingway's "remorseless honesty," however softened and diffused by its symbolism (147).

One of the virtues of Dussinger's 1967 article is that it incorporated the italicized reminiscences in the narrative of the story's present. Harry seems at first to explain away the burden of his reminiscences with some easy notion of determinism; but as those reminiscences progress, that explanation becomes less persuasive, to him and to us. Recognizing this, his "final memory takes the form of a death-wish, for Harry guesses that his state of self-illumination is threatened by time: 'It's a bore. . . . Anything you do too bloody long" (58; *Stories* 73). For Dussinger, Harry's dream-flight is redemptive for its *writing:* he records "faithfully and in precise detail the sensory impressions of his journey," an act that "announces Harry's victory" (59).

MacDonald's essay in 1974 is filled with suggestions that critics in the 1980s might consider. He noted that Hemingway used the italicized reminiscences to indicate that his "protagonist has failed to fulfill his potential," but that "by drawing attention to his own act of creation by his use of italics, . . . Hemingway subtly implies a contrast between the fate of a fictional character who has lost his moral and artistic integrity and the achievement represented by his own story, by a work of art which itself gives evidence of the fact that Hemingway's integrity as a writer remains intact" (72). MacDonald made the further point that Harry remembers all the previous four reminiscences as experiences he "had saved to write" (*Stories* 55); whereas "the last crucial italicized section . . . is the only section during which some direct statement to this effect is not made"; as he noted, this is the one section that "Harry tells Helen he has been 'writing' " (71). That this reminiscence occurs just before the dream-flight raises at least one question. Did Hemingway intend a progression from the italicized sections of reminiscences (the first four of which were clearly remembered and not written), to the last (remembered and imagined as written—the one that begs for death), to end in the last and lasting ascent, that was neither unwritten or, for all its palpable presence on the page, written?

Much has been made of Hemingway's self-destructive use of his own experiences throughout his life and especially in Africa. Little has been made of his attempt, however tentative, to use those experiences in what we, in our latter-day wisdom, know as metafiction.

Works Cited

PRIMARY

Ernest Hemingway: Selected Letters, 1917–1961. Ed. Carlos Baker. New York: Scribner's, 1981.

The Short Stories of Ernest Hemingway. New York: Scribner's, 1938, 52–77.

SECONDARY

Bache, William B. " "*Nostromo* and 'The Snows of Kilimanjaro.' " *Modern Language Notes* 72 (Jan. 1957): 32–34.

Baker, Carlos. *Ernest Hemingway: A Life Story.* 1969. New York: Scribner's, 1988.

———. *Hemingway: The Writer as Artist.* 1952. Princeton: Princeton UP, 1972.

Bassett, Charles W. "Katahdin, Wachusett, and Kilimanjaro: The Symbolic Mountains of Thoreau and Hemingway." *Thoreau Journal Quarterly* 3 (Apr. 1971): 1–10.

Benson, Jackson J. *Hemingway: The Writer's Art of Self-Defense.* Minneapolis: U of Minnesota P, 1969.

Bevis, R. W., M. A. J. Smith, Jr., and G. Brose. "Leopard Tracks in 'The Snows. . . .'" *American Notes and Queries* 6 (Apr. 1968): 115.

Childs, Barney. "Hemingway and the Leopard of Kilimanjaro." *American Notes and Queries* 2 (Sept. 1963): 3.

Crane, John Kenny. "Crossing the Bar Twice: Post-Mortem Consciousness in Bierce, Hemingway, and Golding." *Studies in Short Fiction* 6 (Summer 1969): 361–76.

DeFalco, Joseph. *The Hero in Hemingway's Short Stories.* Pittsburgh: U of Pittsburgh P, 1963.

Dussinger, Gloria R. "Hemingway's 'The Snows of Kilimanjaro.' " *Explicator* 26 (Apr. 1968), Item 67.

———." 'The Snows of Kilimanjaro': Harry's Second Chance." *Studies in Short Fiction* 5 (Fall 1967): 54–59.

Engstrom, Alfred G. "Dante, Flaubert, and 'The Snows of Kilimanjaro.' " *Modern Language Notes* 65 (March 1950): 203–05.

Evans, Oliver. " 'The Snows of Kilimanjaro': A Revaluation." *PMLA* 76 (Dec. 1961): 601–07.

Fisher, Marvin. "More Snow on Kilimanjaro." *Americana Norvegica* 2 (1968): 343–53.

Gordon, Caroline, and Allen Tate. *The House of Fiction.* New York: Scribner's, 1950.

Hanneman, Audre. *Ernest Hemingway: A Comprehensive Bibliography.* Princeton: Princeton UP, 1967.

Howell, John M., ed. *Hemingway's African Stories: The Stories, Their Sources, Their Critics.* New York: Scribner's, 1969.

———. "Hemingway's Riddle and Kilimanjaro's Reusch." *Studies in Short Fiction* 8 (Summer 1971): 469–70.

———. "What the Leopard Was Seeking." *American Notes and Queries* 7 (Jan. 1969): 68.

Johnston, Kenneth G. " 'The Snows of Kilimanjaro': An African Purge." *Studies in Short Fiction* 21 (Summer 1984): 223–27.

Kolb, Alfred. "Symbolic Structure in Hemingway's 'The Snows of Kilimanjaro.' " *Notes on Modern American Literature* 1 (1976), Item 4.

Lewis, Robert W., Jr. *Hemingway on Love.* 1965. New York: Haskell, 1973.

Lewis, Robert W., Jr., and Max Westbrook. " 'The Snows of Kilimanjaro,' Collated and Annotated." *Texas Quarterly* 13 (Summer 1970): 64–143.

———. "The Texas Manuscript of 'The Snows of Kilimanjaro.' " *Texas Quarterly* 9 (Winter 1966): 66–101.

Lynn, Kenneth S. *Hemingway.* New York: Simon, 1987.

MacDonald, Scott. "Hemingway's 'The Snows of Kilimanjaro': Three Critical Problems." *Studies in Short Fiction* 11 (Winter 1974): 67–74.

Meyers, Jeffrey. *Hemingway: A Biography.* New York: Harper, 1985.

Montgomery, Marion. "The Leopard and the Hyena: Symbol and Meaning in 'The Snows of Kilimanjaro.' " *University of Kansas City Review* 27 (June 1961): 277–82.

Oldsey, Bernard. "The Snows of Ernest Hemingway." *Wisconsin Studies in Contemporary Literature* 4 (Spring-Summer 1963): 172–98; rpt. in *Ernest Hemingway.* Ed. Arthur Waldhorn. New York: McGraw-Hill, 1973, 56–82.

Petry, Alice Hall. "Voice Out of Africa: A Possible Oral Source for Hemingway's 'The Snows of Kilimanjaro.' " *Hemingway Review* 4 (Spring 1985): 7–11.

Rovit, Earl. *Ernest Hemingway.* Boston: Twayne, 1963.

Stallman, R. W. *The House That James Built and Other Literary Studies.* East Lansing: Michigan State UP, 1961.

Stephens, Robert O. *Hemingway's Nonfiction.* Chapel Hill: U of North Carolina P, 1968.

———. "Hemingway's Riddle of Kilimanjaro: Idea and Image." *American Literature* 32 (Mar. 1960): 84–87.

Tedlock, Ernest W., Jr. "Hemingway's 'The Snows of Kilimanjaro.' " *Explicator* 8 (Oct. 1949), Item 7.

Thomaneck, Jurgen K. A. "Hemingway's Riddle of Kilimanjaro Once More." *Studies in Short Fiction* 7 (Spring 1970): 326–27.

Tintner, Adeline R. "Wharton's Forgotten Preface to Vivienne de Watteville's *Speak to the Earth:* A Link with Hemingway's 'The Snows of Kilimanjaro.'" *Notes on Modern American Literature* 8 (1984), Item 10.

Walcutt, Charles C. "Hemingway's 'The Snows of Kilimanjaro.'" *Explicator* 7 (Apr. 1949), Item 43.

Waldhorn, Arthur. *A Reader's Guide to Ernest Hemingway.* New York: Farrar, 1972.

Walz, Lawrence A. " 'The Snows of Kilimanjaro': A New Reading." *Fitzgerald/Hemingway Annual* (1971): 239–45.

Winn, Harbour. "Hemingway's African Stories and Tolstoy's 'Illich.'" *Studies in Short Fiction* 18 (Fall 1981): 451–53.

Young, Philip. *Ernest Hemingway: A Reconsideration.* 1952. New York: Harcourt, 1966.

48

Old Man at the Bridge

Composition History (April 1938)

"Old Man at the Bridge," the last story Hemingway was to include in any collected volume in his lifetime, has by all accounts the briefest and least complicated history of its writing. After a two-month uneasy respite from the Spanish Civil War in early 1938, he returned to Europe in March and arrived on 31 May in Barcelona to report on the Loyalists' retreat before the Rebel forces under Franco. He had a contract with North American News Alliance (NANA) and an agreement to contribute to the "sumptuous leftist magazine" *Ken,* recently launched by *Esquire*'s publisher (Baker 327; Watson 155). During the two next two weeks, Hemingway reported on the Rebel drive to the Gulf of Valencia to divide the Loyalist forces. On 15 April, Good Friday, Franco's forces reached Vinaroz on the gulf, driving refugees north across the Ebro to Barcelona.

The story of Hemingway's long and exhausting motor trips from Barcelona to the Ebro delta, the flood of dispatches he sent back to NANA, and his withholding one that was to become "Old Man at the Bridge," is told in dramatic detail in William B. Watson's recent article and the *Hemingway Review* edition of the Spanish dispatches.

Hemingway left at dawn on Easter Sunday, made the grueling drive to Amposta on the Ebro, witnessed the Republican retreat, made his field notes, and returned to Barcelona to write the cable sent before midnight that became "The Old Man at the Bridge." A full day but not an unusual one in this hectic month. The cable might have become another NANA dispatch had Hemingway not been under another deadline from *Ken;* so he sent the three-page untitled cable, bearing a censor's stamp with the date 17 April 1938, to *Esquire* (KL/EH 627). That cable, as Watson noted, went directly to *Ken* where it was printed without revision.

The only evidence for composition, then, lies in the interval between the field notes (transcribed in Watson 154) and the published version. But the notes reveal only some of the details Hemingway recorded—the old man, his steel spectacles, his home town, his twelve-kilometer walk, his concern for the animals he had left behind on the advice of an artillery officer. In the late afternoon and evening of 17 April, Hemingway incorporated these details, changed the three cats to one, the old man's age from sixty-eight to seventy-two, then to seventy-six, and a few bits of the dialogue, and then—as always—noted the weather (Watson 160–61; KL/EH 716).

Although the cable sent to *Ken* has some of the stylistic notes of the NANA dispatches, Watson points out that Hemingway knew a potential "story" when he saw one, and rarely compelled by generic constraints, he sent it off to meet *Ken*'s more pressing deadline (Watson 155–56).

Publication History (19 May 1938; October 1938)

The story's publication on 19 May 1938, only a month after it was written, is something of a record. It appeared in *Ken* with the title *"The Old Man at the Bridge."* On 12 July Hemingway wrote to Max Perkins on the contents for the projected collection of the "first forty eight" stories, but enclosed "that story I cabled to Ken the day we evacuated Amposta. It would make a story for the book I think—An Old Man at a Bridge" (*Letters* 469)—and so it became the forty-ninth.

The one-page copy of the *Ken* publication, used as setting copy for *First Forty-nine* edition and bearing the stamped date 22 August 1938 (KL/EH 627 A) might have been the version Hemingway sent Perkins in July; and so the story became the last to join the collection in October 1938.

Sources and Influences

Carlos Baker's assumption that the story drew immediately upon the events of 17 April 1938, when Hemingway drove from Barcelona south to Amposta on the Ebro, across the pontoon bridge, and returned to compose the cable, is confirmed by William Watson. In the light of this nearly immediate transcription of experience into fiction, the story's transmission by cable, and some of its similarities with the diction and the tone of the confidential insider—"that ever mysterious event called contact" (*Stories* 79)—this story raises complex questions of its genre—is it a "story" or not, whatever Hemingway thought? And if it is, what then of other cables sent to NANA that he later thought of as stories—"The Chauffeurs of Madrid," for example (*By-Line* 268–74)?

These questions are of critical interest when we consider the validity of, say, an interpretation that argues for the shaping force of an archetype, as does Joseph DeFalco's. If, as the field notes suggest, nearly every detail in the story was there at the pontoon bridge over the Ebro at Amposta; and if Hemingway seems simply to have found his story there at hand, can we still say that life imitates art, and leave it at that?

Critical Studies

If few critics have noted the story in detail, none has seriously faulted it—it has the brevity and force of some of the longer *In Our Time* chapters, like "The Revolutionist," and it looks forward to some of the issues of *For Whom the Bell Tolls* and beyond to *The Old Man and the Sea* (Flora 253).

In 1963—a good year for the story—Earl Rovit marked it as one of the few in which the tutor figure "has already achieved a self-containment or self-definition . . . and his further engagement in life will not seriously affect what he *is;* it will only substantiate and clarify that definition" (83–84). Richard Lid considered the dialectic of the story in the context of Hemingway's characters' recurring dilemma: to articulate, but not too much; to recognize the "need for speech" to express the old man's imminent tragedy, but to realize with the soldier-narrator that to say any more would violate his distanced role, and paradoxically through articulation diminish his role and the old man's tragedy (402–03).

It is precisely that sort of insight that is missing from Joseph DeFalco's long labors over the story's Christian imagery: the old man, seen as something of a shepherd and associated with "doves" by the narrator, links him with the narrative's Christ motif on this Easter Sunday. And that is clearly there. But when DeFalco then assigns the narrator the role of a Loyalist with its "anti-clerical implications" precluding the "possibility of his belief in the traditional Saviour," and so personifies him as the "anti-Christ" (125–26), history, Hemingway, and the text call a halt to this reading.

Arthur Waldhorn was the latest to notice the story as something of a prologue to *For Whom the Bell Tolls.* The old man is an "exemplary hero who defines his humanity by his concern for others and sustains his own dignity by quiet uncomplaining courage" (169). Though it looked forward to that novel, "Old Man at the Bridge" is probably more important as an epilogue to those stories that Hemingway honored in the last collection of his lifetime.

Works Cited

PRIMARY

By-Line: Ernest Hemingway. Ed. William White. New York: Scribner's, 1967.

Ernest Hemingway: Selected Letters, 1917–1961. Ed. Carlos Baker. New York: Scribner's, 1981.

The Short Stories of Ernest Hemingway. New York: Scribner's, 1938, 78–80.

SECONDARY

Baker, Carlos. *Ernest Hemingway: A Life Story.* 1969. New York: Scribner's, 1988.

DeFalco, Joseph. *The Hero in Hemingway's Short Stories.* Pittsburgh: U of Pittsburgh P, 1963.

Flora, Joseph M. *Hemingway's Nick Adams*. Baton Rouge: Louisiana State UP, 1982.

Lid, Richard W. "Hemingway and the Need for Speech." *Modern Fiction Studies* 8 (Winter 1962–63): 401–07.

Rovit, Earl. *Ernest Hemingway*. Boston: Twayne, 1963.

Waldhorn, Arthur. *A Reader's Guide to Ernest Hemingway*. New York: Farrar, 1972.

Watson, William B. " 'Old Man at the Bridge': The Making of a Short Story." *Hemingway Review* 7 (Spring 1988): 152–65.

The Fifth Column and Four Stories of the Spanish Civil War
(August 1969)

49

The Denunciation

Composition History (May-September 1938)

"The Denunciation" was the first of the four Spanish Civil War stories collected in 1969 and the first of the three that Hemingway thought of as "Chicote" stories, named for their setting in the "best bar in Spain," if not the best in the world (*Four Stories* 90).

The manuscripts, like the published version, seem tortured. The first is a heavily revised two-page Hemingway typescript, a failed attempt to begin the story. The second is a seven-page Hemingway typescript, with another false start and a four-page insert. It begins: "They had butchered a cow at the Embassy . . ." (*Four Stories* 90); it ends with Emmunds and John leaving Chicote's to cook the narrator's share of that cow, before the confessional phone call to Pepé at Seguridad. Of most interest is the four-page insert, one in manuscript, for page 6, which includes the long recollection of gambling with Delgado at San Sebastian and Emmunds's self-condemnation (*Four Stories* 95 ["All right, I said"] to 97 [" . . . the buzzing in the head"]). This incomplete typescript bears two provisional titles, "The Denunciation" and "A Client of Chicote's." The fourth page of the insert, in manuscript, is a rejected dialogue in which Emmunds tries to explain to John what Chicote's was like before the war, "sort of like the Stork Club in New York"; but the only American club John knows is the "John Reed Club," and he wonders whether the Stork "maybe was a fascist sort of John Reed Club"—Emmunds leaves it at that. The third item is an uncorrected typescript close to the final version.

William Watson's unpublished article on "The Denunciation" argues for the close connection with Hemingway's attack on John Dos Passos in "Treachery in Aragon," written 15–25 May 1938, and for that date as the story's inception (Watson, "Hemingway's 'Denunciation,' " and correspondence with author, 5 November 1987).

When Hemingway arrived in New York from Paris on 31 May 1938, he told reporters he was going to work on "some short stories and a novel" (Baker 330, 626); on 11 June he wrote to Max Perkins he had one story ready for revision—this could well have been the second Hemingway typescript of the story—and on 3 August he wrote again to say he had completed "two stories about Chicote's Bar, 3,000 and 4,200 words in length, both 'imperfect' " (Baker 626). Of the three Chicote stories, the only one approximating 4,200 words is "The Denunciation"; the other is "The Butterfly and the Tank."

Their imperfections probably were worked out in August and September, for the two were published soon after in *Esquire*.

Publication History (November 1938; August 1969)

By 22 October 1938 Hemingway was writing Arnold Gingrich of *Esquire* about the "third Chicote story" ("Night Before Battle") and so had sent him both "The Denunciation" and "The Butterfly and the Tank" (*Letters* 472). The first was published in the November issue of that magazine, the second in the following month.

Only three months after the publication of *The First Forty-nine*, Hemingway was considering another volume of short stories. He suggested to Perkins a list of titles including the three Chicote stories, "Nobody Ever Dies" (to appear in *Cosmopolitan* in March), "Landscape with Figures" (*Complete Stories* 590–96), and "three very long ones I want to write now." Two would have been derived from his Spanish Civil War dispatches, and the third became *The Old Man and the Sea* (*Letters* 479, 7 February 1939). So there is this much justification for the posthumous publication of some of these stories, if only in 1969.

Sources and Influences

Until recently, those critics who have noticed "The Denunciation" have seen in it—as in its companion stories—Hemingway's rather fitful efforts to work out his attitudes toward the Spanish Civil War that were partially resolved in the writing of *For Whom the Bell Tolls*, begun in March of 1939, and after which the notion of another short story volume was forgotten. Earl Rovit and others have found a turning point in the African stories and *To Have and Have Not* away from the social isolation of *A Farewell to Arms* to the social commitment of *For Whom the Bell Tolls* in this period. But both this story and "Under the Ridge," the latter finished only weeks before beginning the Spanish novel, contemplate and variously affirm something like Frederic Henry's "separate peace."

For that reason alone, one might wonder why in "The Denunciation" Hemingway returned to the issue of a writer's engagement and responsibility in the political controversies surrounding a war he observed as a foreigner. All three Chicote stories are explicit exercises with a writer-narrator contemplating both his aesthetic and moral involvement in his material. And so they represent an end, and not a happy one, to a theme in the earliest of the Nick Adams stories in which Hemingway contemplated that young writer's "need to write."

Something of that consideration supports William Watson's argument that "The Denunciation" is a near allegory of Hemingway's final and violent break with John Dos Passos, so virulently expressed in his *Ken* article, "Treachery in Aragon," of 30 June 1938. Watson recounted Dos Passos's insistent attempts to discover the fate of José Robles Pazos, a Johns Hopkins professor and Dos Passos translator executed as a Fascist by the Loyalists. Hemingway, feeling that Dos Passos's inquiries might "jeopardize the propaganda film ["The Spanish Earth"] they were making with Joris Ivens," attacked him in the "Treachery" article for "cowardice and treason," to say nothing of squeamish and naive liberalism. But, as Watson argued, his attack was "designed to cover up his own unwillingness to help Dos Passos find out the truth about Robles's death." At this point Robles exits, and Hemingway's denunciation of Dos Passos provides the biographical analogue with the denunciation of the story. For Watson, both the self-deprecating remarks in the story about the writer's motives, founded in "righteousness and Pontius Pilatry" and ending in the sentimental admission of guilt to preserve the integrity of the waiters at Chicote's, are analogous to Hemingway's admission of guilt and conciliatory gesture to Dos Passos, implying that, after all, they both shared a love for the people of Spain transcending political antagonisms (Watson).

This detailed argument, only sketched in here, goes some way to explain the curious confessional, if not self-flagellating, moments in the narration; they are too intense, too particular to be only another stage in Hemingway's abiding interest in the abstract topic of the narrator-as-writer. There is a deep sense of shame at the heart of this fiction.

Critical Studies

The two earliest studies of "The Denunciation," Martin Light's and Julian Smith's, reviewed all four of the Civil War stories in 1969 just before they were collected. Light was compelled to summarize much of the plot of the story, but he managed to isolate most of its major elements: the symbolic setting of Chicote's bar, once a nonpolitical place but now ironically the scene of a fatal political act; the contrast between the ebullient flyer, John the Greek, and the inexplicable figure of Delgado; the thin line between the waiter's and the narrator's conception of "responsibility"; and the narrator's complicity in the denunciation and his sense of betrayal of not only "Delgado, but a revered place and his own principles." If the article seems to gloss the story's tangled conflicts rather too simply, it did bring the story to critical attention and suggested in passing that it bore some resemblance to the controversy between Hemingway and Dos Passos over the Robles affair (67–69).

Julian Smith turned his attention to the story's "perverted world in which the code of conduct makes it less painful to be betrayed by a friend than by a waiter," a world in which "the one sane voice is that of a Greek comrade named John." John's two apparently digressive experiences, one in which he is buried by an explosion and the other in which he is confronted by an octopus in a deep-sea dive, seem to have marked him with a wisdom that places him "somehow above political differences." Henry Emmunds, the narrator, at first refuses to participate in the denunciation, then does, and in so doing "denounces himself to the reader both as man and writer" (7). That irony runs through the religious symbolism that Smith found emerging in this story and evident in the others: in Chicote's, once a place of communion, Emmunds buys three party tracts for thirty centavos, is "told by the old woman that God will bless him, a prophecy he doubts. Immediately the denunciation begins" (9).

Jay Gertzman's article of 1979 followed Light's and Smith's implications further into the complex moral and literary questions this story raises, questions that had been called with Stephen Spender's attack in a general review of books on the Spanish war in 1969. Spender had deplored the narrator's providing the Seguridad telephone number and then assuming that much guilt to protect the waiter, Chicote's, and whatever that represents. For him it was a "maudlin, hideously inverted sentimentality" that stained the story and its "disguised narrator," Hemingway, as "morally repugnant" (Spender 6).

Here, in a later political arena, is the critical issue that complicated for so long the argument of "The Short Happy Life of Francis Macomber." In the controversy between Warren Beck and Mark Spilka over that story, the central issue was whether there was a "necessary style" that identified the values of the narrator or a central character with those of Hemingway. If that is the issue here, as it seems to be, then the question is whether or not one can exonerate the narrator (and so Hemingway) by the arguments Emmunds gives, while admitting their near identity; or whether one can exonerate Hemingway with the argument that he has, as in "The Short Happy Life," presented a morally flawed and impercipient witness or narrator of the event.

Gertzman struggled with that complex issue in a remarkably candid manner. He recognized the "presence of Hemingway" in the story, with which those of Mark Spilka's persuasion would agree, but then asked whether that presence is "detrimental to the story" (245). Put in perhaps belligerent terms, he asked whether Hemingway meant to justify himself *by* justifying his narrator, or in more neutral terms, exonerate himself by condemning his narrator. In either case, Hemingway's investment in this story is considerable.

His argument was relentless—to a point. He agreed too easily with Martin Light's notion that Emmunds is afflicted with what E. M. Halliday called Frederic Henry's "torpor brought on by too many months living close to the war" (247)—a misconception of both Henry and "Enrique" Emmunds. But Gertzman asked the almost final question: What does Emmunds sacrifice? Not his honor or his reputation; nor does his admission of complicity "effect any meaningful atonement"; rather "it seems to show lack of imagination, a very literal-minded reliance on the apparent rightness of a Reverend Cause and an Ideal Bar" (247–48). If that is so, then the phone call "is a pathetic atonement, because as an outsider, an intellectual, a writer, he cannot identify himself with the cause he supports." More than that, his "phone call to Pepé [admitting his responsibility in the denunciation] is as close as he gets emotionally and psychologically to the Spanish Loyalists." And that act is "almost a kind of *hubris* in that he tries to create in himself a sensibility which he really does not possess" (247–50). Gertzman concluded that Hemingway presented a writer who had failed to distance himself from the events he witnessed and, if only in giving a phone number available to anyone, engaged himself in those events and their fatal outcome. As he said, the burden of the story "rests on the insinuations about the behavior, function, and perspective proper to the writer as he moves in and observes the real world, as he must, despite its dangers" (252). A fine perception.

Again in 1979, Kenneth Johnston noted that the story was one of "self-denunciation," an admission of "Pontius Pilatry" (*Four Stories* 97), but that the confession was more than a personal statement, for he was also "denouncing the U. S. State Department policy of nonintervention," which Hemingway had castigated in a *Ken* article of 16 June 1938 (372, 377, 381 n. 4). Johnston followed and supported earlier critics, like Light and Smith, who had cited the story as one of betrayal. He added an interesting linguistic note that the "Spanish word 'delgado' means 'thin,' 'delicate,' 'tenuous'; the phrase 'hilar delgado,' means, colloquially, 'to hew close to the line,' 'to split hairs'" (380).

That, most certainly, is what Emmunds is doing in the story's last line, "Luis Delgado was an old client of Chicote's and I did not wish him to be disillusioned or bitter about the waiters there before he died" (*Four Stories* 100); and almost as certainly Hemingway was hewing close to the line in his almost casuistical consideration of his denunciation of Dos Passos.

Works Cited

PRIMARY

The Complete Short Stories of Ernest Hemingway. New York: Scribner's, 1987.

Ernest Hemingway: Selected Letters, 1917–1961. Ed. Carlos Baker. New York: Scribner's, 1981.

The Fifth Column and Four Stories of the Spanish Civil War. New York: Scribner's, 1969, 89–100.

SECONDARY

Baker, Carlos. *Ernest Hemingway: A Life Story.* 1969. New York: Scribner's, 1988.

Gertzman, Jay A. "Hemingway's Writer-Narrator in 'The Denunciation.'" *Research Studies* 47 (Dec. 1979): 244–52.

Johnston, Kenneth G. "Hemingway's 'The Denunciation': The Aloof American." *Fitzgerald/Hemingway Annual* (1979): 371–82.

Light, Martin. "Of Wasteful Deaths: Hemingway's Stories about the Spanish War." *Western Humanities Review* 23 (Winter 1969): 29–42; rpt. in *The Short Stories Ernest Hemingway: Critical Essays.* Ed. Jackson J. Benson. Durham: Duke UP, 1975, 64–77.

Rovit, Earl. *Ernest Hemingway.* Boston: Twayne, 1963.

Smith, Julian. "Christ Times Four: Hemingway's Unknown Spanish Civil War Stories." *Arizona Quarterly* 25 (Spring 1969): 5–17.

Spender, Stephen. "Writers and Revolutionaries." *New York Review of Books,* 25 September 1969.

Watson, William B. "Hemingway's 'Denunciation'—A Final Gesture to Dos Passos." Unpublished paper presented at the Third International Hemingway Conference, Madrid, June 1984, 1–14.

50

The Butterfly and the Tank

Composition History (July-September 1938)

Hemingway's letter to Max Perkins of 3 August 1938, telling him he had "completed 2 stories about Chicote's Bar, 3000 and 4200 words in length, both imperfect" (Baker 626), argues that he had worked through the various false starts and his own heavily revised typescripts and manuscript of "The Butterfly and the Tank" in July (KL/EH 300, 301, 303) but still had to work out their imperfections for the later typescripts in early September (KL/EH 302, 304).

The story's most troublesome imperfection was the ending. He had some difficulty getting started in his first typescript (300), found his pace in another (301), and then continued it in manuscript (303; from *Four Stories* 108 ["It seems he was feeble . . ."] on). This manuscript introduces a deleted ending that was followed in the later uncorrected typescript fragments (304). All these might have been the unperfected work of July. The remaining titled typescript (302) probably followed the letter of 3 August, for it includes the ending of the published version. If this was the sequence, Hemingway found his final ending, with the exception of the last sentence (*Four Stories* 109), in his early typescript (301); then he added a long dialogue between the narrator and the manager over the symbolic appropriateness of the "tank" in the title, omitting the concluding paragraph recollecting the victim's wife's last words, rejected that, and returned to his original conception.

Publication History (December 1938; August 1969)

The record for the publication of "The Butterfly and the Tank" follows that of "The Denunciation" described in the previous chapter. This second "Chicote" story appeared in the December 1938 issue of *Esquire* and was collected with the other Spanish Civil War stories in 1969.

Sources and Influences

The most evident source for the story is the pointless shooting of Pedro, "the flit-king," recalled in two other works: Hemingway's own "The Fifth

375

Column," and Langston Hughes's autobiographical *I Wonder as I Wander*. In "The Fifth Column," Dorothy Bridges, with her "Vassar" sensibilities, tells the same anecdote with many of the same details. Philip replies, "Poor chap," and she reminds him of his similar behavior "the other night with a spitoon. Trying to provoke trouble there in Chicote's," when he could be doing "something *political* or *military* and fine" (*Four Stories* 22–23). Although Langston Hughes knew the anecdote secondhand, he heard it from the originals for the English couple, "the forceful woman" and her boyish companion (Hughes 362–65; *Four Stories* 102).

The anecdote, then, was familiar to many in Madrid in the dark fall of 1937; but whether Hemingway witnessed the shooting or was simply as impressed as others with its ironic point is, so far, a matter of conjecture, even though Hughes, like John Steinbeck, naturally assumed he had been at the bar when it happened (Baker 337).

Whether he had seen it or not, the earlier version of the event in the play underlines Hemingway's sense of identification with the joyful victim—if one assumes that Philip's caper with the spitoon was a similar gesture—and his sense of its meaning. In the play, Philip's laconic "Poor chap" rejects Dorothy's appeal for something "fine," as does the story's rejection of the manager's interpretation of the allegory of the butterfly and the tank.

Critical Studies

There are only two commentaries on "The Butterfly and the Tank" that are more than cursory. Martin Light, in his review of the Civil War stories, saw a progression in the narrator's conception of the anecdote: he first thought of it as a "comedy of little people acting foolishly"; then in response to others who see it thematically as "misunderstood gaiety coming in contact with deadly seriousness," he objects, preferring "an account without imposed meanings and artificial symbols" (71). The narrator, after dismissing the event, as Philip did in "The Fifth Column" with "poor chap," is caught between those like the forceful English woman, who would censor the event as prejudicial to the Republican cause, and the manager—a writer manqué—who would similarly "censor" the ironic futility of the event by investing the protagonists with the symbolic roles of the butterfly and the tank.

Julian Smith, in his review of the Civil War stories, suggested that the narrator, caught in this dilemma, does not simply settle for the ironic facts of the matter, but sees it "ritualized through the magical three": three waiters, three rejections, three attackers, three screaming girls, and so on (9). So the "flit king" becomes an ironic version of Christ, a simple "bringer of joy," whose death "ironically improves things" the next morning (10).

Martin Light seemed closer to the real issue of the story, for he was concerned with the narrator's dilemma, while Julian Smith at least implied that the dilemma is resolved in a narration that finds its meaning in a portrayal of an ironic Christ figure. However many triplets in the story, they do not resolve its central issue, whether to explain, even explain away, the meaning of the event through political or religious metaphors and so dismiss the fact that no one, not even the police if they knew, could answer the wife's question, "Who has done this to thee, Pedro?" (*Four Stories* 109).

Works Cited

PRIMARY

The Fifth Column and Four Stories of the Spanish Civil War. New York: Scribner's, 1969, 101–09.

SECONDARY

Baker, Carlos. *Ernest Hemingway: A Life Story*. 1969. New York: Scribner's, 1988.

Hughes, Langston. *I Wonder as I Wander*. New York: Octagon, 1974.

Light, Martin. "Of Wasteful Deaths: Hemingway's Stories about the Spanish Civil War." *Western Humanities Review* 23 (Winter 1969): 29–42; rpt. in *The Short Stories of Ernest Hemingway*. Ed. Jackson J. Benson. Durham: Duke UP, 1975, 64–77.

Smith, Julian. "Christ Times Four: Hemingway's Unknown Spanish Civil War Stories." *Arizona Quarterly* 25 (Spring 1969): 5–17.

51
Night Before Battle

Composition History (September-October 1938)

"Night Before Battle," the third and last of the Chicote stories, must have been written sometime in the latter part of September and the first two weeks of October 1938, and at a furious pace. On 22 October Hemingway sent the story to Arnold Gingrich at *Esquire* and mentioned "another swell story done that [I] only need to go over . . . and two chapters done on a novel" (*Letters* 472); it is likely he is referring to either "Under the Ridge" or "Nobody Ever Dies" and the early chapters of *For Whom the Bell Tolls*.

Although one of his sources for the story was published in May 1938 (see Julian Smith below), and Hemingway could have been working intermittently on it since then, his one remaining typescript, titled and heavily revised, seems more like the work of that fall (KL/EH 607). The only other typescript is a carbon of that sent to *Esquire* with some corrections, a word count, and serial rights noted; its original was probably that sent on 22 October.

Publication History (February 1939; August 1969)

With its *Esquire* publication in February 1939, Hemingway toyed with the idea of another collection of stories—"The Denunciation," "The Butterfly and the Tank," "Night Before Battle," "Nobody Ever Dies," to be published in March, two others he was about to write, and one, "Landscape with Figures," still to be sent out. The only other one he had in mind became *The Old Man and the Sea* (*Letters* 479, 7 February 1939). But by the end of the following month, he had over fifteen thousand words done on *For Whom the Bell Tolls*, "20 times better than that Night Before Battle which was flat" (*Letters* 482, 25 March 1939). That judgment, which might apply as well to most of his Spanish Civil War stories, was enough to scotch the proposed collection, and the story went uncollected until 1969.

Sources and Influences

Hemingway had at hand his three NANA dispatches to assist his recollection of the details of filming the fighting at Casa del Campo in the story's opening episode; and the first of them ends with a near encounter between "a big trimotor Junker" and a "Government biplane" that might have recalled Baldy's story of shooting down another Junker (Dispatches 6, 7, and 9 from 9, 11, and 20 April 1937; Watson 23-29, 33-36).

When Hemingway contrasted "Night before Battle" with his burgeoning novel in that letter of March 1939, he remarked that the story was "flat where this [the novel] is rounded and recalled where this is invented" (*Letters* 482). And the story, such as it is, echoes with notes of recollected dialogue—drunken, ironic, exhausted remarks from random and faceless figures that drift in and out of Chicote's, the narrator, Edwin Henry's, room at the Hotel Florida, and the Gran Via restaurant. Out of that welter of characters, two death-haunted figures loom with larger meaning, Al Wagner, the tank captain, and Baldy Jackson, the flyer. Although Wagner's original has not been identified, Jackson's has, and his experiences, at least, mark the story as "recalled."

Julian Smith has identified Baldy's prototype in Harold E. "Whitey" Dahl, whose experiences were recounted in Frank Glasgow Tinker's *Some Still Live* and match Baldy's "detail for detail" as Tinker's awe for Whitey's character is matched by the other flyer's affection for Baldy (12). Hemingway had followed the serialization of Tinker's book in the *Saturday Evening Post* and in May 1938 purchased three copies through Scribner's (*Letters* 467; Reynolds 192).

Finally, the story has another of those dark and prophetic notes one finds in Hemingway's fiction. Three times Baldy asks rather pathetically, "Where's Frank?" but he has left; a few months after the story was published, Frank Tinker committed suicide, and Hemingway regretted having missed the chance to talk him out of it (*Letters* 494-95).

Critical Studies

Martin Light's review of the story in 1969 isolates the two figures Al Wagner and Baldy Jackson and places Edwin Henry, the observer of both war and warriors, between them. The scene at Chicote's, where talk against Prime Minister Largo Caballero's direction of the recent battle is unwise, is balanced by a scene at the "anarchist" restaurant on the Gran Via, where the waiters are corrupt (*Four Stories* 114-15, 125-26). In both scenes Edwin Henry offers food, drink, and a night with a woman to distract Al from his premonition of dying in the next morning's now futile battle. He fails, and the tanker's death is forecast in his last words, "Tomorrow night at Chicote's. We don't have to go into the time" (*Four Stories* 138). Over against him is the gloriously drunk Baldy Jackson, whose function, it seems, is to recount his downing a Junker and then being shot down when he "started watching the spectacle" and lost the protection of his echelon. His first account is mockingly literary with both clichéd and sentimental metaphors: the burning Junker "like a blast furnace" and the parachutes like "big beautiful morning glories." When his fellow flyers ridicule this version, he agrees to tell them "what happened, really," and he does in the technical language of those who fight the war and must beware of "sightseeing" (*Four Stories* 134-35).

Martin Light distinguishes between the tanker and the flyer with Robert Jordan's reflection on the "right mood for a soldier: 'All the best ones . . . were gay'" (*For Whom* 17) like the flyer, and those who have lost their gaiety and are left only with a deep anger at the prospect of dying uselessly (Light 73).

Julian Smith, after an unpersuasive attempt to resurrect Christian and archetypal imagery from the story, adds to the opposition between the tanker and the flyer both the political and artistic elements. Al, the tanker, pities the flyers because they are mercenaries, and so perhaps can afford their gaiety, while he has a political commitment to the war. Both men engage in combat and together mark the "difference between the soldier fighting the war and the artist reporting it" (13), the narrator. At the outset, Henry's refusal to get in close to the combat is justified by the concern for the cameras—no tanker or flyer has that excuse. After this raucous night, however, Henry admits to his filmmaking colleagues that "We've got to get closer tomorrow," and one replies, "Much closer. I am glad you know" (*Four Stories* 137). The two major characters, then—the mercenary with a kind of literary gaiety with which he distances himself and the politically engaged soldier—represent degrees of engagement and risk in the conflict, and for the observing artist present a dilemma he must resolve during his night before battle.

Lately, Kenneth Johnston has found an ironic note in Al Wagner's plan to return to his unit through the Plaza de España and the flyers' return to Alcala. In that plaza there is the famous statue of Don Quixote and Sancho Panza, and Alcala was the birthplace of Cervantes. Thus, Al becomes the Knight of the Sad Countenance, the short man with thick glasses, his Sancho, the tank his Rosinante, and the war a futile quest, even though Hemingway's "vision contained both knight and squire" (26-28). Hemingway may have risked "gambling heavily on the reader's knowledge of the landmarks of Madrid" (26); but if he did he played against his own story, for Al Wagner is hardly charging windmills in a benighted chivalric quest.

Works Cited

PRIMARY

Ernest Hemingway: Selected Letters, 1917-1961. Ed. Carlos Baker. New York: Scribner's, 1981.

The Fifth Column and Four Stories of the Spanish Civil War. New York: Scribner's, 1969, 110–39.

For Whom the Bell Tolls. New York: Scribner's, 1940.

SECONDARY

Johnston, Kenneth G. "Hemingway's 'Night before Battle': Don Quixote, 1937." *Hemingway Notes* 6 (Fall 1980): 26–28.

Light, Martin. "Of Wasteful Deaths: Hemingway's Stories about the Spanish Civil War." *Western Humanities Review* 23 (Winter 1969): 29–42; rpt. in *The Short Stories of Ernest Hemingway: Critical Essays.* Ed. Jackson J. Benson. Durham: Duke UP, 1975, 64–77.

Reynolds, Michael S. *Hemingway's Reading: 1910–1940.* Princeton: Princeton UP, 1981.

Smith, Julian. "Christ Times Four: Hemingway's Unknown Spanish Civil War Stories." *Arizona Quarterly* 25 (Spring 1969): 5–17.

Watson, William B., ed. "Hemingway's Civil War Dispatches." *Hemingway Review* 7 (Spring 1988): 4–92.

52

Nobody Ever Dies

Composition History (October-November 1938)

In a letter written from Paris to Arnold Gingrich on 22 October 1938, Hemingway went through the list of stories he had sent him. He mentioned that when he started on "the third Chicote story I got this instead," the typescript of "Night Before Battle" he was enclosing. He went on to mention "another swell story done that only need to go over (maybe best ever wrote, anyway one of them)." Carlos Baker thought it possible the new story was "Under the Ridge," on the understandable assumption that Hemingway could not have thought of "Nobody Ever Dies" as one of the best he ever wrote (*Letters* 472–73). But he was nearly finished with that Cuban epilogue to the Spanish Civil War in late October and probably had it typed in early November. (A typist's bill is attached to the carbon typescript, KL/EH 612). By 7 February 1939, Hemingway suggested a new collection including the story, but did not mention "Under the Ridge" until 25 March. So the swell story of late October 1938 must have been the one every critic considers the weakest of this late period, "Nobody Ever Dies."

Other than the untitled Paris typescript (KL/EH 612), all that remains is a forty-four-page manuscript, titled "The Flower of the Party" (KL/EH 610), and some eight pages of discarded manuscript related to it (KL/EH 611). Again, Hemingway's trials came with the story's ending. Both the manuscript and the typescript do not include the two maudlin paragraphs associating Maria with Joan of Arc and ending with an egregious pun ("She sat there holding herself very still . . . her face shining in the *arc* light," *Cosmopolitan* 76; *Complete Stories* 480)

The manuscript is missing page 42, but both it and the typescript end with the sentence "Fifty dollars is a lot of money now in La Havana." Either there is a missing typescript or Hemingway added the two sentimental paragraphs and the published ending to the original of this Paris typescript. That ending returns to the allusion to Joan of Arc, promising some final victory, for the Negro's "blue voodoo beads . . . could not help his fear because he was up against an older magic now" (*Cosmopolitan* 76; *Complete Stories* 481).

Sources and Influences

The only source for the story has been suggested by Kenneth Johnston, the only critic who has taken it seriously. He noted that Enrique, the wounded young Cuban, must have served in the "XV International Brigade with the American volunteers in the Abraham Lincoln Battalion, which had its baptism of fire in the Jarama River valley, southeast of Madrid, in late February 1937," establishing the date of the story, fifteen months later, in June of 1938 (54–55). That identification serves also to date the writing of the story, for as Johnston noted, its theme, with its abundant imagery of rebirth in nature, closely resembles Hemingway's eulogy for the Lincoln Battalion in "The American Dead in Spain," published a month before the story appeared. Finally, Johnston argued persuasively that in this story Hemingway was sketching out an analogue for the ending of *For Whom the Bell Tolls:* in both the story and the novel, the heroes "part with their Marias" in strikingly similar ways.

Critical Studies

Kenneth Johnston's article is, again, the only serious critical study of "Nobody Ever Dies" His analysis centers on the ironic juxtaposition of images: the allusions to the laurel trees, the classical wreath of victory, is most often associated with the police informer, who, like the mockingbird Enrique sets free, wears a coat of gray and betrays the wounded veteran. And the "high seriousness of the opening section is" ironically lightened with puns and the counterpoint of the "best-of-all-possible worlds of the radio commercials with the imperfect one in which Enrique is trapped" (55–56).

Johnston's essay is a noble and necessary effort that succeeds in demonstrating that the story has been unjustly ignored. But reading the story in *Cosmopolitan,* with its lurid illustration suggesting Maria is about to be raped, recalls attention to the "melodrama and sentimentalism" Johnston acknowledged (58).

If it were not for the fact that one of the best of these late stories, "Under the Ridge," appeared in this magazine some six months later, one might argue that the most pervasive and insidious influence on "Nobody Ever Dies" was *Cosmopolitan,* whose editors must have added the exclamation point to its title in that publication.

Works Cited

PRIMARY

The Complete Short Stories of Ernest Hemingway. New York: Scribner's, 1987, 470–81.

Ernest Hemingway: Selected Letters, 1917–1961. Ed. Carlos Baker. New York: Scribner's, 1981.

"Nobody Ever Dies!" *Cosmopolitan* 106 (Mar. 1939): 28–31, 74–76.

"On the American Dead in Spain." *New Masses,* 14 Feb. 1939: 3.

SECONDARY

Johnston, Kenneth G. " 'Nobody Ever Dies': Hemingway's Neglected Story of Freedom Fighters." *Kansas Quarterly* 9 (1977): 53–58.

53

Under the Ridge

Composition History (February 1939)

When Hemingway left for Cuba on 14 February 1939, he had just written to Max Perkins that he was going to finish three long stories, two of which would be about the Civil War, the battle at Teruel, and the "storming of the Guadarrama pass by the Polish lancers." When he arrived, he dropped that plan and "wrote one about the war, Pauline thinks among best I've ever written, called Under The Ridge" and turned again to the fifteen thousand words he had written on *For Whom the Bell Tolls* (*Letters* 478, 7 February; 482, 25 March 1939). Two months later he wrote to Charles Scribner that he had a "good story to sell to Cosmopolitan now that I wrote in February when was warming up before this [*For Whom the Bell Tolls*] but so far haven't taken the time out to get it re-written and copied" (*Letters* 486, 23 May 1939).

So it is probable that he began a manuscript or typescript of the story in the last two weeks of February, rewrote it and sent a finished typescript to *Cosmopolitan* sometime in the early summer of 1939. If these manuscripts exist, there is no record of them in any of the major manuscript collections.

Publication History (October 1939; August 1969)

"Under the Ridge" was published in the October 1939 issue of *Cosmopolitan*. In his letter to Max Perkins of 25 March 1939, Hemingway was still thinking of a new collection of stories for which he had "The Denunciation. The Butterfly and the Tank. Night Before Battle. Nobody Ever Dies. Landscape With Figures. And this new one [,] Hell, that makes six" (*Letters* 482). But by then he was absorbed in his Spanish novel, and once that was published, he must have recognized that a collection of the stories with which he "warmed up" for the novel would have been an anticlimax.

The story was finally collected in *The Fifth Column and Four Spanish Civil War Stories* of 1969.

Sources and Influences

As with the other Spanish Civil War stories, Hemingway's recollections of his experience contributed largely to "Under the Ridge," but in a more general way than for, say, "Old Man at the Bridge" or "The Butterfly and the Tank." Wayne Kvam is tempted by the similarity between two paragraphs of Hemingway's sixth NANA dispatch and the opening paragraph of the story to suggest that the dispatch's "setting and physical sensations . . . figure prominently in 'Under the Ridge.'" From that he concluded that Hemingway based his story on "what really happened in action" (the phrase is from *Death in the Afternoon*) and was "operating on the raw experience of journalism" (226–28). But the dispatch of 9 April 1937, which recalls his first experience in combat outside of Madrid at Morata de Taruña three days earlier, provided only those few details, while the experience itself could not have included all the dramatic details and counterpointed conflicts of the story. Hemingway, in Cuba and two years after the events of the spring of 1937, was clearly trying out the fictional possibilities for the Spanish novel that was by then his first concern.

Martin Light and Wayne Kvam have noted those elements in the story that foreshadow *For Whom the Bell Tolls:* a narrator, both engaged in the action and at a distance from it, who is friends with a general—Lucasz, named in the novel—but rejected by the Extremaduran—as Robert Jordan is by Pablo—and who hears a tale of Paco's execution—as Jordan hears from Pilar of Loyalist brutality (Light 75–76; Kvam 239–40, nn. 29, 32, 36).

That the story was something of an exercise for the novel is not to detract from its considerable achievement as a story, as Wayne Kvam seemed to assume, but rather to demonstrate how far Hemingway had come from his dispatches and from those stories that hewed so closely to experience and to some of his own bravado mannerisms—this difference makes the story stand out at the end of this sequence of stories, just as "Old Man at the Bridge" did at its beginning.

Critical Studies

For Julian Smith the "versions of Christian sacrifice and communion" in the first three Civil War stories are concluded in "Under the Ridge" with the "quasi-Biblical description of Paco's last supper and death" and the dismissal of the narrator "without benediction." More interesting is Smith's sense of the story's informing principles of ironic contradiction and reversal: "Paco shot himself so he might live but was executed; the French soldier walked away to live but died . . .; a French tank commander who got drunk to be brave will be shot . . .; the Russian general warns the narrator not to get killed but is himself killed; tanks returning in defeat are ironically reversed on film where they 'advanced over the hills irresistibly . . . toward the illusion of victory'" (15–16).

That last image is crucial, for although the story "seems to be about exterior events [it] is actually about the state of mind of the nameless narrator." He "sublimates his . . . fear of death . . . by dwelling on the fears and deaths of others"; he is scrupulously "conscious and aware as opposed to his cameraman"; and although "divided by his understanding of the French deserter as a man and by his recognition of the necessity of the harsh discipline meted out by battle police," he becomes the "cold observer who can tell us in one sentence that a good friend has been killed and in the next observe with professional blandness that the 'oddest thing about that day was how marvelously the pictures we took of the tanks came out'" (16).

Wayne Kvam, drawing on a variety of Hemingway's pronouncements on the role of the writer in wartime, considered "Under the Ridge" to be a "story about how a writer writes a story" (228). The process Kvam extracts from this fiction begins with the writer's "acute sensitivity to place" (231); from that sensitivity not only to the physical scene but also to the moral or emotional position of others in that scene, the writer derives human understanding. Kvam drew on the remarkable paragraphs in which the narrator identifies with the Frenchman walking away from the battle (Kvam 232–33; *Four Stories* 146–47). For all the writer's "responses as a *man*" to the scene and its weary figures, the final act is to refuse "as a *writer,* to be misled by them [and to shape] his 'truth' in the tragic dialectic between necessary discipline and the individual's will to live" (236).

The "truth in a tragic dialectic" is a fine notion, but something in the story resists it or any suggestion of resolution it might bear. Just as in the story the battle is in the past and we are present witnesses to an ignominious retreat, so the story itself is told long after the event—after the general was killed and the films had been developed. In that retreat we hear of Paco's execution in the past, hear the execution of the Frenchman beyond the ridge, and learn that the tank commander will die in the morning. If there is any dialectic at the end of the story it turns on the idea of victory. There is the momentary victory of the Frenchman, but it "only lasted until he had walked halfway down the ridge." The narrator and his companions walk past the dead man "still wearing his blanket," to "the staff car that would take us to Madrid." What they have brought from the war are the films of the tanks crawling "toward the illusion of victory we screened" (*Four Stories* 151).

Those films became "The Spanish Earth," which, of course, did not record the brutal lesson of Paco's death or the futile victory of the proud Frenchman. But "Under the Ridge" does, and so may approach something of a confession, not in terms of a tragic dialectic—all that is political talk in the story—but in the final image of a dead man, senselessly killed, in his last place under the ridge.

Works Cited

PRIMARY

Ernest Hemingway: Selected Letters, 1917–1961. Ed. Carlos Baker. New York: Scribner's, 1981.

The Fifth Column and Four Stories of the Spanish Civil War. New York: Scribner's, 1969, 140–51.

SECONDARY

Kvam, Wayne. "Hemingway's 'Under the Ridge.' " *Fitzgerald/Hemingway Annual* (1979): 225–40.

Light, Martin. "Of Wasteful Deaths: Hemingway's Stories about the Spanish Civil War." *Western Humanities Review* 23 (Winter 1969): 29–42; rpt. in *The Short Stories of Ernest Hemingway: Critical Essays.* Ed. Jackson J. Benson. Durham: Duke UP, 1975, 64–77.

Smith, Julian. "Christ Times Four: Hemingway's Unknown Spanish Civil War Stories." *Arizona Quarterly* 25 (Spring 1969): 5–17.

The Complete Short Stories of Ernest Hemingway: The Finca Vigia Edition
(November 1987)

54/55

Get a Seeing-Eyed Dog
and
A Man of the World

Composition History "Get a Seeing-Eyed Dog" (March 1954-July 1956)
"A Man of the World" (May-June 1957)

Although the last two stories published in Hemingway's lifetime, "Get a Seeing-Eyed Dog" and "A Man of the World," were written at least one and possibly three years apart, their contrasting visions of blindness, with characters as different as a Wyoming brawler and a novelist recollecting his past in a Venetian hotel, unites them in the opposition that led Hemingway to offer them as "Two Tales of Darkness" in the *Atlantic* of November 1957. For this reason and that the limited commentaries on the tales draw on one to illuminate the other, they will be considered together here.

"Get a Seeing-Eyed Dog": The latest date for the writing of this story is established with a letter to Charles Scribner, Jr., on 14 August 1956 that listed it along with five unpublished World War II stories. He mentioned that Mary Hemingway had just "copied" them, and it is possible that the last titled typescript for the story (KL/EH 425) was completed then. But in that letter he distinguished between the war stories and the "one I wrote to get going after Africa" and the two disastrous air crashes in late January 1954 (*Letters* 868). With a "full-scale concussion, . . . ruptured liver, spleen, and kidney," various broken bones, burns, and a "temporary loss of vision in his left eye," Hemingway went ahead with plans for a fishing trip on the coast near Zanzibar, gave it up, and sailed to Venice to convalesce (Baker 522-23).

The story's setting, its painful reminiscences, the fragile relationship between the suffering writer and his companion, even the story's fragmentary, sketchlike quality, all suggest that this story was, as Hemingway said, "one I wrote to get going after [meaning *immediately* after] Africa." The only revisions in his first typescript (KL/EH 424) are insignificant, with the exception of naming the writer "Tommy," not Philip as in the published version, perhaps linking him with the narrator of "A Man of the World."

"A Man of the World": The spring of 1957 was a dismal season for Hemingway. In a state of depression, he responded to the *Atlantic*'s request for a contribution to their centenary issue by beginning a memoir of Scott Fitzgerald, so starting the process that would end with the posthumous publication of *A Moveable Feast*. Carlos Baker argued that something in that effort at recollecting his early Parisian years, writing out answers to George Plimpton's questions for a *Paris Review* "interview," and what he thought of as anecdotal betrayals of Dylan Thomas led him to give up the Fitzgerald memoir and turn instead to writing "A Man of the World" sometime between mid-May and mid-June (Baker 537–38; Hemingway to H. Breit letter cited, 663).

There is a single Hemingway typescript with two holograph additions, one of which is of interest: the addition of the ending from "Have a drink, Blindy." to the end (*Complete Stories* 495). The original of an uncorrected and titled carbon (KL/EH 535) was probably sent to the *Atlantic*.

Publication History (November 1987)

With "A Man of the World" in hand for the *Atlantic* at the end of June, Hemingway was visited sometime in July by Edward Weeks's editorial representative, who agreed to accept *two* stories for the centenary issue, and Hemingway was able to—finesse may be too critical a term—send them "Get a Seeing-Eyed Dog" as well. Then, when he received a check for a thousand dollars he wrote to Weeks on 20 August 1957 that if they were willing to pay that for one story, they should double the fee for two since he "could sell these two stories I sent you for at least four times the price" Weeks had offered (*Letters* 880).

The two stories were published then in the November 1957 centenary issue of the *Atlantic,* but reversed from their sequence of composition, with "A Man of the World" followed by "Get a Seeing-Eyed Dog." Edward Weeks may have taken that raise in the ante with equanimity or not. In any case, the two stories carry an editorial note recognizing Hemingway as a Nobel Prize winner, a writer of "swift and revealing dialogue" with a "veneration for courage," but also one "with a capacity to share and inflict [!] suffering" (*Atlantic* 65)—to the tune of a thousand dollars on the *Atlantic?*

In the recent *Finca Vigia* edition of the stories the texts are taken from the *Atlantic*'s publication but the order of the stories is reversed (*Complete Stories* 487–95), perhaps in recognition of their sequence of composition.

Sources and Influences

Carlos Baker dismissed both these stories as trivial, and there is always the off chance that he was right. That suspicion is supported by some of the lonely and rather strenuous articles that see these two stories as the "capstone"—not the tombstone—of Hemingway's career (Smith 9, Wylder 53). Once again, when Julian Smith turned from his earlier study of the Spanish Civil War stories, he noted a persuasive similarity with Hemingway's earlier works, particularly the earlier "Snows of Kilimanjaro," and with the later novel, *Across the River and into the Trees*. But his most interesting insight followed upon Baker's placement of the latter story in the period when he began the retrospective *A Moveable Feast* (14–15). Delbert Wylder was less restrained, for he found analogues for these two stories in Shirley Jackson's "The Lottery," Hawthorne's "Young Goodman Brown" and "My Kinsman, Major Molineux," Frost, Poe, Melville, and on, until both stories sink under the weight of better fiction (54 ff.)

There may be undiscovered and persuasive sources in other writers for these two stories, but so far they derive their primary interest from their relationship with Hemingway's own, last, desperate, and dying attempts to dramatize his own agony as an artist in the late years of the 1950s.

Critical Studies

Julian Smith attempted to redeem these stories from critical disdain with the argument that "A Man of the World" shares a symbolic setting with "A Clean, Well-Lighted Place" and an action as portentous. But it is not Blindy's story, although he is "like Christ, . . . a man of all the world," for its drama rests in the reaction of the three others at the bar: Frank, the bartender, "who knew and told" Blindy's story; Tom, the narrator, "who knew and would not tell"; and the "stranger who seeks to know and is told." So the story becomes an "interior monologue, perhaps even an examination of conscience" as Tom recalls the "personal and moral implications of what he has witnessed" (12).

Yet the story's western setting, reluctant narrator, uninitiated listener, and grimly exaggerated details could turn us from the passion of Christ to Mark Twain and the tradition of the tall tale—after all, the narrator is named Tom and the man who bit out Blindy's eyes, Sawyer.

Smith found a connection between the two stories in the contrast between Harry Morgan and Richard Gordon in *To Have and Have Not*: Blindy is to Morgan—a maimed but manly hero—as Philip (of "Get a Seeing-Eyed Dog") is to Gordon—an unmanned writer (13). But the more interesting associations are those he drew between this story of remembering and "The Snows of Kilimanjaro" and the late recollection of Paris in *A Moveable Feast*. Tom's story of Blindy may have been one of the "twenty good stories" from the American West that Harry of "The Snows" had never written. Philip, like Harry, spent his days remembering the past, as Hemingway was to do in his last years; and through this intricate analogy, the Venetian sketch and the western tale become "Hemingway's final payments on Harry's last dream and testament" (15).

Works Cited

PRIMARY

The Complete Short Stories of Ernest Hemingway. New York: Scribner's, 1987, 487–95.

Ernest Hemingway: Selected Letters, 1917–1961. Ed. Carlos Baker. New York: Scribner's, 1981.

"Two Tales of Darkness." *Atlantic* 100 (Nov. 1957): 64–66.

SECONDARY

Baker, Carlos. *Ernest Hemingway: A Life Story.* 1969. New York: Scribner's, 1988.

Smith, Julian. "Eyeless in Wyoming, Blind in Venice—Hemingway's Last Stories." *Connecticut Review* 4 (1971): 9–15.

Wylder, Delbert E. "Internal Treachery in the Last Published Stories of Ernest Hemingway." *Hemingway: In Our Time.* Ed. Richard Astro and Jackson J. Benson. Corvallis: Oregon State UP, 1973.

Epilogue: Excluded Stories, 1921–1987

To establish a canon of Hemingway's short stories, even for a survey such as this one, is to raise a variety of questions, some as controversial as definitions of the genre itself, others just as complicated by issues of authorial intention and the "true" text.

Some would argue that all eighteen of the *in our time* chapters of 1924 deserve inclusion in this book, not only the two he simply retitled, "A Very Short Story" and "The Revolutionist," at one time titled "An Even Shorter Story." But here Hemingway's final intention, whatever his motives, held sway.

Others may question the generic distinction between a fable and a story and expect a discussion of "A Divine Gesture," written in the summer of 1921 and published in the *Double Dealer* (May 1922), at the beginning of his career, and "The Good Lion" and "The Faithful Bull," written in early 1950 and published in *Holiday* (March 1951), near its end. No critic has ventured to state what the first means, if anything; the last two occasional pieces have some slight biographical interest, but little to warrant their study as stories.

They may question, too, the exclusion of "One Trip Across," published in *Cosmopolitan* (April 1934) and "The Tradesman's Return," in *Esquire* (February 1936); but the two became chapters in a "Key West-Havana novel" soon after their first publication (*Letters* 447), and have been so read since then.

Since Hemingway's death three books have included variously edited versions of unpublished manuscripts. The first was *The Nick Adams Stories* (New York: Scribner's, 1972). Of the eight unfinished sketches and rejected passages of other stories, two have been considered here with the original stories of which they were a part: "Three Shots" with "Indian Camp" and "On Writing" with "Big Two-Hearted River."

Two manuscripts published as stories in this edition deserve a note. "Summer People" was written in the late summer of 1924. A very personal story, it is intimately related to some of the memories in the rejected conclusion of "Big Two-Hearted River." It, rather than "A Lack of Passion," was the one of "two long stories [that was] not much good" he mentions in a letter of 15 August 1924 (*Letters* 122)—it was tactless if not libelous. He never completed the typescript version of the original manuscript, even though he considered using its title for "The Three-Day Blow" and at one time thought of substituting the story for "My Old Man." The text published here is corrupt, with a misreading of the nickname "Stut" for "slut" and the elision of a full page of the manuscript, first noticed by Peter Griffin but cited later as evidence of Hemingway's attitude toward women.

The other is "The Last Good Country," intermittently written between April 1952 and July 1958. The manuscripts clearly show Hemingway embarked on a novel, with two related plots. The published text disguises that intent; and, as Philip Young admitted, cuts were made "where the text was wordy, the pace slow, or the taste dubious" (6)—that is to say, revealing and dirty.

The second book to print unpublished manuscripts was Peter Griffin's *Along with Youth* (Oxford: Oxford UP, 1985). Since they show Hemingway's development of strategies begun in his published school fiction and realized in "Up in Michigan," those manuscripts are reviewed in the Prologue.

The third is the recent collection of *The Complete Short Stories of Ernest Hemingway* (New York: Scribner's, 1987). Although "Stut" is no longer a slut, the page is still missing from "Summer People" and "The Last Good Country" is still rewritten and bowdlerised. This text lists five works presented as stories. They were neither intended as stories nor meant to be published—indeed some were never meant to be read. They are "An African Story" gathered from the recently published *The Garden of Eden* (New York: Scribner's, 1986); "Black Ass at the Crossroads," a sketch from Hemingway's World War II adventures; "Landscape With Figures," sketch from Spain in 1938; and two family anecdotes from the 1950s, "I Guess Everything Reminds You of Something" and "Great News from the Mainland."

With one or two possible exceptions, none of these manuscripts adds significantly to our understanding of Hemingway's art of the short story, while some diminish it. Hemingway, through the forty years from 1921 until his death, seems to have agreed with that judgment. And, in any case, as someone—probably Mark Twain—has said, "Books are never finished, they're just abandoned."

Works Cited

PRIMARY

Ernest Hemingway: Selected Letters, 1917–1961. Ed. Carlos Baker. New York: Scribner's, 1981.

SECONDARY

Griffin, Peter. "A Substantive Error in the Text of Ernest Hemingway's 'Summer People.' " *American Literature* 50 (1978): 471–73.

Philip Young. " 'Big World Out There': *The Nick Adams Stories.*" *Novel* 6 (Fall 1972): 5–29.

Index of Hemingway's Works

Across The River and Into the Trees, 91, 272, 282
"African Story, An," 396
"After the Storm," xviii, *240–45,* 246, 265, 291
"Alpine Idyll, An," xvii, *132–37,* 141
"Art of the Short Story, The," *(Paris Review),* 99, 125–28, 138, 224, 225, 333, 336
"Ash Heel's Tendon, The," xxvii, 142
"Banal Story," xvi, xvii, 105, *110–14,* 235
"Battler, The," xvi, 12, 44, 76, 87, 96, *115–21,* 128, 142, 148, 260, 280, 323
"Big Two-Hearted River" (including "On Writing"), xi, xvi, 12, 35–37, 65, 73, 81, *85–101,* 104–6, 116, 118–20, 162, 174, 175, 177, 182, 272, 273, 280, 305, 310, 313, 395
"Black Ass at the Crossroads," 396
"Butterfly and the Tank, The," xx, 370, *375–77,* 378, 385, 386
"Canary for One, A," xvii, xviii, 6, 82, *159–63,* 164, 165, 168, 198, 199, 207, 254
"Capital of the World, The," xix, *321–26,* 349, 351
"Cat in the Rain," xvi, 6, 7, 16, 18, 19, *43–49,* 50, 56, 82, 161, 207, 254
"Che Ti Dice la Patria?" xvii, *193–96,* 198, 204, 291
"Clean, Well-Lighted Place, A," x, xi, xviii, 181, 182, 206, 271, *277–88,* 330, 393
"Cross-Country Snow," xvi, 19, 69, *81–84,* 118, 136, 161, 207, 254
"Crossroads—An Anthology," xxvii, 6
"Current, The," xxvii, 127

"Day's Wait, A," xviii, 218–20, 291, *302–6,* 312
Death in the Afternoon, xviii, 76, 104–6, 113, 162, 189, 190, 218, 224, 231, 233–35, 237, 240, 246, 248, 264, 265, 289, 323, 386
"Denunciation, The," xx, *369–74,* 375, 378, 385
"Divine Gesture, A," 395
"Doctor and the Doctor's Wife, The," xvi, *61–67,* 68, 81, 120, 199, 309
"End of Something, The," xvi, 43, 44, *50–55,* 56, 62, 118, 169
"Faithful Bull, The," 395
Farewell to Arms, A, xviii, 27, 31, 38, 47, 77, 87, 91, 166–68, 172, 173, 175, 217, 218, 231, 232, 240, 245, 252, 253, 270, 272, 289, 292, 299, 325, 339, 370, 373
"Fathers and Sons," xviii, xix, 51, 62, 63, 66, 199, 201, 218–21, 232, 238, 304, *307–17*
"Fifth Column, The," 375, 376
"Fifty Grand," xvii, 12, 104, 118, *125–31,* 142, 143, 149, 243, 265, 280
For Whom the Bell Tolls, xx, 113, 312, 339, 364, 370, 378, 380, 383, 385, 386
"Gambler, the Nun, and the Radio, The," xviii, 12, 219, 258, 271, 280, *289–96,* 307
Garden of Eden, The, xvii, xix, 226, 227, 396
"Get a Seeing-Eyed Dog," xx, *391–94*
"God Rest You Merry, Gentlemen," xviii, 181, *246–51,* 265
"Good Lion, The," 395
"Great News from the Mainland," 396
Green Hills of Africa, xix, 113, 142, 292, 312, 321, 327, 328, 332–34, 339, 356

397

"Hills Like White Elephants," xvii, xviii, 6, 7, 19, 21, 84, 160, 161, 173, 198, *204-13*, 221, 254
"Homage to Switzerland," xviii, 246, *252-56*, 271
"I Guess Everything Reminds You of Something," 396
"In Another Country," xvii, 71, 87, 156, 160, *164-71*, 172, 180, 206, 250, 269, 272, 280, 305
"Indian Camp" (including "Three Shots"), xvi, 12, *34-42*, 43, 44, 50, 51, 53, 61, 62, 66, 68, 71, 118, 120, 141, 162, 169, 199, 201, 280, 305, 309, 312, 395
"Interview with Ernest Hemingway, An," *(Paris Review)*, 138, 207, 392
"Judgment of Manitou," xxv, xxvi, 37
"Killers, The," xi, xvii, 13, 34, 110, 118, 119, 128, 132, 134, *138-53*, 154, 156, 157, 159, 160, 164-66, 181, 182, 206, 250, 261, 280, 323
"Lack of Passion, A," 69, 102, 133, 204, 395
"Landscape with Figures," 370, 385, 396
"Last Good Country, The," 63, 66, 117, 118, 199, 312, 396
"Light of the World, The," xxvi, 118, 148, 246, *257-63*, 269
"Man of the World, A," ix, xx, *391-94*
"Matter of Colour, A," xxv, xxvi, 127
"Mercenaries, The," xxvii
"Mother of a Queen, The," xviii, 246, *264-67*, 291
Moveable Feast, A, xv, xix, 3, 16-19, 35, 50, 56, 87, 91, 98, 99, 138, 185, 186, 353, 392, 393
"Mr. and Mrs. Elliot," xvi, xix, 45, 62, 68, *75-80*, 115, 189, 226
"My Old Man," xv, xvi, 3, 4, *10-15*, 17, 18, 36, 75, 81, 104, 118, 126, 128, 265, 396
"Natural History of the Dead, A," xviii, 134, 189, 219, 223, *231-39*, 246, 268, 270, 307, 310
"Night Before Battle," xx, 370, *378-81*, 382, 385
"Nobody Ever Dies," xx, 370, 378, *382-84*, 385

"Now I Lay Me," xvii, 66, 71, 87, 90, 165-68, *172-79*, 180, 194, 198, 199, 269, 272, 280, 305, 310
Old Man and the Sea, The, 95, 106, 156, 157, 280, 364, 370, 378
"Old Man at the Bridge," ix, xix, xx, *362-65*, 386
"On the Quai at Smyrna" (Introduction by the Author), xvii, *189-92*, 234
"One Reader Writes," xviii, xxvii, 246, 291, *297-301*
"One Trip Across," 321, 330, 395
"Out of Season," xi, xv, xviii, 4, 6, *16-22*, 35, 36, 44-46, 82, 161, 206, 207, 254
"Portrait of Three, or The Paella," 264, 269
"Portrait of the Idealist in Love," xxvii
"Pursuit Race, A," xvii, xviii, 12, 164, 172, 173, *180-84*, 185, 189, 198
"Revolutionist, The," xvi, *30-33*, 364, 395
"Sea Change, The," xix, 113, *223-30*, 246
"Sepi Jingan," xxv, 37
"Short Happy Life of Francis Macomber, The," xi, xix, 211, 280, 285, 322, 323, *327-48*, 349, 352, 372
"Simple Enquiry, A," xvii, xviii, 164, 172, 173, 180-82, *185-88*, 189, 198
"Snows of Kilimanjaro, The," xix, 211, 280, 285, 323, *349-61*, 393, 394
"Soldier's Home," xvi, *64-74*, 87, 93, 118, 166, 167, 272
"Spanish Earth, The," 371, 387
"Summer People," 51, 395, 396
Sun Also Rises, The, xvi, xvii, 77, 78, 83, 86, 87, 94, 132, 159, 165, 167, 177, 249, 250, 299, 325
"Ten Indians," ix, xvii, 38, 53, 59, 63, 120, 125, 132, 138, 139, 154, 193, *197-203*, 204, 270
"Three-Day Blow, The," xvi, 43, 44, 50-52, 54, *56-60*, 62, 83, 116, 118, 120, 199, 282, 312, 396
To Have and Have Not, xix, 128, 243, 323, 325, 328, 330, 339, 352, 370, 393
"Today is Friday," xvii, 138, 139, 141, 142, *154-58*, 159

Torrents of Spring, The, xvii, 5, 71, 112, 141, 310
"Tradesman's Return, The," 321, 330, 395
"Undefeated, The," xvi, xvii, 12, 69, *102-9*, 126, 128, 129, 133, 135, 156, 165, 206, 280
"Under the Ridge," xx, 382, 383, *385-88*
"Up in Michigan," ix, x, xv, xvi, xvii, xxvii, *3-9*, 17, 18, 36-38, 46, 66, 71, 76, 77, 102, 115, 116, 396

"Very Short Story, A," xvi, *25-29*, 30, 395
"Visiting Team, The," 272
"Way You'll Never Be, A," xix, 71, 87, 91-93, 165-67, 169, 175, 235, 246, *268-76*, 280, 313
"Wine of Wyoming," xviii, *217-22*, 224, 246, 269, 291, 312
Woppian Way, The (The Passing of Pickles McCarty), xxvii, 70, 127, 134, 272

General Index

Adair, William, 91
Alger, Horatio, 142
American Caravan, The, 133, 134
Anderson, Margaret, 226
Anderson, Paul Victor, 96
Anderson, Sherwood, xi, xv, 3, 5, 11–14, 36, 37, 71, 150
Aristotle, 52, 107
Armistead, Myra, 135
Armstrong, Richard and Jane, 298, 302
Arnold, Aerol, 65, 66
As Stable Pamphlets, The, 154, 155
Atkins, Anselm, 243, 244
Atlantic Monthly, xx, 126, 391, 392

Babbitt, Irving, 232, 234–36
Bache, William, 119, 284, 331, 353
Baker, Carlos, xviii, 3, 4, 6, 7, 10, 13, 18–20, 26, 27, 31, 34–37, 44, 48, 57, 64, 69, 70, 75, 82, 83, 88, 89, 102, 110, 112, 115, 116, 125–27, 132–35, 143, 156, 157, 161, 167, 174, 182, 186, 193–95, 204, 206, 207, 217, 219, 224, 234, 240, 246–48, 252–55, 258–60, 264, 268, 270, 273, 278, 279, 281, 285, 291, 292, 297–99, 302, 303, 307, 312, 321, 328, 335, 342, 352–56, 363, 369, 370, 375, 376, 382, 391, 392
Baker, Sheridan, 13, 87, 90, 92, 98, 128, 129, 150, 156, 157, 186, 236, 255, 259, 274, 284, 293, 303, 332
Balzac, Honoré de, 68, 310
Barba, Harry, 52
Barbour, James J., 260, 262
Bardacke, Theodore, 335
Barnes, Daniel R., 279, 280, 284
Barnes, Djuna, 69
Barney, Nathalie, 226

Barthes, Roland, 28
Bassett, Charles, 353
Beach, Sylvia, xv, 34, 226
Beck, Warren, 336–38, 340–42, 344, 345, 372
Beckett, Samuel, 285
Beebe, Maurice, 291
Beegel, Susan F., 105, 125, 126, 232, 234, 235, 240, 242–44
Beerbohm, Max, 19
Bell, H. H., Jr., 339
Bell, Millicent, 164
Bender, Bert, 340, 341
Benert, Annette, 284, 285
Bennett, Warren, 47, 48, 277, 278, 281, 283
Benson, Jackson J., 58, 65, 149, 162, 166, 168, 201, 284, 314, 315, 334, 343, 358
Bernard, Kenneth, 40
Bevis, R. W., 354
Bierce, Ambrose, 353
Bird, William, 4, 25, 26, 104
Bloom, Harold, 242
Bluefarb, Sam, 284
Bookman, The, 51, 232, 310
Booth, Wayne, 286
Boulton, Eddy, 62, 312
Boulton, Prudence, 37, 63, 66, 197, 199, 312
Boulton, Richard, 62, 63, 199
Boutelle, Ann Edwards, 200, 201, 314, 315
Boyd, John D., 72
Brenner, Gerry, 12, 14, 40, 53, 92, 93, 177, 182, 187, 201, 236, 237, 243, 266, 339
Brooks, Cleanth, 143–49, 285, 286
Brose, G., 354
Brosnahan, Leger, 328
Browning, Robert, 254, 265, 266

401

Bruccoli, Matthew J., xxv, 259, 260
Brumback, Theodore, 265
Bryher, (Annie Ellerman McAlmon), 226
Buber, Martin, 284
Bunyan, John, 88
Burhans, Clinton D., 64
Burke, Jackson, 333
Burns, Stuart L., 58, 59
Burton, Harry, 330

Callaghan, Morley, 103, 224–26
Camus, Albert, 285
Canby, Henry S., 232
Carabine, Keith, 90, 91, 96
Carroll, Lewis, 259
Cass, Colin S., 166, 169
Cervantes, Miguel de, 380
Cézanne, Paul, 86, 97, 98
Chaucer, Geoffrey, 259
Chekhov, Anton, 310
Chesterton, G. K., 57
Chicago Tribune, 191
Childs, Barney, 354
Christensen, Francis, 106
Clark, John A., 236
Clendening, Logan, 246, 247, 297–300
Cohen, Louis H., 247, 248
Colburn, William E., 281
College Humor, 126
Colliers, 126
Collins, Seward, 232, 234
Conrad, Joseph, 14, 88, 96, 150, 240, 242, 244, 245, 353
Cooperative Commonwealth, 70
Cosmopolitan, xx, 4, 10, 11, 240–42, 252, 253, 321, 327, 328, 330, 331, 351, 352, 370, 382, 383, 385
Cowley, Malcolm, 88, 90, 94, 143, 173, 174, 273
Crane, John Kenny, 353
Crane, R. S., 144, 145, 147, 331, 335, 342, 345
Crane, Stephen, 88, 142, 280, 331
Criterion, 45
Crosby, Caresse, 233
Crosby, Harry, 307
Cunliffe, W. Gordon, 161

Dahl, Harold E., 379

D'Annunzio, Gabriele, 68, 69, 194, 195, 270
Dante, Alighieri, 274, 275
Davidson, Arnold E., 344
Davies, Phillips G. and Rosemary R., 126, 127, 129, 143
Davis, Robert Murray, 65, 66
Davis, William V., 147
DeFalco, Joseph, 19, 27, 31, 38, 39, 52, 65, 71, 73, 78, 79, 83, 93, 94, 98, 107, 112, 118, 119, 128, 129, 135, 141, 142, 148, 149, 156, 157, 162, 167, 176, 177, 186, 201, 208, 209, 211, 227, 228, 243, 248, 255, 260, 261, 273, 274, 284, 292, 299, 300, 303, 304, 313, 323, 324, 335, 338, 339, 342, 355, 357, 363, 364
Descartes, René, 88, 95
Dolch, Martin, 142, 146, 147, 161, 281
Donaldson, Scott, 27, 126, 159, 160, 162, 205, 260, 262
Doran, George H., 36, 86, 87
Dorman-Smith, E. E. (Chink), 31, 191, 332, 335
Dos Passos, John, 116, 240, 289, 321, 323, 369, 371–73
Douglas, Norman, 69
Dussinger, Gloria R., 355–58

Edelson, Mark, 299
Einstein, Albert, 255
Eliot, T. S., xi, 16, 18, 19, 43–45, 47, 76–78, 151, 161, 167, 206, 234, 244, 248, 275, 280, 285, 299
Elliott, Gary D., 208, 258
Ellis, Havelock, 69
Engstrom, Alfred G., 357
Esquire, xx, 321, 322, 350–53, 362, 375, 378
Evans, Oliver, 147, 355, 356
Evans, Robert, 94
Ewell, Nathaniel M., 281

Fadiman, Clifton, 268–70
Faulkner, William, 254, 311
Fenton, Charles A., xxvi, 17, 142, 181, 248, 299
Ficken, Carl, 96

General Index 403

Fiedler, Leslie A., 7, 311, 314, 335, 337
Fielding, Henry, 117
Finch, Edith, 154, 155
Fisher, Marvin, 353
Fitzgerald, F. Scott, xx, 11, 12, 16, 18, 19, 36, 44, 51, 88, 99, 103, 104, 112, 116, 125, 132, 141, 161, 164, 172, 180, 204, 275, 352, 392
Flanner, Janet, 226
Fleming, Robert E., 200, 201, 204, 206, 228, 229, 312, 334
Fletcher, Mary, 208
Flora, Joseph M., 8, 41, 51, 53, 57, 66, 82, 83, 88, 92, 95, 98, 118, 119, 133, 135, 136, 142, 150, 162, 167, 169, 170, 177, 199, 201, 218–21, 229, 237, 258–61, 274, 275, 303–5, 310, 312–15
Fontana, Ernest, 182, 183
Ford, Ford Madox, 34, 35, 43, 68–70, 82, 85
Ford, Hugh, 233
Forster, E. M., 282
Forum, The, 110–13, 223, 235
Fox, Stephen, 65
Franklin, Sidney, 264, 265, 267
Frazer, James George, 356
Friend, Krebs, 62, 70
Frost, Robert, 88, 95, 136, 393
Frye, Northrop, 107, 108, 149
Fulkerson, Richard, 64, 65

Gabriel, Joseph F., 281, 282
Gaillard, Thomas L., Jr., 334
Gajdusek, Robert E., 56, 57
Galantière, Lewis, xv, 218
Gamble, James, 27, 94, 191
Garcia, Manuel "Espartero," 105
Garcia, Manuel "Maera," 104–6, 111–13
Gerogiannis, Nicholas, 117
Gertzman, Jay A., 372, 373
Gibb, Robert, 90
Gibbs, Arthur Hamilton, 112
Gingrich, Arnold, 264, 302, 321, 322, 327, 378, 382
Gordon, Caroline, 355, 356
Graves, Robert, 326

Grebstein, Sheldon N., 5, 13, 65, 78, 96, 97, 106, 157, 182, 195, 208–11, 219, 220, 227, 228, 236, 266, 274, 293, 303, 304, 313, 325
Greco, Anne, 343
Green, Gregory, xxvi
Griffin, Peter, x, xxvii, 6, 27, 69, 94, 142, 175, 299, 396
Grimes, Larry E., 39, 182, 315
Groseclose, Barbara, 32
Gurko, Leo, 64, 167

H. D. (Hilda Doolittle), 69, 226
Hagemann, E. R., xv, 271, 273
Hagemann, Meyly Chin, 97
Hagopian, John V., 46–48, 142, 146, 147, 161, 279, 281–83
Halliday, E. M., 373
Hanneman, Audre, x, 352
Hannum, Howard L., 89, 92, 96
Harkey, Joseph H., 334
Harper and Brothers, 68, 69, 81, 82
Harrison, G. B., 334
Harrison, J. M., 191
Hattam, Edward, 134
Hawthorne, Nathaniel, 89, 150, 228, 229, 259, 393
Hays, Peter L., 70, 248, 249, 303
Heap, Jane, 76, 110, 111
Hegel, Georg W. F., 107
Hellenga, Robert R., 340
Hemingway, Carol, xxvi, 63, 311
Hemingway, Clarence E., 37, 62–64, 201, 217, 226, 232, 238, 256, 307, 312
Hemingway, Elizabeth Hadley Richardson, xv–xvii, 16, 21, 25, 31, 34, 43–45, 50, 78, 82, 87, 94, 104, 159–61, 164, 168, 202, 204, 205, 207, 253
Hemingway, George, 37
Hemingway, Grace Hall, 34, 43, 50, 63, 226, 257, 265
Hemingway, Gregory, 303
Hemingway, John H. N. (Bumby), 44, 302, 303, 307, 311
Hemingway, Leicester, xxvi, 63, 143, 174, 314
Hemingway, Madelaine, 70
Hemingway, Marcelline, 226

Hemingway, Mary Walsh, 281, 391
Hemingway, Patrick, 217, 269, 303
Hemingway, Pauline Pfeiffer, xvii, 140, 160, 164, 204, 206, 217, 219, 224–26, 252, 254, 269, 278, 279, 289, 321, 332, 349, 385
Hemingway, Willoughby, 307
Henry, O., xxvi, 53, 127, 142, 162
Herndon, Jerry A., 334
Herrick, Robert, 232, 235
Hewlett, Maurice, 57, 58
Hickok, Guy, 173–75, 193, 194, 204, 207, 241, 291
Hill, John S., 343
Hirsch, E. D. Jr., 337
Hoffman, Steven K., 279, 280, 285, 286
Holland, Robert B., 342
Hollander, John, 207, 209–11
Hotchner, A. E., 143, 263, 269–71
Housman, A. E., 88
Hovey, Richard B., 92, 164, 176, 177, 182, 187, 236
Howe, E. W., xxvii, 5, 6
Howell, John M., 241, 243, 254, 328, 330, 332, 354
Howells, William Dean, 150
Hughes, Langston, 376
Hunt, Anthony, 31, 32
Hunt, Holman, 258, 259
Hurley, C. Harold, 283, 335
Hutton, Virgil, 335, 341, 342

Ingman, Trisha, 162
Ivens, Joris, 371

Jackson, Paul R., 20, 344
Jackson, Shirley, 393
Jackson, Thomas J., 330
James, Henry, 14, 88, 135, 144, 150, 160, 161, 219, 229, 236, 281, 299, 353
James, William, 280
Jerome, Judson, 279
Johnston, Dorothy, 110
Johnston, Kenneth G., 18–20, 31, 32, 51, 57–59, 143, 177, 178, 204, 209, 211, 220, 221, 352, 353, 356, 373, 380, 382, 383
Jones, Horace P., 72
Jones, Waring, 246

Joost, Nicholas, 112
Josephs, Allen, 175
Joyce, James, xi, xv, 17, 36, 37, 47, 56, 57, 69, 70, 77, 78, 85, 88, 99, 103, 169, 199, 200, 254, 255, 259, 261, 291, 323

Kafka, Franz, 142
Kann, Hans-Joachim, 277
Kansas City Star, 94, 181, 248
Kashkin, Ivan, 289
Ken, 362, 363, 371
Kerner, David, 282–84
Killinger, John, 285, 335
Kinnamon, Keneth, 106
Kipling, Rudyard, 88, 127
Kobler, J. F., 195, 208, 228, 229, 335, 344
Kolb, Alfred, 356
Krause, Sidney J., 13
Kroeger, F. P., 281
Kruse, Horst H., 47
Kurowsky, Agnes von, 25–27
Kvam, Wayne, 110–13, 386, 387
Kyle, Frank B., 96, 119, 120

Lanford, Ray, 13
Lardner, Ring, xxv, 127
Lawler, Charles A., 328, 330
Lawrence, D. H., 12, 70, 185, 287
Lawrence, T. E., 256
Leach, Henry G., 111, 113, 223
Leiter, Louis, H., 191, 192
Lengel, William C., 241, 252, 254
Lewis, Robert W., Jr., 13, 14, 73, 74, 165, 200, 233, 332, 333, 342, 343, 350, 351, 354, 355, 357, 358
Lewis, Sinclair, 206
Liberty, 126
Lid, Richard W., 364
Light, Martin, 371–73, 376, 377, 379, 380, 386
Little Review, 16, 25, 62, 76, 111, 115
Livingston, Howard, 146
Locklin, Gerald, 266
Lodge, David, 48, 282
Loeb, Harold, 115, 116
London, Jack, xxvi, 88, 117
Lorimer, George, 102–4
Lounsberry, Barbara, 340

Lynes, George Platt, 155
Lynn, Kenneth S., x, xxv, 18, 27, 226, 265, 266, 268, 269, 273, 333, 352

McAleer, John, 323, 324
McAlmon, Robert, 4, 17, 69, 97, 102, 104, 207, 224–27
McCann, Richard, 315, 316
MacDonald, Scott, 105–8, 282, 283, 358
MacFadden, Bernarr, 294
McKenna, John J., 335, 336
MacLeish, Archibald, 140, 231, 233, 291
Magee, John D., 47
Mahony, Patrick J., 304
Maloney, Russell, 235, 236, 355
Maloy, Barbara, 259
Markham, Beryl, 353
Marlowe, Christopher, 167
Marryat, Frederick, xi, 331, 332, 335
Martine, James J., 127–30, 149, 258, 260
Marvell, Andrew, 45
Mason, Jane, 253, 254, 268, 270, 333
Maupassant, Guy de, 68, 258, 259
Maurois, André, 335
May, Charles E., 281, 282
Melville, Herman, 73, 89, 119, 150, 187, 393
Mencken, H. L., 206
Meredith, George, 57, 58
Meyer, Hans, 354
Meyers, Jeffrey, x, 6, 13, 18, 27, 44, 88, 194, 226, 268, 273, 328, 332, 333, 335, 352
Monteiro, George, 38, 40, 58, 59, 72, 247, 248, 250, 279, 291
Montgomery, Constance, xxv, xxvi, 6, 37, 51, 64, 199, 258, 259
Montgomery, Marion, 292, 293, 353, 355
Moore, L. Hugh, Jr., 148
More, Paul Elmer, 232, 234, 235
Morris, William, 146
Morton, Bruce, 90
Murolo, Frederick L., 292
Murphy, Gerald and Sara, 159, 254, 323

Nabokov, Vladimir, 135
Nagel, James, 343, 344
National Geographic, 256
National Review, 236
Nelson, Oscar, 117
New Masses, 133
New Republic, xvii, 193–95, 198, 204
New Yorker, The, 235

O'Brien, Edward J., 11, 17, 34, 44, 62, 68, 75, 81
O'Conner, William Van, 355, 356
Oldsey, Bernard, 85, 97, 98, 323, 325, 327, 329, 357
O'Neil, David, 81, 82
O'Neil, George, 82
O'Neill, Eugene, 323
Organ, Dennis, 208
Ortiz, 264
Owen, Charles A., Jr., 146, 148

Park, Mungo, 232, 234, 235
Parker, Alice, 53, 54
Parker, Dorothy, 207, 209
Penner, Dick, 39–41
Percival, Philip, 332, 354
Perkins, Maxwell, 4, 111, 126, 132, 133, 138, 141, 160, 164, 165, 172, 180, 185, 189, 193, 194, 204, 205, 207, 217, 218, 224, 225, 232, 246, 269, 290, 298, 303, 307–9, 328, 330, 349, 351, 352, 363, 369, 370, 375, 385
Peterson, Marvin V., 336
Peterson, Richard K., 28, 325
Petry, Alice Hall, 7, 8, 353
Pierce, Waldo, 240, 246
Pinter, Harold, 150, 151
Plato, 241, 342
Plimpton, George, 138, 207
Poe, Edgar Allan, 89, 393
Poore, Charles, 231, 268, 270
Pope, Alexander, 227
Portz, John, 236
Pound, Ezra, xv, xvi, 3, 4, 16, 17, 25, 31, 35, 36, 43–45, 68–70, 77, 78, 292
Pyle, Howard, 303

Quinn, John, 62

Reardon, John, 149
Reid, Stephen, 324–26
Reinert, Otto, 281
Remarque, Erich Maria, 232, 235
Reusch, Richard, 354
Reynolds, Michael, x, xxv–xxvii, 5, 6, 10, 12, 26, 27, 62, 63, 69, 105, 110, 173, 175, 189, 226, 234, 255, 256, 258, 299, 373
Roberts, John J., 73
Robles, Jose, 371, 372
Rodgers, Paul C., Jr., 290, 294, 295
Rodrigues, Eusebio L., 208
Romaine, Paul, 289
Rosenfeld, Paul, 133
Rovit, Earl, 5, 64, 88, 128–30, 135, 149, 156, 167, 169, 175, 242, 243, 266, 274, 280, 285, 293, 325, 339, 356, 364, 370
Rudnick, Lois P., 161

St. John, Donald, 51, 62, 312
Sampson, Edward C., 145, 147, 148
Sandburg, Carl, 111
Sartre, Jean-Paul, 284
Saturday Evening Post, xxvi, xxvii, 6, 102–4, 126, 379
Saunders, Eddie (Bra), 240, 242, 244
Scafella, Frank, 178
Schafer, William J., 262
Schlepper, Wolfgang, 150, 151
Scholes, Robert, 28
Schwartz, Delmore, 293
Scribner, Charles Jr., 281, 283, 391
Scribner's Magazine, xvii, 126, 132, 133, 141, 159, 160, 165, 172, 218, 252, 253, 257, 271, 277–79, 290, 291, 294
Seed, David, 12
Seydow, John J., 341
Shakespeare, William, 57, 146, 227, 335
Shaw, George Bernard, 111
Shelley, Percy Bysshe, 356
Shepherd, Allen, 76–78, 303
Singer, Glen W., 117
Sipiora, Phillip, 209
Smith, Chard Powers, 75, 78, 79
Smith, Julian, 161, 162, 165, 167, 168, 177, 248, 249, 371–73, 376–80, 386, 387, 393

Smith, M. A. J., Jr., 354
Smith, Paul, xxviii, 3, 6, 17, 20, 21, 35, 37, 91, 97, 128, 134, 138, 142, 198, 199, 201, 202, 205, 279, 299
Smith, William B., 51, 57, 115, 240
Somers, Paul, 12
Spender, Stephen, 372
Spilka, Mark, xi, 331, 332, 335–42, 344, 345, 372
Stallman, R. W., 355, 357
Stanley, Edward, Bishop of Norwich, 234
Stearns, Harold, 70
Steffens, Lincoln, 4, 10, 11, 207
Stein, Gertrude, x, xv, 3–5, 17, 19, 34, 44, 62, 69, 71, 85–87, 97, 105, 155, 204, 207
Stein, William Bysshe, 94, 260
Steinbeck, John, 376
Steinke, James, 167, 168, 170, 178
Stendhal (Marie Henri Beyle), 68
Stephens, Robert O., 11, 51, 232, 235, 331, 332, 353, 354
Stephens, Rosemary, 166
Stetler, Charles, 266
Stewart, Donald Ogden, 26, 36, 86, 115
Stewart, Jack F., 94, 95
Stock, Ely, 280
Stone, Edward, 143, 145, 291, 293–95
Stoppard, Tom, 151, 183
Strater, Henry (Mike), 44, 246
Stuckey, W. J., 149
Svoboda, Frederic J., 86, 116, 117, 299

Tabeshaw, Billy, 62, 63
Tanselle, G. Thomas, 39, 40
Tate, Allen, 355, 356
Tedlock, Ernest W., Jr., 355
This Quarter, 86–88, 103, 223–25
Thomaneck, Jurgen K. A., 354
Thomas, Peter, 258, 261
Thomson, George H., 283, 284
Thoreau, Henry David, 88, 353
Thurston, Jarvis A., 201
Tilman, H. W., 354
Tinker, Frank Glasgow, 379
Tintner, Adeline R., 355
Titus, Edward, 224, 226
Tolstoy, Leo, 331, 353
Toronto Star, xvi, 10, 16, 31, 34, 37, 87, 91, 104, 105, 194, 195, 254, 272, 353

Transatlantic Review, 35, 36, 43, 61–63, 70, 82, 84, 85
transition, 173, 198, 205
Trilling, Lionel, 178, 206, 209–11
Turgenev, Ivan, 282, 310
Twain, Mark, xxvi, 88, 117, 119, 236, 393, 396
Twichell, James, 92
Tzara, Tristan, 36

Van Loan, Charles E., 103
Vanity Fair, 234
Villalta, Nicanor, 104
Villon, François, 219, 221, 357

Walcutt, Charles C., 355
Waldhorn, Arthur, 13, 38, 72–74, 82, 83, 89, 106, 119, 129, 142, 148–50, 157, 167, 169, 175, 186, 201, 237, 260, 266, 274, 280, 303, 304, 339, 358, 364
Walker, Robert G., 241, 242
Walpole, Hugh, 57
Walsh, Ernest, 86, 102, 103, 115
Walz, Lawrence A., 146
Ward, J. A., 142
Warren, Robert Penn, 143–49, 279, 284
Waterman, Arthur E., 338
Watson, James Gray, ix, 339, 344
Watson, William B., 362, 363, 369, 371, 379
Watteville, Vivienne de, 350, 354, 355
Watts, Emily Stipes, 97
Weeks, Edward, 392
Weeks, Lewis E., Jr., 208, 236
Weeks, Robert P., 148

Wells, Elizabeth J., 96
West, Ray B., 284, 335, 356
Westbrook, Max, 350, 351, 355, 357
Weston, Jesse L., 248, 249
Wharton, Edith, 355
White, Gertrude, 47, 48
White, Gilbert, 234
White, Stewart Edward, xxvi, 331
White, William, 333
Whitt, Joseph, 52
Wilkinson, Myler, 310
Williams, Wirt, 107, 108, 128, 129, 135, 149, 157, 182, 195, 199, 237, 293, 299, 300, 303, 305, 313
Wilson, Edmund, 11, 12, 111, 181, 186, 189, 332, 335, 342
Wimberly, Lowry Charles, 142
Winn, Harbour, 331
Wister, Owen, xxvi, 232
Witherington, Paul, 192
Woolf, Virginia, 207
Wordsworth, William, 38
Wright, Austin, 211
Wylder, Delbert E., 393

Yanella, Philip Y., 110–13
Yokelson, Joseph B., 274
Young, Philip, 5–7, 12, 18, 40, 52, 56, 64, 87, 89, 90, 92, 98, 106, 117, 119, 128, 134, 142, 143, 147, 148, 156, 161, 167, 169, 175, 176, 199, 227, 260, 273, 280, 292, 293, 331, 335, 352, 353, 396
Yunck, John A., 236